The Audubon Society
Field Guide to
North American Birds

A Chanticleer Press Edition

The Audubon Society Field Guide to North American Birds

Eastern Region

John Bull and John Farrand, Jr.,
The American Museum of Natural
History

Visual Key by Susan Rayfield

Alfred A. Knopf, New York

This is a Borzoi Book
Published by Alfred A. Knopf, Inc.

All rights reserved. Copyright 1977
under the International Union for the
protection of literary and artistic works
(Berne). Published in the United States
by Alfred A. Knopf, Inc., New York,
and simultaneously in Canada by
Random House of Canada Limited,
Toronto. Distributed by Random
House, Inc., New York.

Prepared and produced by
Chanticleer Press, Inc., New York.

Color reproductions by Nievergelt
Repro AG, Zurich, Switzerland.
Type set in Garamond by
Dix Type Inc., Syracuse, New York.
Printed and bound in Japan.

Published July 26, 1977
Reprinted fifteen times
Seventeenth Printing, October 1988

Library of Congress Catalog Card
Number 76-47926
ISBN 0-394-41405-5

CONTENTS

THE AUDUBON SOCIETY

The National Audubon Society is among the oldest and largest private conservation organizations in the world. With over 560,000 members and more than 500 local chapters across the country, the Society works in behalf of our natural heritage through environmental education and conservation action. It protects wildlife in more than seventy sanctuaries from coast to coast. It also operates outdoor education centers and ecology workshops and publishes the prizewinning AUDUBON magazine, AMERICAN BIRDS magazine, newsletters, films, and other educational materials. For further information regarding membership in the Society, write to the National Audubon Society, 950 Third Avenue, New York, New York 10022.

ACKNOWLEDGMENTS

The authors are very grateful to Dean
Amadon for reading and commenting
on the manuscript, to Davis W. Finch
for his great help with problems
of field identification, to Joseph M.
Cadbury, Miklos D. F. Udvardy, and
Edith Bull for numerous helpful
suggestions, and to Angus Cameron for
much practical advice.
They would especially like to thank
Paul Steiner and the staff at Chanticleer
Press for the creative contributions and
effort that made this guide possible:
Milton Rugoff, Gudrun Buettner,
Massimo Vignelli, Susan Rayfield,
Mary Suffudy, Kathy Ritchell, Helga
Lose, and Carol Nehring.
Range maps were researched by David
Ewert, John Dunn, and Kimball Garett
and coordinated by Jill Farmer.

THE AUTHORS

John Bull, a leading authority on birds of the Northeast, has been on the staff of the Ornithology Department of the American Museum of Natural History since 1962. He is the author of two classics on Eastern birds, *Birds of the New York City Area* (1964) and *Birds of New York State* (1974), and has contributed articles on birds to various books and magazines. He has also served as a nature guide on tours around the world as well as in the United States, the Caribbean, and Australia. He has been a delegate to many meetings of the International Ornithological Congress and received a National Science Foundation grant in 1973.

John Farrand, Jr., has been on the staff of the Ornithology Department of the American Museum of Natural History since 1973. After studying birds at Cornell University, the University of Oklahoma, and Louisiana State University, he served in the Division of Birds at the Smithsonian Institution. He has published papers on birds in *The Wilson Bulletin* and other journals and made field trips throughout the United States and in South America, Europe, and Africa.

INTRODUCTION

Each year thousands of people take up the absorbing hobby of bird-watching or "birding." Regardless of their motives, their first goal is learning to identify the hundreds of species in their own region.

It is to make this step as simple—and pleasurable—as possible that this book has been prepared. Its pocket size and its format make it easy to carry into the field and consult on the spot. Take it with you. And welcome to the hobby, or sport, or science, of birding.

Geographical Scope A number of American bird guides divide North America into eastern and western regions at the 100th meridian. This is an arbitrary line that bears no relationship to natural habitats. We have chosen a line (see map) that follows the 100th meridian from the Edwards Plateau in Texas and cuts northward through the Oklahoma panhandle but then curves west and runs along the Rockies through eastern Colorado, Wyoming, and Montana, and, in Canada, along the eastern foothills of the Rocky Mountains. Thus our line for the most part follows the Rockies, a natural barrier in the range of many eastern and western birds. Of course, many birds can and do pass over this barrier in both directions.

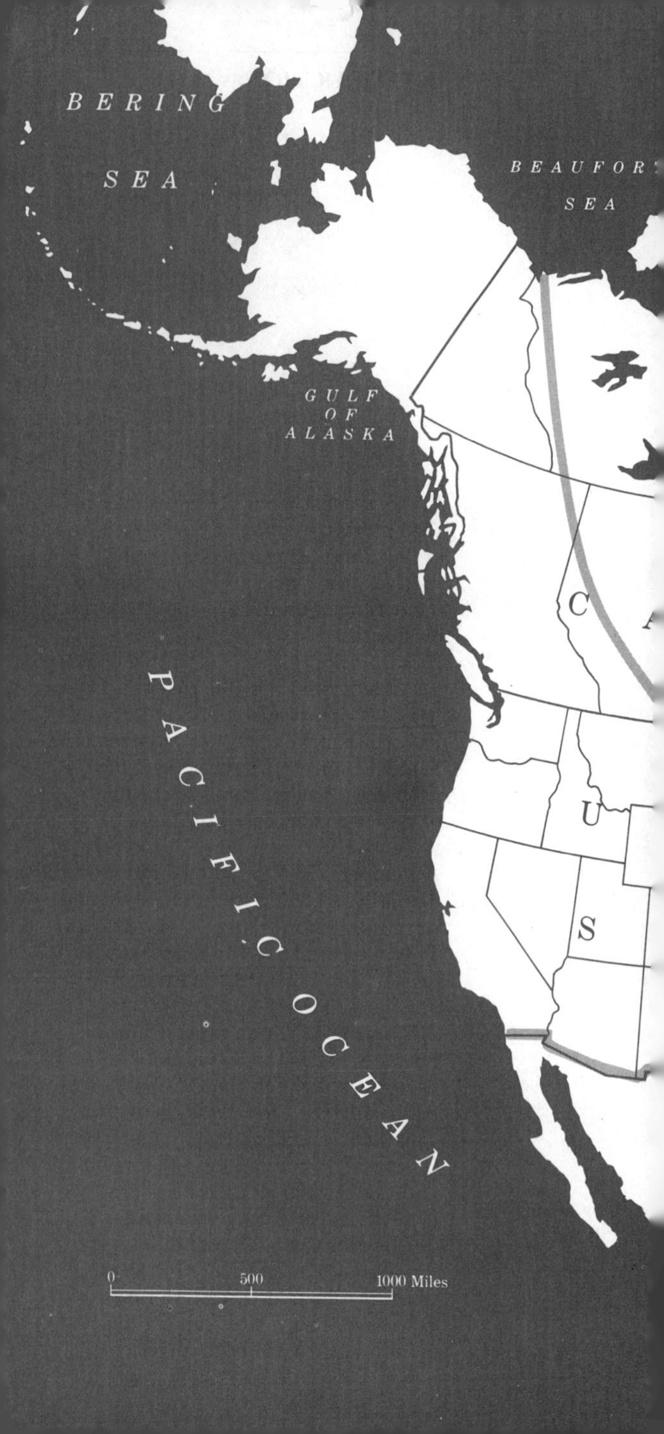

BERING SEA

BEAUFORT SEA

GULF OF ALASKA

PACIFIC OCEAN

0   500   1000 Miles

Slowly but surely the number of identical species found on both sides is increasing. Indeed, one ornithologist has predicted that by the year 2000 all the species in the United States will have reached California.

Photographs as a Visual Guide

There are two major ways of illustrating bird guides, each with its advantages and disadvantages: One is the traditional way, by means of paintings, and the other is a newer way, by means of photographs. We have chosen to use color photographs because it has become possible in recent years to get superb portrait photographs of almost every bird seen regularly in America. In using the work of America's leading bird photographers, we believe we are adding an exciting new dimension to what generally appears in guides illustrated by an artist. Every artist's rendering of a bird is his interpretation, whereas a good photograph captures the natural color and stance of birds as you will usually see them. In most instances it also shows birds in their habitat or natural setting, making identification that much easier. Finally there is the beauty itself of pictures made by outstanding photographers: this guide is meant to be a delight to look at as well as use.

How the Guide Works

Most field guides to birds are arranged according to families, that is, according to the bird's structural features. But these are often invisible or not evident to a novice. What a beginner or even an experienced watcher first notes when he glimpses a bird is its size, shape, and color. But if he then consults a standard field guide, organized by families, he must know what family the bird belongs to—whether it is a warbler, a vireo, a finch, or such—before he can locate it in the guide. What he generally does is page laboriously through the book until he comes on a drawing that resembles the bird he has seen. He must go through this trial-and-error procedure each time he uses the guide.

To avoid this hit-or-miss approach the photographs in this guide have been organized on visual principles, that is, by what you see. Thus the 584 photographs are arranged (in the first half of the book) according to a bird's shape and, in most cases, its color. Captions under each pictured species include the plate number (which refers to the photograph), the size of the bird, and the number of the page on which the species is described. If the photograph is not of a breeding male, that is also indicated.

Since you may be afforded only a brief glimpse of a bird, you must learn to note essential details quickly. Such essentials include the following:

Field Marks When you see a new bird, make note of such points as the size and shape of the bill (whether long or short, slender or stout, curved or straight), the tail (long or short, rounded, squared, wedge-shaped, notched, or forked) and the wings (long or short, rounded or pointed). Note any distinctive features such as a crest, or eye-rings, or wing bars, or a flashing white patch in the wings, tail, or rump. Many species have color patterns that identify them at a glance; by studying the pictures in this book in advance, you may be able to identify many species at first sight.

Relative Size It is useful to keep in mind the sizes of a few common species like the House Sparrow, Blue Jay, American Robin, and Common Crow so that you can quickly estimate the relative size of an unfamiliar bird.

Behavior Note what the bird is doing. Is it alone or in a flock? Is it foraging on the ground like a thrasher or is it walking like a starling or hopping like a sparrow? Is it foraging on high or feeding in foliage, like a warbler or vireo? Is it creeping about on the trunk of a tree; if so, is it hitching up the tree like a woodpecker or a creeper, or is it working its way headfirst down the trunk like a nuthatch? If the bird is in flight, is it flapping or soaring? If soaring, are the wings held horizontally, as in gulls and most hawks, or in a shallow V, as in the Turkey Vulture, Rough-legged Hawk, and Marsh Hawk? If in the water, is it feeding at the surface or diving? Make note also of the bird's voice or call.

What the Photographs Show
Most of the photographs show adult males, since these are characteristic of a species, but pictures of females, immatures (imm.), and males in winter plumage are also included when they differ significantly from the breeding male.

The photographs are grouped according to (*a*) obvious similarities in appearance, such as "Long-legged Waders" or "Duck-like Birds," or (*b*) a visible similarity in behavior or habitat, as in "Tree-clinging Birds." Sometimes (*a*) and (*b*) will coincide, as in "Chicken-like Marsh Birds," many of which not only look like each other but have much the same "life-style" and live in the same kind of habitat.

Groups
The groups are as follows:

Long-legged Waders
Gull-like Birds
Upright-perching Waterbirds
Duck-like Birds
Sandpiper-like Birds
Chicken-like Marsh Birds
Upland Ground Birds
Owls
Hawk-like Birds
Pigeon-like Birds
Swallow-like Birds

Tree-clinging Birds
Perching Birds

These broad categories are of course not foolproof and are intended to serve only as a starting point.

Within each of these major categories the birds are grouped according to other similarities. Thus, among the Duck-like Birds the photographs of the Canvasback and Redhead, or of the American Goldeneye and Barrow's Goldeneye, are shown together so that they can be compared at a glance. Similarly, among the Tree-clinging Birds all the woodpeckers with barred backs are placed together for easy comparison.

Silhouette and Thumbprint Guides Preceding the photographs is a section showing silhouettes of birds typical of their groups. For example, the group Long-legged Waders is represented by a silhouette of an ibis; and each type of bird within the group, such as spoonbills and bitterns, is also represented by a typical silhouette. To make it easy to locate each group a silhouette typical of the group has been inset as a "thumbprint" on the left of all the picture spreads in that section.

Perching (Song) Birds Grouped by Color The perching birds are by far the largest category, but the term is now technically restricted to the small songbirds that make up the group known as the passerines. But we have included additional species that we thought belonged best in this section, such as cuckoos and kingfishers. Because songbirds are so numerous these birds are arranged according to their most prominent color (whether overall color or only a distinctive patch) in the following eight groups:

Yellow
Orange/Rust
Red

Gray
Blue
Olive/Green
Brown
Black

This color arrangement of the perching birds depends, of course, on such factors as the light in which a bird is seen or even on individual judgment as to color, and a few birds, such as the multicolored Painted Bunting, do not fit into any simple color category. We have placed each species in the color category where it seemed to fit best. Since most birds the average birder will see are perching birds, this color key will help you make a more rapid initial identification.

Females are usually much duller in coloring and can sometimes be identified only when one knows the male. But after a little practice the reader will surely find our inclusion of distinctive females helpful.

We have also included the different plumages or color phases of some species. For a few birds that are uncommon or of very restricted range no satisfactory color photographs were available. These birds are fully described in the text and each is shown in a drawing next to the description.

Finally, following this Introduction, under the title "How to Use the Keys" is a sample of how to use this book to identify a particular bird.

Text Descriptions Arranged by Habitat
In the text, birds have been grouped according to their primary habitats, giving the reader an additional check on the identification that began in the picture section. The habitat groups are as follows:

Open Ocean
Seashore
Salt Marshes
Freshwater Marshes

Lakes, Ponds, Rivers
Florida Swamps and Keys
Grasslands
City Parks and Suburban Areas
Thickets and Second Growth
Texas Thickets and Second Growth
Deciduous Forests
Coniferous Forests

Note that two of the above categories are partly geographical as well as ecological: "Texas Thickets" and "Florida Swamps and Keys." Both Texas and Florida have a number of species found nowhere else in the eastern United States and grouping these together makes identification in those states much easier.

Before setting out on a field trip to a particular habitat, the reader should glance through the section in the text describing the birds in that habitat in order to get some idea of the species likely to be encountered. Thus in a coniferous forest the birder knows that the owl seen will be one of five species and not a dozen others.

Species Descriptions English and Scientific Names

The English, or common, names of birds are those accepted in the 1957 edition of the American Ornithologists' Union's *Check-list of North American Birds,* as revised in the 32nd supplement in 1973, and in the 33rd supplement in 1976. Where a bird's name has been changed recently by the A.O.U. we have included its former name in quotation marks.

Every bird has a scientific name consisting of two Greek or Latin words. The first word is the genus and the second is the species. The genus, which is always capitalized, includes a number of species. Thus, the scientific name of the Mallard, *Anas platyrhynchos,* tells us that it is a member of the genus *Anas,* which includes most of the surface-feeding or dabbling ducks in North America and elsewhere. The species name, *platyrhynchos,* describes the Mallard duck specifically. Since a bird's common name varies not only from country to country but often from region to region, its scientific names identify it everywhere and provide ornithologists with an international language. These scientific names also tell us what species are in the same genus, family, and so forth. Often the Latin or Greek names reveal an interesting fact about the history or biology of a species or they honor an ornithologist or bird artist; we have included such information wherever it seems particularly interesting.

Under the species name we have given the family name in Latin and its English equivalent, or where there are several large groups in a family, the names of each group.

The description of each species covers all or almost all of the following:

Size   Measurements of average overall length (from tip of bill to tip of tail) of each species are given in inches, along with the metric equivalent. Since measurements of either living birds or museum specimens depend on the way they are measured as well as the individual bird, such measurements are approximate.

Wingspread measurement (W.) is given for many of the larger birds.

Description: This opening paragraph covers physical
Color and   characteristics and plumage. In general,
Plumage   the most striking or distinctive features or field marks are italicized. While a few species like the Blue Jay and the Common Crow look much the same throughout the year and at every age, in many birds the plumage varies with age, sex, or season. In the Starling, for example, adults of both sexes look alike, but young birds, instead of being glossy black like the adults, are grayish-brown; adults have white spots,

and in summer a yellow bill. Breeding plumage is usually the brightest plumage in both sexes and is generally worn in spring and summer.

The young of some species, such as the Herring Gull, pass through a number of distinct plumages before they acquire the final adult plumage. In many species the male and female differ in appearance, but the young bird looks like the female; in the Cardinal, for example, the adult male is bright red, while the female and young are duller and browner. Many species show seasonal variation: male Scarlet Tanagers are bright red during the breeding season but in the fall acquire an olive-green plumage not unlike that of the female. These variations in plumage may be puzzling at first, but one soon learns to recognize the major variations in each species.

Where several species resemble each other closely, we have described the features that distinguish them.

Certain birds such as some of the hawks, ducks, swallows, and gulls are likely to be glimpsed in flight. To help in recognizing them on the wing many drawings of birds in flight have been added.

Voice Since most species have distinctive call notes and songs, a brief description or a simple phonetic transcription is given for all species. Indeed, a few birds are more readily identified by voice than by appearance. Although one can now obtain recordings of voices of many species, a knowledge of calls is best gained by experience with birds in the field.

Habitat We next describe the habitat or habitats that this species prefers— beach, lake, deciduous forest, grassland, city park, suburb, and so forth—as well as the type of area preferred within the habitat. When a species has a different habitat during the winter from that occupied during the breeding season, that, too, is indicated. All the major habitats in eastern America are described in the pages preceding the species descriptions.

Nesting The eggs, nests, and breeding habits of each species are described. The number of eggs given is that normally found in a nest; sometimes a larger clutch may be found, perhaps due to the fact that a second female has laid eggs in a nest.

Range The geographic range is given for all species, even where the range extends beyond the area covered by the book. The breeding range is described first, followed by information on the North American portion of the winter range. Following a common practice, we have generally given the range of each species in clockwise fashion, that is, from west to east and then from north to south. In most instances we have named enough localities for the reader to be able to draw a usable line between the various points. Thus, when we say that the Nashville Warbler breeds from Saskatchewan, Quebec, and Newfoundland south to Connecticut, Pennsylvania, and Nebraska, a line drawn through the first three localities gives the northern limits of the species and another line drawn through the last three localities gives the southern limits in the East.

Range statements may be given in more detail in the West because there the mountains or local differences in rainfall create irregularities in the distribution of a species.

Range Maps In addition to a statement of the geographic range, a range map is provided for species of more than irregular or casual occurrence within the area covered by this book. No range maps are provided for exclusively oceanic species. On these maps the following designations are used:

Breeding rage

Winter range

Areas in which a species occurs in both winter and summer are indicated by cross-hatching.

Permanent range

Notes   At the end of each species descripion notes have been added on such subjects as behavior and feeding habits, population status, and lore.

How to Find   Although it is almost impossible to go
Birds   outdoors without seeing at least a few birds, some advance planning will enable you to increase the number of species you see on a field trip. Many birds tend to confine their activity to one particular habitat, so you should plan to visit as many different habitats as possible during a day of birding. A good system is to begin your field trip at dawn, going first to a freshwater marsh. Rails, bitterns, and other marsh birds are most active and vocal at that hour, and a few minutes in a marsh at sunrise can be more productive than several hours later in the day. From the marsh you can go on to woodlands, fields, or thickets. Until the middle of the morning most songbirds are busily searching for food and singing and are relatively easy to see. From midmorning until late in the afternoon land birds are quiet, while the birds of the beaches, lakes, and other aquatic or marine habitats are active all day. This, then, is the time to search for herons, cormorants, ducks, and sandpipers. Late in the day land birds start singing and foraging again, so you can return to woods and other inland habitats to spot

the species you may have missed in the morning. To round out a full day of birding, make an after-dark visit to a forest or wooded swamp to listen for owls.

The greatest variety of birds can be seen during the migration seasons. It is, therefore, a good idea to plan several field trips during the spring and fall. In spring the best time to search is during the latter half of April and the first half of May, when most of the songbirds migrate north through eastern North America. Most migrating birds fly at night, breaking their journey during the day, when they rest and feed. They tend to gather in quiet places where food is easy to find. In a light woodland along a stream, where there are newly opened leaves and an abundance of small insects, it is possible to see as many as two dozen species of warblers in a single spring morning. Migrating songbirds also concentrate in isolated groves of trees along the coast or in the prairie, and in well-planted city parks. When the land bird migration tapers off in late May, sandpipers and plovers are still flying through. Now is the time to visit beaches, lakes, and marshes. The fall migration is under way by August, when the first of the sandpipers and plovers reappear. In September and October most of the song birds pass through. The migration of ducks, geese, and other water birds continues into November; visits to lakes and bays will pay dividends then. While many species are rather tame, others are shy or secretive. Learn to move slowly and quietly and to avoid wearing brightly colored clothing. Some of these elusive birds can be lured into view by an imitation of the sound of a bird in distress, or by a whistled imitation of a Screech Owl. Rails and certain other secretive species can be attracted by playing tape recordings of their calls.

PARTS OF A BIRD

The generalized drawing of a bird on the following two pages shows the external parts of a bird that are mentioned frequently in the species descriptions in this book. Definitions of terms that are not in everyday use may also be found in the Glossary, on pp. 749–754.

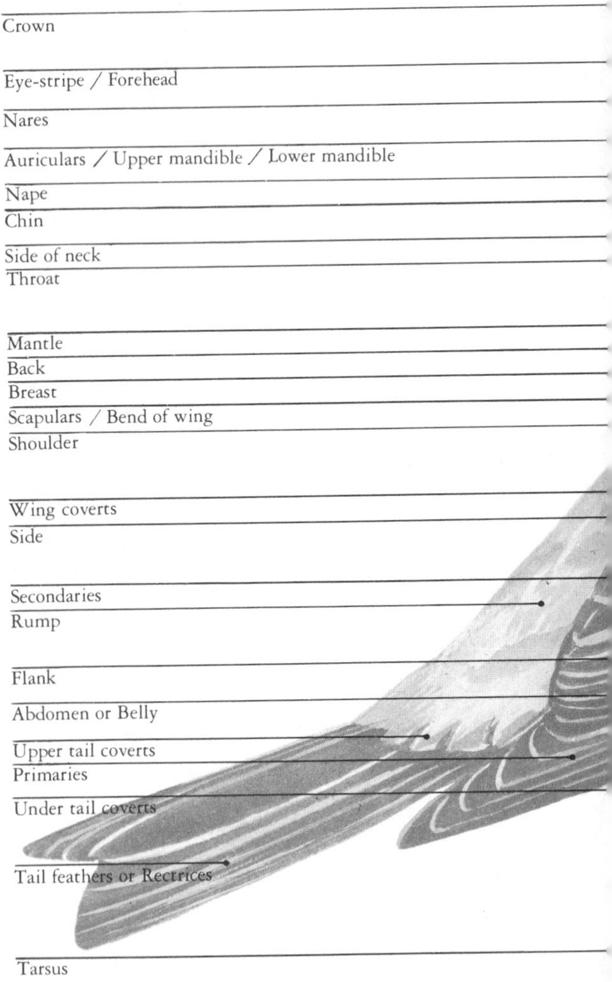

Crown

Eye-stripe / Forehead

Nares

Auriculars / Upper mandible / Lower mandible

Nape

Chin

Side of neck

Throat

Mantle

Back

Breast

Scapulars / Bend of wing

Shoulder

Wing coverts

Side

Secondaries

Rump

Flank

Abdomen or Belly

Upper tail coverts

Primaries

Under tail coverts

Tail feathers or Rectrices

Tarsus

HOW TO USE THE KEYS

Example
A Bird Clinging
to a Tree Trunk

You have seen a streamlined, sparrow-sized bird with a longish bill creeping down the trunk of a maple or other deciduous tree. It was grayish blue, with a white face, black cap and light-colored breast.

1. To make sure it is one of the Tree-clinging Birds, check the typical silhouettes preceding the entire color section.
2. Turn to the photographs in the group labeled Tree-clinging Birds.
3. Among the 20 photographs in this color group, all showing birds clinging to the trunks of trees, some have red on cap or body, several have black, and one is brown. Only two, the White-breasted Nuthatch and the Red-breasted Nuthatch, have grayish blue backs and a black cap.
4. Under the photographs you find the numbers of the pages on which the two nuthatches are described. The Red-breasted Nuthatch is described in the habitat section labeled Coniferous Forest, while the White-breasted Nuthatch is described among the Deciduous Forest birds and, like the bird you saw, it has white underparts. Although both habitually creep downward on tree trunks, your bird was plainly the White-breasted Nuthatch.

Example   You have seen several birds flying
Birds Flying   overhead that have white bodies with
Over a Beach   gray backs, white tails, yellow feet, and
yellow and black bills.

1. You turn to the bird silhouettes at the
   opening of the color section and find
   that your birds look most like the gulls
   found on Plates 31–39 and 41–57.
2. After glancing at the color plates, you
   find that the Herring Gull, Ring-billed
   Gull, and Glaucous Gull all resemble
   the birds you saw. But the Glaucous
   Gull has no black on its wingtips or
   bill, and the Herring Gull has pinkish
   legs and no black on its bill. Only the
   Ring-billed Gull seems to fit.
3. In the captions under the plates you
   find the page numbers on which these
   three birds are described. The
   descriptions confirm that the birds you
   saw were Ring-billed Gulls.

Part I
Color Key

Keys to the Color Plates

The color plates in the following pages are divided into thirteen groups:

Long-legged Waders
Gull-like Birds
Upright-perching Water Birds
Duck-like Birds
Sandpiper-like Birds
Chicken-like Marsh Birds
Upland Ground Birds
Owls
Hawk-like Birds
Pigeon-like Birds
Swallow-like Birds
Tree-clinging Birds
Perching Birds

Thumb Prints To make it easy to locate a group, a typical outline of a bird from that group is inset as a thumb print at the left edge of each double-page of plates. Thus you can find the Long-legged Waders by flipping through the color pages until you come to a series of thumb prints showing the outline of a typical wading bird.

Silhouettes of the Families in Each Group To help you recognize birds by their general shape, the color plates are preceded by pages showing you silhouettes of the families in each group. If the bird you saw looks like one of these silhouettes, you will find the bird in that group.

Captions The caption under each photograph gives the common name of the bird, its size, and the page number on which it is described. The color plate number is repeated in front of each description as a cross reference.
Most of the photographs show birds in typical breeding plumage. Certain birds, as indicated in the caption, are also shown in distinctive immature or winter plumage.

Symbol	Category
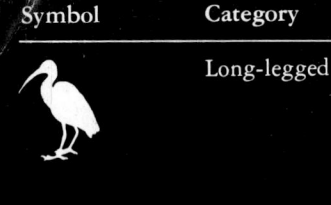	Long-legged Waders

Family Symbols	herons, egrets	Plate Numbers

Family Symbols		Plate Numbers
	herons, egrets	1–8, 10, 13–16, 18–22
	storks	9
	spoonbills	11
	flamingos	12
	bitterns	17, 24
	limpkins	23
	ibises	25–28
	cranes	29–30

Symbol	Category
	Gull-like Birds

Family Symbols		Plate Numbers
	gulls	31–39, 41–57
	shearwaters	40, 79–81
	terns	58–69, 71–75
	skimmers	70
	gannets, boobies	76–78
	storm-petrels	82–83
	frigatebirds	85–86

Symbol	Category
	Gull-like Birds
 	Upright-perching Waterbirds
	Duck-like Birds

Family Symbols		Plate Numbers
	skuas, jaegers	84, 87–89
	tropicbirds	90
	auks, murres, puffins	91–98
	cormorants	99, 101–103
	anhingas	100, 104
	surface-feeding ducks	105–108, 112, 115, 119, 133, 135–144, 164
	diving ducks	109–110, 116–118, 120–127, 129–132, 145–158, 160

Duck-like Birds

Family Symbols		Plate Numbers
	stiff-tailed ducks	111, 159
	mergansers	113–114, 128, 161–163
	coots	134
	whistling-ducks	165–168
	geese	169–172
	swans	173–174
	pelicans	175–176
	grebes	177–185
	loons	186–190

Symbol	Category
	Sandpiper-like Birds
	Chicken-like Marsh Birds

Family Symbols		Plate Numbers
	sandpipers	191–193, 197–202, 209–232, 245–246
	plovers, turnstones	194–196, 233–241
	phalaropes	203–208
	oystercatchers	242
	avocets, stilts	243–244
	gallinules	247–248
	rails	249, 251–254
	jaçanas	250

Symbol	Category
	Upland Ground Birds
	Owls

Family Symbols		Plate Numbers
	snipes, woodcocks	255–256
	quails, partridges, pheasants	257–258, 267, 274
	grouse	259–266, 268, 270
	turkeys	269, 273
	roadrunners	271
	chachalacas	272
	nightjars	275–278
	true owls	279–290, 292
	barn owls	291

Symbol	Category
	Hawk-like Birds

Family Symbols		Plate Numbers
	hawks	293–301, 311, 319
	kites	302–304, 320
	eagles	305, 307–308
	ospreys	306
	harriers	309–310
	caracaras	312
	falcons	313–316
	vultures	317–318

Symbol	Category
 	Pigeon-like Birds
	Swallow-like Birds
	Tree-clinging Birds
	Perching Birds

Family Symbols		Plate Numbers
	pigeons, doves	321–328
	swallows	329–334, 336
	swifts	335
	woodpeckers	337–352
	nuthatches	353–354, 356 .
	creepers	355
	wood warblers	357–361, 363–380, 382, 402–404, 444–448, 455–457, 460, 503–505, 509, 514, 563–564
	vireos	362, 383, 449–454

Symbol	Category
	Perching Birds

Family Symbols		Plate Numbers
	titmice	381, 427–428, 431–432, 511
	cardinals, grosbeaks	384, 399, 405–408, 414, 424, 439, 561–562
	buntings, finches, sparrows	385–386, 401, 409–413, 429, 437–438, 476–478, 513, 520, 527–545, 547–554, 557–559, 566
	orioles, blackbirds	387–388, 393–398, 515–519, 555, 560, 567–576, 583
	tanagers	389, 416–417, 442, 473–475
	flycatchers	390, 415, 418, 423, 426, 461–472, 512
	meadowlarks	391–392
	thrushes	400, 440–441, 498–502, 510

Symbol	Category
	Perching Birds

Family Symbols		Plate Numbers
	mockingbirds, thrashers	419–420, 494–497
	shrikes	421–422
	jays, magpies	425, 435–436, 483, 584
	becards	430
	kingfishers	433–434, 482
	gnatcatchers, kinglets	443, 458–459
	hummingbirds	479–481
	parrots	484

Symbol	Category
	Perching Birds

Family Symbols		Plate Numbers
	wrens	485–493
	waxwings	506–507
	bulbuls	508
	cuckoos	521–523, 577 578
	weaver finches	524–526
	pipits	546
	larks	556
	starlings	565
	crows	579–582

The color plates on the following pages are numbered to correspond with the number preceding each species description in the text. Most of the birds shown are adult males but also shown are some distinctive females and immatures and a few instances of seasonal changes in plumage.

Long-legged Waders

These are medium to large-sized water birds with long legs adapted for wading in fresh or salt water. Most of these species, such as herons, egrets, cranes, ibises, spoonbills, and flamingos, are conspicuously patterned and many are entirely white. Others are pink but some have concealing colors which make them difficult to detect.

1 Snowy Egret breeding plumage, 20–27", p. 380

2 Great Egret breeding plumage, 35–41", p. 406

3 Reddish Egret white phase, 30″, p. 330

4 Cattle Egret breeding plumage, 20″, p. 490

5   Snowy Egret non-breeding plumage, p. 380

6   Great Egret non-breeding plumage, p. 406

7 Little Blue Heron imm., 25–30″, p. 406

8 Cattle Egret non-breeding plumage, 20″, p. 490

9 Wood Stork, 40–44", p. 478

10 "Great White Heron", 39–52", p. 478

11 Roseate Spoonbill, 30–32″, p. 380

12 American Flamingo, 48″, p. 479

13 Louisiana Heron, 25–30″, p. 381

14 Great Blue Heron, 39–52″, p. 444

15 Reddish Egret dark phase, 30″, p. 330

17   Least Bittern, 11–14″, p. 407

19   Yellow-crowned Night Heron, 22–27″, p. 408

20   Black-crowned Night Heron, 23–28″, p. 409

21 Yellow-crowned Night Heron imm., p. 408

22 Black-crowned Night Heron imm., p. 409

23 Limpkin, 25–28", p. 480

25 White Ibis, 23–27", p. 382

27 Glossy Ibis, 22–25″, p. 382

28 White-faced Ibis, 22–25″, p. 383

29 Whooping Crane, 45–50″, p. 384

30   Sandhill Crane, 34–48″, p. 410

Gull-like Birds

These waterbirds spend much of their time in flight. All have long, pointed wings. Gulls, terns, gannets, and boobies are predominantly white, while frigatebirds are black. Most of these birds occur along seacoasts or on the ocean, but some of the gulls and terns are found on inland waters.

31   Iceland Gull imm., 23″, p. 330

32   Ivory Gull, 17″, p. 331

33   Glaucous Gull imm., 28″, p. 332

34 Iceland Gull, 23″, p. 330

35 Thayer's Gull, 24″, p. 333

36 Glaucous Gull, 28″, p. 332

37   Herring Gull, 23–26″, p. 445

38   Ring-billed Gull, 18–20″, p. 446

39   Black-legged Kittiwake, 16–18″, p. 333

40 Northern Fulmar, 18″, p. 314

41 Lesser Black-backed Gull, 23″, p. 334

43 Laughing Gull, 15–17″, p. 385

44 Sabine's Gull, 13–14″, p. 314

46 Black-headed Gull, 15″, p. 447

47 Little Gull, 11″, p. 448

49 Ivory Gull imm., 17″, p. 331

50 Herring Gull imm., 23–26″, p. 445

52 Ring-billed Gull imm., 18–20″, p. 446

53 Bonaparte's Gull imm., 12–14″, p. 449

55   Bonaparte's Gull winter plumage, 12–14″, p. 449

56   Laughing Gull winter plumage, 15–17″, p. 385

58 Common Tern winter plumage, 13–16″, p. 450

59 Sandwich Tern winter plumage, 16″, p. 336

60 Forster's Tern winter plumage, 14–15″, p. 385

61 Common Tern, 13–16″, p. 450

62 Roseate Tern, 14–17″, p. 336

63 Arctic Tern, 14–17″, p. 337

64 Royal Tern, 18–21″, p. 338

65 Caspian Tern, 19–23″, p. 451

66 Forster's Tern, 14–15″, p. 385

67   Sandwich Tern, 16″, p. 336

68   Gull-billed Tern, 13–15″, p. 386

69   Least Tern, 8–10″, p. 339

70 Black Skimmer, 18″, p. 340

71 Sooty Tern, 16″, p. 341

73 Brown Noddy, 15″, p. 342

74 Black Noddy, 12″, p. 343

76 Gannet, 35–40″, p. 344

77 Brown Booby, 30″, p. 316

79 Cory's Shearwater, 20–22″, p. 317

80 Greater Shearwater, 18–20″, p. 318

82   Wilson's Storm-Petrel, 7″, p. 321

83   Leach's Storm-Petrel, 8–9″, p. 322

85 Magnificent Frigatebird, 38–40″, p. 345

86 Magnificent Frigatebird ♀, 38–40″, p. 345

88 Pomarine Jaeger, 22″, p. 325

89 Parasitic Jaeger, 17″, p. 326

Upright-perching Waterbirds

 These birds are usually seen perching on rocks or trees at the edge of the water. In most cases, their feet are located far back on the body, which gives the birds a distinctive upright posture when perching. The auks, murres, and puffins are patterned in black-and-white, while the cormorants and anhingas are largely or entirely black.

91   Razorbill, 17″, p. 346

92   Black Guillemot, 13″, p. 347

93   Thick-billed Murre, 18″, p. 347

94   Common Murre, 17″, p. 348

95   Common Puffin, 12″, p. 349

96   Dovekie, 8″, p. 349

97 Common Puffin, 12″, p. 349

99 Double-crested Cormorant, 30–35", p. 451

101 Olivaceous Cormorant, 25″, p. 453

103 Double-crested Cormorant, 30–35", p. 451

Duck-like Birds

Included here are the many ducks, geese, and swans, as well as other birds that, like the ducks, are usually seen swimming. Many of the male ducks, and breeding-plumaged loons and grebes, are boldly patterned, while female ducks and winter-plumaged loons and grebes are clad in modest browns and grays.

105 Green-winged Teal, 12–16", p. 413

07 Mallard, 18–27″, p. 454

109 Redhead, 18–22″, p. 455

11 Ruddy Duck, 14–16″, p. 416

113 Red-breasted Merganser, 19–26″, p. 351

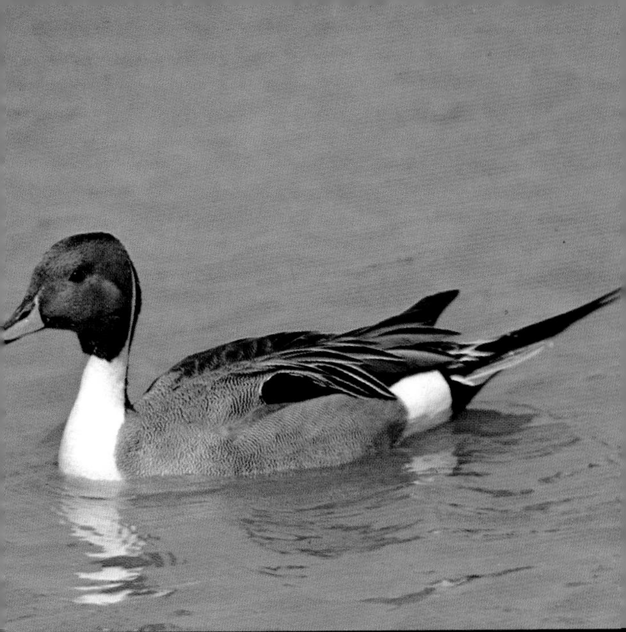

115 Pintail, 25–30″, p. 418

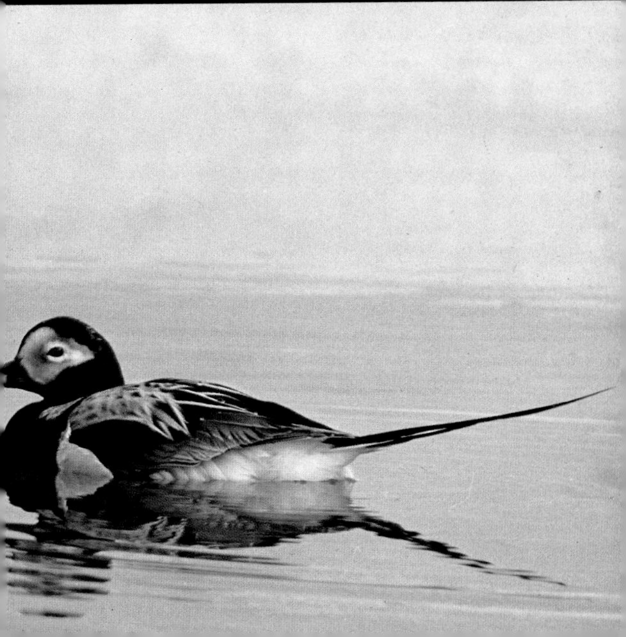

117 Common Eider, 23–27", p. 353

119 Wood Duck, 17–20″, p. 457

120 Harlequin Duck, 14–20″, p. 354

121   Ring-necked Duck, 14–18″, p. 458

122   Tufted Duck, 17″, p. 459

123 Lesser Scaup, 15–18″, p. 460

124 Greater Scaup, 15–20″, p. 461

125   Barrow's Goldeneye, 20–23″, p. 355

126   Common Goldeneye, 16–20″, p. 356

127 Bufflehead, 13–15″, p. 357

129　Surf Scoter, 17–21″, p. 358

131 Black Scoter, 17–21″, p. 359

132 European Wigeon, 18–20″, p. 415

133   Black Duck, 19–22″, p. 387

134   American Coot, 15″, p. 419

135 Gadwall, 18–21″, p. 420

136 Blue-winged Teal, 14–16″, p. 421

137   Mallard ♀, 18–27″, p. 454

138   Pintail ♀, 21–23″, p. 418

139 Gadwall ♀, 18–21″, p. 420

141   Cinnamon Teal ♀, 14–17″, p. 417

143 Northern Shoveler ♀, 17–20″, p. 416

144 Green-winged Teal ♀, 12–16″, p. 413

145 Common Eider ♀, 23–27″, p. 353

146 King Eider ♀, 18–25″, p. 353

47 White-winged Scoter ♀, 19–24″, p. 359

149   Barrow's Goldeneye ♀, 16–20", p. 355

151   Bufflehead ♀, 13–15″, p. 357

153 Redhead ♀, 18–22″, p. 455

155 Tufted Duck ♀, 17″, p. 459

157 Lesser Scaup ♀, 15–18″, p. 460

159 Ruddy Duck ♀, 14–16″, p. 416

161 Common Merganser ♀, 22–27″, p. 456

63 Hooded Merganser ♀, 16–19″, p. 461

165 Fulvous Whistling-Duck, 18–21″, p. 422

167 Black-bellied Whistling-Duck, 20–22″, p. 422

169 White-fronted Goose, 27–30″, p. 423

171 Snow Goose blue and white phases, p. 388

172 Brant, 22–30″, p. 390

173   Mute Swan, 58–60″, p. 424

174   Whistling Swan, 48–55″, p. 463

175 White Pelican, 55–70″, p. 425

177 Least Grebe winter plumage, 8–10″, p. 464

179 Least Grebe, 8–10", p. 464

181 Eared Grebe winter plumage, 12–14″, p. 361

83 Eared Grebe, 12–14″, p. 361

185 Red-necked Grebe, 18–20″, p. 465

187 Arctic Loon, 24″, p. 363

189   Red-throated Loon winter plumage, p. 363

Sandpiper-like Birds

This is a large group of small to medium-sized birds that have long legs and slender bills and are usually seen foraging on the beach or along the margins of lakes, ponds, marshes, or streams. Although these birds are collectively called "shorebirds," a few, such as the Killdeer, are often found on bare ground, far from water. Many of these birds are cryptically colored, but some, like the American Oystercatcher and the avocets and stilts, are boldly patterned in black-and-white.

191   Red Knot winter plumage, 10½", p. 364

192   Dunlin winter plumage, 8½", p. 365

94   American Golden Plover winter plumage, p. 366

95   Black-bellied Plover winter plumage, p. 367

197   Spotted Sandpiper winter plumage, 7½", p. 467

198   Purple Sandpiper winter plumage, 9", p. 369

200 Stilt Sandpiper winter plumage, 8½″, p. 391

201 Short-billed Dowitcher winter plumage, p. 391

203   Northern Phalarope winter plumage, 7", p. 326

204   Wilson's Phalarope winter plumage, 9", p. 427

206 Northern Phalarope ♀ summer plumage, p. 326

207 Wilson's Phalarope ♀ summer plumage, p. 427

209   Dunlin, 8½″, p. 365

210   Curlew Sandpiper winter plumage, 8″, p. 370

212 Short-billed Dowitcher, 12″, p. 391

213 Long-billed Dowitcher, 12½″, p. 393

215 Spotted Sandpiper, 7½", p. 467

216 Solitary Sandpiper, 8½", p. 428

218 Upland Sandpiper, 12″, p. 490

219 Pectoral Sandpiper, 9″, p. 429

221 Semipalmated Sandpiper, 6½″, p. 371

222 Western Sandpiper, 6½″, p. 371

224   Buff-breasted Sandpiper, 8″, p. 491

225   Baird's Sandpiper, 7½″, p. 372

226   White-rumped Sandpiper, 7½″, p. 373

227   Lesser Yellowlegs, 10½″, p. 394

228   Greater Yellowlegs, 14″, p. 395

229   Willet, 15″, p. 392

230 Stilt Sandpiper, 8½″, p. 391

231 Marbled Godwit, 18″, p. 396

233   Snowy Plover, 5–7″, p. 373

234   Piping Plover, 6–7″, p. 374

236 Semipalmated Plover, 6–8″, p. 375

237 Wilson's Plover, 7–8″, p. 376

239 American Golden Plover, 9–11″, p. 366

240 Black-bellied Plover, 10–13″, p. 367

242 American Oystercatcher, 17–21″, p. 376

243 Black-necked Stilt, 13–16″, p. 397

245 Whimbrel, 17", p. 398

Chicken-like Marsh Birds

These are small to medium-sized marsh
birds, most of which keep themselves
well concealed in the reeds or marsh
grasses. The bill may be long and
slender, as in the Clapper Rail or
Virginia Rail, or stubby and chicken-
like, as in the Sora. The two gallinules,
allied to the modestly plumaged rails
that make up the rest of this group, are
more often seen in the open and are
more brightly colored.

247 Common Gallinule, 13″, p. 430

248 Purple Gallinule, 11–13″, p. 431

249 Sora, 8–10″, p. 432

251 Yellow Rail, 6–8″, p. 433

253 Clapper Rail, 14–16″, p. 399

Upland Ground Birds

This group contains the familiar game birds—grouse, quails and pheasants—as well as certain other cryptically colored birds of woodlands, such as the woodcocks, snipe, and the nightjars. Many of these birds are difficult to detect against a background of dead leaves or grass until they flush unexpectedly into the air.

255 Common Snipe, 10½–11½″, p. 435

257 Bobwhite, 8–11", p. 493

259 Sharp-tailed Grouse, 16–18″, p. 493

261 Greater Prairie Chicken, 16–18″, p. 494

263 Willow Ptarmigan, 15″, p. 674

265 Willow Ptarmigan winter plumage, 15″, p. 674

267 Gray Partridge, 12–14″, p. 496

269 Turkey displaying, 48″, p. 631

271   Roadrunner, 24″, p. 497

273 Turkey, 48″, p. 631

274 Ring-necked Pheasant, 30–36″, p. 497

275   Common Nighthawk, 10″, p. 498

276   Pauraque, 12″, p. 600

77 Whip-poor-will, 10″, p. 632

Owls

This well-known group of birds scarcely needs a description. They are small to large birds with large round heads, loose, fluffy plumage and disk-like faces. Many are nocturnal, and are usually seen roosting quietly in trees during the day, but a few, such as the all-white Snowy Owl or the Short-eared Owl, often hunt by day and may be seen in open country.

279   Screech Owl red phase, 10″, p. 634

280   Screech Owl gray phase, 10″, p. 634

281   Long-eared Owl, 15″, p. 676

282   Great Horned Owl, 25″, p. 677

283   Burrowing Owl, 9″, p. 499

284   Short-eared Owl, 16″, p. 436

285 Barred Owl, 20″, p. 634

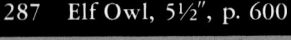

287 Elf Owl, 5½″, p. 600

289   Saw-whet Owl, 7", p. 635

291   Barn Owl, 18″, p. 500

Hawk-like Birds

The hawks and their allies range in size from the American Kestrel, scarcely larger than a Blue Jay, to the huge eagles and vultures. All have sharply hooked bills for tearing their prey, and many are often seen soaring high in the air. The wings may be rounded, as in the Red-tailed and Sharp-shinned Hawks, or pointed, as in the falcons and some of the kites.

293   Cooper's Hawk, 14–20″, p. 636

294   Sharp-shinned Hawk, 10–14″, p. 680

295 Rough-legged Hawk light phase, 19–24″, p. 501

296 Goshawk, 20–26″, p. 681

297   Broad-winged Hawk, 13–15″, p. 637

298   Red-shouldered Hawk, 16–24″, p. 637

09 Swainson's Hawk, 18–22″, p. 502

301 White-tailed Hawk, 21–23″, p. 503

03 White-tailed Kite, 15–16″, p. 504

305 Bald Eagle, 30–31", p. 468

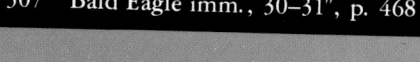
307 Bald Eagle imm., 30–31″, p. 468

309 Marsh Hawk, 16–24″, p. 437

11 Harris' Hawk, 18–30", p. 601

313 Merlin, 10–14", p. 682

315 Peregrine Falcon, 15–21″, p. 470

317 Turkey Vulture, 25–32″, p. 641

319 Short-tailed Hawk, 13–14″, p. 481

320 Everglade Kite, 16–18″, p. 482

Pigeon-like Birds

This group includes the familiar Rock Dove or city pigeon and its allies. These are small to medium-sized birds, small-headed, and clad in soft browns and grays. On the ground they walk with a characteristic mincing gait.

321   White-winged Dove, 12″, p. 602

322   Mourning Dove, 12″, p. 542

323 Ringed Turtle Dove, 12″, p. **542**

325 Ground Dove, 6½″, p. 506

327 Rock Dove, 13½″, p. 543

328 White-crowned Pigeon, 13″, p. 482

Swallow-like Birds

Included here are the swallows and martins and the similar but unrelated swifts. These are small birds that spend most of their time in the air, flying gracefully about in pursuit of their insect prey. They have pointed wings and often gather in large flocks.

329 Barn Swallow, 5¾–7¾″, p. 507

330 Cliff Swallow, 5–6″, p. 508

331   Tree Swallow, 5–6¼″, p. 471

333   Rough-winged Swallow, 5–5¾″, p. 472

335 Chimney Swift, 5½″, p. 545

Tree-clinging Birds

The woodpeckers, nuthatches, and creepers are usually seen climbing about on the trunks of trees, in search of insects hidden in the bark. Most of the woodpeckers are clad in black-and-white, although a few, like the Common Flicker, are mainly brown. The nuthatches are soft gray above and whitish or rusty below, and the creepers are brown and streaked.

337 Downy Woodpecker ♀, 6″, p. 643

338 Hairy Woodpecker ♀, 9″, p. 643

339 Downy Woodpecker, 6″, p. 643

340 Hairy Woodpecker, 9″, p. 643

341 Black-backed Three-toed Woodpecker ♀, 9″, p. 68

342 Northern Three-toed Woodpecker ♀, 8½″, p. 683

343   Black-backed Three-toed Woodpecker, 9″, p. 683

344   Northern Three-toed Woodpecker, 8½″, p. 683

345   Ladder-backed Woodpecker, 7″, p. 605

346   Yellow-bellied Sapsucker, 8½″, p. 644

347 Red-cockaded Woodpecker, 8″, p. 684

349　Red-bellied Woodpecker, 10″, p. 645

351 Red-headed Woodpecker, 10″, p. 508

353 Red-breasted Nuthatch, 4½–4¾", p. 685

355 Brown Creeper, 5–5¾″, p. 647

356 Brown-headed Nuthatch, 4–5″, p. 686

Perching Birds

This very large group includes nearly all of the songbirds, as well as cuckoos, kingfishers and hummingbirds, which, while unrelated, resemble songbirds rather closely. They range in size from the three- or four-inch hummingbirds and kinglets, to the large crows and ravens. They occur in a great variety of habitats and show an even greater variety of patterns and colors.

357 Yellow Warbler, 4½–5″, p. 568

358 Wilson's Warbler, 4½–5″, p. 568

360 Prothonotary Warbler, 5½", p. 648

361 Blue-winged Warbler, 4½", p. 570

363 Prairie Warbler, 5″, p. 571

364 Pine Warbler, 5½″, p. 686

366 Magnolia Warbler, 5″, p. 687

367 Canada Warbler, 5″, p. 688

368 Cape May Warbler, 5″, p. 688

369　Hooded Warbler, 5½″, p. 649

370　Kentucky Warbler, 5½″, p. 650

371　Common Yellowthroat, 4½–6″, p. 572

372 Mourning Warbler, 5½″, p. 651

373 Nashville Warbler, 4–5″, p. 573

375 Black-throated Green Warbler, 5″, p. 690

376 Yellow-throated Warbler, 5″, p. 691

378 Golden-winged Warbler, 4½", p. 574

379 Yellow-rumped Warbler, 5–6", p. 691

381 Verdin, 4–4½″, p. 606

382 American Redstart ♀, 4½–5½″, p. 575

384   Evening Grosbeak, 7½–8½″, p. 693

385   American Goldfinch, 4½–5½″, p. 510

387 Black-headed Oriole, 9″, p. 606

388 Orchard Oriole ♀, 7″, p. 652

390   **Kiskadee Flycatcher, 10½″, p. 607**

391   **Western Meadowlark, 8½–11″, p. 511**

393 Northern ("Baltimore") Oriole, 7–8½″, p. 546

394 Northern ("Bullock's") Oriole, 7–8½″, p. 546

396 Orchard Oriole, 7″, p. 652

397 Lichtenstein's Oriole, 9″, p. 609

399 Black-headed Grosbeak, 7½", p. 653

400 American Robin, 9–11", p. 548

402 American Redstart, 4½–5½″, p. 575

403 Bay-breasted Warbler, 5½″, p. 695

405   Pyrrhuloxia, 7½–8½″, p. 610

407 Cardinal, 8–9″, p. 578

08 Rose-breasted Grosbeak, 8″, p. 654

409 Purple Finch, 5½–6½″, p. 696

410 House Finch, 5–6″, p. 549

411 Common Redpoll, 5–5½″, p. 578

412 Red Crossbill, 5¼–6½″, p. 696

413 White-winged Crossbill, 6–6½″, p. 697

415 Vermilion Flycatcher, 6″, p. 611

416 Scarlet Tanager, 7½″, p. 655

418 Scissor-tailed Flycatcher, 14″, p. 513

419 Mockingbird, 9–11″, p. 549

421   Northern Shrike, 9–10½″, p. 514

422   Loggerhead Shrike, 8–10″, p. 514

424   Pine Grosbeak ♀, 8–10″, p. 698

425   Gray Jay, 10–13″, p. 699

427 Carolina Chickadee, 4–5″, p. 656

428 Black-capped Chickadee, 4¾–5¾″, p. 657

430 Rose-throated Becard, 6½″, p. 612

431 ″Black-crested Titmouse,″5–6″, p. 613

433 Belted Kingfisher, 13″, p. 473

435   Blue Jay, 12″, p. 552

437 Lazuli Bunting, 5–5½″, p. 580

438 Indigo Bunting, 5½″, p. 581

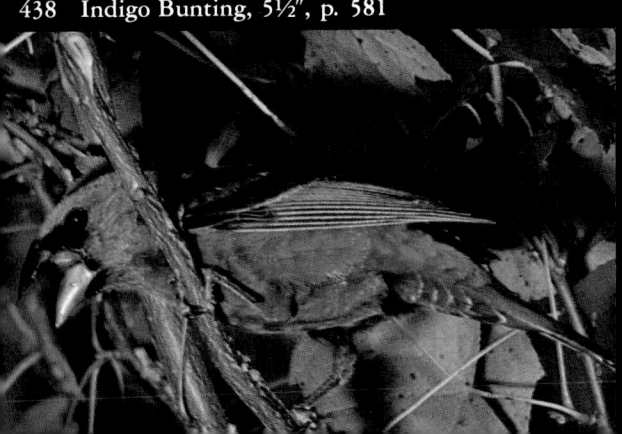

440 **Eastern Bluebird**, 7″, p. 516

441 **Mountain Bluebird**, 7″, p. 517

443 Blue-gray Gnatcatcher, 4½–5″, p. 659

444 Cerulean Warbler, 4½″, p. 660

446 Black-throated Blue Warbler, 5″, p. 700

447 Northern Parula, 4½″, p. 701

448 Northern Parula ♀, 4½″, p. 701

449 Bell's Vireo, 4¾", p. 582

450 Solitary Vireo, 5–6", p. 701

451 Philadelphia Vireo, 6", p. 702

452 Black-whiskered Vireo, 5½″, p. 486

453 Red-eyed Vireo, 5½–6½″, p. 660

455   Bay-breasted Warbler ♀, 5½″, p. 695

456   Orange-crowned Warbler, 4½–5½″, p. 584

458 Golden-crowned Kinglet, 3½–4″, p. 704

459 Ruby-crowned Kinglet, 3¾–4½″, p. 705

460 Connecticut Warbler 5½″, p. 706

461   Acadian Flycatcher, 6″, p. 662

462   Willow Flycatcher, 6″, p. 584

463   Yellow-bellied Flycatcher, 5½″, p. 707

464 Least Flycatcher, 5¼″, p. 663

465 Eastern Wood Pewee, 6½″, p. 664

467 Western Kingbird, 9″, p. 518

468 Tropical Kingbird, 8½″, p. 615

470 Olive-sided Flycatcher, 7½″, p. 706

471 Wied's Crested Flycatcher, 9½″, p. 615

473 Summer Tanager ♀, 7–8″, p. 655

474 Scarlet Tanager ♀, 7½″, p. 655

476 Painted Bunting, 5½", p. 586

477 Painted Bunting ♀, 5½", p. 586

478 Olive Sparrow, 5¾", p. 617

479   Ruby-throated Hummingbird, 3½″, p. 554

480   Rufous Hummingbird, 3½–4″, p. 555

481   Buff-bellied Hummingbird, 4½″, p. 618

482 Green Kingfisher, 8″, p. 475

483 Green Jay, 12″, p. 619

484 Monk Parakeet, 11″, p. 555

485   Short-billed Marsh Wren, 4–4½″, p. 437

486   House Wren, 4½–5¼″, p. 556

487   Winter Wren, 4–4½″, p. 708

488 Long-billed Marsh Wren, 4–5½", p. 438

489 Carolina Wren, 5½", p. 587

491   Canyon Wren, 5½–6″, p. 619

492   Rock Wren, 5–6½″, p. 620

494 Brown Thrasher, 11½″, p. 557

495 Long-billed Thrasher, 11″, p. 621

496 Curve-billed Thrasher, 9½–11½″, p. 622

497 Sage Thrasher, 8½″, p. 623

498 Gray-cheeked Thrush, 6½–8″, p. 709

499 Veery, 6½–7¼″, p. 666

500 Wood Thrush, 8″, p. 666

501 Hermit Thrush, 6½–7½″, p. 709

502 Swainson's Thrush, 6½–7¾″, p. 710

503   Ovenbird, 6″, p. 667

504   Louisiana Waterthrush, 6½″, p. 668

505   Northern Waterthrush, 6″, p. 669

506 Cedar Waxwing, 6½–8″, p. 558

507 Bohemian Waxwing, 7½–8½″, p. 711

508 Red-whiskered Bulbul, 8″, p. 486

509   Worm-eating Warbler, 5½″, p. 670

510   Wheatear, 5½–6″, p. 518

511   Boreal Chickadee, 5–5½″, p. 712

512 Vermilion Flycatcher ♀, 6″, p. 611

513 Indigo Bunting ♀, 5½″, p. 581

515 Brewer's Blackbird ♀, 8–10″, p. 519

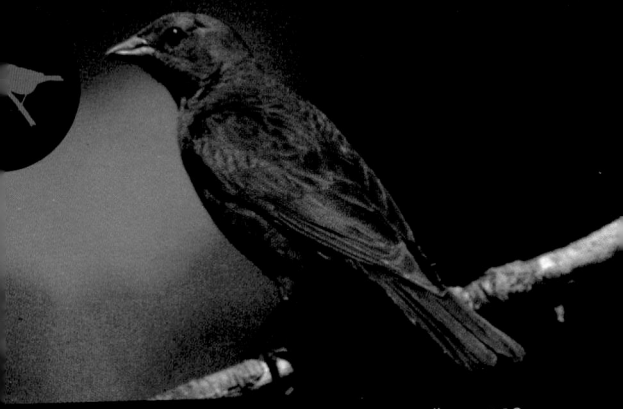

516 Brown-headed Cowbird ♀, 6–8″, p. 559

518 Yellow-headed Blackbird ♀, 8–11″, p. 439

519 Boat-tailed Grackle ♀, 12–13″, p. 402

521   Black-billed Cuckoo, 12″, p. 589

522   Yellow-billed Cuckoo, 10½–12½″, p. 590

524 Eurasian Tree Sparrow, 6", p. 560

525 House Sparrow, 5–6½", p. 560

526 House Sparrow, ♀, 5–6½", p. 560

527   Lark Sparrow, 5½–6½″, p. 521

528   Black-throated Sparrow, 5¼″, p. 624

529   Harris' Sparrow, 7½″, p. 590

530 Chipping Sparrow, 5–5½", p. 561

531 Tree Sparrow, 5½–6½", p. 522

532 Field Sparrow, 5¼", p. 522

533 Sharp-tailed Sparrow, 5½″, p. 440

534 Seaside Sparrow, 6″, p. 402

535 Clay-colored Sparrow, 5–5½″, p. 523

536   Grasshopper Sparrow, 4½–5″, p. 524

537   Henslow's Sparrow, 5″, p. 525

539   White-throated Sparrow, 6–7″, p. 591

540   White-crowned Sparrow, 6–7½″, p. 592

542   Song Sparrow, 5–7″, p. 562

543   Fox Sparrow, 6½–7½″, p. 593

544   Lincoln's Sparrow, 5–6″, p. 712

545   Dickcissel, 6″, p. 528

546   Water Pipit, 6–7″, p. 528

547   Snow Bunting, 6–7¼″, p. 530

548 Savannah Sparrow, 4½–6″, p. 531

549 Lark Bunting ♀, 6–7½″, p. 532

551 Lapland Longspur, 6–7″, p. 533

552 Chestnut-collared Longspur, 5½–6½″, p. 534

554 Smith's Longspur, 5¾–6½″, p. 536

555 Bobolink ♀, 6–8″, p. 537

556 Horned Lark, 7–8″, p. 538

557 Pine Siskin, 4½–5″, p. 713

558 Purple Finch ♀, 5½–6½″, p. 696

559 House Finch ♀, 5–6″, p. 549

560 Red-winged Blackbird ♀, 7–9½″, p. 441

561 Rose-breasted Grosbeak ♀, 8″, p. 654

563 Blackpoll Warbler, 5½″, p. 714

564 Black-and-White Warbler, 5″, p. 671

566 Lark Bunting, 6–7½", p. 532

567 Bobolink, 6–8", p. 537

568 Red-winged Blackbird, 7–9½", p. 441

569 Rusty Blackbird, 9″, p. 715

570 Brewer's Blackbird, 8–10″, p. 519

571 Brown-headed Cowbird, 6–8″, p. 559

572 Common Grackle (Bronzed), 12″, p. 564

573 Common Grackle (Purple), 12″, p. 564

574 Bronzed Cowbird, 8½″, p. 520

575 Boat-tailed Grackle, 16–17″, p. 402

576 Great-tailed Grackle, 16–17″, p. 626

577   Smooth-billed Ani, 14″, p. 539

579 Common Crow, 17–21″, p. 565

581 Common Raven, 21–27", p. 716

583 Yellow-headed Blackbird, 8–11″, p. 439

Part II
Habitat Key

The number preceding each species description in the following pages corresponds to the number of the illustration in the color plates section. If the description has no number there is no color plate but in that case a drawing accompanies the description.

Open Ocean

Pelagic waters, mostly out of sight of land. Much of this water overlies the continental shelf and so is rich in plankton, the microscopic marine organisms that provide food for fish and seabirds.

In addition to the birds treated in this section, one will occasionally see flocks of migrating waterfowl, shorebirds, and songbirds.

40 Northern Fulmar
"Fulmar"
(*Fulmarus glacialis*)
Shearwaters, Fulmars (Procellariidae)

Description: 18" (46 cm). A stocky, gull-like
seabird; typical birds are pale gray on
back and wings, white elsewhere, but
uniformly dark gray individuals occur,
as well as intermediates between pale
and dark gray. Yellow bill. Easily
distinguished from gulls by its flight:
several fast wingbeats followed by a
stiff-winged glide.

Voice: Chuckling and grunting notes when
feeding; various guttural calls during
the breeding season.

Habitat: Rocky cliffs; open seas.

Nesting: 1 white egg on a bare rock or in a
shallow depression lined with plant
material.

Range: Arctic Ocean south to Newfoundland,
wintering at sea south to New Jersey;
also in northern Eurasia.

The Fulmar feeds on fish, squids, and
shrimp and the refuse of the whaling
industry. The expansion of the fishing
industry in this century has caused an
increase in the North Atlantic
population of this species, especially
noticeable in the British Isles. Fulmars
have been reported in greater numbers
on the east coast of America in the last
few years, but this may be due to the
increasing number of observers going
out to sea to look for them.

44 Sabine's Gull
(*Xema sabini*)
Gulls, Terns (Laridae)

Description: 13–14" (33–36 cm). A small, *fork-tailed*
gull with black primaries and *triangular
white patch on rear edge of wing.* Hood
dark in breeding plumage. Bill black
with yellow tip. Immature lacks dark

hood but can be told by forked tail.

Voice: High-pitched grating or squeaking notes.

Habitat: Tundra ponds in summer; open ocean in migration and winter.

Nesting: 3 or 4 olive-brown eggs, spotted with darker brown, placed in a grass-lined depression on the ground. In small colonies.

Range: Coastal tundra around the shores of the Arctic Ocean, farther inland in Alaska. Migrates mainly at sea. Winter range not fully known; some birds winter off the Pacific coast of northern South America.

This delicate gull is seldom seen outside of the breeding season as it is almost exclusively oceanic. On the tundra it gracefully plucks small crustaceans and insects from the surface of the water like a tern. It also takes eggs from nesting colonies of Arctic Terns.

72 Bridled Tern
(*Sterna anaethetus*)
Gulls, Terns (Laridae)

Description: 14–15" (35–38 cm). A stocky oceanic tern, dark gray above, white below, with a black cap; white forehead and eyebrow, and a conspicuous white collar or "bridle" on hindneck. Sooty Tern similar, but lacks collar and is blacker on upperparts.

Voice: Usually silent; various high-pitched barking notes on the breeding grounds.

Habitat: Open ocean; breeds on rocky or sandy islands.

Nesting: 1 white egg, spotted with brown, placed in a shallow depression among rocks on an island. In colonies.

Range: Breeds in tropical Atlantic, Indian, and Pacific oceans; ranges in nonbreeding season to offshore waters from the Carolinas to Florida.

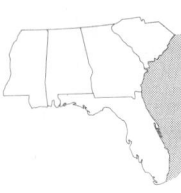

This bird was long thought to be a casual visitor to the North American coast, but as more birders travel out to the Gulf Stream, it is becoming evident that the species is fairly common twenty or thirty miles offshore.

77 Brown Booby
(*Sula leucogaster*)
Gannets, Boobies (Sulidae)

Description: 30″ (76 cm). Adult has dark brown head and upperparts, with a sharply contrasting white breast and belly and white underwing coverts; immature is gray-brown, darker on head, wings, and tail.

Voice: Usually silent, but a variety of quacking, grunting, and screeching calls have been described.

Habitat: Tropical and subtropical seas, breeding on coastal islands.

Nesting: 2 pale blue eggs on the ground in a slight mound of broken shells and scattered vegetation.

Range: Pantropical waters; in America, breeds on islands north to the Gulf of Mexico and the Caribbean Sea; wanders occasionally to the coasts of Florida, Louisiana, and Texas; perhaps occurs regularly on the Dry Tortugas, Florida.

Of the three boobies seen off the beaches of the Gulf of Mexico, the Brown is by far the most plentiful. Related to the larger Gannet, boobies also dive for fish by plunging into the sea. They also skim the surface, catching flying fish that leap clear of the surf. These birds are dependent on a strong wind for takeoff from a tree or other elevated perch. On a calm day they rest in the vegetation or on the ground.

78 Blue-faced Booby
(*Sula dactylatra*)
Gannets, Boobies (Sulidae)

Description: 32" (80 cm). A stocky white seabird
with black tail, black tips and trailing
edges to the wings, and a stout pinkish
or orange bill. In the breeding season,
birds have a patch of bare, bluish skin
at the base of the bill. The Gannet is
similar but larger, with only the wing
tips black.

Voice: Usually silent; a variety of hissing
and quacking notes on the breeding
grounds.

Habitat: Tropical seas.

Nesting: 2 chalky, pale blue eggs in a shallow
depression on the ground. In colonies.

Range: The Bahamas and West Indies, and on
other islands in the tropical Atlantic,
Indian, and Pacific oceans. A casual on
the coasts of Florida, Louisiana, and
Texas.

Like many birds that nest on remote
oceanic islands, these birds have little
fear of man and because of their
tameness, they were easily killed for
food by early mariners, who gave them
the name "Booby" for this reason.
Boobies obtain their food in spectacular
plunges into the sea from the air. A
principal food of this species is flying
fish; These birds are therefore seldom
found in areas where flying fish are
not plentiful.

79 Cory's Shearwater
(*Puffinus diomedea*)
Shearwaters, Fulmars (Procellariidae)

Description: 20–22" (51–56 cm). Dull gray above,
white below; *pale bill (usually yellow)*.
Similar to the Greater Shearwater, but
the dull gray crown of Cory's Shearwater
blends evenly with the white sides of the
face, without the abrupt contrast seen

in the Greater Shearwater.

Voice: Howling, gurgling calls heard only on breeding grounds.

Habitat: Open oceans.

Nesting: 1 white egg laid in a rock crevice or on open ground on an island, less often in caves or burrows. In colonies.

Range: Breeds in eastern Atlantic and Mediterranean, and occurs in summer and fall off the east coast of North America.

This is the only one of our large shearwaters that breeds in the Northern Hemisphere. After the breeding season the birds move westward into American waters, usually becoming common in July and remaining until late in the fall. A powerful bird, it does not resort to burrows for protection from predators during the breeding season. Like the Sooty and Greater Shearwater, it often follows ships in search of food.

80 Greater Shearwater
(*Puffinus gravis*)
Shearwaters, Fulmars (Procellariidae)

Description: 18–20″ (46–51 cm). Narrow-winged, gull-sized seabird usually seen skimming over the waves in the wake of ships. Dull brown above, white below; *dark cap contrasting sharply with white side of face;* may show white at base of tail; *black bill.* Cory's Shearwater is paler, lacks the contrast between crown and face, and has a pale bill.

Voice: Usually silent in our area; a snarling *eeyah,* given by birds resting in flocks on the water.

Habitat: Open ocean.

Nesting: 1 white egg laid in a burrow on a grassy slope. In very large colonies.

Range: Islands of the Tristan da Cunha group, South Atlantic. Spends the northern summer as a nonbreeding visitor to the North Atlantic.

It is incredible that the millions of Greater Shearwaters that appear in the North Atlantic each summer have bred on one small group of islands in the Southern Hemisphere. Like the Sooty Shearwaters, these birds follow a "Great Circle" route around the Atlantic, appearing in North American waters in May, then moving on to the eastern Atlantic in late summer. Expert divers, they feed mainly on small fish and squid.

Audubon's Shearwater
(Puffinus lherminieri)
Shearwaters, Fulmars (Procellariidae)

Description: 11–12" (28–30 cm). A small shearwater with white cheeks, throat, breast, and abdomen; black crown, upperparts, and *black undertail coverts.* Half the size of the Greater Shearwater. The rarer Manx Shearwater has white undertail coverts.

Voice: Twittering calls and mewing notes heard at night in the breeding colonies.

Habitat: Open oceans.

Nesting: 1 white egg laid in a burrow or rock crevice on an island. In colonies.

Range: Islands in tropical seas around the world. Wanders northward, as far north as New York City in the U.S.

Very similar to the Manx Shearwater, this tropical species appears regularly on the Gulf Stream during the summer. There is no evidence that this bird undertakes the great migrations of the other shearwaters. Like the Manx, it is not a ship-follower, and so is often difficult to see closeup.

Manx Shearwater
(*Puffinus puffinus*)
Shearwaters, Fulmars (Procellariidae)

Description: 12½–15″ (32–38 cm). A small
shearwater, *black above and white below.*
Greater Shearwater is nearly twice as
large, and usually shows white at the
base of the tail. Audubon's Shearwater
is almost identical but has *dark
undertail coverts.*

Voice: Cooing and clucking notes heard at
night at breeding colonies.

Habitat: Open oceans.

Nesting: 1 white egg laid in a burrow or rock
crevice on an island. In colonies.

Range: Breeds in the eastern Atlantic. Occurs
as an uncommon visitor (and very rare
breeder) off the east coast of North
America. Allied forms breed in Pacific
and Indian oceans.

Unlike the larger Sooty, Greater, and
Cory's Shearwaters, this species does
not follow ships and is usually seen
skimming past at some distance. Manx
Shearwaters are known to have bred
once in Massachusetts, but because they
are entirely nocturnal on the breeding
grounds, they may have bred more
frequently on our shores and have
simply gone unnoticed. These birds are
great travelers whose movements are
poorly understood; a bird that was
banded in Great Britain was later
recovered in Australian waters.

81 **Sooty Shearwater**
(*Puffinus griseus*)
Shearwaters, Fulmars (Procellariidae)

Description: 16–18″ (41–46 cm). Gull-sized. The
only Atlantic shearwater that appears
all dark sooty brown, paler on the wing
linings. This slender, narrow-winged
seabird skims on stiff wings over the
waves, alternately gliding and flapping.

Voice: Silent except for a variety of cooing and croaking notes heard on breeding grounds.

Habitat: Open ocean.

Nesting: 1 white egg in a burrow lined with plant material. In colonies.

Range: Islands in subantarctic seas. Spends the northern summer in the North Atlantic and North Pacific oceans.

One of the most abundant birds in the world, this species nests in millions on islands off New Zealand. Most that appear off the east coast breed around Tierra del Fuego off the southern tip of South America. After breeding, they begin a great circular migration around the Atlantic Ocean, arriving off the east coast of North America in May, continuing on to Europe, then down the west coast of Africa, returning to their nesting islands in November.

82 Wilson's Storm-Petrel
"Wilson's Petrel"
(*Oceanites oceanicus*)
Storm-Petrels (Hydrobatidae)

Description: 7" (18 cm). A small seabird that skims over the surface like a swallow. Black with a white rump; *tail not forked.* Leach's Petrel is similar, but has a forked tail and butterfly-like flight.

Voice: A soft peeping, heard at close range when the birds are feeding.

Habitat: Open ocean; breeds on rocky cliffs and offshore islands.

Nesting: 1 white egg in a crevice among rocks or in a burrow in soft earth.

Range: Breeds in Antarctic and subantarctic seas; in nonbreeding season ranges over Atlantic, Pacific, and Indian oceans, in the western Atlantic north to Labrador.

One of the most abundant birds in the world, this species, formerly called

"Wilson's Petrel," nests in countless millions on islands in the Southern Hemisphere, and visits the Northern Hemisphere during our summer months. It often hovers at the surface of the water, its wings held over its back and its feet gently touching the water. Although normally a bird of the open ocean, it may occasionally enter bays and estuaries. It is named after the early American ornithologist Alexander Wilson (1766–1813).

83 Leach's Storm-Petrel
"Leach's Petrel"
(*Oceanodroma leucorhoa*)
Storm-Petrels (Hydrobatidae)

Description: 8–9" (20–23 cm). Small, swallow-like seabird, all black with a white rump. Differs from Wilson's Storm-Petrel in having the tail somewhat forked, dark feet, and a flight that is more erratic. Unlike Wilson's, this species seldom follows boats.

Voice: A variety of trills, screams, and cooing notes.

Habitat: Open seas, resorting to rocky islands and coasts to breed.

Nesting: One white egg, often with a faint ring of spots at the large end, placed in a shallow burrow in the ground or under a log or board, often well-concealed. In colonies.

Range: Coasts and offshore islands from Labrador south to Maine, rarely to Massachusetts. Winters on the open ocean. Also breeds in the eastern Atlantic and on both sides of the Pacific Ocean.

Although not uncommon, Leach's Storm-Petrel, until recently called "Leach's Petrel," is seldom seen because it feeds far out at sea, and visits its breeding grounds under cover of darkness.

The presence of the birds is not difficult to detect, however: the nesting burrows have an unmistakable musky odor, caused by an oily orange liquid that the birds emit when disturbed, and the air is filled with their nocturnal calls. These birds are vulnerable to many predators, but their nocturnal habits no doubt save them from heavy predation by their principal enemies, gulls. Like other storm-petrels, they feed mainly on small shrimp and other planktonic animals, which they pluck deftly from the surface of the ocean.

It has been reported that, because of their high oil content, these birds were at one time used as lamps. A cotton wick was inserted in the throat of a dead bird, which when lighted would burn for a considerable length of time.

84 Skua
(*Catharacta skua*)
Jaegers, Skuas (Stercorariidae)

Description: 21" (53 cm). A large, dark, heavy-bodied, gull-like bird, grayish brown with conspicuous white patches in the outer wing. Tail short and blunt. Immatures of the larger gulls lack the white wing patches.

Voice: A harsh *hah-hah-hah-hah;* various quacking and croaking notes.

Habitat: Breeds on open bare ground near the sea; at other times ranges over the open sea.

Nesting: 2 olive-brown eggs with dark brown spots, in a grass-lined nest on the ground. Often in loose colonies.

Range: Nests on Iceland and islands north of Britain, ranging widely over the North Atlantic. Also breeds on islands in the Southern Hemisphere.

Skuas occur off the shores of the Northern Hemisphere most often in late summer and early fall, where they

are abundant on the fishing banks off
Newfoundland. They feed on a variety
of shrimp, fish, rodents, and the eggs
and young of colonial seabirds. They
are vigorous in the defense of their
nests, diving boldly at intruders.

87 Long-tailed Jaeger
(*Stercorarius longicaudus*)
Jaegers, Skuas (Stercorariidae)

Description: 21" (53 cm). Adults similar to light-
phase Parasitic Jaegers, but smaller,
more graceful, and with *very long central
tail feathers*. Upperparts paler than in
other jaegers, and blackish cap smaller
and more sharply defined. Flight more
buoyant.

Voice: A harsh *kreeah;* other yelping and
rattling notes on the breeding grounds.

Habitat: Breeds on tundra and stony hillsides; at
other times ranges over open ocean.

Nesting: 2 olive-brown eggs with brown spots,
in a grass-lined nest placed either on
bare ground or among rocks.

Range: North of the Arctic Circle, wintering
far offshore in both Atlantic and Pacific
oceans.

Smallest of the three jaegers, the Long-
tailed is the rarest in eastern North
America, presumably because it
migrates chiefly in mid-ocean.
Although occasionally, like other
jaegers, it harries terns and gulls, it
feeds mainly by catching its own fish,
taking flying insects in the air, and
sometimes preying on small birds. On
the breeding grounds its staple food is
lemmings.

88 Pomarine Jaeger
(*Stercorarius pomarinus*)
Jaegers, Skuas (Stercorariidae)

Description: 22″ (56 cm). Larger and stockier than the Parasitic Jaeger, with a more extensive white flash in the outer wing and with central tail feathers twisted and blunt, not pointed; breast band often darker and wider; bill heavier; flight more direct. Dark-phase and light-phase individuals occur.

Voice: Harsh chattering calls; a harsh *which-yew*.

Habitat: Swampy tundra; on migration and in winter on the ocean.

Nesting: 2 olive-brown eggs with darker brown spots, in a grass-lined depression on the ground.

Range: Above the Arctic Circle in Alaska, northern Canada, and Greenland; in eastern United States winters mainly south of Cape Hatteras, North Carolina. Also in Eurasia.

Largest of our jaegers, it preys on birds up to the size of terns and small gulls, as well as lemmings, carrion, and the eggs and young of colonial seabirds. Like the Parasitic Jaeger it also pursues gulls and terns, forcing them to disgorge their food, which it catches in mid-air. Although it can be seen from land at times, it is much more often seen far off shore.

89 Parasitic Jaeger
(Stercorarius parasiticus)
Jaegers, Skuas (Stercorariidae)

Description: 21″ (53 cm). A fast-flying, gull-like
seabird. Typical adults are brown
above, white or light dusky below,
with a *gray-brown band across the breast*
and a dark, almost black crown. Dark-
phase birds are uniform dusky brown
with pale cheeks. Intermediates between
the two color phases occur.
Distinguished from other jaegers by
*pointed central tail feathers extending up
to three inches beyond rest of tail* and
moderate white flash in outer wing.
Often seen harrying gulls and terns.

Voice: Usually silent; a variety of mewing and
wailing notes on the breeding grounds.

Habitat: Grassy tundra and stony ground near
inland lakes in summer; at other times
on the ocean.

Nesting: 2 olive-brown eggs with darker brown
spots, in a grass-lined depression on the
ground or among rocks.

Range: Aleutians, northern Alaska, Canada,
and Greenland south to central Canada;
winters in warm waters south to
Argentina. Also in northern Eurasia.

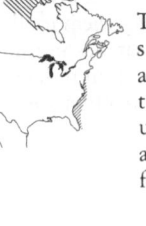

This is the most familiar of our jaegers
since it comes more readily into bays
and estuaries and feeds more often close
to shore. Like the other jaegers, it
usually obtains food by pursuing gulls
and terns and forcing them to drop
food.

203, 206 Northern Phalarope
(Phalaropus lobatus)
Sandpipers (Scolopacidae)

Description: 7″ (18 cm). Sparrow-sized. In summer,
head and back dark, chin and belly
white separated by *chestnut throat and
upper breast.* In winter, much paler and
grayer above, entirely white below. *Bill*

thin. Conspicuous wing stripe.

Voice: Sharp *whit* or *twit*.

Habitat: Open ocean, beaches, flats, lake and river shores.

Nesting: 4 brown-spotted olive eggs in a slight hollow on the ground in marshy tundra.

Range: Arctic and subarctic zones of both hemispheres; in America south to central Canada. Winters at sea in the Southern Hemisphere.

The Northern or "Red-necked Phalarope" belongs to a group in which the female is brighter than the male and the male incubates the eggs. It has fully lobed toes and swims buoyantly. In effect an oceangoing sandpiper, it spends nearly all of its nonbreeding life at sea, although on occasion it wades in pools and feeds in mud like many other shorebirds. Phalaropes often feed by spinning around in the water. The motion of their feet stirs up plankton, which they gather from the surface by rapid jabs of the bill.

205, 208 Red Phalarope
(*Phalaropus fulicarius*)
Sandpipers (Scolopacidae)

Description: 8″ (20 cm). In summer, *rich chestnut,* dark crown, white face; *short, stout, yellow bill* with a black tip. In winter, gray above and white below, bill darker. Paler than the Northern Phalarope with an *unstreaked back* and a less contrasting wing stripe. Like other phalaropes, the female is more brightly colored than the male.

Voice: Sharp metallic *beek.*

Habitat: The most pelagic of all shorebirds, mostly ocean-inhabiting in the nonbreeding season; otherwise it is found in bays, inlets, inland lakes, shores, coasts, and on the tundra in the breeding season.

Nesting: 4 brown-speckled olive eggs placed on the ground in a grass-lined nest on an elevated spot in low marshy areas.

Range: Islands and coasts along the Arctic Ocean of both hemispheres; in America south to northern Canada. Winters at sea, chiefly in the Southern Hemisphere.

Hundreds of these shorebirds may be seen from a fishing boat far at sea, where they look like bobbing corks or miniature gulls riding the waves. The greater part of their diet while they are at sea is made up of tiny marine animals known as plankton. On land they forage around the tundra pools for aquatic larvae of mosquitoes, midges, and beetles. After egg-laying the male takes over the duties of hatching and rearing the young.

Seashore

Open sandy beaches, mudflats, and dunes, the latter covered with beach grass. This section includes the birds most likely to be seen on the water from shore.

3, 15 Reddish Egret
(*Egretta rufescens*)
Herons, Bitterns (Ardeidae)

Description: 30″ (76 cm). W. 46″ (1 m). Medium-sized heron. Slaty with shaggy rufous head and neck; *black legs; pink bill with black tip.* Also a white phase.

Voice: Squawks and croaks.

Habitat: Salt and brackish waters, breeding in shallow bays and lagoons; in mangroves (Florida); among cacti, willows, and other shrubs (Texas).

Nesting: 3 or 4 bluish-green eggs in a grass and stick nest in mangroves, low bushes, or on the ground.

Range: Local in extreme southern Florida and along the Texas coasts, south to the West Indies and Mexico.

This egret feeds on fish, frogs, and crabs, pursuing its prey with rapid rushes and upraised wings as it twists and turns. It is uncommon and rather local throughout its range. Both color phases may be seen on the Gulf Coast, the dark one predominating in Florida waters, the white in Texas, but this varies according to locality; sometimes both occur together. During the nuptial display the plumes on its head, neck, and back stand out in a bristly ruff.

31, 34 Iceland Gull
(*Larus glaucoides*)
Gulls, Terns (Laridae)

Description: 23″ (58 cm). A smaller version of the Glaucous Gull, with a relatively smaller bill. Adults are pearl-gray to white; pinkish bill and feet. Immatures creamy buff.

Voice: Like the Herring Gull, a variety of croaks, squeaks, and screams.

Habitat: Lake and river shores, ocean beaches, sewer outlets, and refuse dumps.

Nesting: 2 or 3 light brown eggs with darker blotches in a nest lined with grass, moss, and seaweed placed either on a cliff or a sandy shore.

Range: Breeds in Greenland and south to Baffin Island. Winters in eastern North America south to New Jersey and the Great Lakes. Also in northern and temperate Europe.

The habits of the two "white-winged" gulls are similar, but the smaller Iceland Gull is more buoyant and graceful on the wing. It is also more of a scavenger and much less predatory. In addition to garbage dumps and sewage outlets, this species frequents places where fish are being cleaned. Both of these pale gulls, being relatively rare, are avidly sought by bird-watchers.

32, 49 Ivory Gull
(*Pagophila eburnea*)
Gulls, Terns (Laridae)

Description: 17" (43 cm). A rather small, *short-legged* gull; adults are pure white with yellowish bill and legs; immatures similar but with *black bars and spots* in varying numbers.

Voice: A harsh *eeeer*.

Habitat: Rocky cliffs or stony ground; winters at the edge of the pack ice in Arctic seas.

Nesting: 2 buff-olive eggs marked with dark blotches, in a nest lined with moss, lichens, and seaweed, on bare ground among rocks or on gravel-covered polar ice.

Range: Known to breed in the New World only on Somerset and Ellesmere Islands in the Canadian Arctic; more widespread in Eastern Hemisphere. Winters in the Arctic Ocean, appearing rarely farther south.

With the Eskimos and the polar bear, the Ivory Gull shares the realm of icebergs and ice floes. Indeed, it follows these hunters in quest of food, for it is largely a scavenger, feeding on the remains of their kills—mainly seals. It also eats wolf and fox dung, whale blubber, lemmings, crustaceans, and insects.

33, 36 **Glaucous Gull**
(*Larus hyperboreus*)
Gulls, Terns (Laridae)

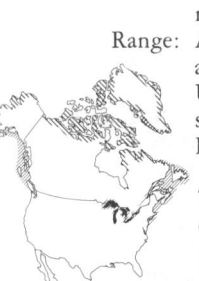

Description: 28″ (71 cm). Large gull. Adults pearl-gray to white; yellowish bill and pinkish feet. Immatures creamy-buff. *No black in wing tips.*

Voice: Hoarse croaks and screams.

Habitat: Shores of lakes, rivers, and the seacoast; also refuse dumps and sewage outflow.

Nesting: 3 light brown eggs with dark chocolate blotches placed in a cliff nest lined with moss and grass.

Range: Arctic and subarctic portions of Alaska and Canada. Winters in the northern United States. Also in the arctic, subarctic, and north temperate areas of Eurasia.

The great white Glaucous Gull is ordinarily rare south of Canada; usually found with flocks of the abundant Herring Gulls when it visits the United States. This is one of the most predatory gulls, capturing and eating alcids, plovers, small ducks, ptarmigan, and songbirds as well as lemmings and fish. It is also a scavenger, feeding on garbage, dead animal matter, and even bird droppings.

35 Thayer's Gull
(*Larus thayeri*)
Gulls, Terns (Laridae)

Description: 24″ (61 cm). In all plumages, very
similar to the Herring Gull, gray
above, white below, but *eye of adult
dark* instead of yellow.

Voice: Mewing and squealing notes.

Habitat: Arctic coasts and islands, usually on
rocky cliffs.

Nesting: 3 bluish or greenish eggs spotted with
brown, in a nest lined with grass,
moss, or lichens placed on high rocky
cliffs.

Range: Greenland and northeastern Canada;
winters chiefly on the Pacific Coast of
North America south to Baja
California. Very rare winter visitor to
southeastern Canada and northeastern
United States.

Until recently this bird was thought to
be a subspecies of the Herring Gull, or
of the Iceland Gull, or even a hybrid
between the two. Experiments with
color-dyed individuals have now
demonstrated that differences in eye
and eye-ring color of Herring, Iceland,
and Thayer's gulls are sufficient to
prevent them from interbreeding.

39, 54, 57 Black-legged Kittiwake
(*Rissa tridactyla*)
Gulls, Terns (Laridae)

Description: 16–18″ (40–46 cm). Small, seagoing
gull. Adult white with pale gray back
and wings; *sharply defined black wing tip,*
as if dipped in black ink; black feet;
yellow bill; slightly forked tail. Winter
adult has dusky gray patch on nape.
Young bird has dusky band on nape,
dark diagonal wing band, and black-
tipped tail.

Voice: Variety of loud, harsh notes. Very noisy
on the breeding ground. With a little

imagination, its common call can be said to resemble its name, *kittiwake*.

Habitat: Cliffs and seacoasts in the Arctic; winters at sea.

Nesting: 2 pinkish-buff spotted eggs in a well-made cup of mosses and seaweed at the top of a cliff or on a ledge. In colonies.

Range: North Pacific and Arctic Ocean to the Gulf of St. Lawrence. Winters from the edge of the sea ice south to the Sargasso Sea. Also in Eurasia.

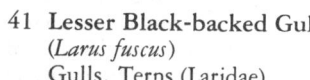

This abundant gull is not commonly seen from shore, for it generally spends the entire winter on the open ocean, where it feeds on small fish and plankton. Most young gulls flee from the nest if disturbed, but the young of this cliff-nesting species stay put no matter how close a human observer gets; to leave a nest on a high, narrow ledge could result in a fatal plunge to the rocks below. This is the only gull that dives and swims underwater to capture food.

---

41 Lesser Black-backed Gull
(*Larus fuscus*)
Gulls, Terns (Laridae)

Description: 23″ (58 cm). Slightly smaller than the Herring Gull. Adult has *yellow legs;* dark slate-gray back and wings. Immatures of this species and the Herring Gull are virtually indistinguishable.

Voice: A strident *kyow,* deeper than that of the Herring Gull.

Habitat: Nearly all types of open country—coasts, islands, fields, lakes, airports, refuse dumps, etc.

Nesting: 3 pale blue-green eggs spotted with brown in a nest sparsely lined with grass or laden with debris, placed on open ground or on rocky islets. Usually in colonies.

Range: Northern Europe south to France;
winters from central Europe south to
central Africa. Rare but regular visitor
to eastern North America.

Although this Old World species is
still rare on the American side of the
Atlantic, it is being seen in and around
larger cities, not only along the coast
but also in the Great Lakes region.
During the colder months it may be
found at garbage dumps, sewer outlets,
and reservoirs.

42, 51 Great Black-backed Gull
(*Larus marinus*)
Gulls, Terns (Laridae)

Description: 30″ (76 cm). Very large gull. Adult has
black back and wings, rest of plumage
white. Bill yellow and legs pinkish.
Immature mottled with brown, has a
black tip to its tail, and a dark bill.

Voice: Similar to that of the Herring Gull
but deeper and more guttural. A deep
keeow.

Habitat: Coastal beaches, estuaries, and lagoons;
also at refuse dumps. Less commonly on
inland lakes and rivers.

Nesting: 3 olive eggs with dark brown blotches
placed in a ground nest, lined with
grass.

Range: Coasts on both sides of the North
Atlantic, south to southern United
States and the Mediterranean.

Our largest gull, this conspicuous bird
accompanies the ever-present Herring
Gull at all times of the year, even
during the summer when they nest
together in mixed colonies. However,
the Black-backed always asserts
dominance over its smaller relative. It
preys on almost anything smaller than
itself, including Dovekies, small ducks,
petrels, fish, and shellfish as well as the
eggs and young of other gulls. It has
extended its breeding range south in

recent years and nests in a number of
places on the shores of Long Island,
New York, and New Jersey. Although
found close to man's habitations, it is a
shyer bird than the Herring Gull.

59, 67 Sandwich Tern
(*Sterna sandvicensis*)
Gulls, Terns (Laridae)

Description: 16″ (40 cm). Robin-sized. White with
gray mantle, black cap, short crest,
and *long, black, yellow-tipped bill.*
Formerly called Cabot's Tern.
Voice: Loud, harsh *curr-it.*
Habitat: Coastal beaches and islands.
Nesting: 2 greenish, black-marked eggs on bare
sand, usually with Royal Terns.
Range: Locally on the Atlantic and Gulf coasts
from Virginia to Florida and Texas; also
in the Caribbean and from Scandinavia
and the British Isles to the
Mediterranean. Winters south to
Panama, Brazil, Africa, and India.

The Sandwich Tern is one of three
crested terns occurring along our coasts.
Its range is most unusual. It breeds
much farther north in Europe than it
does in America because of the
warming influence of the Gulf Stream.
Sandwich Terns feed offshore diving for
fish, shrimp, and squid; inshore they
have been reported to eat marine worms
as well.

---

62 Roseate Tern
(*Sterna dougallii*)
Gulls, Terns (Laridae)

Description: 14–17″ (35–43 cm). Robin-sized.
White with a black cap and *very pale
gray back and wings.* Similar to
Common, Arctic, and Forster's Terns,
but bill usually solid black, upper parts

paler, tail longer and more deeply
forked.

Voice: Loud, harsh *zaap,* likened to the sound
of tearing cloth. Also a softer *cue-lick.*

Habitat: Coastal beaches, islands, and inshore
waters.

Nesting: 2 or 3 spotted buff or olive eggs in a
hollow in the ground, sometimes lined
with dead grass; may be placed in the
open but more often concealed in
vegetation or among rocks. Colonial,
often nesting with other species of
terns.

Range: Along the coast from Gulf of St.
Lawrence south to Venezuela; winters
from Gulf Coast to Brazil. Also breeds
in eastern Atlantic, western Indian
Ocean, and southwest Pacific.

The Roseate Tern is much less
numerous than other terns of similar
size, and its patchy distribution around
the world suggests that it is an old
species, perhaps more abundant and
widespread ages ago. It probably suffers
from competition for nesting sites with
the Common Tern, at least in American
waters, and like that species is sensitive
to disturbance by human beings. For
these reasons our breeding population is
small, and the location of known
colonies is often kept secret by those
eager to protect the birds. It frequently
nests in colonies of Common Terns,
occupying the less favorable, marginal
sites.

63 Arctic Tern
(*Sterna paradisaea*)
Gulls, Terns (Laridae)

Description: 14–17″ (35–43 cm). Whitish, with
white streak below the black cap and
pale gray upperparts. Deeply forked
tail. Similar to Common Tern but
underparts grayer, bill blood-red, legs
shorter, tail longer.

Voice: Harsh *TEE-ar* or *kip-kip-kip-TEE-ar*,
higher in pitch than the Common Tern.

Habitat: Coastal islands and beaches; also on
tundra in summer.

Nesting: 2 spotted olive-buff eggs in a shallow
depression in ground, sometimes lined
with grass or shells. Usually nests on
islands or protected sand spits. In
colonies.

Range: Aleutians, northern Alaska, Ellesmere
Island east to Newfoundland,
Massachusetts, Quebec, northern
Manitoba and British Columbia.
Winters at sea in the Southern
Hemisphere. Also breeds in northern
Eurasia.

Seldom seen south of its breeding
grounds in the East, these terns
annually perform spectacular
migrations, every fall heading eastward
across the Atlantic and down the west
coasts of Europe and Africa to winter in
the Antarctic Ocean. In spring they
retrace the same route, a round trip
totaling as much as 22,000 miles. They
see more daylight than any other living
creature since they are in both the
Arctic and Antarctic during the periods
of longest days. During the northern
winter this species is more truly oceanic
than its close relatives, feeding chiefly
on small seagoing shrimp and other
planktonic animals. Like most other
terns, it vigorously defends its nest,
often making painful attacks on the
heads of human intruders.

64 **Royal Tern**
(*Sterna maxima*)
Gulls, Terns (Laridae)

Description: 18–21″ (46–53 cm). Crow-sized. A
large tern with a heavy *yellow-orange* to
orange-red bill. Black cap, pale gray
back and wings, white forehead, black
crest. Tail moderately forked. Similar

Caspian Tern has blood-red bill, darker underwing, and shorter tail.

Voice: Harsh *Kak,* like the Caspian Tern but higher-pitched.

Habitat: Sandy beaches.

Nesting: Usually a single buff, spotted egg in a sand scrape on an island or a sheltered peninsula.

Range: Breeds along the coast from Virginia to Texas and Mexico, wandering regularly farther north in summer. Winters from the Gulf Coast southward. Also breeds in West Africa.

It nests in large, dense colonies. Nests are sometimes washed away by storm tides but the birds usually make a second attempt, often at a new location. It has fewer young than other terns but maintains its numbers wherever it has protection from disturbance. It feeds almost entirely on small fish, rather than crustaceans and insects taken by most other terns.

69 Least Tern
(*Sterna albifrons*)
Gulls, Terns (Laridae)

Description: 8–10″ (20–25 cm). Size of a large sparrow. *Very small* tern with a *yellow bill* and a fast, shallow wingbeat. White with black cap, pale gray back and wings, and forked tail; *forehead white.*

Voice: Sharp *killick* or *kip-kip-kip-killick.*

Habitat: Sandy and pebbly beaches along the coast; sandbars in large rivers. Often on land fills.

Nesting: 2 or 3 buff, lightly spotted eggs in an unlined scrape on a sand spit or gravel beach. In colonies.

Range: Maine south to Venezuela; occasionally along rivers in the Mississippi Valley; coastal California. Winters from Gulf Coast southward. Also breeds in Eurasia, Africa, and Australia.

This tern, despite its small size, is more tolerant of human disturbance than its larger relatives, often breeding close to heavily populated areas. It suffered greatly in the days when terns were shot for the millinery trade, and long after the shooting stopped it seemed unable to recover its former numbers. Finally, within the last few decades, it began to increase again and has become a familiar sight along the coast. Because of its habit of nesting on low sandbars, whole colonies are sometimes destroyed by extra high tides. It is most often seen hovering over the water, peering downward in search of small minnows and other marine or freshwater organisms.

70 Black Skimmer
(*Rynchops niger*)
Skimmers (Rynchopidae)

Description: 18″ (46 cm). Crow-sized. Black above, white below; red legs. *Bill red with black tip; laterally compressed, bladelike;* unique among birds in having *lower mandible much longer (about one-third) than the upper.*

Voice: In addition to their barking call they have softer cooing notes on the nesting site.

Habitat: Breeds chiefly on sandbars and beaches; feeds in shallow bays, inlets, and estuaries.

Nesting: 3 or 4 brown-blotched buff eggs on bare sand, usually among shell fragments and scattered grass clumps.

Range: Atlantic and Gulf coasts from Massachusetts and Long Island to Florida and Texas and from Mexico to southern South America. Winters regularly north to the Carolinas.

This extraordinary bird can hardly fail to attract attention from even the most blasé observer, especially when in

flight. Usually only one or two individuals are seen as they skim the surface (hence their name) for fish, with the tip of the lower mandible cutting through the water. They also wade in shallow water jabbing at the fish scattering before them. At other times compact flocks may be seen flying in unison, wheeling in one direction and then another—showing first the jet black of the wings, then the gleaming white of the underparts. Black Skimmers have extended their breeding range northward within the past forty years and today nest on the less disturbed sand beaches and dunes of Long Island. They are especially attracted to the sand fill of newly dredged areas; such places contain colonies of up to 200 pairs. These sites are usually temporary, being abandoned as soon as too much grass appears.

71 Sooty Tern
(*Sterna fuscata*)
Gulls, Terns (Laridae)

Description: 16″ (40 cm). Robin-sized. *Adult black above with white forehead; white below.* Deeply forked tail; thin, black bill. Immature birds are dark brown.
Voice: Harsh, squeaky notes and croaks.
Habitat: Coastal and oceanic islands during the breeding season; pelagic at other times.
Nesting: 1 white egg with reddish-brown blotches in a hollow in the sand; occasionally on rocks or ledges. Almost always in large colonies. Has an unusual nine-month breeding cycle.
Range: Tropical seas; in North America breeds only on the Dry Tortugas, Florida.

Sooty Terns are notorious wanderers, and when not nesting they range far and wide over the seas. Perhaps this is why they are so often blown inland, sometimes many hundreds of miles, by hurricanes and tropical storms. These birds have a remarkable homing ability: when individuals marked with a dye were taken fro.n their breeding grounds on the Dry Tortugas, and released along the coasts of North Carolina and Texas, all returned to their breeding grounds in one to seven days. Sooty Terns feed largely at dusk and at night. Unlike most other terns they do not dive, but pluck small fish and squid from the surface of the water. They spend most of their time in the air, rarely perching or alighting on the water.

73 Brown Noddy
(*Anous stolidus*)
Gulls, Terns (Laridae)

Description: 15" (38 cm). Robin-sized. Dark sooty-brown with pale grayish-white crown; wedge-shaped tail; slender, black bill.

Voice: Low *cah,* similar to call of a young crow.

Habitat: Coastal and oceanic islands during the breeding season; pelagic at other times.

Nesting: 1 buff egg, spotted with lilac and brown, in a stick nest lined with seaweed and often bits of shell and coral, placed on rocks, in trees, bushes, or on exposed coral reefs.

Range: Breeds on the Dry Tortugas, Florida. Found nearly throughout the warmer regions of the world.

These dark brown terns with light caps associate commonly with Sooty Terns, at least at breeding colonies. Unlike them, however, the Noddy does not wander northward after the nesting season and, as a result, few are reported in our area north of southern Florida. Noddies get their name from their habit of nodding and bowing to each other during courtship. They catch their food—primarily small fish—by pouncing on it when it comes to the surface rather than diving after it as most terns do. These oceangoing terns are fond of perching on floating pieces of driftwood and occasionally alight on the water and float.

74 Black Noddy
(*Anous tenuirostris*)
Gulls, Terns (Laridae)

Description: 12″ (30 cm). Bill black, top of head white, rest of plumage dark sooty-brown, feet brownish-black. Bill long, thin, and straight; tail wedge-shaped.

Habitat: Small oceanic and coastal islands in the breeding season; otherwise wanders at sea.

Nesting: One egg, whitish spotted with brown, laid in a stick nest lined with grass or seaweed in a tree or bush.

Range: Tropical portions of the Atlantic, Pacific, and Indian oceans. In the East found only in the Dry Tortugas, off southern Florida.

This pantropical tern is of extremely local occurrence in North America, but each year since 1960 one or two individuals have been found among nesting Brown Noddies in the Dry Tortugas. Although occurring there regularly, the Black Noddy has not yet been known to nest there. This species may easily be told from the Brown Noddy by its smaller size, blacker color, and white rather than gray cap; it is sometimes called the White-capped Noddy.

76 Gannet
(*Morus bassanus*)
Gannets, Boobies (Sulidae)

Description: 35–40″ (89–102 cm). Goose-sized. Adult white with black wing tips; head tinged with rich orange-buff in breeding season. Long, pointed tail and wings. Immature bird is dark gray speckled with white. Alternately flaps and glides in flight—shaped like a flying cross.

Voice: Guttural croak or grunt, heard only on the breeding islands.

Habitat: Large colonies on rocky cliffs of coastal islands.

Nesting: 1 bluish-white egg that soon changes to brown is placed in a shallow nest of dried seaweed high on a precipitous cliff or along the top of a bluff. Nests are close together.

Range: Breeds on a few islands off Newfoundland, in the Gulf of St. Lawrence, and off Nova Scotia. Winters in coastal waters south to Florida. Also the west coast of Europe.

This strictly maritime species, the only northern member of the Booby family, is one of the most spectacular birds. During migrations they may be observed offshore, either gliding above the water or diving into the sea after fish, sometimes plunging headlong from heights as great as 50 feet or more. A remarkable system of interconnected air sacs under the skin of the breast serves as a cushion to protect the bird from the shock of striking the water. A trip to the breeding colony on Bonaventure Island, off the Gaspé Peninsula, Quebec, yields one of the great sights in the bird world: over 15,000 pairs of gannets incubating, brooding their young, or searching for food. Gannets, like other members of the family, take part in an elaborate series of displays. When one bird returns to the nest site it is greeted by its mate. Both birds raise their heads and cross bills, which they clash together like fencers, then bow to each other with wings and tails raised. This is followed by mutual preening of the head and neck. Usually the bird who has been relieved at the nest will pick up sticks or seaweed to present to its mate. Finally, the departing bird stands with head and neck extended straight up and wings raised over the back, then launches itself into the air with an upward leap.

85, 86 Magnificent Frigatebird
(*Fregata magnificens*)
Frigatebirds (Fregatidae)

Description: 38–40″ (96–102 cm). W. 90″ (2.5 m). Black with very long, pointed wings, deeply forked tail, and long hooked bill. Male has a brilliant red throat pouch in breeding season and inflates it to huge size during courtship; female has a white breast. Young have white head and underparts.

Voice: Usually silent; harsh, guttural notes during courtship.

Habitat: Mangrove islets in shallow waters.

Nesting: 1 white or greenish-white egg in a stick nest in mangrove clumps.

Range: Local on islets in Florida Bay. In the nonbreeding season, ranges to the coasts of Florida, Louisiana, and Texas. Also south to Peru and Brazil.

Frigatebirds, also known as Man-o'-War-birds, are masters of flight—whether soaring on outstretched wings, circling in the sky, swooping down on flying fish, or giving chase to boobies and other seabirds. They have the largest wingspread in proportion to weight of any bird. A frigatebird will harass a booby until the latter drops its catch, which the frigatebird deftly snatches in midair. These birds have been known to eat squid, jellyfish, young sea turtles, and nestling seabirds. They never alight on land or water because their short legs and broad wings make it difficult for them to take off except from a height, such as the limb of a tree or a rock.

---

91 Razorbill
(*Alca torda*)
Auks (Alcidae)

Description: 17″ (43 cm). A crow-sized diving bird. Black above, white below. Very deep bill, laterally compressed.

Voice: Low croaks and growls.

Habitat: Coastal waters.

Nesting: 1 brown-spotted bluish egg placed on or under rocks.

Range: Greenland south to Maine and from northern Europe to France. Winters south as far as New Jersey and the Mediterranean.

These birds can often be recognized at a distance on the water by their large heads, stout bills, and upward-pointed tails. As with many alcids, Razorbills migrate southward after severe cold spells and visit our shores in the midst of winter. They are hardy birds, spending most of their time at sea and approaching land only after strong easterly gales. During the breeding season they prefer rocky coasts, where they lay their eggs and raise their young. Razorbills feed mostly on fish, shrimp, and squid. They are very adept at diving and have been caught in gill nets as deep as sixty feet.

92 Black Guillemot
(Cepphus grylle)
Auks (Alcidae)

Description: 13" (33 cm). Pigeon-sized. In summer, *all black with a large white wing patch; bright red feet;* pointed bill. In winter the black is largely replaced by white. Locally called Sea Pigeon.

Voice: Shrill mouselike squeaks.

Habitat: Rocky coasts, even in winter.

Nesting: 2 whitish eggs with dark brown blotches placed under rocks, either on a bare surface or on loose pebbles.

Range: Circumpolar, breeding south to Maine, the British Isles, Scandinavia, and Alaska. Winters south to Long Island (rarely), France, and Alaska.

In summer plumage these jet-black seabirds with their large white wing patches and bright red feet are conspicuous, especially when in flight. A characteristic field mark is their habit of dipping their bills into the water. Guillemots are hardy birds, rarely migrating even in subzero weather. Their food consists primarily of small fish, crustaceans, mollusks, and marine worms.

93 Thick-billed Murre
(Uria lomvia)
Auks (Alcidae)

Description: 18" (46 cm). Crow-sized. Black above, white below; throat white in winter.

Voice: Purring or murmuring, hence the name "murre." Also a guttural croak and higher pitched bleat.

Habitat: Rocky coasts.

Nesting: 1 large bluish-green egg with brown scrawls. They nest in dense colonies of countless thousands on sheer sea cliffs. The single egg, laid on a narrow ledge, is pear-shaped, so that instead of rolling off the cliff it merely rolls around on its own axis.

Range: High Arctic and subarctic coasts of both hemispheres; in America it breeds south to islands in the Gulf of St. Lawrence. Winters on the Pacific Coast south to southern Alaska, on the Atlantic south to New Jersey.

Unlike the other alcids, which are exclusively oceanic, this species occurs very rarely on the Great Lakes and other large inland bodies of water. Murre eggs are a rich source of food for both Eskimos and Indians, while the birds themselves are among the chief prey of Gyrfalcons, Peregrines, and Skuas. In turn the murres feed on fish, squid, and various crustaceans.

94 Common Murre
(*Uria aalge*)
Auks (Alcidae)

Description: 17" (43 cm). Crow-sized. An almost exact counterpart of the previous species, but *bill thin and pointed;* face with more white in winter; dark line above eye projects backward.

Voice: Similar to the Thick-billed Murre.

Habitat: Rocky coasts.

Nesting: 1 blue-green egg with black marks on a bare rock ledge.

Range: Arctic and subarctic shores; breeds in America south to California on the Pacific side but only to islands in the Gulf of St. Lawrence on the Atlantic. Winters south to California and Massachusetts.

On the Pacific Coast this species breeds much farther south than the Thick-billed Murre, but curiously enough not on the Atlantic coast. Much more abundant on the Pacific side. The murres, like all alcids, use their wings for swimming and diving, and seem to fly through the water.

95, 97 Common Puffin
(*Fratercula arctica*)
Auks (Alcidae)

Description: 12″ (30 cm). Short, stocky bird. Black above and white below, with a white face and red legs; its remarkable *triangular bill is brilliant red and yellow.* In fall the horny outer covering of the bill peels off, leaving the bill smaller and duller in appearance.

Voice: Deep, throaty purrs and croaks. One call sounds like *Hey, Al.*

Habitat: Chiefly rocky coasts.

Nesting: 1 white egg in a burrow in soft soil or a rock crevice. Nest cavity is lined with grass.

Range: Greenland and arctic Europe south to Maine and Portugal. It is essentially nonmigratory and winters chiefly offshore in the breeding range.

This clown of the sea is a comical-looking bird with a short dumpy figure, red-rimmed gleaming yellow eyes, gaudy triangular bill, and a habit of waddling around, jumping from rock to rock. It nests in much smaller colonies than do most of the other alcids. Puffins hunt their food in rocky coastal waters and also at sea. Their food consists of small fish, shellfish, and shrimp. They are excellent swimmers and divers. An attempt is being made to reintroduce the puffin into a former breeding area on the Maine coast. Nestlings from Newfoundland have been hand-reared on islands with the hope that they will return to this area as adults.

96, 98 Dovekie
(*Alle alle*)
Auks (Alcidae)

Description: 8″ (20 cm). Starling-sized. Very small, chunky, black-and-white seabird. Black above, white below. Bill very short.

Voice: Lively chattering.

Habitat: Breeds on rocky cliffs and winters chiefly at sea.

Nesting: 1 bluish-white egg in a rock crevice.

Range: High Arctic south to Greenland. Winters south to New Jersey.

The little Dovekie, smallest of Atlantic Alcidae, exists in countless thousands in the cold Arctic regions and is considered by some to be the most abundant bird in the world. Greenland Eskimos catch large numbers of them in long-handled nets, eating the birds raw and making shirts from their skins. Great flocks move southward during severe cold spells, but the vast majority winter far out at sea. On occasion, during migration in November, powerful easterly gales may blow them great distances inland, where they usually succumb to the elements or die of starvation. Dovekies feed on phytoplankton, krill, small fish, and crustaceans.

102 Great Cormorant
(*Phalacrocorax carbo*)
Cormorants (Phalacrocoracidae)

Description: 35–40″ (89–102 cm). Goose-sized. Adult black with white throat and yellow chin pouch; in breeding plumage it has white flank patches. Immatures are dull brown, paler below, often white on belly.

Voice: Deep, guttural grunts.

Habitat: Cliffs, rocks, and trees of coastal inlands.

Nesting: 3 or 4 pale blue-green eggs overlaid with a chalky coating, placed in seaweed-lined stick nests.

Range: Greenland and locally in Atlantic Canada south to southwestern Nova Scotia. Winters south to New Jersey. Also in the Old World.

Largest of all cormorants, in the Orient this species is trained to catch fish. Cormorants dive from the surface of the water and are excellent swimmers. They feed largely on fish but also take crustaceans and mollusks. The Great Cormorant has increased in numbers within the past quarter century, and dozens may now be observed in winter on offshore rocks in the northeast.

113, 162 Red-breasted Merganser
(*Mergus serrator*)
Swans, Geese, Ducks (Anatidae)

Description: 19–26" (48–66 cm). Male has a green head, *gray sides, white neck-ring, and rusty breast.* Female grayish, with brown head shading gradually into white of breast. Both sexes are crested and have red bills.

Voice: Usually silent; various croaking and rasping notes during courtship.

Habitat: Northern lakes and tundra ponds; in winter, principally on the ocean and in salt bays.

Nesting: 8–10 olive-buff eggs in a down-lined depression on the ground concealed under a bush or in a brush pile.

Range: Alaska, Baffin Island, and Labrador south to Maine, Michigan, and British Columbia. Winters chiefly along the coast south to the Gulf Coast and northern Mexico. Also breeds in northern Eurasia.

This is the only one of our three mergansers commonly found on salt water. Like the others it lives mainly on fish, which it captures in swift underwater pursuit, aided by its long, pointed bill lined with sharp toothlike projections.

116, 152 Oldsquaw
(*Clangula hyemalis*)
Swans, Geese, Ducks (Anatidae)

Description: Males 19–22″ (48–56 cm); females 15–
17″ (38–43 cm). Male boldly patterned
in black and white (chiefly white in
winter, chiefly black in summer), with
very long, slender central tail feathers.
Females are duller and lack the long tail
feathers. In all plumages has *all-dark,
unpatterned wings.*

Voice.   Various clucking and growling notes; a
musical *ow-owdle-oo,* frequently
repeated, during courtship.

Habitat: Tundra; in winter on open bays and
inshore waters.

Nesting: 6–9 pale buff eggs, in a down-lined
cup of grass and twigs, concealed under
a bush or in a hollow on the tundra.

Range: Aleutian Islands, northern Alaska
eastward along the arctic coast of
Canada and the islands to Greenland,
south to southern Hudson Bay and
northern British Columbia. Winters
along the coast south to Oregon and the
Carolinas. Also in Eurasia.

The Oldsquaw is one of the very few of
our diving ducks that travels under
water by using its wings; other species
propel themselves with their feet. This
fact may explain the birds' ability to
dive to such great depths—as deep a
80 fathoms. Their food consists of
shrimps, small fish, and mollusks.
These very noisy birds are noisiest in
early spring, when males gather and
utter their mellow, barking courtship
calls; this pleasing sound is audible
for a mile or two on a still, spring
morning.

117, 145 Common Eider
(Somateria mollissima)
Swans, Geese, Ducks (Anatidae)

Description: 23–27" (58–68 cm). Our largest duck. Male has *black underparts; white back,* breast, and head; dark crown; back of head has greenish tinge. Female is mottled brown. Long, sloping bill gives the bird a distinctive profile.

Voice: During courtship the male gives a human-like moan. Female quacks.

Habitat: Rocky coasts and coastal tundra.

Nesting: 4–7 olive or buff eggs in a substantial mass of grass thickly lined with down. Often several pairs form a loose colony.

Range: Alaska across the Arctic to Greenland and south to Maine. Winters along the coast south to Alaska and Long Island. Also breeds in northern Eurasia.

Eiders are best known for their down— very soft feathers plucked from the breast of the female. For hundreds of years down has been gathered from nests in northern Europe and used to make pillows and quilts. Only eiders in the Arctic are strongly migratory; in the warmer parts of their range they may remain near the breeding grounds all year. Their principal foods are mussels and other shellfish, which are swallowed whole and crushed by muscles in the bird's stomach. Since the persecution of eiders was ended after the turn of the century, there has been a spectacular increase along the Maine coast and they are once again nesting in large numbers.

118, 146 King Eider
(Somateria spectabilis)
Swans, Geese, Ducks (Anatidae)

Description: 18–25" (46–63 cm). A large duck. Similar to the Common Eider, but male has a *black back* and a conspicuous orange-yellow bill and "shield" on forehead. Female similar to female Common Eider but bill is shorter, not extending as far back toward eye, and lacks the distinctive sloping profile.

Voice: A guttural croaking.

Habitat: Rocky coasts and islands.

Nesting: 4–7 buff-olive eggs in a down-lined depression on rocky tundra, often some distance from the edge of the water.

Range: Usually in freshwater ponds and lakes in Alaska and Arctic islands east to Greenland, south locally to Hudson Bay. Winters along coasts south to southern Alaska and New Jersey; rarely farther south and on the Great Lakes. Also breeds on Arctic coasts of Eurasia.

Although the world population of the King Eider is large, the birds are seldom seen in the United States; most winter farther north and favor deeper water than the Common Eider. They often dive far for food, and have been caught in nets as much as 150 feet below the surface. Like the Common Eider, they take large numbers of mussels and other shellfish, but vary their diet with small fish, squids, sand dollars, and sea urchins. Their breeding grounds are so remote that their down is not collected as extensively as that of the Common Eider.

120, 160 **Harlequin Duck**
(*Histrionicus histrionicus*)
Swans, Geese, Ducks (Anatidae)

Description: 14–20″ (35–51 cm). A small, dark duck. Male is blue-gray, appearing black at a distance, with chestnut flanks and distinctive white patches on the head and body. Female is dusky brown with three whitish patches on sides of face. In flight, this species lacks white patches on the wings.

Voice: Call has been described as a mouse-like squeak; hence the local name "Sea mouse."

Habitat: Swift-moving streams in summer; rocky, wave-lashed coasts and jetties in winter.

Nesting: 5 or 6 pale buff eggs in a mass of down concealed in a crevice in rocks along a stream.

Range: Alaska, Baffin Island, and northern Quebec south to Labrador and California. Winters along the coast south to Long Island and central California. Also breeds in Asia and Iceland.

In the Northeast these ducks are known locally as "Lords and Ladies." They spend most of their lives on salt water, visiting inland streams only during the breeding season. As soon as the female begins incubating, her mate returns to the ocean and undergoes the annual molt. The preferred habitat—rugged seacoasts—offers food that few other species can exploit. The birds are adept at riding a wave up against the rocks and quickly tearing loose snails, limpets, and barnacles. They also feed on small shrimp, crabs, and small fish, which they catch by diving. In their stay on freshwater streams, they feed mainly on larvae of aquatic insects.

125, 149 **Barrow's Goldeneye**
(*Bucephala islandica*)
Swans, Geese, Ducks (Anatidae)

Description: 16½–20″ (42–51 cm). Male has a white body, black back, and black-appearing (actually glossed with purple) head. Similar to male Common Goldeneye, but has more black on sides, a stubbier bill, and a *crescent-shaped—instead of round—white spot in front of eye*. Female gray with white collar and brown head; differs from female Common Goldeneye in having steeper forehead, duller (less warm brown) head, and smaller white wing patches.

Voice: A harsh croak.

Habitat: Forested lakes and rivers; in winter on open bays and estuaries along coast.

Nesting: 9 or 10 pale green eggs on a bed of down in a hollow tree or, in treeless areas, under a rock.

Range: Alaska south in mountains to central California and Colorado, and along the coast of Labrador; winters along Pacific coast and in smaller numbers from Maritime Provinces south to Long Island. Also breeds in western Greenland and Iceland.

Barrow's Goldeneye favors alpine lakes, often breeding at elevations of 10,000 feet or more. Its patchy distribution suggests that it is an ancient species, perhaps now in decline. In the East it is outnumbered by the Common Goldeneye, but may occur in flocks of hundreds in the Maritimes.

126, 150 **Common Goldeneye**
(*Bucephala clangula*)
Swans, Geese, Ducks (Anatidae)

Description: 16–20″ (40–51 cm). Male has a white body; black back; black-appearing (actually glossy greenish) head; and a *large, round, white spot in front of the bright yellow eye.* Female is grayish with white neck ring and warm brown head. Both sexes have a distinctive puffy head shape and a large white wing patch in flight.

Voice: In February and March, one can often hear the nasal, rasping calls of courting males even when the birds themselves cannot be seen.

Habitat: Nests on lakes and ponds in the North; in migration and winter mainly along the coast in bays and inlets.

Nesting: 8–15 pale green eggs in a mass of down

in a natural tree cavity, sometimes as
high as 60 feet aboveground.

Range: Alaska and Labrador south to northern
New England, Minnesota, and British
Columbia. Winters south to northern
Mexico, the Gulf Coast, and Florida.

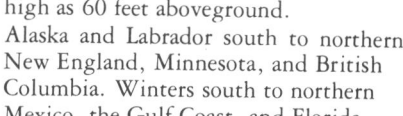

Called the "Whistler" because the loud
sound produced by the wings identifies
it even at night, when the birds fly
overhead from one feeding ground to
another. In the courtship display,
which begins in late winter, the male
stretches his head forward along the
water, then throws it rapidly upward
over his back, bill pointed skyward,
while uttering a loud rasping note.
Then he swings his orange feet forward,
sending up a spray in front of him. In
winter these ducks feed mainly on
mollusks; in summer, mostly on
aquatic plants and insects.

127, 151 Bufflehead
(*Bucephala albeola*)
Swans, Geese, Ducks (Anatidae)

Description: 13–15″ (33–38 cm). Small, chubby
duck. Male largely white, with black
back, black head with greenish- and
purplish gloss, and *large white patch
from eye to top and back of head*. Female
all dark with a single whitish patch on
cheek. It is a fast flier and has a rapid
wingbeat.

Voice: A squeaky whistle (male); a soft, hoarse
quack (female).

Habitat: Northern lakes and ponds; in winter,
mainly on salt bays and estuaries.

Nesting: 8–12 pale buff eggs in a mass of down
placed in a woodpecker hole up to 20
feet aboveground.

Range: Alaska, Mackenzie, and Ontario south
to Manitoba and the mountains of
California. Winters on both coasts
south to Mexico, the Gulf Coast, and
Florida.

The Bufflehead, or "Butterball" as it is known to hunters, is a smaller relative of the goldeneyes and like them breeds in tree cavities. Its courtship is similar to that of the Common Goldeneye. It is one of the most familiar ducks along the coast in winter. Usually in small parties, it does not form great rafts as do scaups, Redheads, and Canvasbacks.

129, 148 Surf Scoter
(Melanitta perspicillata)
Swans, Geese, Ducks (Anatidae)

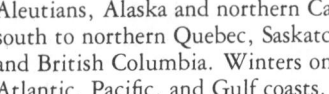

Description: 17–21″ (43–53 cm). Male black with white patches on the crown and nape; hence the local name "Skunk-head." Bill swollen at the base and bearing a large black spot. Female brownish-black with two whitish patches on cheek. Both sexes lack white wing patch.

Voice: A low, guttural croaking.

Habitat: Northern lakes; winters almost entirely on the ocean and in large coastal bays.

Nesting: 7–9 pale buff eggs in a down-lined depression concealed under bushes or in marshy vegetation.

Range: Aleutians, Alaska and northern Canada south to northern Quebec, Saskatchewan, and British Columbia. Winters on Atlantic, Pacific, and Gulf coasts.

The Surf Scoter is the only one of the three scoters confined to the New World. These birds are similar in habits to White-winged Scoters but are more likely to be seen diving for mollusks and crustaceans along the line of breaking surf. When alighting on the water they have a distinctive habit of holding their wings up over their backs while coasting to a stop. Because they consume little plant food, hunters do not consider their flesh good to eat; nevertheless, many thousands are shot annually for sport.

130, 147 White-winged Scoter
(*Melanitta fusca*)
Swans, Geese, Ducks (Anatidae)

Description: 19–24" (48–61 cm). Male black with *bold white wing patches* and yellow bill with a large black knob at the base. Females are dull brown with two whitish facial spots and white wing patches.

Voice: A hoarse croak.

Habitat: Large lakes; in winter most birds move to the ocean or coastal bays, but a few remain on big lakes in the interior.

Nesting: 8–12 buff-pink eggs in a hollow under bushes or crevice near water.

Range: Aleutians, Alaska and Manitoba south to North Dakota and Washington. Winters regularly south to British Columbia, Colorado, Louisiana, and South Carolina. Also in Eurasia.

During the height of migration, in October and November, the long, irregular lines of thousands of scoters migrating southward just offshore provide a most impressive sight. This scoter, known in Europe as the Velvet Scoter, is the most widespread of the three species. It feeds chiefly on mollusks, which it collects from mussel beds at depths of 15 to 25 feet. Unlike most diving ducks, which propel themselves underwater with their feet, scoters may also use their wings.

131 Black Scoter
"Common Scoter"
(*Melanitta nigra*)
Swans, Geese, Ducks (Anatidae)

Description: 17–21" (43–53 cm). Male black; black bill with large yellow knob at base, hence the local name "Butterbill." Female duller, with pale cheeks and all dark bill.

Voice: In spring a musical, whistled *cour-coo*.
Habitat: Ponds in boreal forest; winters on the ocean and in large salt bays.
Nesting: 6–8 pale buff eggs in a down-lined cup of grass hidden in a rock crevice or clump of grass near the edge of water.
Range: Western Alaska, Labrador, and Newfoundland. Winters along the coast south to California and South Carolina, more rarely in the interior. Also found in Eurasia.

The Black Scoter, formerly called Common Scoter, is actually the least common of three species, being more abundant in the Old World than in North America. Like the others it preys heavily on mussels and other mollusks, but also spends much time tearing barnacles and limpets from submerged rocks and reefs. Newly hatched young remain on fresh water for several days, feeding on freshwater mussels and the larvae of aquatic insects, but then move to salt water.

176 Brown Pelican
(*Pelecanus occidentalis*)
Pelicans (Pelecanidae)

Description: 45–54″ (114–137 cm). W. 90″ (2.5 m). Very large, stocky bird with a dark brown body and a massive bill and throat pouch. Head whitish in adults, dark brown in young. Usually rests its bill on its breast.
Voice: Adults are silent but young birds in nesting colonies are very noisy, emitting loud grunts and screams.
Habitat: Sandy coastal beaches and lagoons.
Nesting: 2 or 3 whitish eggs in a mass of sticks and grass placed in a tree or low bush, or on the ground on an island. In colonies.
Range: Atlantic Coast from North Carolina south to Venezuela; on the Pacific Coast from British Columbia to Chile.

Unlike its larger relative, the White Pelican, it is an expert diver, often plunging spectacularly in pursuit of fish just beyond the breakers. Its pouch is not used to store or carry fish as is generally believed, but rather serves to separate the fish from the water. Since the fish that form their principal diet retain insecticides dissolved in the water, these substances build up in the birds' bodies and cause their eggs to be thin-shelled and easily broken. As a result, some breeding colonies fail to produce a single young bird, and the species has ceased to breed in large parts of its former range.

181, 183 Eared Grebe
(*Podiceps nigricollis*)
Grebes (Podicipedidae)

Description: 12–14" (30–36 cm). A *small, slender-necked,* slender-billed diving bird. In breeding plumage head and back are black; *golden ear tufts* and *black crest.* In winter plumage dark gray above, white below. Similar in winter to Horned Grebe, but chunkier, and *bill appears slightly upturned,* sides of face are smudged with gray, with a white patch behind ear.

Voice: Froglike cheeping notes, usually heard only during breeding season.

Habitat: Marshy lakes and ponds; open bays and ocean in winter.

Nesting: 4 or 5 white, stained eggs set on a mass of floating vegetation in a marsh. In colonies.

Range: British Columbia and Manitoba south to Texas, New Mexico, and Southern California. Winters on Pacific Coast, rarely in interiors and on Atlantic.

Although most Eared Grebes migrate southwestward in the fall to the Pacific, a very few turn up each year on the East Coast. Unlike the Horned Grebe, which supplements its diet with small fish, the Eared Grebe feeds almost exclusively on aquatic insects and small crustaceans. These birds are highly gregarious, not only nesting in large, dense and noisy colonies but assembling in large flocks in winter.

182, 184 Horned Grebe
(*Podiceps auritus*)
Grebes (Podicipedidae)

Description: 12–15″ (30–38 cm). Small, slender-necked, with a short, sharply pointed bill. In breeding plumage, dark body, rufous neck, blackish head, and *conspicuous buff ear plumes.* In winter, dark upper parts and white chin and neck. The commonest saltwater grebe in the East.

Voice: Usually silent, but on the breeding grounds it gives a loud series of croaks, shrieks, and chatters.

Habitat: Marshes and lakes in summer; in winter, mainly on salt water but also on the Great Lakes.

Nesting: 4 whitish, stained eggs in floating vegetation anchored to marsh plants.

Range: Alaska and northern Canada southeast to Wisconsin. In winter, Aleutians and along Atlantic Coast to Texas. Also breeds in Eurasia.

Although it breeds in freshwater marshes, each fall most of the American population moves to the coast; it is therefore thought of as a saltwater bird. These grebes are rarely seen in flight; once on the wintering grounds they seldom fly, and they migrate almost entirely at night. Like other grebes, the young can swim and dive immediately after hatching, but are often seen riding on the parent's back. Grebes have a remarkable ability to control their specific gravity so that they can swim high in the water or almost submerged.

186, 189 Red-throated Loon
(*Gavia stellata*)
Loons (Gaviidae)

Description: 24–27" (61–68 cm). Goose-sized.
Large, long-bodied bird seldom seen
away from salt water. In breeding
plumage, *gray head and neck, rusty
throat,* black back spotted with white.
In winter, similar to the Common Loon
but smaller, paler, with bill thinner
and *seemingly upturned.*

Voice: Its call, more rarely heard than that of
the Common Loon, is a high-pitched
wail. More often heard is a low,
goose-like growl.

Habitat: Salt bays and tundra ponds during the
summer; bays and estuaries and ocean
in winter.

Nesting: 2 olive-buff, spotted eggs in
vegetation, at the edge of or in water.

Range: Aleutian Islands and coastal tundra
south to Newfoundland and northern
Manitoba. In winter, south to Florida
and the Gulf Coast. Also breeds in
northern Eurasia.

The attractive breeding plumage of this
loon is seldom seen in southern
latitudes, for it is acquired just before
the birds depart for their nesting
grounds. Loons have difficulty walking
on land because their legs are located at
the extreme rear of their bodies, so they
are seldom seen away from the water.
They are extremely vulnerable to oil
pollution; many have been killed along
both coasts as a result of recent spills.

187 Arctic Loon
(*Gavia arctica*)
Loons (Gaviidae)

Description: 24" (60 cm). A *small* loon with a *slender
straight bill.* In breeding plumage, head
pale gray, neck and back black with
white stripes, throat black with purple

reflections. In winter plumage blackish above, white below. Red-throated Loon in winter has paler, brownish upperparts and an upturned bill; Common Loon is larger, with a stouter bill.

Voice: A harsh *kok-kok-kok-kok*.

Habitat: Tundra, lakes, ponds, and sloughs; in winter, coastal bays and inlets but also on the ocean.

Nesting: 2 spotted olive-brown eggs laid directly on the bare ground or in a slight depression lined with stems and roots, never far from water.

Range: High Arctic regions of both hemispheres; in America, south and east to Hudson Bay. Winters chiefly on the Pacific Coast, but ranges east in migration to the northern portions of Manitoba, Ontario, and Quebec. Very rare in northeastern United States.

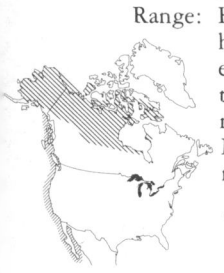

This little-known species is the rarest of the three loons in the East. Its diet consists mainly of fish, but on the breeding grounds it also takes crustaceans.

191, 211 Red Knot
(*Calidris canutus*)
Sandpipers (Scolopacidae)

Description: 10½″ (26 cm). Robin-sized. In spring, *rufous underparts and gray upperparts;* in fall, whitish below; short, almost plover-like bill. In flight it shows a whitish rump.

Voice: Soft *quer-wer*. Also a soft rolling trill.

Habitat: Tundra; in migration on tidal flats and rocky shores, and on beaches in inland areas.

Nesting: 4 olive-buff, brown-spotted eggs in a lichen-lined slight depression on dry ground, often among rocks.

Range: Arctic coasts of both hemispheres. Winters from southern United States to southern South America.

Knots in breeding plumage, with their rich rufous underparts set off by marbled gray backs, are among the handsomest of shorebirds. They make a nearly 20,000-mile round trip between the Arctic and Antarctic oceans each year.

192, 209 Dunlin
(*Calidris alpina*)
Sandpipers (Scolopacidae)

Description: 8½″ (21 cm). Starling-sized. *Fairly long bill with a distinct droop at the tip.* In summer, *reddish back;* white below with a *conspicuous black belly.* In winter, dull gray; paler below.

Voice: *Cheerp* or *chit-lit.*

Habitat: Beaches, extensive mud and sand flats, tidal inlets and lagoons; also inland lake and river shores.

Nesting: 4 brown-splotched olive eggs in a grass clump on a dry hummock on the open tundra.

Range: Arctic coasts on both hemispheres. In America, south to southern Alaska and Hudson Bay. Winters on the Pacific Coast from British Columbia and on the Atlantic Coast from New England south to Mexico and Florida.

These handsome birds, also known as Red-backed Sandpipers, are very tame and thus easy to approach and study. Among the hardiest of shorebirds, thousands sometimes spend the winter months on sandbars or inlets along the coast as far north as Long Island.

193, 220 Sanderling
(*Calidris alba*)
Sandpipers (Scolopacidae)

Description: 8″ (20 cm). Starling-sized. In summer, rufous head and breast and white belly;

in winter the rufous areas are replaced by pale gray; *black bill and legs; conspicuous white wing stripe.*

Voice: Sharp *kip.* Conversational chatter while feeding.

Habitat: Ocean beaches, sandbars, occasionally mud flats; inland lake and river shores.

Nesting: 4 brown-spotted olive eggs in a hollow on the ground lined with grasses and lichens.

Range: Worldwide. In the Americas it breeds along the coasts of the Arctic Ocean south to Hudson Bay. Winters from the United States (both coasts) to southern South America.

Practically every day of the year these birds may be found on any ocean beach. As a wave comes roaring in, the birds run up on the beach just ahead of the breaker, then rush after the retreating surf to feed on the tiny crustaceans and mollusks stranded by the outgoing water.

194, 239 American Golden Plover
(*Pluvialis dominica*)
Plovers (Charadriidae)

Description: 9–11″ (23–28 cm). Quail-sized. Dark brown above, with black throat, breast, and belly; bold white stripe from forehead, over the eye, and down the side of the neck. In winter, underparts dusky whitish. Lacks the white wing stripe and the black patch under the wing of the larger and paler Black-bellied Plover.

Voice: A mellow *quee-lee-lee.*

Habitat: Tundra; in migration, on coastal beaches and mudflats and inland on prairies and plowed fields.

Nesting: 3 or 4 spotted buff eggs in a shallow depression lined with reindeer moss, usually on a ridge or other elevated spot in the tundra.

Range: Eastern Siberia, northern Alaska, and

Devon Island south to southern Alaska and Baffin Island. Winters to southern South America and in India, Australia, and the South Pacific.

The American Golden Plover annually performs one of the longest migrations of any American bird. In late summer, birds from the eastern Arctic gather in Labrador and Newfoundland, where they fatten on crowberries and other small fruits before beginning their nonstop flight to the northern coast of South America, a journey of some 2500 miles. Smaller numbers move southward in the fall across the Great Plains. Relatively few of these birds are found along the east coast of the United States. Once in South America, they make another long flight across the vast Amazon Basin, finally arriving at their principal wintering grounds on the pampas of Argentina, Patagonia, and Tierra del Fuego. Here in former times they gathered in enormous numbers, but heavy shooting in both North and South America took a serious toll from which the species has not fully recovered. In the spring the birds return to the Arctic, but at that time they move north by way of the Great Plains.

195, 240 **Black-bellied Plover**
(*Pluvialis squatarola*)
Plovers (Charadriidae)

Description: 10–13″ (25–33 cm). Quail-sized.
Similar to the American Golden Plover but larger, grayer, with a bold white stripe on the wing visible when the bird flies. In flight it always shows a *black patch under the wing.* At any season it has a *white rump;* the rump is dark in the American Golden Plover.

Voice: Clear, whistled *pee-a-weee* reminiscent of the Wood Pewee.

Habitat: Tundra; in migration and in winter it occurs on beaches and coastal marshes, less commonly on inland marshes, lakeshores, and plowed fields.

Nesting: 3 or 4 spotted buff eggs in a shallow hollow lined with moss, lichens, and grass in tundra.

Range: Northern Alaska and Arctic islands to southern Alaska, Southampton Island, and southern Baffin Island. Winters to northern South America. Also breeds in northern Eurasia.

It seldom travels in large flocks like the American Golden Plover; it is usually found singly or in small groups. Our largest plover, it is conspicuous among its usual companions, the smaller plovers, turnstones, and sandpipers. It is wary and is usually the first to fly off when approached, commonly flying out over water, circling, and landing again behind the observer. It is one of the familiar winter shorebirds along the Atlantic Coast, and a few—mostly fledged the previous summer—spend the summer south of the breeding range. Its principal foods are small crabs and sandworms.

196, 241 Ruddy Turnstone
(*Arenaria interpres*)
Sandpipers (Scolopacidae)

Description: 8–10″ (20–25 cm). A stocky shorebird with orange legs. Upperparts rusty red in summer, duller in winter; white below. Face and breast have conspicuous black markings, duller but still visible in winter. Because of their striking flight pattern they are sometimes called "Calico-backs."

Voice: A metallic but musical *netticut* or *kek-kek*.

Habitat: Coastal tundra; in winter on rocky, pebbly, and sandy coasts and beaches.

Nesting: 4 buff-olive spotted eggs in a shallow

hollow sparsely lined with grass and dead leaves and concealed under low bushes.

Range: Islands and coasts in the Arctic. Winters regularly from California and the Carolinas south to South America, in smaller numbers farther north. Also breeds in Arctic Eurasia and in the interior of central Asia.

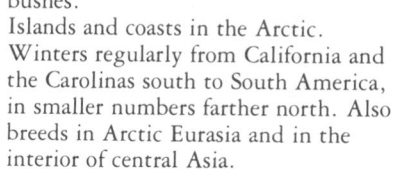

Turnstones are named from their method of feeding, in which they walk along the beach, deftly rolling small stones and pebbles and seizing the animals hiding underneath. They also dig holes in the sand, often larger than themselves, in pursuit of burrowing crustaceans. Although turnstones are usually encountered in small groups, they are very abundant; during the winter they scatter over a huge area, regularly occurring as far south as Australia, New Zealand, southern Africa, and South America as well as on remote islands in the South Pacific, where they sometimes prey on nesting terns' eggs.

198, 217 Purple Sandpiper
(*Calidris maritima*)
Sandpipers (Scolopacidae)

Description: 9″ (23 cm). *Dark slate* with *orange-yellow legs;* bill dull orange with black tip. Paler and more streaked in winter.
Voice: Single or double *twit.*
Habitat: Rocky coasts and promontories.
Nesting: 4 brown-spotted buff eggs in a depression lined with grass and leaves on the ground.
Range: Arctic and subarctic Canada. Winters on the Atlantic Coast south to South Carolina. Also in arctic, subarctic, and temperate regions of Europe.

These hardy birds remain through the coldest winters on wave-washed rocks

along the ocean front. Sometimes flocks of as many as fifty or more may be found on stone jetties. Purple Sandpipers are among the tamest of shorebirds and can be approached closely. In recent years these birds have been found lingering later in spring, and a few nonbreeders have been reported even in summer as far south as Long Island. Their food consists of small crustaceans and mollusks such as periwinkles and snails.

210 Curlew Sandpiper
(*Calidris ferruginea*)
Sandpipers (Scolopacidae)

Description: 8" (20 cm). In summer, rich cinnamon or chestnut; in winter, gray above and white below. Curved bill. White rump is visible in flight.

Voice: A soft, dry *chirrip*.

Habitat: Tundra; chiefly coastal mud flats on migration.

Nesting: 4 pale yellow eggs with dark brown spots, in a depression on the ground in the tundra.

Range: Northern Siberia; winters in Africa, Asia, and Australia. In America, a rare but regular migrant on the Atlantic Coast.

Except for a small area on the arctic coast of Alaska, this Old World species breeds solely in northern Siberia. During spring migration the adults are in their bright chestnut breeding plumage and, with their curved bills and white rumps, are easily distinguished in the field from their usual associates, the Knots and Dunlins. However, on fall migration in their dull winter plumage they are much more difficult to spot among the hordes of other shorebirds.

221 Semipalmated Sandpiper
(*Calidris pusilla*)
Sandpipers (Scolopacidae)

Description: 6½″ (16 cm). Brownish-gray above, white below; short, straight bill; *black legs.*

Voice: A soft *krip.* Also a conversational chatter while feeding.

Habitat: Coastal beaches, lake and river shores, flats, and pools in salt marshes.

Nesting: 4 brown-marked buff eggs in a depression on the ground.

Range: Northern Alaska and Canada south to Hudson Bay. Winters from the southeastern U.S. and Mexico to South America.

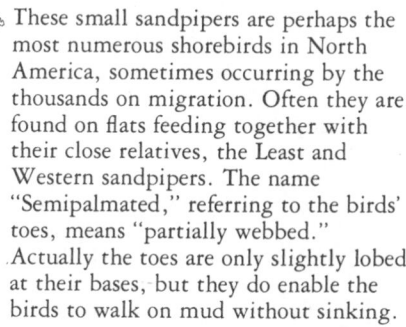

These small sandpipers are perhaps the most numerous shorebirds in North America, sometimes occurring by the thousands on migration. Often they are found on flats feeding together with their close relatives, the Least and Western sandpipers. The name "Semipalmated," referring to the birds' toes, means "partially webbed." Actually the toes are only slightly lobed at their bases, but they do enable the birds to walk on mud without sinking.

222 Western Sandpiper
(*Calidris mauri*)
Sandpipers (Scolopacidae)

Description: 6½″ (16 cm). Sparrow-sized. Similar to the Semipalmated Sandpiper, but *bill longer with a droop at the tip.* In summer, *crown and upper back rusty;* in winter, *dull gray.*

Voice: *Cheep* or *kreep,* higher and thinner than the Semipalmated.

Habitat: Shores, mud flats, grassy pools, and wet meadows.

Nesting: 4 creamy eggs with red-brown spots in a grass-lined depression on either wet or dry tundra.

Range: Coasts of Alaska and eastern Siberia.
Winters from the coasts of southern
United States to South America.
Migrates both on the coasts and less
commonly in the interior.

This species often associates with the
slightly smaller Semipalmated
Sandpipers. Western Sandpipers usually
feed in deeper water than the other
small "peeps" and sometimes immerse
their bills completely. In all other
respects these sandpipers are much alike
in their behavior and are difficult to
separate in the field.

225 Baird's Sandpiper
(*Calidris bairdii*)
Sandpipers (Scolopacidae)

Description: 7½" (19 cm). Bluebird-sized. Buff-
brown with dark greenish legs; when
the bird is at rest, the *wings project
beyond the tail*. Back appears scaly
because of the pale edges of its feathers.
Voice: *Kreep,* also a loud trill similar to that of
other "peeps."
Habitat: Chiefly inland areas with grassy pools,
wet meadows, and lake and river
shores; in summer on the tundra.
Nesting: 4 dark-spotted, tawny eggs in a dry
depression on the ground, often among
rocks.
Range: Arctic coasts of northeastern Siberia,
Alaska, Mackenzie, the islands in the
Canadian Arctic, and Greenland.
Winters at high elevations in the Andes
in South America. Migrates chiefly
through the center of the continent.

Baird's Sandpiper is the least common
of the sandpiper group known as
"peeps;" and is often overlooked because
of its similarity to other small
sandpipers. It was named in honor of
Spencer Fullerton Baird, an early
American ornithologist (1823–1887).

226 White-rumped Sandpiper
(*Calidris fuscicollis*)
Sandpipers (Scolopacidae)

Description: 7½" (19 cm). Small sandpiper with a short, straight bill and a *white rump*. In summer, rufous above; in winter, gray with *conspicuous white eye-stripe*. About the same size as Baird's Sandpiper; larger than Least, Semipalmated, and Western sandpipers; distinctly smaller than Pectoral Sandpiper.

Voice: Mouselike *jeet-jeet* or swallow-like twitter.

Habitat: Tundra; flats, grassy pools, wet meadows, and shores in winter.

Nesting: 4 brown-spotted olive eggs in a grass-lined nest in a slight depression on the ground. Because of the remoteness of its breeding grounds relatively few nests have been found.

Range: Northern Alaska, Yukon and the Arctic islands south to northern Hudson Bay. Winters in southern South America, east of the Andes from southern Brazil southward.

A long-distance flyer, it performs annual migrations between the Arctic and the subantarctic. On the wintering grounds in Argentina this is the commonest of the smaller sandpipers. With its conspicuous white rump this species is the easiest to identify of the "peeps," as these smaller sandpipers are called.

233 Snowy Plover
(*Charadrius alexandrinus*)
Plovers (Charadriidae)

Description: 5–7" (13–17 cm). Whitish with pale brown upperparts, black legs, *slender black bill,* and a small black mark on each side of the breast. The similar Piping Plover has a stubbier, yellow bill and yellow legs.

Voice: Plaintive *chu-we* or *o-wee-ah*.

Habitat: Flat, sandy beaches; alkali beds; and sandy areas with little vegetation.

Nesting: 2 or 3 black-spotted buff eggs in a sand scrape lined with a few shell fragments or bits of grass.

Range: Locally from Washington, Colorado, and Oklahoma to South America, and along the Gulf Coast as far east as northwestern Florida. Winters from California and the Gulf Coast south. Also breeds in the Old World.

The Snowy Plover's patchy distribution, not only in North America but elsewhere in the world, is due to its specialized habitat requirements. Keeping to large, flat expanses of sand, it avoids competition for food in a habitat in which few other species can exist. Here these tiny birds, with their pale coloration, are difficult to see even when they run nimbly over the hard, pavement-like ground. In England the species is usually found only on the southern coast in the counties of Kent and Sussex, and is called the Kentish Plover.

234 Piping Plover
(*Charadrius melodus*)
Plovers (Charadriidae)

Description: 6–7" (15–17 cm). Sparrow-sized. Pale whitish with complete or incomplete black breast band; yellow legs; bill yellowish in spring, dark in fall.

Voice: Clear, whistled *peep-lo*.

Habitat: Bare, dry, sandy areas, both inland and on the coast.

Nesting: 4 buff-white eggs evenly marked with small dark spots, laid in a depression in the sand that is often lined with pebbles and bits of shells. Usually in loose colonies.

Range: Lakes in interior Canada and Newfoundland south along the Atlantic

Coast to Virginia, rarely to the Carolinas. Winters on the Atlantic and Gulf coasts, north regularly as far as the Carolinas. Also south to the West Indies and Mexico.

The color of dry sand, the Piping Plover is difficult to see on the beach. The eggs and downy chicks also blend with the sand. With the rapid expansion of summer resorts along the Atlantic Coast, many of the former nesting sites have been destroyed. This species arrives much earlier in spring and departs for the South much earlier in fall than does the Semipalmated Plover.

236 Semipalmated Plover
(*Charadrius semipalmatus*)
Plovers (Charadriidae)

Description: 6–8″ (15–20 cm). A dark-backed shorebird with white underparts and a *conspicuous black breast band* from which it gets its common name of "Ring-necked Plover." Bill stubby, yellow-orange, with dark tip. The Piping Plover is similar but is much paler above. The larger Killdeer has two black breast bands.

Voice: Plaintive two-noted whistle: *tsuwee*. Also a soft, rather musical chuckle.

Habitat: Beaches and tidal flats, shallow pools in salt marshes; lakeshores in the interior during migration.

Nesting: 4 brown-spotted buff eggs in a shallow scrape lined with shell fragments, pebbles, or bits of vegetation on the tundra or on a beach.

Range: Breeds from the Aleutians, Alaska and the islands of the Canadian Arctic south to Nova Scotia, Quebec, northern Manitoba, and northern British Columbia. Winters regularly from California and the Gulf Coast south; in smaller numbers farther north.

This is one of the most familiar American shorebirds. The birds usually migrate in flocks, but otherwise tend to scatter when feeding. They have the typical plover habit of running along the beach for several paces, then stopping abruptly and raising their heads.

237 Wilson's Plover
(*Charadrius wilsonia*)
Plovers (Charadriidae)

Description: 7–8″ (17–20 cm). Starling-sized. Male brown above and white below with a broad black eye patch and neck band; *heavy black bill* and *pinkish-gray legs.* Female similar but bands are gray.

Voice: Clear, whistled *queet.* Also *quit-quit.*

Habitat: Sand beaches and mud flats.

Nesting: 3 or 4 buff eggs with small spots and blotches placed in a slight depression on the open sand or occasionally in the dunes.

Range: Atlantic and Gulf coasts from southern New Jersey (rare) to Florida and Texas. Winters chiefly along the Gulf Coast south to northern South America.

Its stouter, longer bill enables this bird to partake of a more varied diet than other plovers, including small crabs, shrimps, beach fleas, beetles, spiders, and the smaller shellfish. This is the largest of the "ring-necked" plovers and can be most easily identified by its thick black bill.

242 American Oystercatcher
(*Haematopus palliatus*)
Oystercatchers (Haematopodidae)

Description: 17–21″ (43–53 cm). Chicken-sized. Boldly patterned in blackish-brown and white. Long red bill, pink feet. Shows a bold white wing patch in flight.

Voice: Piercing *kleep!* Also a plover-like *cle-ár*.

Habitat: Sandy and pebbly beaches, mud flats, borders of salt marshes.

Nesting: 2–4 spotted blackish-buff eggs in a shallow scrape lined with a few shell fragments on beaches.

Range: Along the coast from Baja California and Massachusetts south to Argentina and Chile. Winters from North Carolina southward.

Oystercatchers are large, conspicuous birds that were quickly shot out along the Atlantic Coast. Given total protection, they have once again become numerous and now nest in numbers as far north as Massachusetts, where just a few years ago they were very rare. Oystercatchers insert their long, bladelike bills into mussels and other bivalves, severing the powerful adductor muscles before the shells can close. They also feed on barnacles and snails. Although they do not breed in colonies, these birds gather in large flocks on migration and in winter.

580 Fish Crow
(*Corvus ossifragus*)
Jays, Magpies, Crows (Corvidae)

Description: 17″ (43 cm). All black, somewhat smaller than the American Crow, but size is deceptive in the field. May be best told by its voice.

Voice: Two calls, both distinct from the American Crow's familiar *caw*—a nasal *kwok* and a two-noted nasal *ah-ah*—but in the breeding season young American Crows have a similar *kwok* call.

Habitat: Low coastal country, near tidewater in the North; in the South also lakes, rivers, and swamps far inland.

Nesting: 4 or 5 greenish eggs with brown blotches in a stick nest lined with pine needles, grass, hair, or bark flakes placed in an evergreen or deciduous tree.

Range: Atlantic and Gulf coasts from Massachusetts and extreme southern New England south to Florida and west to Texas. Also inland along the larger rivers north to Arkansas, southwestern Tennessee, central Virginia, and south-central Pennsylvania.

Nearly all the heronries on the coast have attendant Fish Crows ever ready to plunder the heron nests for eggs. An omnivorous feeder like all crows, it consumes corn, insects, lizards, wild and cultivated fruits, and often carrion and dead fish—hence its name.

Salt Marshes

Tidal marshes of brackish or salt water, along creeks and estuaries and behind barrier beaches. At low tide there are often extensive mudflats.

Besides the birds treated in this section, one may find some of the birds of freshwater marshes, and during migration, hawks and swallows are sometimes numerous here.

1, 5 Snowy Egret
(*Egretta thula*)
Herons, Bitterns (Ardeidae)

Description: 20–27″ (51–68 cm). W. 38″ (1 m). A
small white heron with a *slender black
bill,* black legs, and *yellow feet.* In the
breeding season it has long lacy plumes
on its back. Similar to young of the
Little Blue Heron, but that species has
a stouter, bluish-gray bill and greenish-
yellow legs and feet.

Voice: Harsh squawk.

Habitat: Salt marshes, ponds, rice fields, and
shallow coastal bays.

Nesting: 3 or 4 pale blue eggs on a platform of
sticks in a bush or reedbed. In colonies,
often with other species of herons.

Range: Northern California, Oklahoma, and
Maine to southern South America.
Winters regularly north to California
and South Carolina.

During the 19th and early 20th
centuries, Snowy Egrets were
slaughtered almost to extinction for
their fine plumes, used to decorate hats.
Fortunately, complete protection has
enabled them to increase their numbers
again. Snowies are agile, often seen
sprinting about in shallow water, or
even hovering as they seek small
shrimps and minnows. Although they
breed on freshwater marshes in the
West, in the eastern states, where large
freshwater marshes are scarce, they are
best known as salt marsh birds.

---

11 Roseate Spoonbill
(*Ajaia ajaja*)
Ibises, Spoonbills (Threskiornithidae)

Description: 30–32″ (76–81 cm). W. 53″ (1.3 m).
Brilliant pink with white neck and
back, orange tails. Straight bill with
broad spatulate tip, hence its name.
Immatures are white.

Voice: Low croak or cluck.
Habitat: Mangroves.
Nesting: 3–5 dull white eggs with dark spots
and blotches in stick nest, in low dense
bushes or trees.
Range: Locally on the coasts of southern
Florida, Louisiana (rare), and Texas.
Also West Indies, Mexico, and Central
and South America.

These birds spend much time feeding
on shrimps and fish in the shallow
waters of Florida Bay and the Gulf of
Mexico. They obtain food by sweeping
their bills from side to side and
scooping up whatever they encounter.
Early in the century their numbers were
severely depleted by plume hunters
but, with protective laws, they have
increased once again.

13 Louisiana Heron
(*Egretta tricolor*)
Herons, Bitterns (Ardeidae)

Description: 25–30" (63–76 cm). W. 38" (1 m).
A gray-blue heron with rufous neck and
white belly.
Voice: Guttural croaks and squawks.
Habitat: Swamps, bayous, coastal ponds, salt
marshes, mangrove islands, mud flats,
and lagoons.
Nesting: 3 or 4 blue-green eggs in a stick nest in
a tree, on the ground, or among reeds.
Range: Atlantic and Gulf coasts from
Massachusetts southward. Winters
north to Virginia. Also in South
America.

Also called the "Tricolored Heron," this
is one of the most numerous herons in
the Deep South. It is extremely slender
and with graceful movements searches
about for frogs or fish. Like bitterns, it
has a habit of standing motionless
among the grasses with bill pointing
straight up in an attempt to avoid
detection.

25, 26 White Ibis
(*Eudocimus albus*)
Ibises, Spoonbills (Threskiornithidae)

Description: 23–27" (58–68 cm). W. 38" (1 m).
Adult white with black wing tips
(usually hidden at rest); bare face and
downcurved, red bill; red legs in
breeding seasons, otherwise slate-
colored. Immature birds are brown
above and white below with brown bill
and legs.

Voice: Grunts and growls.

Habitat: Marshy sloughs, mud flats, lagoons,
and swamp forests.

Nesting: 3–5 pale blue, green, or buff eggs with
dark spots or blotches in a stick nest in
trees over water.

Range: Coastal from South Carolina to Florida
and Texas. South to northern South
America.

Around their colonies, ibises eat crayfish,
which in turn devour quantities of fish
eggs. By keeping down the numbers of
crayfish, the birds help increase fish
populations. In addition, their
droppings fertilize the water, greatly
increasing the growth of plankton, the
basic food of all marsh life.

27 Glossy Ibis
(*Plegadis falcinellus*)
Ibises, Spoonbills (Threskiornithidae)

Description: 22–25" (56–63 cm). W. 37" (0.9 m).
A large, all-dark marsh bird with a
downcurved bill. Plumage rich chestnut;
wings glossy greenish. The White-
faced Ibis of the Southwest is similar
but has a narrow band of feathers
around the base of the bill and around
the eye.

Voice: Low grunt and higher-pitched bleats.

Habitat: Marshes, swamps, flooded fields, coastal
bays, and estuaries.

Nesting: 2–4 pale blue eggs in stick nests in

bushes and trees, rarely on the ground. In colonies, often along with herons.

Range: On or near the coast, chiefly from Maine to Florida and Texas. In recent years, inland to the Great Lakes. Also in the Old World.

The Glossy Ibis probably crossed the Atlantic from Africa to northern South America in the 19th century, dispersing northward into the United States by way of the Caribbean region. In recent years it has expanded its range considerably and is now a common breeder in areas where it was rare or absent. Inland it frequently eats crayfish, but along the coast it feeds mostly on fiddler crabs. It also eats insects and snakes, including the poisonous water moccasin.

28 White-faced Ibis
(*Plegadis chihi*)
Ibises, Spoonbills (Threskiornithidae)

Description: 22–25" (56–63 cm). W. 37" (0.9 m). A large, chestnut-bronze marsh bird with a long, curved bill. Very similar to the Glossy Ibis but has a *band of white feathers around the base of the bill, under the chin, and behind the eye.* The Glossy Ibis may show white skin at base of bill. In winter the White-faced loses this band and becomes virtually impossible to distinguish from the Glossy.

Voice: Low croak or grunt.

Habitat: Salt marshes and brushy coastal islands in Louisiana and Texas, freshwater marshes in the West.

Nesting: 3–5 pale blue eggs in a shallow cup of reeds lined with grass and placed in low bushes in a marsh.

Range: Oregon and Nebraska south into Mexico and east to coastal Louisiana. Winters north to the Gulf Coast. Also breeds in South America.

This western bird enters our area only in western Louisiana and Texas where the White-faced Ibis is common and the Glossy Ibis is rare; therefore most dark ibises can be assumed to be the White-faced. This bird probably represents an earlier invasion of the New World by the Glossy Ibis, which in isolation evolved into a separate species.

29 Whooping Crane
(*Grus americana*)
Cranes (Gruidae)

Description: 45–50″ (114–127 cm). W. 90″ (2.3 m). A very large bird, *pure white with jet-black wing tips* and red on forehead and cheeks. Immature birds are similar but head and neck are brown.

Voice: Trumpet-like call that can be heard for several miles.

Habitat: Breeds in northern freshwater bogs; winters on coastal prairies.

Nesting: 2 dark-blotched buff eggs in a mound of marsh vegetation.

Range: South-central Mackenzie, Canada (Wood Buffalo Park). Winters on the Gulf Coast of Texas at Aransas National Wildlife Refuge.

This extremely rare crane is one of our most spectacular birds. In the last few years a few eggs have been taken and placed in the nests of Sandhill Cranes. The young Whooping Cranes are reared by their foster parents. In this way it is hoped that the population of Whooping Cranes can be increased beyond its present limit of about 50.

43, 56 Laughing Gull
(*Larus atricilla*)
Gulls, Terns (Laridae)

Description: 15–17" (38–43 cm). In summer the
adult has a *black hood* and dark gray
back and wings; hind edge of wing is
white; *wing tip is black, without white
spots.* Lacks a hood in winter. Young
bird is dark brown with *contrasting
white rump.* The similar Franklin's Gull
has a black wing tip separated from the
gray wing by a white band.

Voice: Loud, high-pitched *ha-ha-ha-ha-haah-
haah-haah-haah.*

Habitat: Salt marshes, bays, and estuaries. Very
rare inland.

Nesting: 3 olive-brown eggs with dark blotches
in a ground nest lined with grass and
weed stems on sand or salt marsh.

Range: Maine to the Caribbean. Winters
regularly north to Virginia, in smaller
numbers farther north.

The common summer gull along the
Atlantic and Gulf coasts, it has
declined in numbers in recent years
perhaps due to the destruction of
coastal marshes and the increase in
Herring Gulls, which prey on its eggs
and young. Very agile on the wing,
Laughing Gulls easily catch bits of food
tossed into the air. In winter they feed
on beaches and in harbors.

60, 66 Forster's Tern
(*Sterna forsteri*)
Gulls, Terns (Laridae)

Description: 14–15" (35–38 cm). White with pale
gray back and wings, black cap, and
deeply forked tail. Orange bill with
black tip. Similar to the Common Tern,
but *wing tips* are *frosty white* and, at very
close range, outer web of outermost tail
feathers white instead of dusky. Lacks
black cap in winter but has distinctive

black mark behind eye.

Voice: Harsh nasal *beep*.

Habitat: Salt marshes in the East; freshwater marshes in the West.

Nesting: 3 or 4 buff, spotted eggs on a large platform of dead grass lined with finer grasses. Usually placed on masses of dead marsh vegetation. In colonies.

Range: Breeds along the Atlantic Coast from Maryland to Texas and in the interior from Alberta and California east to Illinois. Winters from Virginia to Guatemala.

One of the few exclusively North American terns, it is so similar to the Common Tern that, until 1831, it was not recognized as a distinct species. Its preference for marshes enables it to avoid competition with the Common Tern, which favors sandy or pebbly beaches and rocky islands. It was named after Johann Reinhold Forster (1729–1798), a German pastor-naturalist who accompanied Captain Cook around the world, in 1772.

68 Gull-billed Tern
(*Gelochelidon nilotica*)
Gulls, Terns (Laridae)

Description: 13–15″ (33–38 cm). Pigeon-sized. Very pale with almost white back and wings, black cap, and *stout black bill*; tail not as deeply forked as in other terns. Winter birds lack the black cap.

Voice: Rasping *katy-did* similar to the sound made by that insect.

Habitat: Coastal marshes and sandy beaches.

Nesting: 2 or 3 spotted buff eggs in a shell-lined shallow depression (occasionally a well-made cup of dead marsh grasses) on a sandy island in a salt marsh. In colonies. Often breeds with other species of terns.

Range: Long Island south to the Gulf of Mexico and the West Indies. Winters

from the Gulf Coast to northern South America. Also in Eurasia, Africa, and Australia.

In addition to the usual tern diet of fish and crustaceans, this bird catches insects in flight, and pursues them on the ground in plowed fields or croplands. Although not numerous, it is widespread, breeding in scattered colonies. In America it was one of the species hardest hit by the millinery trade and has never recovered its former numbers, although recently it has slowly extended its range to the north.

133 Black Duck
(*Anas rubripes*)
Swans, Geese, Ducks (Anatidae)

Description: 19–22″ (48–56 cm). Sooty brown with conspicuous white wing linings, olive or greenish bill. Sexes alike. The female Mallard is paler and sandier and has the bill mottled with orange.

Voice: Typical duck quack.

Habitat: Marshes, lakes, streams, coastal mud flats, and estuaries.

Nesting: 9–12 greenish-buff eggs in a ground nest of feathers and down.

Range: Eastern and central North America, from Manitoba and Labrador to Texas and Florida.

It is believed that widespread interbreeding between Black Ducks and Mallards has resulted in recent years in a decrease of "pure" Blacks. Actually the name is a misnomer, for the bird appears black only at a distance; it was formerly more aptly known as the "Dusky Duck." In areas of heavy shooting, these and other dabbling ducks ingest enough lead shot to cause extensive mortality from lead poisoning. If hunters used steel shot such damage would be much reduced.

Mottled Duck
(*Anas fulvigula*)
Swans, Geese, Ducks (Anatidae)

Description: 21" (53 cm). Mottled dark brown and
sandy. Similar to a female Mallard, but
bill clear yellow or orange yellow, and
tail dark, rather than sandy brown.

Voice: A loud *quack,* like that of a Mallard.

Habitat: Coastal marshes and lagoons.

Nesting: 9–13 pale greenish eggs, in a down-
lined nest of grass, concealed in
vegetation near a shore.

Range: Resident in southern Florida and along
the Gulf Coast of Louisiana and Texas.

This southern duck is a very close
relative of the more widespread
Mallard. Until recently, no other duck
of the genus *Anas* nested in these
coastal marshes, and so the distinctive
male plumage, which among these
birds serves in species recognition, was
gradually lost. After thousands of years
of evolutionary change, the two sexes
are colored alike.

171 **Snow Goose**
including "Blue Goose"
(*Chen caerulescens*)
Swans, Geese, Ducks (Anatidae)

Description: 22–30" (56–76 cm). The white color
phase with black wing tips is most
common in the East, while in the West
and along the Gulf Coast the "Blue
Goose"—dark gray with white head and
neck—is numerous. Pinkish bill and
feet.

Voice: High-pitched nasal barking.

Habitat: Breeds on the tundra and winters in salt
marshes and marshy coastal bays; less
commonly in freshwater marshes and
adjacent grain fields.

Nesting: 5–7 whitish eggs in a large cup of grass
and moss lined with down. Often in
loose colonies.

Range: Arctic regions of North America and extreme eastern Siberia. Winters on the Pacific Coast south to Baja California and along the Atlantic Coast from New Jersey to Texas. In smaller numbers in the interior.

Until recently the two color phases were considered separate species, but it is now known that they interbreed where their ranges overlap. The nesting grounds of the "Blue Goose" were unknown until 1929, when large numbers were discovered breeding on the shores of Foxe Basin, west of Baffin Island. They are now known to breed on Baffin Island and nearby Southampton Island. Each fall virtually the entire population gathers at the southern end of Hudson Bay and makes a single nonstop flight to the Gulf Coast.

Ross' Goose
(*Chen rossii*)
Swans, Geese, Ducks (Anatidae)

Description: 24″ (60 cm). A Mallard-sized edition of the Snow Goose. White wings, black wing tips, pink bill and pink legs. Differs from the Snow Goose in its smaller size, *very stubby bill,* and rounder head.

Voice: Soft cackling and grunting notes.

Habitat: Arctic tundra in the breeding season, salt or fresh marshes in the winter.

Nesting: 4 creamy white eggs in a nest of grass lined with down, placed on a small island in a lake or river.

Range: Breeds in northeastern Mackenzie and on Southampton Island; winters mainly in central California; but occurs occasionally in the lower Mississippi Valley and on the east coast.

This species is very similar to the white phase of the Snow Goose, and

occasionally hybridizes with that species. There is some evidence that many of the Ross' Geese that appear in the eastern United States in the winter are actually hybrids. The great majority of Ross' Geese spends the winter in the Sacramento Valley in California.

---

172 Brant
including "Black Brant"
(*Branta bernicla*)
Swans, Geese, Ducks, (Anatidae)

Description: 22–30" (56–76 cm). Similar to the Canada Goose but smaller, shorter-necked, and lacking the conspicuous white cheek patch. Dark brown above with black head and neck, and an inconspicuous white mark on the side of the neck.

Voice: Low, guttural croaking, unlike the clear, rich honking of Canada geese.

Habitat: Tundra and coastal islands in the Arctic; salt marshes and estuaries in winter.

Nesting: 4 or 5 cream-colored eggs in a large mass of moss and down on the tundra. Often nests in loose colonies.

Range: Breeds in the Arctic; winters along the coasts south to California and the Carolinas.

Its favorite winter food is eelgrass. In the 1930s a disease virtually wiped out this abundant underwater plant in the North Atlantic and the Brant declined drastically, but it is once again a fairly common visitor to our shores. Migrating flocks can be identified at a great distance as they travel in erratic, constantly shifting bunches unlike the V-shaped flocks of Canada Geese or the long, irregular lines of Snow Geese. Birds from far western North America have black underparts and until recently were considered a separate species, the "Black Brant."

200, 230 Stilt Sandpiper
(*Micropalama himantopus*)
Sandpipers (Scolopacidae)

Description: 8½" (21 cm). Robin-sized. *Chestnut head stripes and barring below* are diagnostic in breeding plumage. Nonbreeding birds have much paler plumage with a white line over the eye. Long bill, slightly downcurved at the tip. Has long, greenish legs. Wings unpatterned.

Voice: Simple *tu-tu* similar to that of Lesser Yellowlegs.

Habitat: Grassy pools and shores of ponds and lakes.

Nesting: 4 pale buff eggs with brown markings on open ground in grass tussocks near water.

Range: Breeds in northern Alaska and Canada. Winters in Florida and South America. Uncommon along the Atlantic Coast.

Often associated with dowitchers and yellowlegs, Stilt Sandpipers resemble both species and appear to be intermediate between the two. While yellowlegs move about continually in nervous, jerky motions and dowitchers feed slowly, probing deep into the mud, Stilt Sandpipers move like yellowlegs but cover more ground, at the same time feeding deliberately like dowitchers.

201, 212 Short-billed Dowitcher
(*Limnodromus griseus*)
Sandpipers (Scolopacidae)

Description: 12" (30 cm). Rich rust-brown in spring, gray in fall; very long bill, greenish legs, barred tail, white rump and back.

Voice: Loud, rapid, whistled *tu-tu-tu*.

Habitat: Mud flats, creeks, salt marshes, and tidal estuaries.

Nesting: 4 greenish eggs, spotted with brown,

in a nest lined with grass and moss in a
ground depression on open wet tundra.

Range: Southern Alaska to eastern Canada.
Winters from southern United States to
central South America.

Dowitchers often occur in large
flocks—sometimes in the thousands—
on coastal flats during migrations,
remaining well bunched whether in
flight or feeding in the mud. They
probe deeply with their long bills with
rapid up-and-down movements like
sewing machines, seeking marine
worms, snails, tiny crustaceans, and
aquatic larvae.

202, 229 Willet
(*Catoptrophorus semipalmatus*)
Sandpipers (Scolopacidae)

Description: 15″ (38 cm). Pigeon-sized. Grayish-
brown with *gray legs*. Best told in flight
by its flashy *black-and-white wing
pattern*. The gray legs and thicker bill
distinguish it from the Greater
Yellowlegs.

Voice: Extremely vocal; their *will-will-willet*
calls identify them immediately. They
also utter a rapid *kuk-kuk-kuk-kuk-kuk-kuk*.

Habitat: Coastal beaches, freshwater and salt
marshes, lakeshores, and wet prairies.

Nesting: 4 brown-spotted olive-buff eggs in a
nest lined with weeds or bits of shell in
a depression on open ground or in a
grass clump.

Range: Breeds locally in southern Canada,
United States, and the West Indies.
Winters from southern United States to
central South America.

Willets look quite nondescript on the
ground and superficially resemble
yellowlegs; but once in flight or even
with wings spread out, they are
distinguished by their striking black-
and-white color pattern. They

frequently accompany godwits on
migration.

213 Long-billed Dowitcher
(*Limnodromus scolopaceus*)
Sandpipers (Scolopacidae)

Description: 12¼" (31 cm). A stocky shorebird with
a very long, straight bill. Breeding
birds have rusty underparts and dark,
streaked upperparts; winter birds are
gray. In all plumages shows a
conspicuous white rump and lower
back, most easily seen in flight. Very
similar to Short-billed Dowitcher, but
darker and more coarsely streaked
above, and with a longer bill. Voices
also different.

Voice: A sharp, thin *keek*, very different from
soft *tu-tu-tu* of Short-billed Dowitcher.

Habitat: Breeds in muskeg; in migration and
winter occurs on mud flats, marshy
pools, and margins of freshwater ponds.

Nesting: 4 olive eggs spotted with brown, in a
grass and moss-lined nest on the
ground.

Range: Northeastern Siberia, northern Alaska,
and northwestern Canada. Winters
from southern United States south to
Guatemala.

Dowitchers are most often seen during
migration, when this species favors
freshwater habitats, and the Short-
billed Dowitcher is more partial to salt
water. The main fall migration of
Long-bills takes place in September and
October, when a majority of Short-bills
have already departed.

214 Ruff
(*Philomachus pugnax*)
Sandpipers (Scolopacidae)

Description: 11″ (28 cm). The breeding males have
extraordinarily variable plumage,
showing any combination of black,
white, chestnut, gray, buff, etc. ear
tufts, ruffs, and gorgets; females (called
Reeves) and winter males are much
duller—gray or brown above, white
below; leg color varies from yellow to
green, brown, and red. In flight, two
oval white tail patches are visible. In all
seasons the male is noticeably larger
than the female.

Voice: Usually silent, but occasionally a soft
tu-whit when flushed.

Habitat: Short grassy meadows and marshy
ponds.

Nesting: 4 gray, green, or buff eggs, heavily
marked with deep brown blotches.

Range: Subarctic Europe and Asia south to the
central portions of those continents;
winters south to South Africa, Ceylon,
and Indonesia. In America, a rare but
regular migrant on or near the Atlantic
Coast.

The Ruff is one of the most remarkable
of all shorebirds. It is the only wader in
which the two sexes are different in
color, pattern, and size during the
breeding season. The males also form
leks or "dancing" grounds and engage
in courting. After mating, the females
build their nests away from the
courtship area.

227 Lesser Yellowlegs
(*Tringa flavipes*)
Sandpipers (Scolopacidae)

Description: 10½″ (26 cm). A smaller edition of the
Greater Yellowlegs, with a shorter bill.

Voice: Call is quite different from that of the

Greater Yellowlegs: a flatter, less melodious *tu-tu*, given in doublets rather than triplets.

Habitat: Marshy ponds, lake and river shores, mud flats; in the breeding season, boreal bogs.

Nesting: 4 buff eggs blotched with brown in a slight depression on the open ground near damp places.

Range: Alaska and Canada. Winters from southern United States to southern South America.

This species usually occurs in larger flocks and is a tamer bird than the Greater Yellowlegs, allowing an observer a much closer approach before flying off a short distance. Both species of yellowlegs nod up and down when watching an intruder or just before.

228 Greater Yellowlegs
(*Tringa melanoleuca*)
Sandpipers (Scolopacidae)

Description: 14″ (35 cm). A slender, gray-streaked wader with conspicuous white upper tail coverts and long *yellow legs*. The Lesser Yellowlegs is similar, but smaller, with a more slender bill.

Voice: Far-reaching, penetrating—though musical—series of whistled *whew-whew-whew*s, usually given in threes or fours. This call easily differentiates the Greater Yellowlegs from its relative, the Lesser Yellowlegs.

Habitat: Prefers pools, lakeshores, and tidal mud flats on migration, but open wet tundra and marshy ground in the breeding season.

Nesting: 4 eggs—rich, tawny-colored, heavily marked with brown—in a slight depression on the ground in open, damp areas.

Range: Breeds in southern Alaska and central and southern Canada. Winters along

coast from Carolinas to southern South America.

The larger of the two yellowlegs is a noisy and conspicuous bird. It is also more wary than its smaller relative and flushes at a greater distance. It often wades up to its belly and occasionally even swims. With its long legs it easily obtains food in pools.

231 Marbled Godwit
(*Limosa fedoa*)
Sandpipers (Scolopacidae)

Description: 18″ (46 cm). Crow-sized. A large, pale, buff-brown wader with *cinnamon wing linings* and buffy underparts, and a *long, pinkish upturned bill.*

Voice: Prolonged, far-reaching, whistled *god-wit, god-wit,* or *go-wit, go-wit*—hence its name.

Habitat: Extensive grasslands; on migration, salt marshes, tidal creeks, mud flats, and sea beaches.

Nesting: 4 olive-buff eggs, blotched with brown, in a slight depression on the ground in a grass-lined nest.

Range: South-central Canada and north-central United States. Winters from southernmost United States to Central America and on the Pacific Coast of South America to Chile.

One of our largest shorebirds, it breeds on the vast grassy plains of the West but less abundantly than in former days. Like the Long-billed Curlew, it is a rich buff color, blending perfectly with the brown grass of the plains.

232 Hudsonian Godwit
(*Limosa haemastica*)
Sandpipers (Scolopacidae)

Description: 15" (38 cm). *Underparts rufous* in the
breeding season, otherwise gray above,
whitish below. Conspicuous *black-and-
white tail,* broad white wing stripe, and
black wing lining. Long, slightly
upturned bill.

Voice: Similar to the Marbled Godwit but
higher pitched. Reported as *chip-ta-it*
and *quit-quit*. Usually silent.

Habitat: Tundra; chiefly mud flats on migration.

Nesting: 4 olive-buff eggs in a shallow grass-
lined hollow on the ground.

Range: Breeds on the Canadian tundra and
migrates through the United States;
winters in the southern parts of South
America.

Never common, the Hudsonian Godwit
was for many years hunted for food and
became scarce. Now completely
protected, its numbers have increased
considerably. This large shorebird can
be seen in flocks of up to several dozen
or more during fall passage on the
coastal mud flats of the northeastern
states.

243 Black-necked Stilt
(*Himantopus mexicanus*)
Avocets, Stilts (Recurvirostridae)

Description: 13–16" (33–40 cm). Black above, white
below; head patterned in black and
white; long neck; *very long red legs;*
straight, very thin bill.

Voice: Sharp *kip-kip-kip-kip*.

Habitat: Salt marshes and shallow coastal bays in
the East; also freshwater marshes in the
West.

Nesting: 3 or 4 brown-spotted buff eggs in a
shallow depression lined with grass or
shell fragments in a marsh. In small,
loose colonies.

Range: Oregon and Saskatchewan to the Gulf Coast, and along the Atlantic Coast from Delaware and the Carolinas to northern South America. Winters mainly south of the United States.

These stilts once bred as far north as New Jersey. Noisy and conspicuous, their decline was due to excessive hunting. In the nesting season they are particularly aggressive and will often fly low over an approaching human being, uttering a loud alarm call with their long red legs trailing behind them.

245 Whimbrel
(*Numenius phaeopus*)
Sandpipers (Scolopacidae)

Description: 17" (43 cm). Crow-sized, with long legs. Gray-brown with *striped crown* and medium-length *curved bill*.

Voice: 5–7 loud, clear, whistled notes.

Habitat: Arctic tundra, preferring freshwater pools near the coast. On migration, chiefly coastal salt meadows, mud flats, and grassy slopes along the coast.

Nesting: 4 olive eggs heavily marked with brown in a depression in a moss or sedge clump on the ground.

Range: Northern America and Eurasia. In America winters from Florida and California to southern South America.

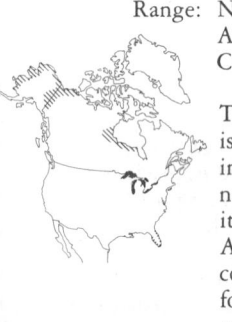

The Whimbrel, or Hudsonian Curlew, is found not only along both coasts but in the center of the continent. It is numerous because of its wary behavior, its remote nesting grounds on the Arctic tundra, and its successful competition with other big shorebirds for food and breeding territory. Like many other tundra breeders, those in the east fly offshore during their autumn migration to South America, returning in spring mainly through the interior.

246 Long-billed Curlew
(*Numenius americanus*)
Sandpipers (Scolopacidae)

Description: 23" (58 cm). Very large, buff-brown shorebird with *very long sickle-shaped bill* and cinnamon wing linings.

Voice: *Cur-lew*, with the second note higher.

Habitat: Chiefly grass plains and prairies; in migration, lake and river shores, mud flats, salt marshes, and sand beaches.

Nesting: 4 brown-spotted olive-buff eggs in a grass-lined nest in a hollow on the ground.

Range: Breeds chiefly in western North America from southern Canada to New Mexico and Texas. Winters from California and Louisiana to Guatemala, and from South Carolina to Florida.

Our largest shorebird, the "Sicklebill," as it was called by hunters, was once a plentiful gamebird of the Great Plains and the formerly extensive prairies to the east. They are now so scarce that they must be protected by law. Their prolonged, musical whistles carry far, signaling their arrival in spring. While they incubate, their golden colors blend with the brown grass, making them difficult to detect. On grasslands they consume grasshoppers, crickets, and beetles; on shores and beaches, during their migration, they feast on small crustaceans and mollusks or on berries and seeds.

253 Clapper Rail
(*Rallus longirostris*)
Rails, Gallinules, Coots (Rallidae)

Description: 14–16" (35–40 cm). Chicken-sized. Long-billed, grayish-brown bird without the rusty underparts of the similar King Rail.

Voice: Harsh clattering *kek-kek-kek-kek-kek*.

Habitat: Salt marshes.

Nesting: 5–15 spotted buff eggs in a shallow
saucer or deep bowl of dead marsh
grasses, often domed.

Range: Breeds along the coasts from California
and Massachusetts to South America.
Winters north to New Jersey, rarely
farther north.

Its call is one of the most familiar
sounds in the salt marshes in summer.
Although generally secretive, the birds
are sometimes forced into view by high
tides, when they may be seen along
roads in the marsh or standing on
floating boards. Otherwise they are
most often glimpsed as they dart across
a tidal creek between sheltering grasses.
This bird may be confused with the
rusty King Rail when the latter enters
the salt meadows for the winter.

Black Rail
(*Laterallus jamaicensis*)
Rails, Gallinules, Coots (Rallidae)

Description: 5–6″ (13–15 cm). Sparrow-sized. Black
with rusty nape and white flecks on the
back; black bill; legs and feet greenish.
Can be confused with the glossy black
young of larger rails.

Voice: *Kee-kee-kerr,* the last note lower in
pitch.

Habitat: Coastal salt marshes, more rarely in
inland freshwater marshes.

Nesting: 4–8 lightly spotted pale buff eggs in a
loose cup of grass concealed under a
mat of dead marsh vegetation.

Range: Breeds along the Atlantic and Pacific
coasts from Long Island and California
to southern South America, locally in
the interior. Winters north to the Gulf
Coast.

This tiny rail may be common in some
areas, but is so secretive that many
consider it rare. The birds spend much
of their time creeping about under mats

of dead marsh grass. The best way to detect them is to enter a salt marsh at night during the breeding season and listen for their high-pitched, piping call notes, which carry as far as a mile. These birds respond to an imitation of their call and may sometimes be lured within range of a flashlight.

316 Gyrfalcon
(*Falco rusticolus*)
Falcons (Falconidae)

Description: 22″ (56 cm). W. 48″ (1.2 m). A very large falcon. Three color phases occur: blackish, white, and gray-brown. All are more uniformly colored than the Peregrine Falcon, which has dark mustaches and hood.

Voice: A chattering scream: *ke-a, ke-a, ke-a.*

Habitat: Arctic tundra and rocky cliffs, usually near water. At rare intervals it moves south to coastal beaches and marshes.

Nesting: 4 heavily spotted reddish-brown eggs on a rock ledge lined with sticks, grass, moss, and even the bones of its prey.

Range: Circumpolar; in America, breeding from Alaska, Canada, and Greenland south only to central Canada. Winters mostly in the breeding range, but on occasion as far south as northern United States.

This magnificent falcon is a very rare visitor from the Arctic. It is a memorable occasion when one is sighted on a coastal salt marsh or over open country inland. In the Far North they feed mainly on ptarmigans, but during the summer months they also take shorebirds, eiders, and gulls, and make frequent raids on the great colonies of murres and dovekies.

519, 575   Boat-tailed Grackle
(*Quiscaluis major*)
Orioles, Blackbirds (Icteridae)

Description: Males 16–17″ (40–43 cm); females 12–
13″ (30–33 cm). Tail very long and
keel-shaped. Male black, *iridescent blue
on back and breast; yellow or brown eyes.*
Female smaller, brown with a paler
breast. Common Grackle is smaller;
female lacks paler breast. Great-tailed
Grackle of western Louisiana and Texas
has iridescent purple back and breast,
and always has yellow eyes.

Voice: Harsh *jeeb-jeeb-jeeb-jeeb,* unlike the
whistles and clucks of the Great-tailed
Grackle.

Habitat: Marshes along the coast; in Florida also
in farmlands.

Nesting: 3 or 4 pale blue eggs, spotted and
scrawled with brown and purple, in a
bulky cup of grass, mud, and decayed
vegetation 2 to 10 feet up in marsh
grass or bushes.

Range: Resident along the coast from New
Jersey south to Louisiana; also inland in
peninsular Florida.

This species and its close relative the
Great-tailed Grackle were thought to
be a single species until it was recently
found that both nest in southwestern
Louisiana without interbreeding.

534   Seaside Sparrow
including "Dusky Seaside Sparrow"
and "Cape Sable Seaside Sparrow"
(*Ammospiza maritima*)
Grosbeaks, Buntings, Finches,
Sparrows (Fringillidae)

Description: 6″ (15 cm). A dark, gray-streaked
salt marsh sparrow with a dull yellow
mustache and dull yellow spot in front
of the eye.

Voice: Two short, sharp notes followed by a
buzzy *zeeee.*

Habitat: Exclusively grassy salt marsh, favoring the wetter portions.

Nesting: 4 or 5 white eggs with brown blotches in a woven grass nest placed in a grass tussock above the high-tide line.

Range: Salt marshes of the Atlantic and Gulf coasts from southern New England to Florida and Texas, wintering in the southern portions of this range.

Literally a seaside bird, few other sparrows have so restricted a habitat. Favoring the wetter sections of salt marsh, it feeds much less on seeds than do other sparrows, but eats tiny young crabs, snails, and other small marine animals along the tidal creeks of salt meadows. Like all birds living near the ground in grass, it is difficult to detect until almost underfoot, whereupon it flushes, flies for a short distance, drops down into the thick grass, and runs along like a mouse. The best opportunity to view one is when it is in song atop a grass stem or small shrub. Two distinctively plumaged populations of this bird in Florida were formerly considered separate species, called the "Dusky Seaside Sparrow" and the "Cape Sable Seaside Sparrow."

Freshwater Marshes

Shallow fresh water with a growth of
cattails, sedges, reeds, or bulrushes.
Such marshes often include some open
water; in these may be found the birds
we cover in our Lakes, Ponds, Rivers
section. Around the edge of the marsh,
on damp ground, there may be stands
of willows, alders, or red maples, in
which may be found birds treated in
our Thickets and Second Growth
section. Finally, during migration,
flocks of swallows may often inhabit
such marshes.

2, 6 Great Egret
(*Casmerodius albus*)
Herons, Bitterns (Ardeidae)

Description: 35–41" (89–104 cm). W. 55" (1.4 m).
A large, all-white heron with a *yellow bill and black legs*. In Florida the white form of the Great Blue Heron, known as the "Great White Heron," is similar but larger, with greenish-yellow legs.

Voice: Deep guttural croak. Also loud squawks when in the nesting colony.

Habitat: Freshwater and salt marshes, marshy ponds, and tidal flats.

Nesting: 3 or 4 pale blue eggs on a platform of sticks in a tree or bush. In colonies, often with other species of herons.

Range: Oregon, Wisconsin, and Massachusetts to southern South America. Winters regularly north to South Carolina and the Gulf Coast. Also breeds in warmer parts of the Old World.

Formerly known as the "American Egret," "Common Egret," "Large Egret," "White Egret," "Great White Egret," and "Great White Heron," its official name in North America is now Great Egret. One of the most magnificent of our herons, it has fortunately recovered from long persecution by plume hunters. Like the Great Blue Heron, it feeds alone, stalking fish, frogs, snakes, and crayfish in shallow water. Each year individual birds wander far to the north of the breeding grounds.

7, 16 Little Blue Heron
(*Egretta caerulea*)
Herons, Bitterns (Ardeidae)

Description: 25–30" (63–76 cm). W. 41" (1 m).
Adult slate blue with maroon neck; immature is white, usually with dark tips to primaries. Grayish bill with black tip; greenish legs. Young birds

acquiring adult plumage have a piebald
appearance.

Voice: Usually silent. Squawks when alarmed.
Croaks, grunts, and screams at the nest
site.

Habitat: Freshwater swamps and lagoons in the
South; coastal thickets on islands in the
North.

Nesting: 4 or 5 pale bluish-green eggs in a stick
nest in small trees or bushes near the
ground.

Range: East coast from New York to Texas and
inland to Oklahoma. Winters north to
South Carolina. Also in South America.

This is one of the most numerous
herons in the South and may be
observed in large mixed concentrations
of herons and egrets. It eats more
insects than the larger herons and is
sometimes seen following a plow to
pick up exposed insect larvae. Unlike
the egrets, it has no fancy plumes and
was thus spared by plume hunters.

17 Least Bittern
(*Ixobrychus exilis*)
Herons, Bitterns (Ardeidae)

Description: 11–14″ (28–35 cm). A tiny heron with
blackish back and *conspicuous buff wing
patches* and underparts. Female and
young are similar but duller.

Voice: Soft *coo-coo-coo,* easily unnoticed.

Habitat: Freshwater marshes where cattails and
reeds predominate.

Nesting: 4 or 5 small bluish eggs on a flimsy
platform of dead cattails or reeds,
usually over water.

Range: Southern Canada and northern United
States to southern Texas and the West
Indies. Winters from the Gulf Coast
south. Also breeds in South America.

Although locally common, this heron is
very secretive. It is reluctant to fly,

depending on its cryptic color pattern to escape detection. It often runs and climbs rapidly through reeds and cattails. The best way to see it is to wait at the edge of a cattail marsh—eventually one may rise, fly over the cattails, and drop out of sight again. The very rare rufous form, once thought to be a separate species, is called "Cory's Least Bittern."

19, 21 Yellow-crowned Night Heron
(*Nycticorax violacea*)
Herons, Bitterns (Ardeidae)

Description: 22–27" (56–68 cm). W 44" (1.1 m). Medium-sized heron. Adult is slate-gray with black head, *white cheeks, yellowish crown and plumes,* black bill, and orange legs. In flight the feet extend beyond the tail. Immature birds are grayish, finely speckled with white above, like young Black-crowned Night Herons but with a thicker bill and longer legs.

Voice: *Quawk* like that of Black-crowned Night Heron but higher in pitch.

Habitat: Wooded swamps and coastal thickets.

Nesting: 4 or 5 pale blue-green eggs in stick nest in trees or on the ground. Singly or in small colonies; occasionally with other herons.

Range: Massachusetts to Florida and west to Texas; mainly near the coast, but north along the Mississippi River and its larger tributaries, rarely to the central states. Also warmer portions of Middle and South America and West Indies.

As with several herons having a southerly distribution, this species has increased and expanded its range northward. Contrary to popular opinion, herons do not stab a fish (it would then be difficult to release) but grasp it in their bill, toss it in the air, and swallow it head-first.

20, 22 Black-crowned Night Heron
(*Nycticorax nycticorax*)
Herons, Bitterns (Ardeidae)

Description: 23–28″ (58–71 cm). W. 44″ (1.1 m).
A medium-sized, stocky, rather short-
necked heron with *black crown and back,*
gray wings, and *white underparts;* short,
black bill; pinkish or yellowish legs. In
breeding season it has two or more long
white plumes on back of head. Young
birds are dull gray-brown lightly
spotted with white. May be confused
with young Yellow-crowned Night
Herons and American Bitterns.

Voice: Harsh, barking *quawk!,* most often
heard at night or at dusk. A
bewildering variety of croaking,
barking, and screaming calls are uttered
in the nesting colony.

Habitat: Marshes, swamps, and wooded streams.

Nesting: 3–6 pale blue-green eggs in a shallow
saucer of sticks or reeds in a thicket or
reedbed; occasionally in tall trees. In
colonies, sometimes with other species
of herons.

Range: Washington, Saskatchewan, Minnesota,
and New Brunswick, to southern South
America. Winters in southern half of
the United States. Also occurs in
southern Eurasia, Africa, and East
Indies.

As its name implies it is largely
nocturnal, spending daylight hours
roosting in trees or reedbeds. It is
therefore best known for its call. These
birds are less likely to nest in mixed
colonies than other herons. When they
do, they usually keep a separate corner
for themselves.

24 American Bittern
(*Botaurus lentiginosus*)
Herons Bitterns (Ardeidae)

Description: 23–34″ (58–86 cm). A medium-sized, brown heron. *Outer wing appears blackish in flight,* contrasting with mustard brown of inner wing and body. At close range the bird shows a black streak on each side of the throat.

Voice: Peculiar pumping sound, *oong-KA-chunk!*, repeated a few times and often audible for half a mile.

Habitat: Freshwater and brackish marshes and marshy lake shores.

Nesting: 3–7 olive eggs on a platform of reeds concealed in the marsh. Not in colonies.

Range: British Columbia, Manitoba, and Newfoundland to Maryland, Kansas, and southern California; also in Texas, Louisiana, and Florida. Winters north to British Columbia, Ohio, and Delaware, occasionally farther north.

Its call has given such names to the bird as "Thunder-pumper" and "Stake-driver." It is secretive, preferring to freeze and trust its concealing coloration when approached rather than flush like other herons. When an observer is nearby it will often raise its head, point its bill skyward, and sway slowly from side to side, as if imitating waving reeds. If the observer gets too close the bittern will fly off, uttering a low barking call.

30 Sandhill Crane
(*Grus canadensis*)
Cranes (Gruidae)

Description: 34–48″ (86–122 cm). W. 80″ (2 m). Very tall, with long neck and long legs. Largely gray with red forehead. Plumage often appears rusty because of iron stains from the water of tundra ponds. Unlike herons, cranes fly with the neck outstretched and with the upstroke faster than the downstroke.

Voice: Loud, rattling *kar-r-r-o-o-o.*

Habitat: Large freshwater marshes, prairie ponds, and marshy tundra; also on prairies and grainfields during migration and in winter.

Nesting: 2 brown-spotted buff eggs in a large mound of grass and uprooted plants in an undisturbed marsh.

Range: Northeastern Siberia, Alaska, and Arctic Islands south to Michigan, Minnesota, and California; also in Gulf states from Florida to Texas. Winters in Arizona, Texas, Mexico, and California. Also breeds in Cuba.

Apparently this species was always more numerous than the larger Whooping Crane, and the fact that it breeds mostly in the remote Arctic has saved it from the fate of its relative. It is sensitive to human disturbance, and the draining of marshes has reduced nesting populations in the United States. These cranes migrate in great flocks and assemble in vast numbers at places like the Platte River in Nebraska. Here it is possible to see what must have been a common sight when the species bred over most of the interior United States.

The mating dance of the cranes is spectacular. Facing each other, they leap into the air with wings extended and feet thrown forward. Then they bow to each other and repeat the performance, uttering loud croaking calls.

45 Franklin's Gull
(Larus pipixcan)
Gulls, Terns (Laridae)

Description: 13–15″ (33–38 cm). Adult has black
hood and gray back and wings. Similar
to Laughing Gull of seacoasts but
smaller, paler, with *black wing tip
separated from gray by a white band.*
Young bird much like young Laughing
Gull but breast and forehead whiter.

Voice: A strident *ha-ha-ha-ha-ha-ha,* similar to
Laughing Gull's but higher in pitch.
Also utters clucks, screams, and mews.

Habitat: Prairie marshes and sloughs. Often
feeds in plowed fields.

Nesting: 3 buff-brown, spotted eggs on a loose
platform in a marsh. Breeds in large,
noisy colonies.

Range: Prairie marshes from southern Canada
to South Dakota and southwestern
Minnesota. Migrates to Gulf Coast and
winters south to Chile.

A freshwater version of the Laughing
Gull, it is sensitive to habitat
destruction and will breed only in large
colonies. When agriculture encroaches
on prairie marshes and these become
too small for a large colony, the birds
move elsewhere. They are much less
numerous than formerly, but migrating
flocks of these "Prairie Doves" are still a
familiar sight in spring on the southern
plains.

75 Black Tern
(Chlidonias nigra)
Gulls, Terns (Laridae)

Description: 9–10″ (23–25 cm). A medium-sized
tern with *solid black head and underparts;*
gray wing and moderately forked gray
tail; in fall and winter the head and
underparts are white, with dusky
smudging around the eyes and back of
the neck.

Voice: Sharp *kick;* when disturbed, a shrill *kreek.*

Habitat: Freshwater marshes and marshy lakes in summer; sandy coasts in migration and in winter.

Nesting: 2 spotted olive-buff eggs in a hollow on a mass of floating marsh vegetation or a well-made cup of dead grass. Colonial.

Range: Breeds from Quebec, Alaska, Mackenzie, and south to Pennsylvania, Missouri, and California. Winters in South America.

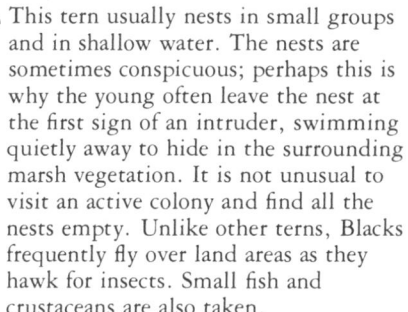

This tern usually nests in small groups and in shallow water. The nests are sometimes conspicuous; perhaps this is why the young often leave the nest at the first sign of an intruder, swimming quietly away to hide in the surrounding marsh vegetation. It is not unusual to visit an active colony and find all the nests empty. Unlike other terns, Blacks frequently fly over land areas as they hawk for insects. Small fish and crustaceans are also taken.

**105, 144 Green-winged Teal
including "Common Teal"**
(*Anas crecca*)
Swans, Geese, Ducks (Anatidae)

Description: 12–16″ (30–40 cm). A small, dark duck. Male has chestnut head, green ear patch, flashing *green speculum,* pale gray sides, and pinkish breast with a vertical white stripe down the side. Female is dark brown without distinctive markings.

Voice: Clear repeated whistle. Females quack.

Habitat: Marshes, ponds, and marshy lakes.

Nesting: 10–12 whitish or pale buff eggs in a down-lined cup in tall grass, often several hundred yards from water.

Range: Aleutians, northern Alaska, Manitoba, and Quebec south to New York, Nebraska, and California. Winters

south to Central America and the West Indies. Also breeds in temperate Eurasia.

Until recently the North American and Eurasian forms were considered distinct species. Eurasian males have a horizontal white stripe along the side of their bodies instead of a vertical stripe down the breast. Each year a few males—and probably females—of the Eurasian form turn up in North America, giving rise to speculation that somewhere in North America a few of these so-called "Common Teal" may be breeding. Green-winged Teal are among the fastest flying ducks and are therefore popular gamebirds. They wheel in compact flocks like shorebirds. They are hardy, being among the last ducks to reach their winter habitat in fall and the first to depart in spring.

106, 140   American Wigeon
(Anas americana)
Swans, Geese, Ducks (Anatidae)

Description: 18–23″ (46–58 cm). Male is brownish with *white crown,* green ear patch, and bold white shoulder patches easily visible in flight. Female is mottled brown with grayish head and whitish shoulder patch. Pale blue bill and feet in both sexes.

Voice: Distinctive whistled *whew-whew-whew.* Also quacks.

Habitat: Marshes, ponds, and shallow lakes.

Nesting: 8–10 whitish or cream-colored eggs in a down-lined hollow in grass, often several hundred yards from water.

Range: Alaska, Mackenzie, and Minnesota south to Nebraska and northern California. Rarely farther east. Winters south to Central America and the West Indies.

The American Wigeon, or "Baldpate," is a wary species, often seen on marshy ponds in the company of diving birds such as coots, Redheads, and Canvasbacks. They wait at the surface while the other birds dive, then snatch the food away when the birds reappear. They also visit grain fields and meadows to graze, like geese, on tender shoots. The birds found in winter along the Atlantic coast seem to come mainly from the Far North, while birds in the interior of the continent move south to the Gulf Coast and West Indies.

132 European Wigeon
(*Anas penelope*)
Swans, Geese, Ducks (Anatidae)

Description: 18–20" (46–50 cm). Male has *rusty head, buff crown,* pinkish-buff breast, and gray body. Female is streaked brown. Bill dull blue. The female American Wigeon is very similar but has a gray-tinged head.

Voice: Piping *whee-ouu;* seldom heard in America.

Habitat: Marshes, ponds, and lakes; resorts to tidal flats in nonbreeding season.

Nesting: 7 or 8 buff-cream eggs in a nest lined with grass and down, concealed in vegetation often some distance from water.

Range: Eurasia; an uncommon visitor to North America, mainly along the coast.

An Old World relative of the American Wigeon, this bird in recent years has become an uncommon but regular visitor to our area, usually found in a flock with its American cousin. Known in Europe as one of the shyest of ducks, it is a popular gamebird. Wigeons often feed at night, and unlike most other ducks they obtain a good deal of food by grazing.

108, 143 Northern Shoveler
"Shoveler"
(*Anas clypeata*)
Swans, Geese, Ducks (Anatidae)

Description: 17–20″ (43–51 cm). Large "shovel" bill. Male has green head, white body, and *chestnut flanks*. Female streaked brown with pale blue wing patches; similar to female Blue-winged Teal but larger, with the distinctive bill. Both sexes have *pale blue shoulder patches*.

Voice: Low croak, cluck, or quack.

Habitat: Marshes and prairie potholes. Sometimes on salt or brackish marshes.

Nesting: 8–12 pale olive or greenish eggs in a down-lined cup of grass concealed in vegetation, often some distance from water.

Range: Alaska, northern Mackenzie and Manitoba, south to Nebraska, Colorado and Southern California; occasionally farther east and south. Winters north to British Columbia and Georgia, and in smaller numbers to New England. Also breeds in Eurasia.

Like the closely related Blue-winged Teal, the Northern Shoveler, formerly called "Shoveler," is among the first ducks to arrive in the fall and the last to leave in the spring. It feeds on minute aquatic animals by straining water through comblike teeth along the sides of its long, expanded bill. It also eats seeds and aquatic plants. Because it often feeds in stagnant ponds, it is particularly susceptible to botulism, a fatal bacterial food poisoning.

111, 159 Ruddy Duck
(*Oxyura jamaicensis*)
Swans, Geese, Ducks (Anatidae)

Description: 14–16″ (35–40 cm). A small, chunky duck with a long tail that is often held straight up. Male in breeding plumage has a chestnut body, black crown, and *white cheeks*. Female and winter male are dusky brown with whitish cheeks— crossed by a brown stripe in the female. Bill of male is blue in breeding season, black at other times.

Voice: Mostly silent. Courting male makes a series of clucking notes.

Habitat: Freshwater marshes, marshy lakes and ponds; sometimes shallow salt bays and rivers in winter.

Nesting: 5–15 buffy-white eggs in a floating nest of dry stems of water plants lined with down, concealed among reeds or bulrushes in a marsh.

Range: Breeds from British Columbia, Mackenzie, and Quebec south to the Gulf Coast and through Central America to northern South America. Winters north to British Columbia and Massachusetts.

This duck is one of the most aquatic members of the family, and like a grebe can sink slowly out of sight. They seldom fly, escaping from danger by diving or concealing themselves in marsh vegetation. Once airborne, however, they are fast fliers, annually covering long distances in migration. Largely vegetarian, they favor marsh plants and seeds in summer, wigeon grass in winter. The male has a bizarre courtship display, raising and spreading his tail as he produces bubbles by expelling air trapped under his breast feathers.

112, 141 Cinnamon Teal
(*Anas cyanoptera*)
Swans, Geese, Ducks (Anatidae)

Description: 14–17″ (35–43 cm). Male bright rufous, with a pale blue patch along the leading edge of each wing. Female mottled sandy brown and dusky, with pale blue wing patches; not distinguishable in the field from female Blue-winged Teal.

Voice: A soft *quack;* various chattering and clucking notes.

Habitat: Prairie marshes, ponds, and slow-moving streams bordered with reeds.

Nesting: 4–16 pale buff eggs in a cup nest of grass and feathers concealed in grass or weeds, usually near water.

Range: Western North America from Aleutian Islands, regularly east to Saskatchewan, Nebraska, and western Texas, and casually east to New York and the Carolinas. Also in South America.

This western relative of the Blue-winged Teal often associates with that species in areas where both occur. Like the Blue-wing, these birds migrate south in late summer and early fall, a month or two ahead of the other dabbling ducks. Records of the Cinnamon Teal from east of their normal range are based on sightings of adult males, because the females are indistinguishable from female Blue-wings.

115, 138 Pintail
(*Anas acuta*)
Swans, Geese, Ducks (Anatidae)

Description: Males 25–30″ (63–76 cm), females 21–23″ (53–58 cm). Slim, graceful duck with a slender neck. Male has *brown head and white neck with white line extending up the side of the head.* Central tail feathers long, black, and pointed. Female streaked brown, similar to female Mallard but paler, grayer, and slenderer, with brown speculum that is bordered with white at the rear edge only; tail is more pointed than in female Mallard.

Voice: Distinctive two-toned whistle. Females quack.

Habitat: Marshes, prairie ponds, and tundra;

sometimes salt marshes in winter.

Nesting: 7–10 pale greenish-buff eggs in a shallow grass bowl lined with down and hidden in grass, often some distance from water.

Range: Breeds from Alaska and Greenland south to western Pennsylvania, Nebraska, and California. Locally and occasionally farther east. Winters south to Central America and the West Indies. Also breeds in Eurasia.

The Pintail, a widely distributed and common duck, is a strong flier and long-distance migrant like the Mallard. Seeds of aquatic plants are its main food, but in winter small aquatic animals are also taken; when freshwater habitats freeze over, it resorts to tidal flats, where it feeds on snails and small crabs. A popular gamebird because of its tasty flesh and fast flight, it is one of our wariest ducks.

134 American Coot
(Fulica americana)
Rails, Gallinules, Coots (Rallidae)

Description: 15″ (38 cm). *Slate-gray* with a conspicuous *white bill;* greenish legs and lobed feet.

Voice: Variety of calls, some fowl-like clucking, and cackles, grunts, and other harsh notes.

Habitat: Open ponds and marshes; in winter, also in saltwater bays and inlets.

Nesting: 8–10 brown-spotted pinkish eggs in a shallow platform of dead leaves and stems of marsh plants, usually on the water but anchored to a clump of reeds.

Range: Southern Canada to northern South America.

Coots are the most aquatic members of their family, moving on open water like ducks and often feeding with them. They are excellent swimmers and

divers, and they eat various aquatic plants. They also come out on land to feed on seeds, grass, and waste grain. They often become tame when fed scraps and bits of bread. These birds must patter over the water before becoming airborne.

135, 139 Gadwall
(*Anas strepera*)
Swans, Geese, Ducks (Anatidae)

Description: 18–21" (46–53 cm). A medium-sized duck with a *white patch on hind edge of wing*. Male mottled gray with a black rump and sandy brown head. Female similar but brown.

Voice: Duck-like quack. Also utters *kack-kacks* and whistles.

Habitat: Freshwater marshes, ponds, and rivers; locally in salt marshes.

Nesting: 7–12 whitish eggs in a nest made of dead grass, usually well concealed near water but sometimes in upland fields.

Range: Alaska and New England south to North Carolina and California. Winters north to southern New England. Also breeds in Eurasia and North Africa.

This relative of the Mallard has the widest range of any duck, breeding almost throughout the North Temperate Zone. Known to hunters as the "Gray Duck," it is a popular gamebird and is abundant in winter in southern marshes. It feeds mainly on seeds, leaves, and stems of aquatic plants. This species has recently appeared as a breeder on the Eastern seaboard, and now nests along the coast from Nova Scotia to the Carolinas.

136, 142 Blue-winged Teal
(*Anas discors*)
Swans, Geese, Ducks (Anatidae)

Description: 14–16″ (35–40 cm). A small brownish duck with *pale blue shoulder patches*. Male has a gray head and *white crescent* in front of eye. Female mottled brown, similar to female Green-winged Teal but grayer, with pale blue shoulder patches like the male.

Voice: Soft lisping or peeping note. Female utters a soft quack.

Habitat: Marshes, shallow ponds, and lakes.

Nesting: 7–10 whitish eggs in a down-lined hollow concealed in grass near the edge of water.

Range: British Columbia, Quebec, and Newfoundland to North Carolina, the Gulf Coast, and southern California. Winters south to northern South America.

On low marshy prairies in the central part of the continent, where this duck is most numerous, virtually every pond and pothole has a breeding pair. The male commonly "stands guard" on the pond while the female is incubating. Unlike other dabbling ducks that form pairs in the fall, this teal begins courting in the spring and often does not acquire the familiar breeding plumage until December or January. Like most ducks they go through an eclipse plumage and molt most of their feathers, including the primaries, and so are flightless until new feathers grow in. This species migrates early, often passing through the United States in August and September; most Blue-wings winter south of the United States.

165, 166 Fulvous Whistling-Duck
"Fulvous Tree Duck"
(Dendrocygna bicolor)
Swans, Geese, Ducks (Anatidae)

Description: 18–21″ (46–53 cm). A long-legged, long-necked, goose-like duck. Body mainly *tawny, with a white stripe on the side;* rump and undertail coverts are white.

Voice: Clear double whistle. Called "Squealer" by hunters.

Habitat: Rice fields, freshwater marshes, and wet meadows.

Nesting: 12–15 buff-white eggs in a shallow cup of grass or a well-woven basket of reeds in a marsh.

Range: Resident in southern California, Texas, and southern Florida, and locally southward to Brazil. Also breeds in East Africa and India.

Although Fulvous Whistling-Ducks in North America breed only in southern Texas and southern California, they occasionally wander; small flocks have turned up as far away as Utah and Nova Scotia. These long-legged ducks do most of their feeding on land, eating green grass, seeds, and acorns. This species was formerly known as "Fulvous Tree Duck." The name "fulvous" refers to its tawny color.

167, 168 Black-bellied Whistling-Duck
"Black-bellied Tree Duck"
(Dendrocygna autumnalis)
Swans, Geese, Ducks (Anatidae)

Description: 20–22″ (51–56 cm). Long neck and legs; rich chestnut crown, back, and breast; gray face and throat; black lower belly; bright red bill; pink legs; large white wing patch in flight. Female duller.

Voice: Shrill, often repeated whistle.

Habitat: Wooded streams and ponds.

Nesting: 12–14 white eggs, placed without a nest lining, in tree cavity or nest box, occasionally on the ground.

Range: Extreme southern Texas and Arizona to tropical portions of South America.

These handsome, conspicuous birds often rest on large tree branches, stakes, or poles in the water or, less commonly, on the ground. Almost entirely herbivorous, they feed in shallow water on tubers and other aquatic vegetation, as well as in grain fields. Unlike many ducks, this species is largely nocturnal, migrating at night and resting and feeding during the day. They are easily domesticated and are quite tame even in the wild. This species was formerly known as "Black-bellied Tree Duck."

169 White-fronted Goose
(Anser albifrons)
Swans, Geese, Ducks (Anatidae)

Description: 27–30" (68–76 cm). A dusky-brown goose with conspicuous white belly and undertail covers; *white patch on front of face;* underparts barred and flecked with black. *Only goose in the East with orange legs.*

Voice: Distinctive two-note or three-note bark, *kla-ha!* or *ka-la-ha!,* very different from the calls of other geese.

Habitat: Marshy tundra; winters on marshes and bays.

Nesting: 4–6 creamy-buff eggs in a down-lined grassy depression on the tundra.

Range: Breeds in Alaska, the Northwest Territories, and Greenland. Winters from British Columbia and Illinois to southern Mexico and the Gulf Coast. Also breeds in northern Eurasia.

This is the least common goose in the eastern states, occurring in numbers only along the western Gulf Coast in

Louisiana and Texas; its winter headquarters is the Sacramento Valley of California. Along the eastern edge of the Great Plains the birds often migrate at night, when they are identified by their distinctive call. Like other geese, they often leave the marshes to feed in nearby stubble fields; here they are frequently concealed from view until the observer is very close, when they explode noisily into the air. Hunters call them "Speckle Bellies." The Tule Goose of the west coast is considered a large race of the White-fronted Goose, but its status is still uncertain and its nesting ground is unknown.

173 Mute Swan
(*Cygnus olor*)
Swans, Geese, Ducks (Anatidae)

Description: 58–60" (147–152 cm). W. 95" (2.3m). All white; bill of adults is orange with black knob at the base. Young birds are similar, but dingy.

Voice: Unlike other swans, it is usually silent except for some hissing and grunting notes. It does have a loud trumpeting call, but this is rarely heard.

Habitat: Ponds, rivers, coastal lagoons, and bays.

Nesting: 6–8 eggs in a huge mound-like nest lined with feathers and down, conspicuously placed at the edge of a pond or marsh.

Range: Introduced from Europe into the northeastern United States; most frequent in southern New England, southeastern New York, New Jersey, and Maryland; also established locally in Michigan.

With its wings arched over its back and its neck in a graceful S-curve, the male is extremely handsome on the water. A breeding pair will defend the nest and young against all comers, including humans, using their powerful wings and strong bills.

175 White Pelican
(Pelecanus erythrorhynchos)
Pelicans (Pelecanidae)

Description: 55–70″ (140–179 cm). W. 96″ (2.8 m). *Huge white bird* with a massive yellow bill and black wing tips. Usually rests bill on breast.

Voice: Low grunts or croaks on the nesting ground, but usually silent.

Habitat: Marshy lakes and along the Pacific and Texas coasts. Winters chiefly in coastal lagoons.

Nesting: 2 or 3 whitish eggs on a low mound of earth and debris on a marshy island; occasionally on barren islands in desert lakes. In colonies.

Range: Breeds from British Columbia and Mackenzie south to western Ontario and California; also on the Texas coast. Winters from Florida and southern California south to Panama.

A flock of migrating White Pelicans is a majestic sight—a long line of ponderous birds, flapping and sailing in unison. These birds ride rising air currents to great heights, where they soar gracefully in circles. They often capture fish cooperatively, forming a long line, beating their wings and driving the prey into shallow water, where they seize the fish in their large, pouched bills. They take in water as well as fish, and so first hold their bills vertically to drain the water out before swallowing the food.

178, 180 Pied-billed Grebe
(*Podilymbus podiceps*)
Grebes (Podicipedidae)

Description: 12–15″ (30–38 cm). Pigeon-sized. A stocky, uniformly brownish water bird; stubby bill, whitish with a prominent black band, lacking in winter.

Voice: Series of hollow *cow-cow-cow* notes somewhat like those of the Yellow-billed Cuckoo.

Habitat: Marshes, ponds; salt water in winter if freshwater habitats freeze.

Nesting: 5–7 whitish, stained eggs in a well-concealed floating mass of dead marsh vegetation anchored to adjacent plants.

Range: British Columbia to southern Mackenzie and Nova Scotia to southern Argentina. Winters as far north as New England.

This is the most common grebe in eastern North America. Although easily overlooked, it announces itself in the breeding season with its loud barking call notes. It eats small fish, crustaceans, and aquatic insects but is especially fond of crayfish, which it easily crushes with its stout bill. When alarmed, it slowly sinks below the water, surfacing again out of sight among the reeds; this trick has earned it the local name of "Hell-diver." It is also called "Dabchick" and "Water Witch."

199, 223 Least Sandpiper
(*Calidris minutilla*)
Sandpipers (Scolopacidae)

Description: 6″ (15 cm). Sparrow-sized; smallest of American shorebirds. Brownish with *yellowish or greenish legs,* a short thin bill, and a streaked breast. Grayer in winter plumage.

Voice: A loud clear *treep;* when feeding, a soft chuckle.

Habitat: Grassy pools, bogs, and marshes with open areas; also flooded fields and mud flats.

Nesting: 4 brown-spotted pinkish-buff eggs in a nest lined with moss and grass on a dry hummock in a depression on boggy tundra.

Range: Breeds in Aleutians, Alaska and Canada. Winters from southern United States to central South America.

These are probably the tamest of shorebirds and at times fly off only when almost underfoot. They look like miniature Pectoral Sandpipers, and like Pectorals they prefer grassy areas to the more open flats frequented by most shorebirds. The name *minutilla* is Latin for "tiny."

204, 207 **Wilson's Phalarope**
(*Phalaropus tricolor*)
Sandpipers (Scolopacidae)

Description: 9″ (23 cm). A strikingly patterned shorebird with pearl gray head and back, white underparts, a *black stripe through eye and down the neck, and chestnut markings on breast and back.* In fall plumage pale gray above, white below; in this plumage its pale color, more terrestrial habits, and slender bill distinguish it from other phalaropes.

Voice: Soft *quoit-quoit-quoit.*

Habitat: Prairie pools and marshes, lake and river shores, marshy pools along the coast.

Nesting: 4 pale buff, brown-spotted eggs in a grass-lined nest in a slight depression on the ground near water.

Range: From southwestern and south-central Canada to central and western United States. Winters chiefly in southern South America.

Wilson's is larger than the Red and Northern phalaropes and has a much

longer, thinner bill. Unlike the others, this species does not have fully lobed toes and so rarely swims, spending no time at sea. When it does feed in water, however, it spins more rapidly than the other two. It is limited to the Western Hemisphere and breeds much farther south than the others.

216 Solitary Sandpiper
(*Tringa solitaria*)
Sandpipers (Scolopacidae)

Description: 8½″ (21 cm). Dark legs, white tail barred with black, *prominent eye-ring;* wing linings dark. Has distinctive, swallow-like flight when flushed.

Voice: *Peet-weet-weet,* like that of the Spotted Sandpiper but higher pitched.

Habitat: Inland ponds and bogs, wet swampy places, and woodland streams.

Nesting: 4 pale green or buff eggs thickly spotted with gray and brown, laid in deserted tree nests of thrushes, jays, or blackbirds in northern spruce forests.

Range: Breeds in Alaska and Canada. Winters from Central America to southern South America.

As its name suggests, this bird is most often seen by itself—a single migrant foraging along the margin of a wooded pond or stream. It is rather shy, and when approached will spring quickly into the air, uttering its ringing call note, and dart away. In the spring, most Solitary Sandpipers seem to migrate north through Central America, and here an observer may be surprised to see flocks of several dozen feeding in flooded fields.

219 Pectoral Sandpiper
(*Calidris melanotos*)
Sandpipers (Scolopacidae)

Description: 9" (23 cm). A chunky, somewhat short-legged wader, with *heavily streaked breast* sharply delimited by the *unmarked white of the belly. Yellow legs.* In flight the wings are dark and have no stripe.

Voice: Sharp *brrrrp.* Courting males inflate the throat and breast and utter a series of booming, resonant calls.

Habitat: Wet, short-grass areas; grassy pools; golf courses and airports after heavy rains; and salt creeks and meadows.

Nesting: 4 buff-white, dark-spotted eggs on the ground in a slight depression in boggy tundra.

Range: Breeds on the Arctic coasts of eastern Siberia, Alaska, and Canada south to Hudson Bay. Winters chiefly in southern South America.

In the days when shorebirds were shot as game, hunters called this species the "Grass Snipe," referring to its liking for grassy meadows, or "Krieker" because of its grating snipe-like call when in flight. They are as numerous in the interior as on the coasts and are another of the many shorebirds that make the long migration from the Arctic to the Antarctic and back again.

244 American Avocet
(*Recurvirostra americana*)
Avocets, Stilts (Recurvirostridae)

Description: 16–20" (40–51 cm). Pigeon-sized. Slender and long-legged. Upperparts and wings patterned in black and white; underparts white. Head and neck rust-colored in summer, white in winter. *Bill very thin and strongly upturned.*

Voice: Loud repeated *wheep.*

Habitat: Freshwater marshes and shallow marshy

lakes; breeds locally in salt or brackish marshes. Many move to the coast in winter.

Nesting: 4 spotted buff eggs in a shallow scrape on a beach or mud flat, with sparse lining of grass. Often in loose colonies.

Range: Washington and Manitoba south to Texas and California. Winters from southern Texas and California to Guatemala. Uncommon but regular on Atlantic coast in fall.

During their southward migration every fall, a few Avocets stray eastward to the Atlantic coast, where they may be seen singly or in small flocks on shallow lagoons and coastal ponds. In the 19th century there was a small breeding population in southern New Jersey, but they were shot out by hunters. Avocets feed much like Spoonbills, sweeping their bills from side to side along the surface of the water to pick up crustaceans, aquatic insects, and floating seeds. Recently given complete protection, they seem to be gaining in numbers and before long may be reported breeding on the Atlantic coast once again.

247 Common Gallinule
(Gallinula chloropus)
Rails, Gallinules, Coots (Rallidae)

Description: 13″ (33 cm). A duck-like swimming bird that constantly bobs its head while moving. Slaty gray with a prominent red bill with yellow tip and red frontal shield (adults); *white under its tail* which it cocks up.

Voice: Squawking notes similar to those of coots. Other calls sound like frogs and are rather harsh in tone.

Habitat: Freshwater marshes and ponds with cattails and other aquatic vegetation.

Nesting: 9–12 cinnamon-buff eggs, lightly spotted with brown; in a shallow platform of dead cattails, rushes, and other marsh plants; usually built up a few inches above water level.

Range: Nearly cosmopolitan in distribution. In the Americas, from southern Canada to southern South America.

Gallinules—or "Moorhens" as they are known in the Old World—are closely related to coots and rails but do not swim out in the open water as much as coots and hide in reeds much less than rails. Males build several nests on the pair's territory; these are used by the female and newly hatched young as "dormitories" at night.

---

248 Purple Gallinule
(*Porphyrula martinica*)
Rails, Gallinules, Coots (Rallidae)

Description: 11–13″ (28–33 cm). Chicken-sized. Rich purplish-blue with green upperparts, white undertail coverts, yellowish-green legs, red-and-yellow bill, and light blue frontal shield.

Voice: Squawking and cackling. Also guttural grunts.

Habitat: Freshwater marshes with lily pads, pickerelweed, and other aquatic vegetation.

Nesting: 6–10 pinkish-buff eggs with fine dark spots in a nest of dead stems and leaves of water plants placed on a floating tussock or in a clump of sawgrass or thicket over water.

Range: The Carolinas and Tennessee to Florida and Texas; wanders to the northern states. South to southern South America.

This beautiful bird is often observed walking on lily pads, using its very long toes, and may even sometimes be seen climbing up into low bushes. When walking or swimming it constantly jerks its head and tail. Its flight is slow and weak, and its yellow legs hang down. On rare occasions these birds have wandered north and have been found in gardens or city parks. They have landed on ships 300 miles from shore and on remote oceanic islands.

249 Sora
(*Porzana carolina*)
Rails, Gallinules, Coots (Rallidae)

Description: 8–10″ (20–25 cm). Quail-sized. *Gray-breasted* with a black face and *stubby yellow bill.* Upperparts mottled brown; lower abdomen banded with black and white. Young birds in fall lack the black face and have buff breasts.

Voice: Most familiar call is a musical series of piping notes rapidly descending the scale. When an intruder approaches a nest the adults come boldly into view, uttering an explosive *keek!*

Habitat: Chiefly freshwater marshes and marshy ponds; rice fields and salt marshes in winter.

Nesting: 6–15 pale yellow-buff, spotted eggs in a cup of cattails and dead leaves, usually placed in a clump of reeds in a more open part of the marsh.

Range: British Columbia, Mackenzie, and Newfoundland south to Pennsylvania, Oklahoma, and Baja California; winters north to California and to the Carolinas.

These birds are especially numerous in fall and winter in southern marshes and rice fields, where they are primarily seed-eaters. Although shot in large numbers every year, their high reproductive rate enables them to maintain a stable population. The greatest threat to them is the destruction of the freshwater marshes where they breed: they have consequently become scarce in heavily populated areas.

251 Yellow Rail
(*Coturnicops noveboracensis*)
Rails, Gallinules, Coots (Rallidae)

Description: 6–8″ (15–20 cm). Sparrow-sized.
Brownish-buff with a short yellow bill
and yellow feet. Shows a *white wing
patch* in flight.

Voice: Series of clicks in groups of two or
three: *click-click, click-click-click.*
Usually heard at night.

Habitat: Grassy marshes and wet meadows.

Nesting: 7–10 buff eggs, with a ring of dark
spots around larger end, in a firm cup
of grass well-concealed in a grassy
marsh.

Range: Central Canada south to North Dakota,
and in New Brunswick, Quebec, and
Maine. Winters from the Carolinas,
Florida, and the Gulf Coast.

All rails are secretive, but none more
than this tiny bird. It is also rare, and
many veteran bird-watchers have never
seen one. It can conceal itself in very
short grass and can seldom be induced
to fly. The best way to see one is to
follow a mowing machine in a damp
meadow in the Deep South during
September or October. When the uncut
grass is reduced to a small patch, one or
more birds may flush into view, fly
weakly away, and disappear into the
nearest patch of tall grass.

252 Virginia Rail
(*Rallus limicola*)
Rails, Gallinules, Coots (Rallidae)

Description: 9–11″ (23–28 cm). A small rail with a
long *reddish bill,* rusty underparts, and
gray cheeks. The much larger King Rail
has buff cheeks. Fall immatures are
similar to adults, but have blackish
breasts.

Voice: Series of descending grunts and a far-carrying *ticket-ticket-ticket-ticket*.

Habitat: Freshwater and brackish marshes. May visit salt marshes in winter.

Nesting: 5–12 spotted pale buff eggs in a shallow and loosely constructed saucer often woven into surrounding marsh vegetation.

Range: Breeds from British Columbia, Minnesota, and Newfoundland south to Guatemala. Winters regularly north to Virginia, occasionally farther north.

This common but elusive marsh bird is most often detected by its call. It seldom flies, preferring to escape intruders by running through protecting marsh vegetation. When it does take wing, it often flies only a few yards before dropping out of sight into the marsh. Despite its apparently weak flight, it annually migrates long distances, having even been recorded as far offshore as Bermuda. Like all rails, its body is compressed laterally so that it can more easily slip between the stems of rushes and cattails.

254 **King Rail**
(*Rallus elegans*)
Rails, Gallinules, Coots (Rallidae)

Description: 15–19" (38–48 cm). A secretive, chicken-sized marsh bird with a long, slightly curved bill. *Head, neck, and underparts rusty;* back mottled brown. Similar to Virginia Rail but larger and without gray face patch. Clapper Rail is grayer.

Voice: Series of deep resonant notes, *beep-beep-beep-beep,* etc., usually more rapid at the end.

Habitat: Freshwater marshes and roadside ditches; wanders to salt marshes in fall and winter.

Nesting: 6–16 spotted buff eggs in a deep bowl of grass, often with surrounding marsh grass pulled down and woven into a dome.

Range: Minnesota and Massachusetts south to
Florida, Texas, and northern Mexico.
Winters regularly from the Gulf Coast
southward. Also breeds in Cuba.

This large rail is common in the larger
freshwater marshes of the interior.
Although difficult to see, its loud call,
consisting of deep grunting and
clucking notes, often reveals its
presence. It occasionally hybridizes
with the Clapper Rail where freshwater
and salt marshes occur together. They
may eventually be found to be two
forms of a single species.

255 **Common Snipe**
(*Capella gallinago*)
Sandpipers (Scolopacidae)

Description: 10½–11½" (26–29 cm). A long-billed,
brownish shorebird with striped back,
usually seen when flushed from the
edge of a marsh or a pond. Fast, erratic
flight.
Voice: Sharp, rasping *scaip!* when flushed.
Habitat: Freshwater marshes, ponds, flooded
meadows, and fields; more rarely in salt
marshes.
Nesting: 4 pale olive-brown eggs, spotted with
black, in a grass-lined depression
concealed in a grass tussock in a marsh.
Range: Alaska, Hudson Bay, and Labrador
south to Massachusetts, Indiana, and
California; more rarely farther south.
Winters regularly north to British
Columbia and Virginia. Also breeds in
Eurasia.

Although snipes commonly migrate in
flocks at night, during the day they
scatter and usually feed alone. They
seek food early in the morning and in
late afternoon, and seem to be more
active on cloudy days. In addition to
the alarm note described above, these

birds have a variety of calls heard only
on the breeding ground, and they
perform a spectacular territorial display
in which the feathers of the tail produce
an eerie whistling sound. They are not
as numerous as formerly but are still a
popular gamebird. This species was
formerly called "Wilson's Snipe," after
the Scottish-American ornithologist
Alexander Wilson (1766–1813).

284 Short-eared Owl
(*Asio flammeus*)
True Owls (Strigidae)

Description: 16″ (40 cm). Crow-sized. A long-
winged, tawny-brown owl of open
country, rather heavily streaked, and
with a blackish patch around each eye.
The very short ear tufts are rarely
visible.

Voice: Usually silent; on the nesting ground
gives a variety of barks, hisses, and
squeals.

Habitat: Freshwater and salt marshes; open
grassland, prairies, dunes; open country
generally during migration.

Nesting: 5–7 white eggs in a grass-lined
depression on the ground, often
concealed in weeds or beneath a bush.

Range: Breeds locally from Alaska and northern
Canada south to New Jersey and
California; winters in the southern part
of the breeding range and south to
Guatemala. Also in South America and
most of the Old World.

This owl is most commonly seen late in
the afternoon, as it begins to move
about in preparation for a night of
hunting. It can often be identified at a
great distance by its habit of hovering;
its flight is erratic and bounding.
Occasionally several birds may be seen
at once, an indication that small
rodents—their major prey—are
especially numerous.

309, 310 Marsh Hawk
(*Circus cyaneus*)
Hawks, Eagles (Accipitridae)

Description: 16–24" (40–61 cm). W. 42" (1.1 m).
Long-winged, long-tailed hawk with a
white rump, usually seen soaring
unsteadily over marshes with its wings
held in a shallow "V". Male has a pale
gray back, head, and breast. Female
and young are brown above, streaked
below, young birds with a rusty tone.

Voice: Usually silent. At the nest it utters a
kee-kee-kee-kee or a sharp whistle.

Habitat: Marshes and open grasslands.

Nesting: 4 or 5 pale blue or white eggs,
unmarked or with light brown spots,
set in a mound of dead reeds and grass
in a marsh or shrubby meadow.

Range: Eastern Aleutians, Alaska, Mackenzie,
and Newfoundland to Virginia and
northern Mexico. Winters north to
British Columbia, Wisconsin, and New
Brunswick. Also breeds in Eurasia.

This is the only North American
member of a group of hawks known as
harriers. All hunt by flying close to the
ground, taking small animals by
surprise. They seldom pursue their prey
in the air or watch quietly from an
exposed perch as do other hawks and
falcons. Harriers are thought to have
keener hearing than other hawks; their
disk-shaped faces, not unlike those of
owls, are believed to be able to amplify
sound.

485 Short-billed Marsh Wren
(*Cistothorus platensis*)
Wrens (Troglodytidae)

Description: 4–4½" (10–11 cm). A tiny, secretive
wren of grassy marshes. Buff-colored,
with finely streaked crown and back.
Best distinguuished by voice and
habitat.

Voice: A series of harsh notes, sounding like tapping two pebbles together; often heard at night.

Habitat: Grassy freshwater marshes and sedges; also brackish marshes and wet meadows in winter.

Nesting: 5–7 white eggs in a globular mass of marsh grass with a side entrance; lined with feathers and hair that has been woven into the top of a dense stand of grass or sedge.

Range: Saskatchewan, Manitoba, and New Brunswick south to Delaware, Missouri, and Kansas; Central America south to Tierra del Fuego and the Falkland Islands. Winters north to New Jersey and Tennessee. Very local.

Sometimes more aptly called "Sedge Wren," it is most often seen as it is flushed from grass and flies off only to drop from view a few feet away. Its flight is distinctive, the wings vibrating stiffly as the bird seems to float over the ground. Like other wrens it builds "dummy" nests, often hidden in dense marsh grass.

---

488 Long-billed Marsh Wren
(*Cistothorus palustris*)
Wrens (Troglodytidae)

Description: 4–5½" (10–14 cm). Smaller than a sparrow. Brown above, pale buff below, with a *bold white eyebrow and white streaks on the back.*

Voice: Liquid gurgling song ending in a mechanical chatter.

Habitat: Fresh and brackish marshes with cattails, reeds, bulrushes, or sedges.

Nesting: 5 or 6 pale brown eggs speckled with dark brown. Nest is a globular mass of reeds and cattails with a side entrance lined with feathers and cattail down, anchored to reeds.

Range: British Columbia, Manitoba, and New Brunswick south to Florida, the Gulf

Coast, and northern Mexico. Winters north to New Jersey, along the Gulf Coast, and on the Pacific coast north to Washington.

The male has a number of mates, each of which builds a nest of her own. In addition, the male may also build up to half a dozen "dummy" nests, often incomplete, one of which may be used as a roost. Thus a marsh frequented by these birds often contains many nests in various stages of completion. Locating a nest with eggs or young in it can take much time—which may be the purpose of these dummy nests.

518, 583 **Yellow-headed Blackbird**
(*Xanthocephalus xanthocephalus*)
Orioles, Blackbirds (Icteridae)

Description: 8–11" (20–28 cm). Robin-sized. Male much larger than the female; *head, neck and upper breast bright yellow, blackish elsewhere;* and conspicuous white markings on the wings. Female duller and lighter; yellow on the chest, throat, and face; no white wing marks.

Voice: Harsh, incessant *oka-wee-wee* and *kruck* call, coming from many individuals in a colony, blends into a loud, wavering chorus.

Habitat: Freshwater marshes.

Nesting: 3–5 brown-speckled whitish eggs in a basket woven around several strong stalks. Breeds in colonies.

Range: Basically a western bird, extending into the prairie states and provinces.

Visiting a blackbird colony in a marsh or slough in spring is an exciting experience. The surrounding water provides safety but often limits the nesting habitat; crowding is thus inevitable. Some males are always in display flight, with head stooped, feet and tail drooped, wings beating in a

slow, accentuated way. Some quarrel
with neighbors over boundaries while
others fly out to feed. Approaching
predators are mobbed by clouds of
blackbirds and neighboring Redwings,
which nest in the drier stands of
cattails.

---

533 **Sharp-tailed Sparrow**
(*Ammospiza caudacuta*)
Grosbeaks, Buntings, Finches,
Sparrows (Fringillidae)

Description: 5½″ (14 cm). The combination of a
dark cap, gray ear patch, and a bright
orange-buff triangular area on the face
distinguishes this species from the only
other salt-marsh sparrow, the Seaside
Sparrow.

Voice: A dry, insect-like *kip-kip-zeeeee*.

Habitat: Along the coast, in the drier, grassy
portions of salt marsh and inland to
grassy, freshwater marshes.

Nesting: 4 or 5 brown-dotted pale blue eggs in a
loosely woven cup of grass set in
tussock above the high-tide line or
locally in freshwater marsh grass.

Range: Locally from central Canada to the
middle Atlantic states; winters chiefly
on the south Atlantic and Gulf coasts.

These birds spend most of their lives in
dense, coarse marsh grass, and by the
end of the breeding season their
plumage is so badly worn that little of
the distinctive pattern remains visible.
Indeed, there are few birds more
unprepossessing than a threadbare
Sharp-tail in August. A month later,
however, when they have acquired a
fresh coat of feathers, they are among
our most attractive sparrows.

541 Swamp Sparrow
(*Melospiza georgiana*)
Grosbeaks, Buntings, Finches,
Sparrows (Fringillidae)

Description: 5" (13 cm). A chunky, *dark* sparrow
with unstreaked underparts, *bright
rufous cap, and rusty wings;* back and tail
dark brown; face and breast gray; throat
white. The White-throated Sparrow has
a striped crown and lacks rusty
coloration in the wings.

Voice: Sweet, musical trill, all on one note.

Habitat: Freshwater marshes and open wooded
swamps; in migration with other
sparrows in weedy fields, parks, and
brush piles.

Nesting: 4 or 5 blue-green eggs with brown
blotches in a grassy cup on the ground,
well hidden in dense tussocks or marsh
vegetation.

Range: From east-central Canada south to east-
central United States; winters south to
the Gulf of Mexico.

A bird of the wetlands during the
breeding season, the Swamp Sparrow
appears in a variety of other habitats
during migration and winter. It is
rather shy, but responds readily to any
squeaking noise, and can usually be
lured into view by a patient observer. It
is never seen in large flocks like the
White-throated and White-crowned
Sparrows, but is usually found singly,
foraging on the ground in rather dense
cover.

560, 568 Red-winged Blackbird
(*Agelaius phoeniceus*)
Orioles, Blackbirds (Icteridae)

Description: 7–9½" (17–24 cm). Smaller than a
Robin. Male is black with *bright red
shoulder patches.* Female and young are
heavily streaked with dusky brown.

Voice: Rich, musical *O-ka-LEEEE!*

Habitat: Marshes, swamps, and wet and dry meadows; pastures.

Nesting: 3–5 pale blue eggs spotted and scrawled with dark brown and purple. Nest a well-made cup of marsh grass or reeds attached to growing marsh vegetation or built in a bush in a marsh.

Range: Breeds from Alaska and Newfoundland south to Florida, the Gulf Coast, and central Mexico. Winters regularly north to Pennsylvania and British Columbia.

Although primarily a marsh bird, the Red-wing will nest near virtually any body of water and occasionally breeds in upland pastures. Each pair raises two or three broods a season, building a new nest for each clutch. After the breeding season, the birds gather with other blackbirds in flocks sometimes numbering in the hundreds of thousands or millions and have come to be viewed as a health hazard. Attempts have been made to reduce such flocks by spraying and other methods.

Lakes, Ponds, Rivers

Open water that supports swimming
and diving birds, as well as birds that
characteristically feed around its edges.

14 Great Blue Heron
(*Ardea herodias*)
Herons, Bitterns (Ardeidae)

Description: 39–52" (99–132 cm). W. 70" (1.8 m). A common, *large, grayish* heron with a yellowish bill. Flies with neck folded, whereas the Sandhill Crane flies with the neck extended. In Florida an all-white form, the "Great White Heron," differs from the Great Egret in having greenish-yellow rather than black legs.

Voice: Hoarse, guttural squawk.

Habitat: Lakes, ponds, rivers, and marshes.

Nesting: 3–5 pale greenish-blue eggs on a platform of sticks, lined with finer material, usually in a tree but sometimes on the ground or concealed in a reedbed. In colonies.

Range: Alaska, Quebec, and Nova Scotia south to Mexico and the West Indies. Winters as far north as New England and southern Alaska. Also breeds in the Galapagos Islands.

This large heron is frequently found standing at the edge of a pond or marshy pool, watching for fish or frogs, which are its principal food. It also feeds on small mammals, reptiles, and occasionally birds. Most Great Blue Herons migrate south in the fall, but a few remain in the North during the winter; such lingering birds often fall victim to severe weather.

18 Green Heron
(*Butorides striatus*)
Herons, Bitterns (Ardeidae)

Description: 15–22" (38–56 cm). Crow-sized. A small dark heron with *bright orange or yellowish legs.* Head and neck chestnut, crown black with a small crest, back and wings dark green-gray.

Voice: Explosive, rasping *skyow!* Also croaks.

cackles, and clucks.

Habitat: Lake margins, streams, ponds, and marshes.

Nesting: 3–6 pale blue-green eggs in a flimsy saucer of sticks and twigs in a bush or thicket near water. Occasionally breeds in colonies.

Range: British Columbia, Minnesota, and New Brunswick south to southern South America. Winters north to South Carolina, the Gulf Coast, and California. Also in tropical portions of Africa and Southeast Asia.

The most common heron in much of its range, all it requires is a pond or stream with thick bushes or trees nearby for nesting and soft, muddy borders in which to search for its prey. It stretches its neck and bill forward as if taking aim, nervously flicking its short tail, and, after a few elaborately cautious steps, seizes the fish with a jab of its bill. A retiring bird, it is often first noticed when it flushes unexpectedly from the edge of water and flies off uttering its sharp call note.

37, 50 Herring Gull
(*Larus argentatus*)
Gulls, Terns (Laridae)

Description: 23–26" (58–66 cm). Adult white with light gray back and wings; black wing tip with white spots. *Feet pink or flesh-colored.* First-year birds brownish.

Voice: Loud rollicking call, *kuk-kuk-kuk, yucca-yucca-yucca,* and other raucous cries.

Habitat: Lakes, rivers, estuaries, and beaches; common in all aquatic habitats.

Nesting: 2–4 heavily spotted olive-brown eggs in a mass of seaweed or dead grass on the ground or a cliff; most often on islands. In colonies.

Range: Breeds from Alaska and Greenland

south to the Carolinas, and is spreading. Also in Eurasia.

This is the common "sea gull" inland and along the coast. In recent years it has become abundant, probably due to the amount of food available at garbage dumps, and has extended its range southward along the Atlantic Coast, often to the detriment of colonial birds such as terns and Laughing Gulls. Although a scavenger, it also eats large numbers of aquatic and marine animals, and feeds on berries. It often drops clams and other shellfish on exposed rocks or parking lots in order to break the shells and get at the soft interior.

38, 52 Ring-billed Gull
(*Larus delawarensis*)
Gulls, Terns (Laridae)

Description: 18–20" (45–50 cm). Adult silvery gray on back, white on head, tail, and underparts. Similar to Herring Gull but smaller, with *yellow feet* and with narrow black ring around bill. Young birds are mottled brown, paler than a young Herring Gull, and have a blackish tail band and flesh-colored legs.

Voice: Loud, raucous mewing cry, like the Herring Gull but higher-pitched.

Habitat: Lakes and rivers; many move to salt water in the winter.

Nesting: 2–4 spotted buff or olive eggs in a hollow in the ground, sometimes lined with grass or debris. Usually on islands in lakes. In the North they sometimes nest in low trees. In colonies, often with other gulls or terns.

Range: Alaska and Labrador south to the Great Lakes and California. Winters from southern New England south to Cuba.

In most of the northern part of the United States the Ring-billed Gull is

known as a winter visitor, less common than the Herring Gull. But in some inland areas and in the Deep South it is the more numerous of the two species. It often nests in very large colonies; as many as 85,000 pairs nest on a single island in Lake Ontario. By contrast, colonies of Herring Gulls seldom number more than a few score pairs.

46 Black-headed Gull
(*Larus ridibundus*)
Gulls, Terns (Laridae)

Description: 15" (38 cm). A small gull with gray back and inner wings and *flashing white primaries.* In breeding plumage has a dark brown hood. Red bill and legs. Immature is darker above, but shows some white in primaries, and has narrow black tip to tail. *In all plumages, under surface of primaries is blackish.* Bonaparte's Gull is smaller, has black bill, and lacks dark undersurface of primaries.

Voice: A harsh *kwup;* various squealing notes.

Habitat: Bays and estuaries.

Nesting: 3 buff-brown eggs with black blotches, in a nest lined with grass, sticks, and seaweed in trees, bushes, on rocks, or on the ground. Colonies located on sand dunes, beaches, marshes, and open fields.

Range: Northern portions of Europe and Asia south to their southern parts; winters from the southern portions of the breeding range south to Africa and southern Asia. Uncommon but regular winter visitor to eastern North America.

Like the Bonaparte's Gull, with which it is almost always found in America, its flight is light and buoyant, resembling that of a tern more than a gull. Although this Old World gull is uncommon in North America, it may be seen regularly

in small numbers in northeastern coastal
waters. In Europe it is one of the most
familiar gulls.

47 **Little Gull**
(*Larus minutus*)
Gulls, Terns (Laridae)

Description: 11″ (28 cm). The *smallest* gull. Summer
adult has pale gray back and wings,
white underparts, a *black hood,* and
blackish underwings. Winter plumage
similar but head white with partial gray
cap and dark spot behind eye. Dark red
bill and legs. Immature has narrow
black tail tip, a diagonal dark bar on
forewing, and dark primaries.
Voice: A soft *kek-kek-kek-kek.*
Habitat: Inland marshes, meadows, lakes, and
rivers; also coastal bays, flats, harbors,
and estuaries.
Nesting: 3 olive-brown eggs with dark spots, in
a nest lined with grass and leaves,
placed among marsh vegetation.
Range: Central Europe east to southern Siberia;
in recent years, locally in Ontario and
Wisconsin; winters regularly in small
numbers in eastern North America,
especially along the coast from New
Brunswick to New Jersey and on the
Great Lakes.

This tiny gull was known for decades as
a rare winter visitor to the Northeast
before it was found nesting in Ontario.
Its flight is rather buoyant and tern-like,
and it often plucks food from the
surface while on the wing, or dives
from the air after minnows and aquatic
insects.

48, 53, 55 Bonaparte's Gull
(*Larus philadelphia*)
Gulls, Terns (Laridae)

Description:  12–14" (30–35 cm). A small, delicate gull, silvery-gray above with conspicuous white patches on the leading edge of the outer wing. Black on head of breeding adults is lacking in winter. Young birds have dark markings on the upper surface of the wing and a black tail band. The Black-headed Gull is similar, but is larger, has a red bill (Bonaparte's is black), and has dark wing linings.

Voice: Rasping *tea-ar;* a soft, nasal snarling note.

Habitat: Forested lakes and rivers; winters along the coast, in estuaries, and at the mouth of large rivers.

Nesting: 2–4 olive or buff, spotted eggs in a well-made cup of grass, moss, and twigs in a spruce or fir tree near a lake or river.

Range: Breeds in interior of northwestern Canada and in Alaska. Winters along both coasts, on the Atlantic from southern New England southward.

Breeding in the Far North, these beautiful gulls are most often seen on lakes and rivers during migration or along the coast in winter. They keep to themselves, seldom joining the larger gulls at dumps. They feed in tidal inlets and at sewage outlets, picking scraps of food from the water. During spring migration they may often be seen flying northward up large rivers such as the Hudson and the Mississippi. The gull is named after a nephew of Napoleon, Charles Lucien Bonaparte, who was a leading ornithologist in the 1800s in America and Europe.

58, 61 Common Tern
(*Sterna hirundo*)
Gulls, Terns (Laridae)

Description: 13–16″ (33–40 cm). Pigeon-sized. White with black cap and pale gray back and wings. Red bill with black tip. Deeply forked tail. Similar to Forster's Tern but lacks frosty wing tip. Also similar to Arctic and Roseate terns.

Voice: *Kip-kip-kip.* Also *TEEaar.*

Habitat: Lakes, ponds, rivers, coastal beaches, and islands.

Nesting: 2 or 3 spotted olive-buff eggs in a depression in sand or a shallow cup of dead grass on sandy or pebbly beaches or open rocky places; most often nests on islands or isolated peninsulas. In colonies.

Range: Labrador south to the Caribbean and west to Wisconsin and Alberta. Winters from Florida to southern South America. Also in Eurasia.

A grasp of the field marks of other terns is best gained by comparison with these most common of "sea swallows." They are a familiar sight on almost all large bodies of water where protected nesting sites exist. They are seen flying gracefully over the water, searching for small fish and shrimp, which they capture by diving from the air. Sensitive to disturbance during the breeding season, whole colonies often fail to breed successfully because of disruption by humans and, as a result, their numbers are slowly declining. They will attack human intruders in the nesting colonies, often striking them on the head with their bills.

65 Caspian Tern
(Sterna caspia)
Gulls, Terns (Laridae)

Description: 19–23″ (48–58 cm). Gull-sized.
Largely white, with black cap and pale
gray back and wings; heavy *bright red
bill* and *dusky underwing.* The similar
Royal Tern has an orange-red bill, paler
underwing, and is almost never seen
away from the coast.

Voice: Low, hoarse *kraa.* Also a shorter *kow.*

Habitat: Sandy or pebbly shores of lakes and
large rivers, and along seacoasts.

Nesting: 2 or 3 spotted buff eggs in a shallow
depression or a well-made cup of dead
grass, most often on a sandy or rocky
island. Solitary or in small colonies.

Range: Mackenzie, the Great Lakes and
Newfoundland south to the Gulf Coast
and Baja California. Winters north
to California and North Carolina.
Also breeds in Eurasia, Africa, and
Australia.

Much less gregarious than other terns,
Caspians usually feed singly. Pairs
breed by themselves, in small colonies,
or may attach themselves to colonies of
other birds such as the Ring-billed
Gull. Caspians are more predatory than
most other terns, readily taking small
birds or the eggs and young of other
terns.

99, 103 Double-crested Cormorant
(Phalacrocorax auritus)
Cormorants (Phalacrocoracidae)

Description: 30–35″ (76–89 cm). Goose-sized.
Slender-bodied, dark bird with a long
neck and a slender, hooked bill that is
usually tilted upward when swimming.
Orange throat pouch. Stands upright
when perched. Larger than the
Olivaceous Cormorant of the Gulf
Coast, and lacks its white-bordered

throat pouch. Tufts on the crown, from which it gets its name, are rarely visible.

Voice: Deep guttural grunt.

Habitat: Lakes, rivers, swamps, and coasts.

Nesting: 3 or 4 pale, chalky blue eggs in a well-made platform nest of sticks (or seaweed on the coast) in a tree or on a cliff or rocky island. In colonies.

Range: Breeds from Alaska and Newfoundland south to Mexico and the Bahamas. Winters north to Long Island and southern Alaska.

The Double-crested is the most familiar cormorant in the East. Except in the Northeast during the winter, and along the Gulf Coast, it is the only cormorant to be seen. Occupying a wide variety of habitats, it replaces the Great Cormorant (*Phalacrocorax carbo*) which is widespread in the Old World but is here found as a breeder only along the Canadian coast south to the Gulf of Nova Scotia. Cormorants migrate in large, V-shaped flocks like migrating geese but are silent when flying. The word "cormorant" is derived, through French, from the Latin name *corvus marinus,* meaning "sea crow."

100, 104 Anhinga
(*Anhinga anhinga*)
Anhingas (Anhingidae)

Description: 34–36″ (86–91 cm). A blackish bird of southern swamps with a very long, slender neck and long tail. Male's plumage has greenish iridescence; upper surface of wings silvery gray. Female has tawny brown neck and breast, sharply set off from black belly.

Voice: Low grunt similar to that of the cormorant.

Habitat: Freshwater ponds and swamps with thick vegetation, especially cypress.

Nesting: 4 chalky blue eggs in a stick nest lined with fresh green leaves, in trees; often nests in colonies of cormorants.

Range: Atlantic and Gulf coasts from North Carolina to Texas and in the Mississippi Valley north to Arkansas and Tennessee. South to southern South America.

It is also known as the "Snakebird" because its body is submerged when swimming so that only its head and long, slender neck are visible above the water. Its long, dagger-shaped, serrated bill is ideally suited for catching fish, which it flips into the air and gulps down headfirst. Cormorants and Anhingas lack oil glands with which to preen and so must perch with their wings half-open to dry them in the sun. Unlike cormorants, Anhingas often soar in circles high overhead.

101 Olivaceous Cormorant
(*Phalacrocorax olivaceus*)
Cormorants (Phalacrocoracidae)

Description: 25" (63 cm). Duck-sized. Black with olive sheen; orange throat pouch. Double-crested Cormorant is larger, has yellow throat pouch.

Voice: Pig-like grunts.

Habitat: Brackish and fresh water, breeding in trees and low bushes.

Nesting: 4 pale blue eggs with a chalky coating, often red-stained, in a grass-lined stick nest in trees or on rocks.

Range: Coasts of Louisiana and Texas to southern South America.

Smallest of the three cormorants inhabiting the Atlantic and Gulf coasts. Like the other cormorants, it perches on dead branches or posts in the water, where it spreads its wings to dry. These birds sometimes join in communal fishing, lining up across a stream and moving forward with flailing wings to drive the fish into shallow water.

107, 137   Mallard
(*Anas platyrhynchos*)
Swans, Geese, Ducks (Anatidae)

Description: 18–27" (46–68 cm). Male has a *green head, white neck-ring,* chestnut breast, and grayish body. Inner feathers of wing (speculum) are metallic purplish-blue, bordered in front and back with white. Female mottled brown with *white tail* and purplish-blue speculum, bill mottled orange and brown.

Voice: Males utter soft, reedy notes; females, a loud quack.

Habitat: Ponds, lakes, and marshes. Semi-domesticated birds may be found on almost any body of water.

Nesting: 8–10 pale greenish-buff eggs in a shallow bowl of grass lined with down, hidden in marsh grass or on a brush pile near the shore.

Range: Breeds from Alaska and Greenland south to Virginia, Texas, and northern Mexico. Winters south to Central America and the West Indies. Also breeds in Eurasia.

Ancestor of the common white domestic duck, wild Mallards frequently interbreed with domestic stock, producing a bewildering variety of patterns and colors. They also hybridize with wild species such as the closely related Black Duck and even occasionally with Pintails. Strong fliers, Mallards sometimes reach remote oceanic islands where isolated populations may evolve into new species such as the Hawaiian Duck (*Anas wyvilliana*). These often differ from the Mallard mainly in that they lack the colorful plumage of the male.

109, 153 Redhead
(*Aythya americana*)
Swans, Geese, Ducks (Anatidae)

Description: 18–22" (46–56 cm). Male *gray, with brick red head and black breast.* Female duller and browner, with a light area around base of bill; rounder-headed than female Ring-necked Duck. Both sexes have a pale gray wing stripe and a pale blue-gray bill. Similar Canvasback has a whitish body and sloping forehead and bill.

Voice: Like the meow of a cat; also quacks.

Habitat: Nests in marshes, but at other times is found on lakes and bays; often on salt water in winter.

Nesting: 10–15 buff eggs in a woven cup of reeds lined with white down and attached to marsh vegetation.

Range: Breeds from British Columbia, Mackenzie, and Manitoba south to New Mexico, and rarely in eastern states. Winters from California, the Great Lakes, and southern New England south to Guatemala and the West Indies.

Redheads do most of their feeding at night, spending the daylight hours resting on water. This beautiful duck has suffered greatly from hunting and the destruction of its habitat; it has declined in numbers until it is one of the least common North American ducks. In many areas the introduction of carp from Eurasia has caused the destruction of its aquatic food plants.

110, 154 Canvasback
(*Aythya valisineria*)
Swans, Geese, Ducks (Anatidae)

Description: 19–24" (48–61 cm). Male has a *whitish body,* black chest, and reddish head with low forehead. The *long bill gives the head a distinctive sloping profile.* Female

gray-brown, with similar profile. At a
distance males can be distinguished
from Redheads by their white bodies,
the male Redhead's body being largely
gray.

Voice: Males grunt or croak. Females quack.

Habitat: Nests on marshes; winters on lakes,
bays, and estuaries.

Nesting: 7–10 greenish eggs in a floating mass of
reeds and grass anchored to stems of
marsh plants.

Range: Alaska, Mackenzie, and Manitoba south
to Minnesota, Nebraska, and
California. Winters from British
Columbia and Massachusetts south
to the Gulf Coast and to Central
America.

Although they breed mainly in the
West, each fall large numbers migrate
eastward to winter on the Great Lakes
and along the Atlantic Coast. They are
considered among the best-tasting
ducks, and many thousands are shot
annually. In recent years their numbers
have declined drastically, but chiefly
because of the draining of the large
marshes they require to breed. Where
they are still relatively numerous, their
long V-shaped flocks are a striking
sight as they move from one feeding
ground to another. Their principal food
is the aquatic plant known as wild
celery (*Vallisneria*), and part of the
bird's scientific name is a corruption of
that word.

114, 161 **Common Merganser**
(*Mergus merganser*)
Swans, Geese, Ducks (Anatidae)

Description: 22–27" (56–68 cm). Male has *flashing
white sides, green head,* white breast, and
long, thin red bill. Female has gray
body and sides; brownish crested head
sharply set off from white throat. Red-
breasted Merganser is similar, but has

gray sides, white neck-ring, and rust-colored breast.

Voice: Low rasping croak.

Habitat: Wooded rivers and ponds; in winter, also on salt bays.

Nesting: 8–12 pale buff eggs in a down-lined cavity or an abandoned hawk's nest.

Range: Southeastern Alaska, Manitoba, and Newfoundland south to northern New England, Michigan, and California. Winters south to northern Mexico and the Gulf Coast (rare). Also in Eurasia.

Although preferring to feed on lakes, they are often driven to rivers by cold weather; there they are found in flocks of 10 to 20 birds, all facing upstream and diving in pursuit of fish. Formerly, large numbers were shot in the belief that they destroyed valuable gamefish, but it is now understood that these birds are beneficial, preventing overpopulation of fish and thus allowing the survivors to attain greater size. Mergansers have fine tooth-like serrations along the sides of their bills which help in capturing slippery fish.

119, 164 Wood Duck
(*Aix sponsa*)
Swans, Geese, Ducks (Anatidae)

Description: 17–20″ (43–51 cm). A beautiful, crested, multicolored small duck. Male patterned in iridescent greens, purples, and blues with a distinctive white chin patch; red, rather long bill; long tail. Female grayish with broad white eye-ring.

Voice: Loud *wooo-eeek*. Also softer *peet* and *cheep* notes.

Habitat: Wooded rivers and ponds; wooded swamps. Visits freshwater marshes in late summer and fall.

Nesting: Up to 15 whitish eggs in a nest made of down in a natural tree cavity or nest-box sometimes 50 feet or more from the ground.

Range: British Columbia, Nova Scotia, and
Minnesota south to Florida and Texas.
Winters north to Washington in the
West and New Jersey in the East,
rarely farther north. Also breeds in
Cuba.

The Wood Duck's habit of nesting in
cavities enables it to breed in areas
lacking suitable ground cover. The
young leave the nest soon after
hatching, jumping from the nesting
cavity to the ground. Once in the
water, they travel through wooded
ponds with their mother. Snapping
turtles take a heavy toll of them.

121, 156 **Ring-necked Duck**
(*Aythya collaris*)
Swans, Geese, Ducks (Anatidae)

Description: 14–18″ (35–46 cm). Male has black
back and breast; purple-glossed, black-
appearing head; pale gray flanks;
vertical white mark on side of breast.
Female brownish, paler around the base
of the bill, and has a narrow white
eye-ring. Bill pale gray with a white
ring. The shape of the head—high and
angular—distinguishes this bird from
the scaups.
Voice: Soft purring notes, but usually silent.
Habitat: Wooded lakes, ponds, and rivers;
seldom on salt water except in the
southern states.
Nesting: 8–12 buff or olive eggs in a down-lined
cup concealed in vegetation near the
edge of a pond.
Range: Alaska, Manitoba, and Newfoundland
south to Maine, Colorado, and
California. Winters south to Mexico
and the West Indies.

This species might better be called the
"Ring-billed Duck," for its chestnut
neck-ring is usually seen only at close

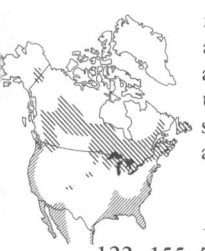

range while the white ring on the bill is a prominent field mark. More partial to acid ponds and lakes in wooded regions than other diving ducks, it eats the seeds of aquatic plants as well as snails and insects.

122, 155 Tufted Duck
(*Aythya fuligula*)
Swans, Geese, Ducks (Anatidae)

Description: 17″ (43 cm). A stocky, blackish duck with flashing *white flanks* and *drooping crest.* Female warm brown, paler on the flanks, with a small white patch at the base of the bill; no crest.

Voice: Various soft, growling notes; low whistles.

Habitat: Wooded lakes, streams, and marshes; in winter often in estuaries and shallow coastal bays.

Nesting: Usually 7–10 pale green eggs in a down-lined bowl of grass, concealed under a bush or tussock and usually near water.

Range: Northern Eurasia; casual in North America, chiefly along the coast in Alaska and the northeastern states.

This Old World bird is a counterpart of the Ring-necked Duck of North America. Indeed, on those rare occasions when a Tufted Duck turns up in our area, it may be seen with a small flock of Ring-necks. In Eurasia these birds gather in very large flocks, often with scaups and coots. In recent years there has been an increase in the number of sightings of this species in our area.

123, 157 Lesser Scaup
(Aythya affinis)
Swans, Geese, Ducks (Anatidae)

Description: 15–18″ (38–46 cm). Similar to the Greater Scaup but crown is higher, giving the head a more angular appearance. Male has its head glossed with purple, not green. Females are dark brown with a small white face patch, not easily distinguishable from the female Greater Scaup. In flight, the white stripe is shorter, whereas in the Greater Scaup the stripe extends three-fourths of the wing's length.

Voice: Seldom heard. Sharp whistles and guttural scolding notes.

Habitat: Ponds and marshes; in migration and winter it occurs on lakes, rivers, and ponds, and in the southern states on salt water.

Nesting: Usually 8–12 olive-buff eggs in a cup of down-lined grass hidden in vegetation often some distance from the edge of the water.

Range: Breeds from interior Alaska and northern Canada south to British Columbia, Montana, and Iowa, and occasionally farther east. Winters regularly from British Columbia and Massachusetts south to the Gulf of Mexico and northern South America.

Confined to the New World, it is thought to be descended from an earlier invasion of North America by the ancestor of both modern species of scaups. Here it evolved into a distinct species, to be joined later by a second arrival, the Greater Scaup, found in both hemispheres. In the northern states, where the Greater Scaup is more common in winter, the Lesser is often found in small parties on fresh water, while in the South it is seen in large flocks on lakes and salt water.

124, 158 Greater Scaup
(Aythya marila)
Swans, Geese, Ducks (Anatidae)

Description: 15–20" (38–51 cm). Male has very light gray body; blackish chest; and *black-appearing, green-glossed head.* Female is a uniform dark brown with white patch at base of bill. Often seen in large flocks on open water.

Voice: Usually silent; discordant croaking calls on the breeding grounds.

Habitat: Lakes, bays, and ponds; in winter, often on salt water.

Nesting: 8–12 olive or buff eggs in a down-lined cup of grass concealed in a clump of grass on land or in marsh vegetation well out from shore.

Range: Alaska and northern Canada east to Hudson's Bay and in Maritime Provinces. Winters mainly along Pacific, Gulf, and Atlantic coasts. Also breeds in Eurasia.

It is most commonly seen in large rafts, often composed of thousands of birds, on big inland lakes. When these lakes freeze over, the birds move to salt water. Although the two scaups can be difficult to tell apart, any very large flock of scaups on the northeast coast in winter may be assumed to be the Greater. Because it dives for many small animals and is not as much of a vegetarian as the Redhead or the Canvasback, the Greater Scaup is not considered as choice a gamebird but is still shot in large numbers annually.

128, 163 Hooded Merganser
(Lophodytes cucullatus)
Swans, Geese, Ducks (Anatidae)

Description: 16–19" (40–48 cm). A small duck with a slender, pointed bill. Male has *white, fan-shaped, black-bordered crest;* dark blackish body; dull rusty flanks; white

breast with two black stripes down the side. Female is dull gray-brown with head and crest warmer brown. Both sexes show a white wing patch in flight.

Voice: Hoarse grunts and chatters.

Habitat: Wooded ponds, lakes, and rivers; sometimes in tidal channels in winter.

Nesting: 8–12 white eggs in a down-lined cup in a natural tree cavity, or sometimes in a fallen hollow log.

Range: Alaska, Manitoba, and Nova Scotia south to Tennessee, Nebraska, and Oregon; occasionally in southeastern states. Winters from British Columbia, Nebraska, and New England south to Mexico and the Gulf Coast.

The smallest of our mergansers, they are most often seen along rivers and in estuaries during the fall and winter. They are usually found in flocks of up to a dozen, and when startled are among the fastest flying of our ducks. They feed chiefly on small fish, which they pursue in long, rapid, underwater dives, but also take frogs and aquatic insects.

---

170 Canada Goose
(*Branta canadensis*)
Swans, Geese, Ducks (Anatidae)

Description: Small races 22–26″ (56–66 cm); large races 35–45″ (89–114 cm). Brownish body with black head and long black neck; conspicuous *white cheek patch*. The smaller Brant lacks the white cheek patch.

Voice: Rich, musical honking.

Habitat: Lakes, bays, rivers, and marshes. Often feeds in open grassland and stubble fields.

Nesting: 4–8 whitish eggs in a large mass of grass and moss lined with down. Usually on the ground near water, but sometimes in an abandoned osprey or eagle nest.

Range: Alaska and Baffin Island south to
Massachusetts, North Carolina, and
California. Winters south to northern
Mexico and the Gulf Coast.
Widespread as a semidomesticated bird
in city parks and reservoirs.

When people speak of "wild geese" it is
generally this species they have in
mind. Familiar in every state and
province; a common sight is their
V-shaped flocks in migration. There is
much geographical variation in size;
some birds are scarcely larger than
Mallards, others are at least twice that
size. Tolerant of man, some even nest
in city parks and suburbs and are
especially noticeable in late summer
and early fall, when they gather on golf
courses and large lawns to molt, often
with one or two acting as sentinels.
When danger approaches they
sometimes crouch low with neck
extended, depending on their coloration
for protection.

174 Whistling Swan
(*Olor columbianus*)
Swans, Geese, Ducks (Anatidae)

Description: 48–55" (122–140 cm). The only swan
likely to be seen in most of the East.
Large, all white; black bill usually with
small yellow spot at base of upper
mandible. Holds neck straight up,
unlike the Mute Swan which bends its
neck in a graceful curve.

Voice: Mellow, rich bugling call, usually
heard from a flock of migrating birds.
Sometimes mistaken for the call of the
Canada Goose.

Habitat: Arctic tundra; winters on marshy lakes
and bays.

Nesting: 4–6 creamy white eggs in a large mass
of grass and moss on an island or at the
edge of a marshy tundra lake.

Range: Breeds in Alaska and northern Canada
east to Baffin Island. Winters in
Aleutians and from Washington to Baja
California and from Maryland to Texas;
occasionally on the Great Lakes.

Each fall large numbers of Whistling
Swans pause briefly on the Great Lakes
before moving to their winter
headquarters along the Atlantic Coast
from Chesapeake Bay to North
Carolina. Often traveling in flocks of
several hundred, they present a
spectacular sight. Many stop on the
Niagara River and are sometimes swept
over the falls to their death. Because
they breed in remote and little
disturbed areas, they have so far escaped
the fate of the closely related
Trumpeter Swan, which was reduced
to near extinction by hunting and
habitat destruction.

177, 179 Least Grebe
(*Podiceps dominicus*)
Grebes (Podicipedidae)

Description: 8–10″ (20–25 cm). Robin-sized.
Grayish with orange eyes and a small,
dark bill. Similar to Pied-billed Grebe
but smaller, with a more slender bill.
Voice: Loud *clang.*
Habitat: Quiet, thickly vegetated ponds and
slow-moving streams.
Nesting: 3–6 white eggs which become stained
with brown, laid in a floating or
anchored nest of reeds, rushes, and
rotten leaves.
Range: Southern Texas and West Indies to
South America.

Smallest North American grebe. Like
most grebes, when leaving the nest the
adults cover the eggs with decayed
vegetation to protect them from
excessive heat of the sun and from
predators. Least Grebes rarely leave the

immediate vicinity of their breeding grounds. They feed mostly on various aquatic insects, and occasionally on small crustaceans such as crayfish. In southern Texas they are often found on ranch ponds.

185 Red-necked Grebe
(*Podiceps grisegena*)
Grebes (Podicipedidae)

Description: 18–20″ (46–51 cm). Largest grebe in eastern North America. A slender water bird with *long rufous neck; whitish cheeks;* dark cap; long, pointed *yellow bill.* Grayish body. Similar in winter, but neck gray. The long yellow bill separates this species from all other North American grebes. In flight it can be distinguished from loons by its smaller size and white wing patches.

Voice: Nasal honk. Also a loon-like wail.

Habitat: Ponds and lakes in summer; bays and estuaries in winter.

Nesting: 3–5 whitish, stained eggs in a floating mass of dead reeds and grass in reedy lakes.

Range: Northern Canada and Alaska southeast to southern Minnesota; more rarely to Quebec and New Hampshire. Winters south to Long Island, rarely to Florida. Also breeds in Eurasia.

Highly aquatic, grebes can swim with only their head above water, concealing themselves in low pond vegetation. The young, striped in black and white, are often seen riding on the parent's back. Like loons, grebes are expert divers, propelling themselves with their lobed feet as they pursue fish, crustaceans, and aquatic insects.

188, 190 Common Loon
(*Gavia immer*)
Loons (Gaviidae)

Description: 28–36" (71–91 cm). Goose-sized.
Heavy, long-bodied water bird with
thick pointed bill held horizontally. In
summer, head and neck black with
white collar; back black with white
spots. In winter, crown, hind neck, and
upperparts grayish; throat and
underparts white. When swimming it
rides low in the water.

Voice: Wild maniacal laugh, also a mournful
yodeled *oo-AH-ho* with middle note
higher, and a loud ringing *kee-a-ree,
kee-a-ree* with middle note lower. Often
calls at night.

Habitat: Forested lakes and rivers; oceans and
bays in winter.

Nesting: 2 olive-brown, lightly spotted eggs in a
substantial mass of vegetation near edge
of water, usually on an island.

Range: Breeds from Aleutian Islands, Alaska,
and Northern Canada south to New
Hampshire, Montana, and California.
Winters south to the Gulf Coast. Also
breeds in Iceland.

It is known for its call, a far-carrying
wail heard on its northern breeding
grounds and occasionally during
migration. Loons are expert divers and
have been caught in nets as much as
200 feet below the surface. Their
principal food is fish, but they also eat
shellfish, frogs, and aquatic insects.
Their feet are located far back on the
body, which aids them in diving; they
travel on land with difficulty,
propelling themselves forward on their
breasts.

197, 215 Spotted Sandpiper
(*Actitis macularia*)
Sandpipers (Scolopacidae)

Description: 7½″ (19 cm). Robin-sized. In breeding
plumage olive-brown above, *many black
spots below;* lacks spotting in fall and
winter.

Voice: Clear *peet-weet;* also a soft trill.

Habitat: Almost anyplace with water nearby,
both in open country and in wooded
areas.

Nesting: 4 buff, brown-spotted eggs in a nest
lined with grass or moss in a slight
depression on the ground.

Range: Northern Alaska and Canada to
southern United States. Winters
from southern United States to South
America.

This is one of the best-known of
American shorebirds. Its habit of
endlessly bobbing the rear part of its
body up and down has earned it the
vernacular name "teeter-tail." When
flushed from the margin of a pond or
stream it is easily identified by its
distinctive flight—short bursts of
rapidly vibrating wingbeats alternating
with brief glides. Most of our
shorebirds breed in the Far North; this
is one of the few that nests in the
United States.

302 Swallow-tailed Kite
(*Elanoides forficatus*)
Hawks, Eagles (Accipitridae)

Description: 22–24″ (56–61 cm). W. 50″ (1.3 m).
A graceful bird of prey, with long,
pointed wings and deeply forked tail.
Head and underparts white, back wings
and tail black.

Voice: Shrill squeals or whistles. Also a soft
twittering.

Habitat: Swamps, marshes, river bottoms, and
glades in open forests.

Nesting: 2–4 creamy white eggs, boldly spotted with dark brown in a stick nest often lined with moss, and usually set in a tall tree.

Range: Breeds mainly on or near the coast from South Carolina to Florida, formerly to Texas; local farther inland in the Gulf states, rare farther north. South to southern South America.

The Swallow-tail's flight as it rides air currents or swoops rapidly after its prey is graceful, buoyant, and effortless. It spends much of the daylight hours on the wing, rarely perching on some dead tree branch. It feeds extensively on lizards and snakes. Much of its food is eaten while aloft, including dragonflies which it snatches out of the air. Like a swallow, it skims the water to drink and bathe.

305, 307   Bald Eagle
(*Haliaeetus leucocephalus*)
Hawks, Eagles (Accipitridae)

Description: 30–31″ (76–79 cm). W. 72–90″ (1.8–2.3 m). A large blackish eagle with *white head, white tail,* and a long, heavy yellow bill. Young birds lack the white head and tail and resemble adult Golden Eagles, but have pale wing linings and a more massive bill.

Voice: Squeaky cackling.

Habitat: Lakes, rivers, marshes, and seacoasts.

Nesting: 2 or 3 white eggs in a huge, conspicuous mass of sticks in the top of a tall tree or, less frequently, on top of a cliff.

Range: Formerly bred throughout most of North America, but now restricted as a breeding bird to Aleutians, Alaska, parts of northern and eastern Canada, northern United States, and Florida. In winter, along almost any body of water, especially the larger rivers in the interior of the continent.

Eating dead fish stranded on beaches and riverbanks has caused many Bald Eagles to absorb large amounts of pesticides, which interfere with the birds' calcium metabolism and result in thin-shelled and often infertile eggs. Once a familiar sight along rivers and coasts, our national bird is today known mainly as an occasional migrant; adults now usually outnumber young birds. Unless these pesticides can be removed from the birds' environment, we may face the loss of one of North America's most magnificent birds.

306 Osprey
(*Pandion haliaetus*)
Ospreys (Pandionidae)

Description: 21–24″ (53–61 cm). W. 54–72″ (1.4–1.8 m). A large, long-winged "fish hawk." Brown above and white below; white head with dark brown line through eye and on side of face. Wing shows distinct bend at the "wrist."

Voice: Loud, musical chirping.

Habitat: Lakes, rivers, and seacoasts.

Nesting: 2–4 white or buff, brown-spotted eggs in a bulky mass of sticks and debris placed in a tree, on rocks, flat ground, or telephone poles.

Range: Breeds from Alaska and Newfoundland south to Florida and the Gulf Coast. Winters regularly from the Gulf Coast and California south to Argentina. Also breeds in Eurasia, North Africa, the East Indies, and Australia.

This hawk is well adapted for capturing fish, which comprise its entire diet. The soles of Ospreys' feet are equipped with sharp, spiny projections that give the bird a firm grip on its slippery prey. It hovers until a fish nears the surface, then plunges feet-first into the water, grasping the fish in its talons.

315 Peregrine Falcon
(*Falco peregrinus*)
Falcons (Falconidae)

Description: 15–21" (38–53 cm). W. 40" (1 m).
Crow-sized. Adults slate-gray above
and pale below, with fine bars and spots
of black; narrow tail; *long pointed wings;*
conspicuous *black "mustaches."* Young
birds darker below and browner.

Voice: Rasping *kack-kack-kack.* Also a long
ascending wail, *WEEchew-WEEchew.*

Habitat: Open country, especially along rivers,
also near lakes, and the coast. Migrates
chiefly along the coast.

Nesting: 2–4 cream-colored, brown-spotted eggs
in a scrape with little lining, placed on
a cliff or in an abandoned eagle's nest.

Range: Formerly bred from Alaska and
Greenland south to Georgia and Baja
California, but now restricted to the
northern parts of its range in the East.
Winters north to British Columbia and
Massachusetts. Also breeds in southern
South America and in Eurasia, Africa,
and Australia.

Spectacular on the wing, in former
times they were a favorite choice for the
sport of falconry, plunging from
tremendous heights at speeds estimated
at 180 miles per hour to capture flying
birds. The Peregrine has been
drastically reduced in numbers by
pesticides (it is said that eating a single
badly contaminated duck can cause a
Peregrine to become infertile) and has
completely disappeared from all but the
most northern parts of its breeding
range. These falcons are quite tolerant
of man and formerly nested on
windowsills and ledges of buildings in
our largest cities, where they preyed on
pigeons.

331 Tree Swallow
(Iridoprocne bicolor)
Swallows (Hirundinidae)

Description: 5–6¼" (13–16 cm). Sparrow-sized. The only swallow in the East with metallic blue or blue-green upperparts and clear white underparts. Young birds are dull brown above but may be distinguished from Bank and Rough-winged swallows by their clear, whiter underparts.

Voice: Cheerful series of liquid twitters.

Habitat: Lake shores, flooded meadows, marshes, and streams.

Nesting: 4–6 white eggs in a feather-lined cup of grass placed in a hole in a tree or in a nest-box.

Range: Alaska, northern Manitoba, and Newfoundland south to Maryland, Nebraska, Colorado, and California. Winters north to the Carolinas, the Gulf Coast, and southern California; occasionally to New York and Massachusetts.

This bird's habit of feeding on bayberries enables it to winter farther north than other swallows. Although most on the East Coast winter in the Carolinas, a few may be found on Long Island or Cape Cod. It is the first of our swallows to reappear in the spring. It sometimes breeds in unusual situations: several pairs once nested on a ferry boat that shuttled across the St. Lawrence River, foraging on both the American and Canadian sides. Tree Swallows often enjoy playing with a feather, which they drop and then retrieve as it floats in the air. They gather in enormous flocks along the coast in fall, where they circle in big eddies like leaves caught in a whirlwind.

333 Rough-winged Swallow
(*Stelgidopteryx ruficollis*)
Swallows (Hirundinidae)

Description: 5–5¾″ (13–14 cm). Sparrow-sized.
Brown back with dusky throat and
upper breast. The similar Bank Swallow
has pure white underparts with the
breast crossed by a narrow brown band.

Voice: Buzzy notes much like Bank Swallow's,
but deeper and more rasping.

Habitat: Streams and rivers, especially in the
vicinity of steep banks and man-made
structures providing nest sites.

Nesting: 5–7 white eggs in a shallow saucer of
grass and debris placed in a cliff
crevice, drainpipe, or at the end of a
tunnel dug by the birds in a sandbank.

Range: British Columbia, Michigan, and New
Brunswick south to northern
Argentina. Winters from Gulf Coast
southward.

The name "Rough-winged" comes from
tiny hooks on the outer primary, which
give the feather a rough feel. The
function of these hooks, found also in a
group of unrelated African swallows, is
unknown. Unlike the Bank Swallow,
Rough-wings do not usually dig their
own nesting burrows, but use ready-
made nesting sites along streams. Thus
they do not nest in large colonies like
the Bank Swallow, although
occasionally a few pairs may be found
close together.

334 Bank Swallow
(*Riparia riparia*)
Swallows (Hirundinidae)

Description: 4¾–5½″ (12–14 cm). Sparrow-sized—
our smallest swallow. Brown above,
dull white below; *breast crossed by a
distinct brown band;* tail notched.
Rough-winged Swallow is warmer
brown, with dusky throat and breast

without distinct brown band.

Voice: Series of buzzy notes, *bzt-bzt-bzt;* also a twitter.

Habitat: Rivers and streams, especially near sandbanks; more widespread during migration.

Nesting: 4 or 5 white eggs in a loosely built cup of grass at the end of a 2- or 3-foot tunnel in a vertical bank, which the bird excavates with feet and bill. Nests in colonies.

Range: Breeds from Alaska and Labrador south to Virginia, Texas, and California. Winters in South America. Also occurs in Eurasia.

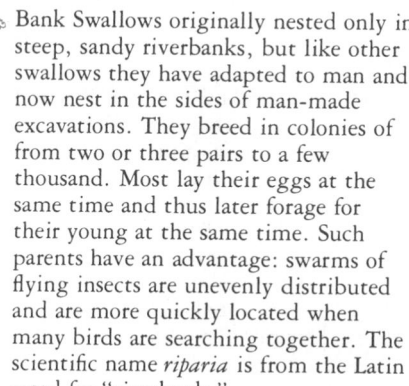

Bank Swallows originally nested only in steep, sandy riverbanks, but like other swallows they have adapted to man and now nest in the sides of man-made excavations. They breed in colonies of from two or three pairs to a few thousand. Most lay their eggs at the same time and thus later forage for their young at the same time. Such parents have an advantage: swarms of flying insects are unevenly distributed and are more quickly located when many birds are searching together. The scientific name *riparia* is from the Latin word for "riverbank."

---

433 Belted Kingfisher
(*Megaceryle alcyon*)
Kingfishers (Alcedinidae)

Description: 13″ (33 cm). Pigeon-sized. *Bushy crest; dagger-like bill;* blue-gray above, white below. Male has a blue-gray breast band; female similar but with a *chestnut belly band.*

Voice: Loud, penetrating rattle, given on the wing and when perched.

Habitat: Rivers, lakes, and saltwater estuaries.

Nesting: 5–8 white eggs in an unlined chamber at the end of a tunnel up to eight feet long, dug in a sand or gravel bank.

Range: Breeds from Alaska and Canada and throughout United States. Winters south to Panama and the West Indies.

Kingfishers often hover like a tern over water where a fish is visible and dive vertically for the prey. They may also take crabs, crayfish, salamanders, lizards, mice, and insects. They often patrol a regular beat along a stream or lake shore, stopping at favorite exposed perches along the way.

434 Ringed Kingfisher
(*Megaceryle torquata*)
Kingfishers (Alcedinidae)

Description: 13″ (33 cm). Pigeon-sized. Similar to the Belted Kingfisher but larger and with more chestnut on belly. Bushy crest and a large, dagger-shaped bill. Blue-gray above, *chestnut below with a white collar.* Female similar but has a gray band across the upper breast.

Voice: Harsh rattle louder than that of the Belted Kingfisher. Also a loud *kleck.*

Habitat: Tree-lined rivers, streams, and lakes.

Nesting: 5–7 white eggs in a burrow dug into a sandbank.

Range: Extreme southern Texas to southern South America. Local on the lower Rio Grande.

Ringed Kingfishers are the largest of the three species of kingfishers in the United States, where they have been found in only two places on the lower Rio Grande in Texas: Laredo and Falcon Dam. Although very local within the United States, the Ringed Kingfisher has been observed regularly at Falcon Dam, but has not as yet bred there.

482 Green Kingfisher
(*Chloroceryle americana*)
Kingfishers (Alcedinidae)

Description: 8″ (20 cm). Robin-sized. Dark green above, white below; *male has a broad rufous breast band, female has a green breast band.* Both sexes have a white collar.

Voice: Instead of the rattle-like call of its larger relatives, the Green Kingfisher has an insect-like buzz and some low clicking notes.

Habitat: Woodland streams and pools.

Nesting: 4–6 white eggs in a cavity at the end of a burrow in a sandy bank.

Range: Extreme southern Texas to southern South America.

Smallest of the three species found in the United States, these birds may be observed in southern Texas near forest-fringed pools and streams of the clearest water, where they sit for long periods on a limb overhanging water until they spot a minnow or other small fish. They then plunge into the water after their prey. At other times, when at a considerable distance from water, they feed on small lizards or grasshoppers.

Florida Swamps and Keys

In southern Florida there are a number
of freshwater and marine habitats that
are grouped together here because of
the distinctive species of birds they
contain. Mangroves are tropical trees
that grow in shallow salt water and
have stiltlike roots and evergreen
leaves. Vast marshes of sawgrass occur
in shallow fresh or brackish water. Keys
are low-lying coral or limestone islands
with tropical vegetation of West Indian
origin, such as gumbo-limbo,
manchineel, Jamaica dogwood,
mahogany, and palms.

9 **Wood Stork**
"**Wood Ibis**"
(*Mycteria americana*)
Storks (Ciconiidae)

Description: 40–44″ (102–112 cm). W. 66″ (1.5 m).
White with black flight feathers and
tail. Head and neck bare, dark gray.
Bill long, stout, and slightly curved,
black in adults and yellow in immatures.
Unlike herons, it flies with its neck
extended.

Voice: Dull croak. Usually silent except
around nest. Young clatter endlessly.

Habitat: On or near the coast, breeding chiefly
in cypress swamps; also in mangroves.

Nesting: 2 or 3 white eggs on a huge stick
platform in colonies in trees.

Range: Breeds in Florida; wanders to South
Carolina and Texas, occasionally
farther. Also in South America.

Often wrongly called "Wood Ibis," this
is a true stork. Its naked gray head has
earned it the local name "flint head."
These birds perch motionless on a bare
branch or slowly stalk through marshes
in search of food. They are sometimes
seen circling high in the air on rising
thermal air currents. They nest in
enormous colonies numbering up to
10,000 pairs, but in recent years their
numbers have declined drastically due
to land development, lumbering, and
draining of their feeding grounds.

10 "**Great White Heron**"
(*Ardea herodias occidentalis*)
Herons, Bitterns (Ardeidae)

Description: 50″ (127 cm). W. 70″ (1.8 m). Largest
of the American herons. White with
yellow bill and legs; Great Egret has
black legs.

Voice: Hoarse croaks.

Habitat: Shallow bays and mangrove islands in
the Florida Keys.

Nesting: 3 pale blue-green eggs in a bulky stick nest placed in a bush or low tree, usually in mangroves.

Range: Islands in the Caribbean Sea and the Gulf of Mexico from Florida Bay to Cuba, Yucatán, and northern Venezuela.

Until recently, the "Great White Heron" was considered a distinct species. But both dark and white young have been found in a single nest, and it is now treated as a white phase of the Great Blue Heron that occurs only in Florida and the Caribbean region. A drive through the Florida Keys on the highway to Key West usually affords a view of several of these stately white birds.

12 American Flamingo
(*Phoenicopterus ruber*)
Flamingos (Phoenicopteridae)

Description: 48″ (122 cm). W. 55″ (1.5 m). Unmistakable. A tall, *long-legged, long-necked pink* bird with a downcurved bill. Wings have black tips and trailing edges.

Voice: Goose-like honking and cackling notes.

Habitat: Shallow coastal lagoons and mudflats.

Nesting: 1 white egg, on a low mound of mud on a mud flat. In colonies.

Range: The Bahamas, West Indies, Yucatán, northern South America and the Galapagos Islands. A casual on the U.S. coast from the Carolinas to Texas.

This species was formerly more numerous, and probably bred at one time along the coast of Florida. Flamingos are extremely sensitive to persecution, and today nest only in a few very isolated localities. The birds use their curiously shaped bills to strain small animals from the mud. Flamingo-like birds, known today only as fossils, lived in western North America 50 million years ago.

23 Limpkin
(*Aramus guarauna*)
Limpkins (Aramidae)

Description: 25–28″ (64–71 cm). Goose-sized. Grayish-brown with white spots and streaks. Long, slender, downcurved bill. Flight is jerky, like that of the cranes, with a rapid upstroke and a slower downstroke.

Voice: Loud, wailing *krrr-ow*.

Habitat: Wooded swamps and marshes.

Nesting: 5–8 buff eggs, with dark brown spots and blotches, laid in a shallow nest of marsh vegetation just above the water; more rarely in a stick nest in low trees or bushes.

Range: Local in southern Georgia and Florida, ranging from the Okefenokee Swamp to the Everglades. South to southern South America.

This bird, related to the cranes and rails, is chiefly nocturnal. It feeds on the freshwater snail *Pomacea,* but also takes frogs, tadpoles, and aquatic insects. Its loud, strident, eerie call, a familiar night sound in the Florida marshes, sounds like a human in distress, so the Limpkin is known locally as the "crying bird."

90 White-tailed Tropicbird
(*Phaethon lepturus*)
Tropicbirds (Phaethontidae)

Description: 32″ (81 cm). W. 37″ (1 m). A white, pigeon-sized seabird with very long central tail feathers, bold black wing markings, and a yellowish bill. Young birds lack the long tail feathers and are finely barred with black above.

Voice: A harsh *ticket-ticket,* repeated frequently
on the wing.

Habitat: Tropical oceans.

Nesting: 1 pinkish egg, spotted with brown,
laid on a bare rock or in a crevice
among rocks on an island.

Range: Bermuda and the Bahamas, and on
islands in the tropical Atlantic, Indian,
and Pacific oceans. A casual on the
coast of Florida and the Carolinas.

These graceful seabirds take their
food—small fish and squids—in
shallow dives from the air. Their flight
is pigeon-like. The birds are able to
travel far out to sea, and after the
breeding season many gather in the
Sargasso Sea, hundreds of miles from
the nearest land.

319 Short-tailed Hawk
(Buteo brachyurus)
Hawks, Eagles (Accipitridae)

Description: 13–14″ (33–35 cm). W. 35″ (1 m).
Crow-sized. A small, chunky hawk
with two phases: the light phase is dark
above and white below; the dark phase
is black above and below except for
light bases to primaries. Both phases
have *banded black-and-white tail.*
Immature is tawny-buff below with
dark streaks.

Voice: Cackles and warning screams, but is
seldom heard except at nest.

Habitat: Chiefly cypress and mangrove swamps.

Nesting: 2 white eggs, spotted or blotched with
brown, in a stick nest lined with leaves,
sometimes decorated with Spanish
moss, in a tree.

Range: Local in southern Florida. Throughout
tropical America.

This rare bird is easily identified in
either color phase, being the only hawk
in the area that is pure black or pure
white below. It often perches low on

poles or trees near swampy areas, and
darts out after birds. It also feeds on
rodents, lizards, and insects.

320 Everglade Kite
(Rostrhamus sociabilis)
Hawks, Eagles (Accipitridae)

Description: 16–18" (40–46 cm). W. 44" (1 m).
Crow-sized. Male dark slate color; its
white tail has a dark broad band; female
is brown, heavily streaked below with
banded tail like male's. Red (male) or
orange (female and young) legs.

Voice: Low cackle, chatter, or neigh, but
seldom heard.

Habitat: Freshwater marshes and lakes.

Nesting: 2–5 white eggs, heavily spotted and
blotched with brown, in a stick nest
placed in low bushes or on the
ground.

Range: Mainly Lake Okeechobee and
Loxahatchee in southern Florida.
Widespread in Central and South
America.

Also called the "Snail Kite," it feeds
exclusively on snails of the genus
Pomacea, found in shallow ponds and
swampy places. The kite's slender,
sharply hooked bill easily extracts the
living animal from the unbroken shell.
The Florida population has become
seriously reduced due to draining of its
habitat but there is evidence that it is
increasing.

328 White-crowned Pigeon
(Columba leucocephala)
Pigeons, Doves (Columbidae)

Description: 13" (33 cm). *Dark gray* with a
conspicuous *white crown.* Melanistic
Rock Doves have shorter tails and white
rather than blackish wing linings.

Voice: *Coo-coo-co-WOOO,* with an owl-like quality.

Habitat: Mangroves and occasionally in tropical hardwoods.

Nesting: 1 or 2 white eggs in a grass-lined stick nest in a tree or bush; often in colonies.

Range: Florida Keys and the West Indies; does not winter in Florida but migrates as far as the southern Caribbean Sea.

In the United States it breeds only in the mangrove swamps of the Florida Keys and, to a lesser extent, among the gumbo-limbo and mahogany trees of the adjacent mainland. In former years great numbers were shot for food, and they became very wary. With the passage of protective laws in 1913, they increased in numbers and nowadays are fairly tame. They are great fruit-eaters but also take insects and seeds.

---

395 Spotted-breasted Oriole
(Icterus pectoralis)
Orioles, Blackbirds (Icteridae)

Description: 8″ (20 cm). Bright orange with black throat, wings, and tail; white patches on wings; *black spots on sides of breast.*

Voice: Like that of other orioles—loud, varied, and continuous.

Habitat: Open country with scattered trees, orchards, gardens, and parks.

Nesting: 4 whitish eggs with black scrawls in a woven basket nest of palm fibers or other vegetable matter.

Range: Southern Mexico to northern Costa Rica. Introduced around Miami, Florida.

This handsome oriole, a native of Mexico, was first reported in the Miami area in 1949, where it was introduced, probably from escaped captives. It has since been found in Florida from Homestead to Fort Lauderdale and appears to be thriving.

426 Gray Kingbird
(*Tyrannus dominicensis*)
Tyrant Flycatchers (Tyrannidae)

Description: 9″ (23 cm). A stocky, large-headed,
pale gray flycatcher of coastal habitats.
Underparts whitish; dusky blackish
patch through eye; bill heavy; tail
notched, without white.

Voice: Buzzy *pe-CHEER-y* and a harsh note.

Habitat: Coastal, in mangrove thickets, on
telephone wires, and in small groves of
palms and oaks.

Nesting: 3 pinkish eggs blotched with brown in
a grass-lined stick nest placed in a
mangrove thicket, usually over or near
salt water.

Range: Coastal regions of South Carolina,
Georgia, Florida, the West Indies, and
smaller islands in the Caribbean.
Winters from the Greater Antilles to
Colombia, Venezuela, and the Guianas.

Like other kingbirds it is fearless, even
chasing hawks and crows. Noisy as well
as belligerent, it frequently emits harsh
notes as it sits on telephone wires or
exposed branches ready to dart after
flying insects.

436 Scrub Jay
(*Aphelocoma coerulescens*)
Jays, Magpies, Crows (Corvidae)

Description: 11–13″ (28–33 cm). Blue Jay-sized.
Wings and tail dull blue, back gray,
with dusky mask, and white throat set
off by a "necklace" of dull blue marks
on the breast. No crest.

Voice: Similar to the Blue Jay's—loud, harsh,
and rasping; also has a sweet song of
trills and low warbles.

Habitat: In Florida confined to scrub oak.

Nesting: 3–6 buff or dull green eggs, spotted
with dark brown, in a bulky mass of
twigs concealed in a dense bush or low
tree.

Range: Breeds from Washington, Wyoming, and Colorado south to Texas and southern Mexico, with an isolated population in central Florida.

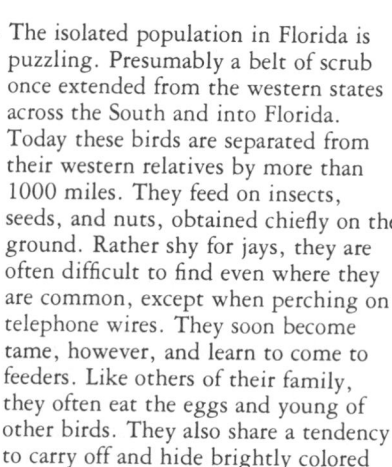

The isolated population in Florida is puzzling. Presumably a belt of scrub once extended from the western states across the South and into Florida. Today these birds are separated from their western relatives by more than 1000 miles. They feed on insects, seeds, and nuts, obtained chiefly on the ground. Rather shy for jays, they are often difficult to find even where they are common, except when perching on telephone wires. They soon become tame, however, and learn to come to feeders. Like others of their family, they often eat the eggs and young of other birds. They also share a tendency to carry off and hide brightly colored objects.

442 Blue-gray Tanager
(Thraupis episcopus)
Tanagers (Thraupidae)

Description: 7″ (17 cm). Larger than a House Sparrow. Pale blue, darker on wings and tail; bend of wing whitish.

Voice: Song weak and squeaky, consisting of short irregular phrases.

Habitat: Residential areas and parks with shade trees.

Nesting: 1 or 2 grayish eggs spotted with brown, in an open cup of dead leaves and grass, placed high in a broadleaved tree.

Range: Native to tropical forests of Central and South America. Introduced in Miami, Florida.

Like many tropical tanagers, these brightly colored birds travel in small flocks in search of insects and fruit. Such flocks include mated pairs regardless of the time of year, for Blue-gray Tanagers remain mated for life.

452 Black-whiskered Vireo
(*Vireo altiloquus*)
Vireos (Vireonidae)

Description: 5½" (14 cm). Similar to the Red-eyed Vireo (olive-green above, white below) but with a *dusky streak below the eye,* giving the bird its name.

Voice: Similar to the Red-eyed Vireo but more abrupt, and in one- to four-note phrases, sometimes described as *whip-Tom-KELLY.*

Habitat: Mangroves, thick scrub, and shade trees.

Nesting: 2 or 3 white eggs with a few small, scattered spots in a nest of grass, leaves, and rootlets in the fork of a branch, usually in mangroves.

Range: Breeds in southern Florida and the West Indies. Winters in northern South America, less commonly in the Lesser Antilles.

They are not shy and come regularly into gardens and shade trees in Key West. They may also be seen in the dense scrub and tropical hammocks in the Upper Keys and occasionally in coconut palms and mangroves around Miami. They eat insects and, rarely, berries and other soft fruits.

508 Red-whiskered Bulbul
(*Pycnonotus jocosus*)
Bulbuls (Pycnonotidae)

Description: 8" (20 cm). Grayish above, whitish below, with a long, conspicuous *black crest, red cheek patch* and undertail coverts, and a black, white-tipped tail.

Voice: Chattering notes; a whistled *queekey!*

Habitat: Residential areas, parks, and gardens.

Nesting: 2–4 pinkish-white eggs, spotted with reddish brown, in a cup of dead leaves and grass, lined with fine roots and hair, in a bush or small tree.

Range: Native to Southeast Asia; introduced and established in Miami, Florida.

This species has long been adapted to living in the vicinity of towns and villages in Southeast Asia, and is now successful in suburban Miami. Bulbuls are noisy, gregarious birds, usually traveling in flocks in pursuit of insects and fruit.

523 Mangrove Cuckoo
(*Coccyzus minor*)
Cuckoos (Cuculidae)

Description: 12″ (30 cm). Blue Jay-sized. Brown above, *rich buff or tawny below;* black facial mask; curved bill. Long, graduated tail with black-and-white spots at tip.

Voice: Low, guttural *gaw-gaw-gaw-gaw-gaw,* almost like a soft bark or the scolding of a squirrel.

Habitat: Only in Florida mangrove swamps.

Nesting: 2 or 3 pale greenish-blue eggs in a stick nest in a low shrub.

Range: Southern Florida through the West Indies and from Mexico to northern South America.

In North America, this species is found only in the Florida Keys and on the adjacent Gulf Coast as far as Tampa Bay. It is difficult to observe, remaining hidden in dense thickets much of the time. Strictly insectivorous, it feeds on hairy caterpillars, grasshoppers, moths, larvae, and spiders.

Grasslands

Included here are natural grasslands such as plains, prairies, and barrens, and man-made grasslands such as pastures, meadows, croplands, airfields, and golf courses.

4, 8   **Cattle Egret**
(*Bubulcus ibis*)
Herons, Bitterns (Ardeidae)

Description: 20″ (51 cm). White with orange-buff head and back plumes during the breeding season. Legs yellow or orange in adults, blackish in immatures. Stocky yellow or orange bill.

Voice: A hoarse croaking.

Habitat: Dry land in open fields where it feeds alongside livestock, but breeds near water with other herons.

Nesting: 3–5 pale blue eggs in a stick nest placed in a bush or tree in a marsh. Usually in colonies.

Range: Chiefly southern and eastern states. Also tropics of Mexico, Central and South America, West Indies, and the Old World.

Originating in the Old World, the Cattle Egret crossed the Atlantic, probably flying from Africa to South America, where this species was first reported early in the present century. The birds gradually spread northward through the West Indies and into Florida, then up the east coast as far as southern Canada by the early 1960s. As sometimes happens when a new species invades a new territory, there has been a population explosion, and they are now abundant throughout the southern part of the country and are breeding as far north as New England. They follow livestock, feeding on insects flushed up from the grass.

218   **Upland Sandpiper**
"Upland Plover"
(*Bartramia longicauda*)
Sandpipers (Scolopacidae)

Description: 12″ (30 cm). Pigeon-sized. *Long neck and tail,* short bill, small head; overall

warm brown with a dark rump and
primaries.

Voice: Well known for its beautiful song,
whistled trills and mournful wind-like
sounds.

Habitat: Open grassland, prairies, and hayfields
in breeding season; also, while on
migration, open country generally.

Nesting: 4 pinkish-buff eggs with brown spots,
placed in a grass-lined nest in a hollow
on the ground.

Range: Alaska and central Canada to central
United States. Winters in southern
South America.

This attractive bird of open grasslands
was formerly shot in great numbers for
food and sport, until it became very
scarce. Now given complete protection,
it has increased once again. It often flies
with wings held stiffly in a downcurve,
like a Spotted Sandpiper, especially on
its nesting grounds. When alighting,
the "Grass Plover," as it was known to
hunters, holds its wings over its back
before folding them down in a resting
position. Until recently this bird has
been called the "Upland Plover."

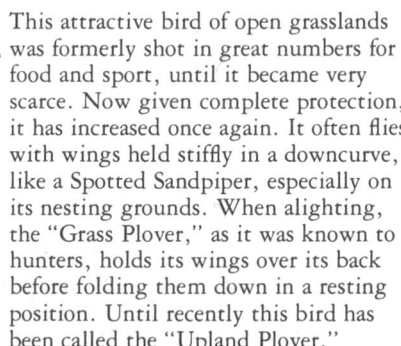

224 Buff-breasted Sandpiper
(*Tryngites subruficollis*)
Sandpipers (Scolopacidae)

Description: 8″ (20 cm). Robin-sized. *Rich buff
underparts and yellow legs;* short, straight
bill.

Voice: Low trilled *preet;* also *tic.*

Habitat: Short-grass fields, meadows, and
prairies. Breeds in dry tundra.

Nesting: 4 pale buff, brown-blotched eggs in a
grass-lined nest on the Arctic tundra.

Range: Arctic Alaska and northwestern
Canada. Scarce fall migrant on the east
coast. Winters on Argentine pampas.

This species looks like a small buff
edition of the Upland Sandpiper, at

times its grassland associate. It is very tame and when approached merely runs through the short grass instead of flying off. Like the American Golden Plover, it undertakes an amazing migration in both spring and fall. After the nesting season in the far Northwest, it migrates southward on a broad front, ending up on the Argentine pampas to spend the winter. On the return passage in spring its movements are much more confined, carrying it chiefly up the Mississippi Valley and to the West, but ultimately back to the arctic shores of Alaska and Canada.

235, 238 Killdeer
(*Charadrius vociferus*)
Plovers (Charadriidae)

Description: 9–11″ (23–28 cm). Robin-sized. Brown above and white below, with *two black bands* on the breast and a blackish bill. In flight, tail appears bright rufous. Often bobs its head.

Voice: Clear *kill-DEEE,* repeated endlessly.

Habitat: Open country generally—plowed fields, golf courses, and short-grass prairies.

Nesting: 4 pale buff, spotted eggs in a slight depression or scrape sparsely lined with grass on bare ground.

Range: Breeds from British Columbia, Mackenzie, and Newfoundland south to the West Indies, Mexico, and Peru. Winters regularly from New Jersey and Ohio southward.

This is probably our most familiar shorebird. Not only is it abundant and conspicuous, but its loud call compels attention. When the nest is approached, the adult feigns injury, hobbling along with wings dragging as if badly wounded. This behavior often succeeds in luring a predator away from the eggs or young; the bird then "recovers" and flies off calling loudly.

257 Bobwhite
(*Colinus virginianus*)
Quail, Partridges, Pheasants
(Phasianidae)

Description: 8–11″ (20–28 cm). A small, chunky,
brown bird; underparts pale and
streaked; *throat and eyebrow white in
males and buff in females.* Usually seen
in groups called coveys.

Voice: Clear whistled *bob-WHITE* or *poor-bob-
WHITE.* The assembly call for a covey
is a *ho-ha,* with each note higher than
the last.

Habitat: Pastures, grassy roadsides, and
farmlands.

Nesting: 10–15 white eggs in a grass-lined
hollow concealed in weeds or grass.

Range: Wyoming, Minnesota, Ontario, and
Massachusetts south to Florida, the
Gulf Coast, and Mexico. Introduced
locally elsewhere.

One of our most popular gamebirds,
the Bobwhite is undoubtedly more
numerous than it was when unbroken
forest covered most of the eastern
United States, but in recent years the
species has declined somewhat due to
the cutting of roadside brush,
trimming of farmland borders, and
gradual replacement of former pastures
with dense stands of young trees.
Outside the breeding season, Bobwhites
gather in coveys of roughly two dozen
birds, vigorously defending their
territory from other coveys.

259, 260 Sharp-tailed Grouse
(*Pedioecetes phasianellus*)
Grouse (Tetraonidae)

Description: 16–18″ (40–46 cm). Similar to the
Greater Prairie Chicken, but speckled
rather than barred and with a *pointed
tail edged with white.*

Voice: Dove-like *coo,* guttural clucks and

cackles. A booming sound during
courtship dance.

Habitat: Prairie grassland and grassy edges of
woodland.

Nesting: 8–12 olive eggs finely speckled with
dark brown in a shallow depression
sparsely lined with down.

Range: Alaska, northern Manitoba, and
Quebec south to Michigan, Colorado,
and Washington.

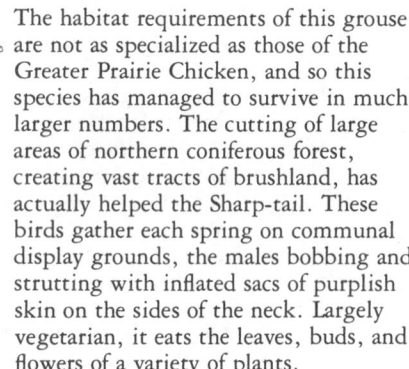

The habitat requirements of this grouse
are not as specialized as those of the
Greater Prairie Chicken, and so this
species has managed to survive in much
larger numbers. The cutting of large
areas of northern coniferous forest,
creating vast tracts of brushland, has
actually helped the Sharp-tail. These
birds gather each spring on communal
display grounds, the males bobbing and
strutting with inflated sacs of purplish
skin on the sides of the neck. Largely
vegetarian, it eats the leaves, buds, and
flowers of a variety of plants.

---

261 Greater Prairie Chicken
(*Tympanuchus cupido*)
Grouse (Tetraonidae)

Description: 16–18″ (40–46 cm). A chicken-like
bird with a short black tail, heavily
barred above and below with grayish
brown. Male has orange air sacs inflated
during courtship display and long black
feathers on sides of neck, erected into
"horns" during courtship; horns of
female shorter.

Voice: Hollow "booming" call during display;
also cackles and clucks.

Habitat: Undisturbed tall-grass prairie.

Nesting: 8–12 olive eggs finely spotted and
blotched with brown in a well-
concealed, shallow, grass-lined
depression in the ground.

Range: Locally in Wisconsin, Illinois, and
Michigan, and from Manitoba south

through the Great Plains to Oklahoma; also on the coastal prairies of Texas.

Once found from the Atlantic Coast west to Wyoming, the Greater Prairie Chicken has been exterminated from much of this vast range through the destruction of the undisturbed prairies on which it breeds. The eastern subspecies, known as the Heath Hen (*Tympanuchus cupido cupido*) became extinct; the form inhabiting the prairies along the Gulf Coast, Attwater's Prairie Chicken (*T. c. attwateri*), may follow its eastern relative into extinction in a few years. Where they still survive, Greater Prairie Chickens perform striking courtship dances on communal display grounds: the males strut about and stamp their feet with "horns" erected and yellow sacs of skin inflated on the sides of the neck, meanwhile uttering a deep cooing call that may carry a mile. They leap and whirl in the air and threaten each other by short runs with tail raised, head down, and feather tufts erected.

262 Lesser Prairie Chicken
(*Tympanuchus pallidicinctus*)
Grouse (Tetraonidae)

Description: 16″ (40 cm). A smaller and paler edition of the Greater Prairie Chicken. In the male, the air sacs on the neck are reddish, rather than yellowish.

Voice: Various cackling and clucking notes; the male "booms" during courtship.

Habitat: Sandy prairies and plains, especially where there is a growth of shrubby oak.

Nesting: 11 to 13 creamy or buff-colored eggs in a grass-lined depression, usually under a low bush or shrub.

Range: Resident in southern Colorado and Kansas, south locally in western Oklahoma, Texas, and eastern New Mexico.

As in the Greater Prairie Chicken, males of this species gather and engage in communal courtship displays in which the birds dance about with the colorful air sacs on their necks inflated and uttering low cooing or "booming" notes. This species replaces the Greater Prairie Chicken in more arid grasslands; some authorities consider the two to be members of a single species.

267 Gray Partridge
(*Perdix perdix*)
Quail, Partridges, Pheasants
(Phasianidae)

Description: 12–14″ (30–35 cm). A small, stocky, chicken-like bird, largely gray with a black "U"-shaped mark on the underparts and a *rust-colored tail*.

Voice: Hoarse *kee-ah*. When flushed, a rapid cackle.

Habitat: Grainfields, agricultural grasslands.

Nesting: 10–20 olive eggs in a shallow depression lined with grass and concealed in vegetation.

Range: Introduced and locally established in Nova Scotia, New Brunswick, northern New York, Ontario, Ohio, Indiana, southern Michigan, Iowa, Minnesota, and across the northern part of the United States to British Columbia. Introduction in the East has been generally unsuccessful. Native to Eurasia.

Also called "Hungarian Partridge," this species is well adapted to areas of intensive agriculture, where no native gamebird can exist. It forms coveys outside the breeding season, like the Bobwhite, but does not defend a territory. In the spring the flocks break up into pairs. While the male takes no part in incubating the eggs, he does help care for the young, which leave the nest soon after hatching. The Gray

Partridge's high reproductive rate enables it to withstand hunting, predators, and cold snowy northern winters, all of which take a heavy toll.

---

271 Roadrunner
(*Geococcyx californianus*)
Cuckoos (Cuculidae)

Description: 24" (61 cm). Crow-sized. A long-legged, gray-brown *long-tailed* ground bird with a *bushy crest*. Bright yellow eyes at close range.

Voice: Clucks, crows, dove-like coos, dog-like whines, and hoarse guttural notes.

Habitat: Open arid country with plenty of thickets to serve as cover.

Nesting: 3–5 ivory-colored eggs in a flat stick nest lined with grass, usually in thick shrub or cactus not far aboveground.

Range: Breeds in Central California, Nevada, Utah, Colorado, Kansas, Oklahoma, Arkansas, and Louisiana south to Central Mexico.

The comical-looking Roadrunner, or "Chaparral Cock" as it is called by cowboys, would rather run than fly. With its twisting and turning in and out of cactus thickets, it can easily outdistance a man. The bird jerks its tail from side to side or up and down; it also elevates its bushy crest when excited. It eats a variety of animal foods, including small snakes, lizards, mice, scorpions, and insects.

---

274 Ring-necked Pheasant
(*Phasianus colchicus*)
Quail, Partridges, Pheasants
(Phasianidae)

Description: 30–36" (76–91 cm). Larger than a chicken, with a long, pointed tail. Male has a red eye-patch, brilliant green head, and white neck-ring; body patterned in soft brown and iridescent russet. Female is a mottled sandy brown with shorter tail.

Voice: Loud crowing *cuck-cuck* accompanied by a resonant beating of the wings. When alarmed they fly off with a loud cackle.

Habitat: Farmlands, pastures, and grassy woodland edges.

Nesting: 6–15 buff-olive eggs in a grass-lined depression concealed in dense grass or weeds

Range: Introduced from British Columbia, Alberta, Minnesota, Ontario and the Maritime Provinces south to New Jersey, Maryland, Oklahoma, and Central California. Native to Asia.

The North American birds of this species are descended from stock brought from several different parts of the Old World and thus are somewhat variable. They are very tolerant of man, often nesting on the outskirts of large cities. Although successful in most grassland habitats, its North American headquarters is the central plains. After the breakup of winter flocks, males establish large territories and mate with several females. At first the chicks feed largely on insects, but soon shift to the adult diet of berries, seeds, buds, and leaves.

---

275 Common Nighthawk
(*Chordeiles minor*)
Nightjars (Caprimulgidae)

Description: 10″ (25 cm). W. 23″ (0.6 m). Blue Jay-sized, usually seen in flight. Dark with long, pointed wings and *white patches on the outer wing.* Perches motionless and lengthwise on branches.

Voice: Loud, nasal, buzzy *peent* or *pee-yah*.

Habitat: Aerial, but open country generally; also cities and towns.

Nesting: 2 eggs, whitish to olive, with dark blotches, laid on soil, rocks, logs, or rooftop gravel.

Range: Canada to Panama and the West Indies; winters in South America.

Its name is somewhat inappropriate, since it is not strictly nocturnal, often flying in sunlight, and it is not a hawk, although it does "hawk," or catch flying insects on the wing. On its breeding grounds the male does a power dive, and then, as it swerves upward, makes a booming sound with its wings. Its capacity to consume insects is prodigious. Analysis of stomach contents has shown that in a single day one bird captured over 500 mosquitoes and another ate 2175 flying ants.

283 Burrowing Owl
(*Athene cunicularia*)
True Owls (Strigidae)

Description: 9″ (23 cm). Pigeon-sized. Short-tailed and long-legged; yellow eyes; no ear tufts; *face framed in white with a blackish collar.*

Voice: Liquid cackling; also a mellow *coo-coooo,* repeated twice.

Habitat: Plains, deserts, fields, and airports.

Nesting: 5–7 white eggs in a long underground burrow nest lined with grasses, roots, and dung.

Range: Southwestern Canada, Florida, and the West Indies to Tierra del Fuego.

This comical little bird is one of the most diurnal of all owls. It often perches near its hole, and when approached too closely will bob up and down and finally dive into its burrow rather than take flight. The burrows have usually been abandoned by prairie dogs or pocket gophers, but the owls are quite capable of digging their own.

291 **Barn Owl**
(*Tyto alba*)
Barn Owls (Tytonidae)

Description: 18" (46 cm). W. 44" (1.1 m). Crow-sized. Buff-brown above and white below, with *heart-shaped face* and numerous small dark dots on white underparts; *dark eyes,* long legs.

Voice: Its weird calls include rapid grackle-like clicks, hissing notes, screams, guttural grunts, and bill snapping.

Habitat: Open country, forest edge and clearings, cultivated areas, and cities.

Nesting: 5–10 white eggs on bare wood or stone in buildings, hollow trees, caves, or even ground burrows.

Range: Nearly worldwide; in America from southernmost Canada to Tierra del Fuego.

This nocturnal ghost of a bird frequents such places as belfries, deserted buildings, and hollow trees. It hunts its food—almost entirely rodents—in garbage dumps, neglected cemeteries, rundown farms, and similar waste lots of large cities. Contrary to popular belief, owls see well by day but their large eyes give them especially good night vision. Recent experiments have shown, however, that Barn Owls depend on keen hearing to locate prey. These owls appear to practice birth control: when food is scarce they lay fewer eggs or do not breed at all.

292 **Snowy Owl**
(*Nyctea scandiaca*)
True Owls (Strigidae)

Description: 24" (61 cm). W. 55" (1.4 m). A big and round-headed owl, from *pure white* to white with dark spotting. Female is larger and darker than the male.

Voice: Usually silent; a hoarse croak and a

shrill whistle are heard on the breeding grounds.

Habitat: Open country: tundra, dunes, marshes, fields, and plains.

Nesting: 5–8 white eggs on open tundra with a lining of feathers, mosses, and lichens.

Range: Circumpolar. Breeds in America, in Aleutians, arctic Alaska, and Canada; winters irregularly south to California, Texas, Missouri, and the Carolinas.

This great white owl is a beautiful sight as it perches upright on a fence post or flies over a marsh. Strictly a bird of open country, it is practically never seen in a tree; it sits on the ground, a rooftop, or other exposed resting place. In the Far North where it breeds, it depends largely on the lemming supply for food. Lemmings undergo periodic population changes (due to population explosion and subsequent epidemics), and when their numbers decrease the owls must migrate southward to avoid starvation. In our latitudes the owls prey on rabbits and other game, or even on dead fish on ocean beaches. In large refuse dumps they prey on Norway rats.

295 Rough-legged Hawk
(*Buteo lagopus*)
Hawks, Eagles (Accipitridae)

Description: 19–24″ (48–61 cm). W. 52″ (1.3 m). A large, long-winged hawk that often hovers. Tail white at the base and dark at the tip; head and neck gray-brown, belly blackish. All-dark and intermediate forms also occur, and can usually be identified by the tail pattern.

Voice: Loud or soft whistles, often in a descending scale.

Habitat: Tundra; winters on open plains, agricultural areas, and marshes.

Nesting: Usually 3 or 4 pale green eggs spotted with black in a mass of moss and sticks placed on a cliff or rocky outcropping in the tundra.

Range: Aleutians, northern Alaska and Baffin Island south to Manitoba and Newfoundland. Winters irregularly south to California and Virginia. Also breeds in Eurasia.

The number of eggs laid by the Rough-leg, like the Snowy Owl, depends on the food supply, with larger clutches occurring in years when lemmings are abundant. At a distance this hawk can be identified by its habit of hovering and by the way it perches: balancing precariously on the most slender twigs at the top of a tree.

299 Swainson's Hawk
(*Buteo swainsoni*)
Hawks, Eagles (Accipitridae)

Description: 18–22″ (45–56 cm). W. 49″ (1.2 m). A large hawk with longer, more pointed wings than the Red-tail. Uniform brown above, white below with brown breast; tail dark brown and indistinctly banded. Young birds similar to immature Red-tails but tend to have darker markings on the breast whereas young Red-tails are more heavily marked on flanks and belly. A rare all-dark form also occurs.

Voice: Long, plaintive, whistled *kreee*.

Habitat: Open plains, grasslands, and prairies.

Nesting: 2–4 white eggs, unmarked or lightly spotted with brown or black, in a nest comprising a large mass of sticks often placed conspicuously in an isolated tree.

Range: Alaska and Mackenzie south to northern Mexico and Texas. Winters chiefly in South America and often migrates eastward to Florida, where small numbers winter.

This species is a highly gregarious *Buteo,* often migrating in great soaring

flocks containing thousands of birds. Its migrations are longer than those of the other species; most individuals go all the way to Argentina to spend the winter, making a round trip of as much as 17,000 miles. On their breeding grounds in the western plains, this hawk preys mainly on rodents and huge numbers of grasshoppers. It is named after the English naturalist William Swainson (1789–1855).

301 White-tailed Hawk
(*Buteo albicaudatus*)
Hawks, Eagles (Accipitridae)

Description: 21–23" (53–58 cm). W. 48" (1.2 m). Adult gray above, white below, with a narrow but conspicuous black band on its white tail and a rufous shoulder patch. Immature birds dark with a gray tail.

Voice: Musical *ke-ke-ke-ke-ke* or *cutta-cutta-cutta-cutta*.

Habitat: Coastal prairie, grassland, and scrub in semiarid country.

Nesting: 2 dull white or very pale blue eggs, unmarked or lightly spotted with brown, in a grass-lined stick nest in low bushes, cacti, and small trees.

Range: Extreme southern Texas to southern South America.

This handsome and conspicuous hawk is a common sight in south Texas where it is found perched along highways on telephone poles, fence posts, or dead trees. Its principal food is rabbits, but it is an opportunist, gathering in flocks with other hawks at brush fires to feed on rodents, rabbits, lizards, and insects driven out by the flames. Like other *Buteo* hawks, it rides the air currents on motionless wings, often soaring to great heights.

303 White-tailed Kite
(*Elanus leucurus*)
Hawks, Eagles (Accipitridae)

Description: 15–16″ (38–40 cm). W. 40″ (1 m). A delicate, graceful, gull-like bird of prey. *Largely white,* with a gray back, black patch on upper and under surfaces of the *pointed wings; tail white.* The back and breast of young birds are streaked with warm brown. Often dangles its feet in flight.

Voice: Whistled *keep-keep-keep.* Also a longer, plaintive *kreep.*

Habitat: Farmlands and prairies with scattered trees or fencerows; mesquite grasslands.

Nesting: 3–5 white, brown-spotted eggs in a well-made platform of twigs lined with grass and placed in a tall tree, usually near water.

Range: Southern California and southern Texas to Chile and Argentina. Formerly occurred also from South Carolina to Florida. Nonmigratory.

The tame, elegant White-tailed Kite was formerly shot in large numbers by farmers who thought it threatened their chickens, although the birds feed almost entirely on insects and a few rodents. The North American population was reduced to a pitiful remnant, and it was feared that the species might become extinct here. Recently, however, it has staged a surprising and unexplained comeback, and is again rather numerous in Texas and California. An allied species in southern Europe and Africa has also increased in numbers, perhaps as a result of some subtle environmental change.

312 Caracara
(Caracara cheriway)
Falcons (Falconidae)

Description: 20–22" (51–56 cm). W. 48" (1.2 m).
Dark brown, with black cap and bare
red face; white throat, neck, base of
tail, and wing tips; black band at tip of
tail.

Voice: High, harsh cackle.

Habitat: Prairies, savannahs, and semi-arid areas
with open groves of palms, mesquites,
and cacti.

Nesting: 2 or 3 white eggs with heavy brown
spots and blotches in a nest made of
twigs, grasses, weeds, and briars lined
with leaves and mosses; set in palmetto
hammocks or live oaks, rarely on the
ground.

Range: Central and southern Florida, where it
is becoming scarce; local in the
southern portions of Texas and Arizona.
South to southern South America.

This scavenger has probably the most
varied diet of any bird of prey. It often
accompanies and dominates vultures at
fresh kills or carrion and also eats small
animals. It is primarily a ground-
inhabiting falcon of open prairies; its
long legs enable it to walk and run
with ease. It is the national emblem of
Mexico.

314 American Kestrel
"Sparrow Hawk"
(Falco sparverius)
Falcons (Falconidae)

Description: 9–12" (23–30 cm). W. 21" (0.5 m).
Jay-sized. Wings long and pointed, tail
long. May be recognized in any
plumage by its *rusty tail and back*. The
adult male has pale blue-gray wings,
rusty in the female. Often seen
hovering.

Voice: Shrill *killy-killy-killy.*

Habitat: Towns and cities, parks, farmlands, and open country.

Nesting: 4 or 5 brown-spotted white eggs placed without nest or lining in a natural or man-made cavity.

Range: Alaska, the Northwest Territories, and Newfoundland south to Tierra del Fuego. Winters from British Columbia, Illinois, and New England southward.

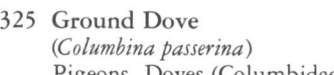

Unlike the larger falcons it has adapted to man and nests even in our largest cities, where it preys chiefly on House Sparrows. In the countryside it takes insects, small birds, and rodents, capturing its prey on the ground rather than in the air like other falcons. The female does most of the incubating and is fed by the male. As he nears the nest with food he calls; the female flies to him and receives the food away from the nest. After the eggs hatch, the male brings most of the food. The young stay with the adults for a time after fledging, and it is not uncommon to see family parties in late summer. This species was formerly called "Sparrow Hawk."

325 Ground Dove
(*Columbina passerina*)
Pigeons, Doves (Columbidae)

Description: 6½" (16 cm). Sparrow-sized. A short-tailed, brown dove with much *rufous in the wings and a heavily scaled breast*.

Voice: Soft cooing with rising inflection.

Habitat: Open areas such as fields, gardens, farmland, and roadsides.

Nesting: 2 white eggs on or close to the ground. The nest is often hidden in a tuft of grass or among weeds.

Range: Southern United States to northern South America. Not migratory.

This bird, as its name implies, spends much of its time on the ground, and is

most commonly seen when flushed from a roadside or path in a brushy pasture. It is a rather retiring bird, and is somewhat locally distributed.

329 Barn Swallow
(*Hirundo rustica*)
Swallows (Hirundinidae)

Description: 5¾–7¾″ (15–20 cm). Sparrow-sized. Our most familiar swallow, and the only one with a *deeply forked tail*. Upperparts dark steel-blue, underparts creamy buff, throat and forehead rusty.

Voice: Constant liquid twittering and chattering.

Habitat: Agricultural land, suburban areas, marshes, lake shores.

Nesting: 4–6 brown-spotted white eggs in a solid cup of mud reinforced with grass, lined with feathers and soft plant material, and placed on a rafter in a building or on a sheltered ledge.

Range: Aleutians west to Unalaska Island, Alaska and the Maritime Provinces to the Carolinas, Arkansas, and Mexico; winters in South America. Also in Eurasia.

The great majority of these birds now nest on or in buildings, but originally they used rocky ledges over streams and perhaps attached their nests to tree trunks in the shelter of branches (as do related species in Africa). Barn Swallows perform long migrations; some that breed in North America winter as far south as Argentina. Like other swallows, they migrate by day, often feeding as they travel. They are swift and graceful fliers, and it is estimated that they cover as much as 600 miles a day in quest of food for their young.

330 Cliff Swallow
(*Petrochelidon pyrrhonota*)
Swallows (Hirundinidae)

Description: 5–6″ (13–15 cm). Sparrow-sized. A
stocky, square-tailed swallow with *pale
buff rump*. Upperparts dull steel-blue,
underparts buff-white; throat dark
chestnut, forehead white. Cave Swallow
of Texas and New Mexico is similar
but smaller, with darker rump and
buff throat.

Voice: Constant squeaky chattering and
twittering.

Habitat: Open country near buildings or cliffs;
lake shores and marshes in migration.

Nesting: 4–6 white eggs in a gourd-shaped
structure of mud lined with feathers
and placed on a sheltered cliff face or
under eaves (in New England they are
called Eave Swallows). In colonies.

Range: Alaska, Ontario, and Nova Scotia south
to Virginia, Missouri, and Central
America. Winters in South America.

As its name implies, this swallow
originally nested on cliffs. The
introduction of House Sparrows was a
disaster for these birds, since the
sparrows usurp their nests and often
cause the swallows to abandon a colony.
Long, cold, rainy spells while the young
are in the nest cause widespread
mortality since the adults are unable to
obtain enough insects.

351 Red-headed Woodpecker
(*Melanerpes erythrocephalus*)
Woodpeckers (Picidae)

Description: 10″ (25 cm). Jay-sized. Strikingly
colored: *entire head red,* wings and tail
bluish-black, white below, *large white
wing patch on each wing* and a white
rump, conspicuous in flight. Immature
resembles the adult except for its gray
head.

Voice: Various chirps, cackles, and squawks. Most often a loud *churr-churr* and *yarrow-yarrow-yarrow*.

Habitat: Open country, farms, rural roads, open park-like woodland, and golf courses.

Nesting: 5 white eggs placed without nest lining in a cavity in a tree, telephone pole, or fence post.

Range: Saskatchewan, Manitoba, and Quebec south to Florida, the Gulf Coast, and New Mexico. Scarce in northeastern states. Winters in southern South America.

These woodpeckers are fond of open agricultural country with groves of dead and dying trees, particularly orchards. They often fly-catch, swooping low across a highway or along the shoulder of a road after flying insects. Red-headed Woodpeckers are driven off by aggressive Starlings, which occupy the nest holes, and by the removal of dead trees. Like the California Woodpecker, they store nuts and acorns, hiding them in holes and crevices. One was observed putting acorns into a hole in a post that was open at the other end; it never discovered where its acorns went.

365 Palm Warbler
(*Dendroica palmarum*)
Wood Warblers (Parulidae)

Description: 5½" (14 cm). An olive-drab, streaked, ground-feeding warbler with bright olive rump, bright yellow undertail coverts, and a *distinctive habit of wagging its tail.* The underparts vary from yellow to dull whitish, depending on age and geography; adults in spring have a *rufous cap.*

Voice: Weak, dry trill like that of a Chipping Sparrow but slower.

Habitat: In summer, bogs in the North; during migration, open places, especially weedy fields and borders of marshes.

Nesting: 4 or 5 white, brown-speckled eggs in a grass nest with shreds of bark lined with feathers and rootlets, placed on the ground in a grass clump, often at the base of a small tree or bush.

Range: Central Canada to the extreme northern portions of the United States. Winters from southern United States to the West Indies and Honduras.

The Palm Warbler is one of the first warblers to arrive in the spring, and at this season is commonly found feeding quietly on the ground, sometimes with flocks of sparrows. It is unusual among warblers of the genus *Dendroica* in nesting on the ground; the only other species that does this is the rare Kirtland's Warbler.

385, 386 American Goldfinch
(*Carduelis tristis*)
Grosbeaks, Buntings, Finches, Sparrows (Fringillidae)

Description: 4½–5" (11–14 cm). Smaller than a sparrow. Breeding male *bright yellow* with a white rump, *black forehead, white edges on black wings and tail,* and yellow at bend of wing. Female and winter male duller and grayer with black wings, tail, and white wing bars. Travels in flocks; undulating flight.

Voice: Bright *per*-chick-*o-ree,* also rendered as *potato-chips,* delivered in flight and coinciding with each undulation.

Habitat: Brushy thickets, weedy grasslands, and nearby trees.

Nesting: 4 or 5 pale blue eggs in a well-made cup of grass, bark strips, and plant down placed in the upright fork of a small sapling or a shrub.

Range: Southeastern British Columbia and Newfoundland south to Georgia, Arkansas, central Oklahoma, southern Colorado, central Utah, and Baja California; widespread in the Northeast.

Winters south to the Gulf Coast and southern Mexico.

This familiar and common species is often called the "Wild Canary." Since their main food is seeds, nesting does not begin until midsummer or late summer, when weed seeds are available. Thus goldfinches remain in flocks until well past the time when other species have formed pairs and are nesting. Because they nest so late, only a single brood is raised each season. In the winter they gather in large flocks, often with other finches such as redpolls and siskins.

391 Western Meadowlark
(*Sturnella neglecta*)
Orioles, Blackbirds (Icteridae)

Description: 8½–11" (21–28 cm). Robin-sized. Streaked brown above, bright yellow below, with a bold black "V" on the breast. Very similar to Eastern Meadowlark, but *upperparts paler, and yellow of throat extending onto cheeks*. Best told by voice.

Voice: Rich, flute-like jumble of gurgling notes, usually descending the scale; very different from the Eastern Meadowlark's series of simple, plaintive whistles.

Habitat: Meadows, plains, and prairies.

Nesting: 3–7 white eggs with dark brown and purple spots in a domed cup of grass and weed stems concealed in grass or weeds.

Range: British Columbia, Manitoba, northern Michigan, and northwestern Ohio south to Louisiana, central Texas, and northern Mexico. Has spread eastward in recent years. Winters north to Nebraska and Utah.

The clearing of eastern North American forests has caused this species to extend its range eastward beyond the Great Lakes, where it has occasionally interbred with the Eastern Meadowlark. They are so similar that it was not until 1844 that Audubon noticed the difference and named the western bird *neglecta* because it had been overlooked for so long. The song of the Western Meadowlark is often heard on Hollywood sound tracks even when the movie setting is far from the bird's range.

392 Eastern Meadowlark
(*Sturnella magna*)
Orioles, Blackbirds (Icteridae)

Description: 9–11" (23–28 cm). Robin-sized. A stocky brown-streaked bird with *white-edged tail; throat and breast bright yellow, breast crossed by a black "V."* Western Meadowlark is very similar, but paler above and the yellow of its throat extends onto cheeks. Best distinguished by voice.

Voice: Clear, mellow whistle, *see-you, see-yeeeer;* a loud rattling alarm note.

Habitat: Meadows, pastures, and prairies; in migration, in open country generally.

Nesting: 3-7 white eggs spotted with brown and dull lavender in a partly domed structure of grass concealed in a depression in a meadow.

Range: Breeds from southeastern Ontario, Nova Scotia, Minnesota, southwestern South Dakota, New Mexico, and Arizona through Central America to northern South America. Winters as far north as New England and Nebraska.

One of the best-known birds of American farmlands, its cheerful song, usually delivered from a conspicuous perch, is familiar in most rural areas. Meadowlarks are often polygamous; more than one female may be found nesting in the territory of a single male.

Because they often breed in hayfields, the nests may be destroyed by mowing; unless the season is well advanced, they will normally nest again. In migration and winter they band together in groups of up to a dozen birds and can be found in almost any open, grassy area.

418 Scissor-tailed Flycatcher
(*Muscivora forficata*)
Tyrant Flycatchers (Tyrannidae)

Description: 14″ (35 cm), of which more than half is a very *long and deeply forked black-and-white tail;* adult has *bright salmon-pink sides and belly;* head, upper back, and breast pale grayish-white.

Voice: Harsh *kee-kee-kee-kee.* Also a chattering and twittering like that of the Kingbird.

Habitat: Open country along roadsides and on ranches with scattered trees and bushes; also fence wires and posts.

Nesting: 5 creamy, brown-spotted eggs in a bulky stick nest lined with soft fibrous material and placed in an isolated tree.

Range: South-central United States north to Missouri and Nebraska. Winters from Mexico to Panama and on the Florida Keys.

These conspicuous flycatchers attract the attention of the most casual passerby. They are especially numerous in southern Texas, and one may see many in a day's drive by watching fence posts and wires along the road. Scissor-tails are as noisy and aggressive as kingbirds and will chase birds much larger than themselves. In spring they put on a wonderful aerial courtship display. With their long scissor-like tail they can maneuver and "sky-dance" gracefully. Nearly all of their food is captured on the wing; included in their diet are many insects harmful to agriculture.

421 Northern Shrike
(*Lanius excubitor*)
Shrikes (Laniidae)

Description: 9–10½″ (23–26 cm). Robin-sized. Pale
gray above, white below, with faint
barring on underparts and a bold black
mask *ending at bill.* Black tail with white
edges. Stout, hooked bill. Usually seen
perched in the top of a tree in the open.

Voice: Mixture of warbles and harsh tones
with a Robin-like quality.

Habitat: Open woodlands and brushy swamps in
summer; open grasslands with fence
posts and scattered trees in winter.

Nesting: 4–6 pale gray eggs spotted with dark
gray and brown. Nest a large mass of
twigs, lichens, moss, and feathers,
usually in a dense conifer.

Range: Alaska and the Labrador Peninsula to
Quebec, Saskatchewan, and northern
British Columbia. Winters south to
Virginia, Texas, and northern
California.

Unusual among songbirds, shrikes prey
on small birds and rodents, catching
them with the bill and sometimes
impaling them on thorns or barbed wire
for storage. Like other northern birds
that depend on rodent populations, the
Northern Shrike's movements are
cyclical, becoming more adundant in
the South when northern rodent
populations are low. At times they hunt
from an open perch, where they sit
motionless until prey appears; at other
times they hover in the air ready to
pounce on anything that moves.

422 Loggerhead Shrike
(*Lanius ludovicianus*)
Shrikes (Laniidae)

Description: 8–10″ (20–25 cm). Robin-sized.
Slightly smaller than a Northern

Shrike, pale gray above, white below, with black face mask *extending over the bill;* dark crown.

Voice: Variety of harsh and musical notes and trills. A thrasher-like series of double phrases.

Habitat: Grasslands, orchards, and open areas, with scattered trees; open grassy woodlands; deserts in the West.

Nesting: 4–6 white eggs, spotted with gray and brown, in a bulky mass of twigs and grass lined with plant down and feathers, set in a thorny shrub or tree.

Range: Breeds from southern British Columbia, central Alberta, central Saskatchewan, southern Manitoba, southern Ontario, southern Quebec, and Maritime Provinces to southern Florida, the Gulf Coast, and Mexico. Winters north to Virginia and northern California.

In the southern half of North America this species is the counterpart of the Northern Shrike of boreal regions of Alaska and Canada. In behavior and choice of habitat the two species are essentially similar although the Loggerhead preys on insects more than its northern relative. Its flight is undulating with alternate rapid fluttering and gliding. Since it has no talons, it impales its prey—usually a small bird, mouse, or insect—on a thorn or barbed wire fence to facilitate tearing it apart then or at a later time; hence its other name, "Butcher Bird."

423 Eastern Kingbird
(*Tyrannus tyrannus*)
Tyrant Flycatchers (Tyrannidae)

Description: 8½" (21 cm). Dark gray above, blackish on head, white below; *black tail with white tip;* usually-concealed red crown patch.

Voice: Harsh and strident notes, often

ascending, like *killy-killy-killy,* and
others that sound like squeaky
chattering.

Habitat: Open country; farms, orchards,
roadsides, and lake and river shores.

Nesting: 3 or 4 creamy white eggs in a stick nest
lined with grass, rootlets, and hair
placed in a tree or bush.

Range: Central Canada to southern United
States. Winters from Peru to Bolivia.

These noisy, conspicuous birds are
named for their aggressive behavior,
often driving away birds much larger
than themselves, such as crows and
hawks, especially near their nests. In
late summer and early fall they often
flock, and large numbers pursue flying
insects; they also feed on wild berries,
which they deftly pluck while on the
wing.

---

440 **Eastern Bluebird**
(*Sialia sialis*)
Thrushes (Turdidae)

Description: 7″ (17 cm). Sexes similar; the male
*bright blue above with a reddish-brown
breast and white belly;* the female is
duller.

Voice: Its call, when flying overhead, is an
unmistakable liquid and musical *turee*
or *queedle.* Song is a soft melodious
warble.

Habitat: Open farmlands with scattered trees.

Nesting: 4–6 pale blue eggs in a loose cup of
grasses and plant stems in natural tree
cavities, old woodpecker holes, fence
posts, and bird boxes.

Range: East of the Rockies from southern
Canada to the Gulf of Mexico and as far
as the mountains of central Mexico.

This beautiful bird is a favorite of many
people and is eagerly awaited in the
spring after a long, cold winter. In
places where Bluebird nest-boxes are

erected and Starlings and House Sparrows are controlled, up to six pairs of bluebirds will nest on as many acres. In the past 25 years bluebirds have become uncommon in the East for reasons not altogether clear. Competition for nest sites may be a critical factor.

441 Mountain Bluebird
(*Sialia currucoides*)
Thrushes (Turdidae)

Description: 7″ (18 cm). Male pure sky blue above, paler blue below, with a white abdomen; female similar but duller and grayer.

Voice: Soft warbling notes.

Habitat: Breeds in high mountain meadows with scattered trees and bushes; in winter descends to lower elevations, where it occurs on plains and grasslands.

Nesting: 5 or 6 pale blue eggs, in a nest of grass and plant fibers in a natural cavity or bird box.

Range: Southern Alaska, Mackenzie, and Manitoba south to western Nebraska, New Mexico, Arizona, and southern California; winters from British Columbia and Montana south through the western United States to central Mexico.

This species has longer wings and a more graceful, swallow-like flight than the Eastern Bluebird. In eastern North America, it is known mainly as a winter visitor to the western plains. These birds usually travel in small parties, and search for food by hovering in the air and dropping down to pick up insects on the ground.

467 Western Kingbird
(Tyrannus verticalis)
Tyrant Flycatchers (Tyrannidae)

Description: 9″ (23 cm). Robin-sized. Pale gray
above, yellow below with white throat;
black tail edged with white.

Voice: Noisy chattering and twittering; also a
sharp *whit.*

Habitat: Open country; ranches, roadsides,
streams, and ponds with trees.

Nesting: 4 creamy white eggs in a stick nest
lined with plant fibers and placed in a
tree or bush.

Range: British Columbia, Manitoba, and
Minnesota, south to Kansas, Oklahoma,
and northern Mexico. Winters mainly
in Central America.

Like the Horned Lark, the Western
Kingbird has benefited from the
cutting of forests; the species has moved
eastward in recent decades. During fall
migration a few are always seen along
the Atlantic Coast. In the Southwest,
especially in arid regions, there are two
other kingbirds, Cassin's and Tropical,
that look like the Western; however,
the Western is distinguished by white
feathers on the sides of the black tail.

510 Wheatear
(Oenanthe oenanthe)
Thrushes (Turdidae)

Description: 5½–6″ (14–15 cm). A very rare,
sparrow-sized bird of open ground.
Warm brown above, buff-pink below;
bold white rump and sides of tail contrast
with black center and tip of tail, which
form an inverted "T."

Voice: Harsh *chak-chak!;* song a jumble of
warbling notes.

Habitat: Barren pastures and beaches in winter;
nests in rocky tundra.

Nesting: 5–7 pale green eggs in a fur-lined cup
of grass concealed under a rock, in a

rabbit burrow, or in a crevice in a wall.

Range: Alaska, Greenland, and northern Canada, appearing very rarely in northern U.S. Also in Eurasia and North Africa.

This Old World species has recently colonized North America from two directions, Siberian birds entering Alaska and European birds crossing to Greenland. Each fall these birds retrace their routes, wintering in Africa where many of the 17 other species of wheatears are found. Occasionally one turns up in populated parts of North America in spring and fall. The scientific name *Oenanthe* is from the Ancient Greek meaning "wine-flower," alluding to the fact that these birds return to Greece in the spring just as the vineyards blossom.

515, 570 Brewer's Blackbird
(*Euphagus cyanocephalus*)
Orioles, Blackbirds (Icteridae)

Description: 8–10″ (20–25 cm). Robin-sized. Male is solid black with purplish-blue iridescent head and yellow eyes. Female is gray with dark eyes. Similar to Rusty Blackbird, but male Rusty has green reflections on head; female Rusty has yellow eyes and jerks its head as it walks.

Voice: Gurgles, squawks, and whistles.

Habitat: Prairies, fields, and farm yards.

Nesting: 3–5 gray eggs with dark brown spots in a nest of coarse grass and twigs reinforced with mud and lined with fine grass and hair, placed on the ground or in a tree. Forms loose colonies of up to 30 pairs.

Range: British Columbia and Manitoba east to the Great Lakes and south to Indiana, Texas, and northern Mexico. Winters north to Tennessee and southern British Columbia.

This blackbird, named for 19th century ornithologist Dr. Thomas M. Brewer of Boston, is best known as a winter visitor to stockyards and farms, where it feeds on spilled grain. It also takes insects that are stirred up by livestock and plows. It nests in hayfields, but its young are usually fledged before the hay is harvested. During breeding season it has an elaborate display that includes fluffing out the feathers, wing quivering, cocking the tail, and pointing the bill upward.

517, 574 Bronzed Cowbird
"Red-eyed Cowbird"
(*Molothrus aeneus*)
Orioles, Blackbirds (Icteridae)

Description: 8½" (21 cm). Sexes similar; bronze-black with bluish-black wings and tail. Prominent red eye can be seen at close range. Brown-headed Cowbird smaller with a distinctive brown head.

Voice: Wheezy and guttural whistling notes and various squeaks and squeals.

Habitat: Pastures, roadside thickets, ranches, open country generally; also parks and orchards.

Nesting: 1–3 blue-green eggs laid in other birds' nests, particularly nests of orioles, tanagers, flycatchers, buntings, and grosbeaks, more rarely thrashers and thrushes.

Range: Southern portions of Arizona, New Mexico, and south central Texas through Mexico and Central America to western Panama.

Until recently called "Red-eyed Cowbird." During courtship both sexes, especially the males, erect their neck feathers into a ruff. The males bow and jump up and down, whistling unmusical squeaky calls, Like their close relatives, the Brown-headed Cowbirds, these birds follow livestock, especially cattle, snapping up insects flushed from the grass. They alight on the backs and necks of livestock to feed on ticks. Cowbirds also feed extensively on seeds and grain. During the colder months these birds form enormous flocks and move around the countryside with other species of blackbirds.

527 Lark Sparrow
(*Chondestes grammacus*)
Grosbeaks, Buntings, Finches, Sparrows (Fringillidae)

Description: 5½–6½" (14–16 cm). Head boldly patterned with black, chestnut, and white; streaked above; white below with a black spot in the center of the breast; tail black with white edges.

Voice: Alternating buzzes and melodious trills.

Habitat: Grassland with scattered bushes and trees; open country generally in winter.

Nesting: 3–5 white eggs, heavily spotted with dark brown and black, in a well-made cup of grass and plant stems on the ground or in a bush.

Range: British Columbia, Saskatchewan, northern Minnesota, and southern Ontario to Alabama, Louisiana, and northern Mexico. Winters from the Gulf Coast and California south to El Salvador. It has long been recorded along the eastern seaboard in fall.

The easiest way to find Lark Sparrows is to drive through grasslands and watch for the birds to fly up into trees along the road. The nests of Mockingbirds have been found with the eggs of both species in them, but it is not clear whether the sparrows have simply taken over an abandoned nest or have driven away the original occupants; since Mockingbirds are very aggressive, the latter seems unlikely.

531 Tree Sparrow
(Spizella arborea)
Grosbeaks, Buntings, Finches,
Sparrows (Fringillidae)

Description: 5½–6½" (14–16 cm). Gray head with
rufous crown and ear-stripe; streaked
brown above; plain gray below with
dark spot in center of breast. Similar to
Field Sparrow but larger and without
white eye-ring or pink bill.

Voice: One or two clear notes followed by a
sweet, rapid warble. Winter feeding call
a silvery *tsee-ler.*

Habitat: Arctic willow and birch thickets, fields,
weedy woodland edges, and roadside
thickets in winter.

Nesting: 4 or 5 pale blue eggs speckled with
brown in a bulky, well-insulated cup of
bark strips and weed stems lined with
feathers and hair, concealed in low
tundra vegetation.

Range: Alaska, northern Saskatchewan, northern
Manitoba, and northern Quebec south to
Newfoundland, central Quebec, and
British Columbia. Winters regularly
south to the Carolinas, Arkansas, and
California.

This northern species is a winter
visitor. Unlike northern finches such as
siskins and crossbills, its number seems
to depend on weather, not on the food
supply—the birds are less numerous in
mild winters. They roam the snow-
covered landscape in flocks, uttering
tinkling calls and often visiting feeders.

532 Field Sparrow
(Spizella pusilla)
Grosbeaks, Buntings, Finches,
Sparrows (Fringillidae)

Description: 5¼" (13 cm). The combination of the
bright pink bill, rufous cap, white eye-ring,
and unstreaked buff breast distinguishes
it from other sparrows.

Voice: Series of soft, plaintive notes, all on the same pitch, accelerating to a trill at the end.

Habitat: Abandoned fields and pastures grown up to weeds, scattered bushes, and small saplings.

Nesting: 4 pale green, brown-spotted eggs in a woven cup-shaped nest of grass lined with rootlets or fine grass and set on or near the ground.

Range: Breeds from northern North Dakota, central Minnesota, northern Wisconsin and central New England south to Georgia, Mississippi, Louisiana, and central Texas. Winters south to the Gulf of Mexico and northeastern Mexico.

When farms and pastures become overgrown with weeds and bushes, birds such as Field Sparrows and Indigo Buntings move in and nest. Although shyer than its close relative the Chipping Sparrow—and thus more difficult to observe—it may be studied at leisure when it sings its sweet plaintive song from a conspicuous perch atop a bush or fence post. During fall migration it may be seen among flocks of mixed sparrows.

535 Clay-colored Sparrow
(*Spizella pallida*)
Grosbeaks, Buntings, Finches, Sparrows (Fringillidae)

Description: 5–5½" (13–14 cm). A small sparrow with streaked crown and upperparts and *clear gray breast;* similar to an immature Chipping Sparrow but brighter, with rump buff-brownish instead of lead gray, sides of neck gray, and buff cheek patch bordered above and below with black. Grasshopper Sparrow has buff underparts.

Voice: Series of four or five toneless, insect-like buzzes.

Habitat: Brushy grasslands and prairies.

Nesting:	3–5 pale blue eggs spotted with dark brown in a bulky cup of hair-lined grass placed in a bush or clump of weeds up to six feet above the ground.
Range:	North-central Canada and Illinois south to Nebraska and Montana; occasionally east to western New York. Winters regularly north to southern Texas and New Mexico.

This western relative of the Chipping Sparrow has been gradually extending its range eastward and now breeds in the eastern Great Lakes region. Each spring and fall a few individuals, most of them immatures, appear on the eastern seaboard, where they can be difficult to distinguish from immature Chipping Sparrows. Such strays often associate with flocks of Chipping Sparrows.

536 Grasshopper Sparrow
(*Ammodramus savannarum*)
Grosbeaks, Buntings, Finches, Sparrows (Fringillidae)

Description:	4½–5″ (11–13 cm). A small, chunky grassland sparrow with a *clear buff breast* and dark rufous, scaly upperparts; has pale central stripe on crown; tail short and pointed.
Voice:	A high-pitched, insect-like *kip-kip-kip, zeeee,* usually uttered from the top of a weedstalk.
Habitat:	Open grassy and weedy meadows, pastures, and plains.
Nesting:	4 or 5 white eggs speckled with red-brown in a cup of grass, often domed, lined with rootlets and hair.
Range:	British Columbia, Manitoba, and New Hampshire south to Florida, the West Indies, and Mexico. Winters north to North Carolina, Texas, and California.

This elusive sparrow—named for its buzzy song—is sensitive to subtle

changes in its habitat. As soon as a weedy field grows up or trees have filled in abandoned pastures, it no longer uses them as breeding sites. In other parts of the country it chooses different habitats, such as palmetto grasslands in Florida. Less of a seed-eater than our other grass sparrows, it feeds largely on insects.

537 Henslow's Sparrow
(*Passerherbulus henslowii*)
Grosbeaks, Buntings, Finches,
Sparrows (Fringillidae)

Description: 5″ (13 cm). Dull olive-green head, red-brown back and necklace of streaks on the breast.

Voice: Explosive, two-note sneeze, *tsi-lick*.

Habitat: Local in moist or dry grassland with scattered weeds and small shrubs.

Nesting: 4 whitish, brown-spotted eggs in a woven grass nest on the ground, usually in a grass clump.

Range: Northeastern United States south to east-central, wintering in the Gulf and south Atlantic states.

This sparrow is secretive and mouse-like, skulking low in the grass. It relies on running rather than flying, and is seldom observed unless perched atop some weed stalk uttering its insect-like "song." These birds are sometimes found in loose colonies of up to a dozen pairs, but one to three pairs are more common. Curiously, it may be present in a certain locality and absent from a seemingly similar habitat not far away. It was named for John Henslow, prominent early 19th century English botanist.

Baird's Sparrow
(*Ammodramus bairdii*)
Grosbeaks, Buntings, Finches,
Sparrows (Fringillidae)

Description: 5–5½" (13–14 cm). A pale, streaked
sparrow, whitish below, breast crossed
by a band of narrow black streaks;
bright ocher crown stripe.

Voice: Three short notes followed by a musical
trill on a lower pitch.

Habitat: Dry upland prairies.

Nesting: 3–5 white eggs blotched and scrawled
with dark brown in a cup of weed stems
and grass concealed in grass or weeds on
the ground.

Range: Saskatchewan and Manitoba south to
Minnesota and Montana. Winters in
Texas, Arizona, and northern Mexico.

These elegant grass sparrows were first
described in 1844 by Audubon, who
named it after Spencer F. Baird, 19th
century ornithologist and Secretary of
the Smithsonian Institution. The total
population is small, and once they leave
the breeding grounds they are difficult
to find. Even on their breeding
grounds, one must search hard for the
habitat that suits them. Here a few
singing males can be found, usually
perched on the tip of weed stalks.

Cassin's Sparrow
(*Aimophila cassinii*)
Grosbeaks, Buntings, Finches,
Sparrows (Fringillidae)

Description: 5" (13 cm). A drab, nondescript
sparrow with finely streaked crown and
back, plain buff-white underparts, and
gray rump and tail.

Voice: Musical trill preceded and followed by
one or more clear notes, usually given
in flight.

Habitat: Sparsely vegetated country; barren
rocky areas with scattered cacti and

yuccas, and short grass. It uses such plants, as well as fence posts and wires, as song perches.

Nesting: 4 white eggs in a deep cup of plant fiber and grass lined with hair and set on the ground in a grass clump or at the base of a bush or a cactus.

Range: From Colorado and Kansas to northern Mexico.

This secretive species, like nearly all grass-inhabiting birds, is difficult to study. It is named for John Cassin, an early 19th century ornithologist at the Philadelphia Academy of Natural Sciences.

538 Le Conte's Sparrow
(*Passerherbulus caudacutus*)
Grosbeaks, Buntings, Finches, Sparrows (Fringillidae)

Description: 5″ (13 cm). Similar to the Sharp-tailed Sparrow of the Great Plains, but crown stripe is white instead of gray; *wide reddish collar* on nape and upper back.

Voice: Two very thin, insect-like hisses.

Habitat: Moist grassland and boggy meadows; also dry fields in winter.

Nesting: 4 whitish, brown-spotted eggs in a grass cup lined with hair and set on the ground, usually in a grass clump.

Range: South-central Canada to north-central United States. Winters in the central and southern states.

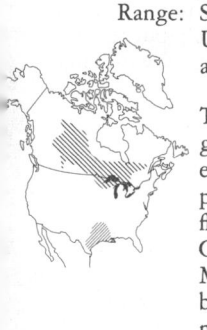

This elusive bird keeps to the thick grass like all grass-loving sparrows except when it mounts an exposed perch to sing. It is almost impossible to flush, for it prefers running to flying. Common in the prairie regions of the Midwest, it inhabits the drier grass borders of rush-grown marshes. It was named for Major John Le Conte of Georgia, an early American naturalist (1818–1891).

545 Dickcissel
(*Spiza americana*)
Grosbeaks, Buntings, Finches,
Sparrows (Fringillidae)

Description: 6″ (15 cm). Male like *miniature
Meadowlark* (yellow breast with black
"V") but has a heavy bill and a *chestnut
wing patch*. Female much like female
House Sparrow, but with narrow
streaks along the sides, and yellowish
throat and breast.

Voice: Song sounds like *dick-dick-cissel,* the
first two notes being sharp sounds
followed by a buzzy, almost hissed
cissel, repeated over and over again from
a conspicuous perch on a fence, bush,
or weed.

Habitat: Open country in grain or hay fields and
in weed patches.

Nesting: 4 or 5 pale blue eggs in a cup of plant
stems and grass set on or near the
ground, often in alfalfa and clover
fields.

Range: Chiefly in the north-central states south
to the Gulf states. Winters from
Mexico to northern South America.

Formerly common in farming regions of
the eastern states, especially on the
Atlantic coastal plain, it disappeared
from that region by the middle of the
last century and is now most numerous
in the Midwest. It appears in small
numbers on the east coast during the
fall migration and rarely but regularly
in winter at feeders, often with House
Sparrows.

546 Water Pipit
(*Anthus spinoletta*)
Pipits (Motacillidae)

Description: 6–7″ (15–17 cm). Sparrow-sized. A
slender brown bird of open country.
Often wags its tail and usually walks
rather than hops. Crown and upperparts

uniform brown, underparts buff with streaks; outer tail feathers white; legs usually black. In contrast, sparrows have conical bills and hop. Sprague's Pipit has a streaked back and yellow legs.

Voice: Paired, high-pitched *pip-pip.* Flight song weak and tinkling trills.

Habitat: Arctic and alpine tundra; in migration and winter it is found on beaches, barren fields, agricultural land, and golf courses.

Nesting: 4 or 5 gray eggs, thickly spotted with brown and streaked with black, in a cup of grass and twigs on the ground in the shelter of a rock or a tussock.

Range: Aleutians, northern Alaska, Mackenzie, the arctic islands, and western Greenland south to Newfoundland, Hudson Bay, and Oregon, and in the mountains to northern Maine and New Mexico. Winters south to Florida, the Gulf Coast, and Guatemala. Also in Eurasia.

Although mainly breeding on the tundra in both hemispheres, some populations in western Europe have colonies on rocky coasts and are known as Rock Pipits. The lack of a breeding species of pipits in the open country of the eastern United States is due to the fact that until recently forests covered this area. In winter large flocks gather in open fields. When disturbed they rise in unison, wheel, turn, and resume their feeding.

Sprague's Pipit
(*Anthus spragueii*)
Pipits (Motacillidae)

Description: 6¼–7" (16–17 cm). Sparrow-sized. A slender-billed, streaked bird with white outer tail feathers; *legs yellow.* Water Pipit is similar, but has black legs and unstreaked back.

Voice: Series of sharp pips. Flight song high in

the air is descending series of tinkling double notes.

Habitat: Short-grass plains and plowed fields.

Nesting: 4 or 5 gray eggs spotted with purple and brown placed in a cup of grass concealed in a tussock on the ground and usually covered by an arch of bent grass stems.

Range: Alberta and Manitoba south to Minnesota and Montana. Winters from Mississippi and Texas to southern Mexico.

This species was named by Audubon for Isaac Sprague (1811–1895), an artist who accompanied him on his trip up the Missouri River. Of the two species found here, it is the only pipit confined to North America. An uncommon and inconspicuous bird, the first specimen was found by Audubon in 1843, and it was not until 16 years later that a second bird was obtained. It is easily overlooked, slipping away through the grass or flying off quickly. Usually seen on breeding grounds, where the males put on a flight display.

---

547 Snow Bunting
(*Plectrophenax nivalis*)
Grosbeaks, Buntings, Finches,
Sparrows (Fringillidae)

Description: 6–7¼″ (15–18 cm). Sparrow-sized. Breeding male has black back with *much white* on head, underparts, wings, and tail. Female similar but duller. Winter birds have brown on crown and upperparts, duller underparts, but still show much white in wings.

Voice: Clear whistle or low soft purring. Song is a sweet warble.

Habitat: Arctic tundra. Winters on windswept grasslands and beaches.

Nesting: 4–6 white eggs with red-brown spots in a ring around the larger end, placed in a cup of grass lined with fur and feathers and concealed among rocks or in tundra vegetation.

Range: Aleutians, northern Alaska and Greenland south to northern Quebec and central Alaska. Winters regularly to Pennsylvania and Oregon.

This circumpolar bird, often called "Snowflake," breeds farther north than almost any other land bird. In severe winters large flocks descend to our northern states, where they favor the most barren places. They can be found at beach parking lots in the dead of winter searching for weed seeds.

---

548 **Savannah Sparrow**
including "Ipswich Sparrow"
(*Passerculus sandwichensis*)
Grosbeaks, Buntings, Finches,
Sparrows (Fringillidae)

Description: 4½–6" (11–15 cm). Pale and streaked, with a bright yellow eyebrow and flesh-colored legs. Tail notched; other grassland sparrows have shorter, more pointed tails.

Voice: High-pitched, buzzy *tsip-tsip-tsip-se-e-e-srr*.

Habitat: Fields, prairies, salt marshes, and grassy dunes.

Nesting: 4–6 pale blue-green eggs, variably spotted and speckled with dark brown, in a cup of grass lined with finer plant material and hair.

Range: Aleutians, Alaska, Mackenzie, and Labrador south to New Jersey, Missouri, and northern Mexico. Winters regularly north to Massachusetts and southeastern Alaska.

This most abundant and familiar of the grass sparrows shows a great deal of color variation over its wide range. One larger and paler form that breeds at Sable Island, Nova Scotia, was until recently considered a separate species, the "Ipswich Sparrow." These birds are able runners; once discovered, they drop into the grass and dart away. In the fall they migrate southward in huge numbers and may then be found almost anywhere—even in city parks.

549, 566 Lark Bunting
(*Calamospiza melanocorys*)
Grosbeaks, Buntings, Finches, Sparrows (Fringillidae)

Description: 6–7½" (15–19 cm). Sparrow-sized. Male black with conspicuous *white wing patches,* most evident in flight. Female duller and streaked with brown, but also shows much white in wings. Usually seen in flocks.

Voice: Long, varied series of trills. Call a soft *hoo-ee.*

Habitat: Open plains and fields.

Nesting: 4–6 pale blue eggs, usually unmarked, in a loose cup of twigs and grass often lined with hair and placed on the ground under a clump of weeds or grass.

Range: Breeds from British Columbia, Manitoba, and Minnesota south to Texas and New Mexico. Winters from southern Texas and Arizona to central Mexico.

Usually seen in large flocks feeding along roadsides. On the breeding grounds they are quite gregarious, several pairs crowding into a few acres of suitable habitat. Since there are few elevated song perches in their grassland breeding area, males advertise their presence with a conspicuous song flight. Often one can see several singing males in the air at one time, providing watchers an easy way to locate a nesting colony. Like many seed-eating birds, they supplement their summer diet with insects.

550 Vesper Sparrow
(*Pooecetes gramineus*)
Grosbeaks, Buntings, Finches,
Sparrows (Fringillidae)

Description: 5–6½" (13–16 cm). A grayish, streaked
sparrow with *white outer tail feathers,
narrow white eye-ring,* and a small patch
of chestnut on the bend of the wing.

Voice: Slow series of four clear musical notes,
the last two higher, ending in a
descending series of trills—sometimes
rendered as *come-come-where-where-all-
together-down-the-hill.*

Habitat: Fields, pastures, and roadsides in
farming country.

Nesting: 4–6 white eggs heavily spotted with
brown in a well-made cup of grass and
rootlets concealed in grass on the
ground.

Range: British Columbia, Ontario, and Nova
Scotia south to the Carolinas, Texas,
Colorado and California. Winters from
New England to the Gulf Coast and
Mexico.

The rich, musical song of this sparrow
is a most distinctive sound on rolling
farmlands. Long known as the "Bay-
winged Bunting," the bird was given
the pleasing if somewhat inappropriate
name Vesper Sparrow by the naturalist
John Burroughs, who thought the song
sounded more melodious in the evening.
The bird is usually found on the ground
but often mounts to an exposed perch
to deliver its song.

551 Lapland Longspur
(*Calcarius lapponicus*)
Grosbeaks, Buntings, Finches,
Sparrows (Fringillidae)

Description: 6–7" (15–17 cm). Sparrow-sized. *The
only longspur in most of the East.* Breeding
male has black face, crown, and upper
breast; chestnut nape; streaked

above and white below with streaked flanks. Female and winter male dull and without bold pattern; best identified by largely black tail with white outermost tail feathers. Smith's Longspur has a similar tail but is always buff above and below and usually shows a small white wing patch.

Voice: Rattling call. Flight song is sweet and bubbling.

Habitat: Arctic tundra; winters in open windswept fields and on grassy coastal dunes. Often found on parking lots along the coast in winter.

Nesting: 4 or 5 pale olive-green eggs heavily spotted with brown and purple in a grass-lined hollow in the ground and concealed under a clump of grass or a dwarf birch.

Range: Aleutians, northern Alaska, the Arctic islands, and Greenland to northern Quebec and southern Alaska. Winters regularly to New York and California. Also in northern Eurasia.

This species is the only one of four longspurs that is found in both hemispheres. Like other longspurs, it is almost invisible on the ground; often a whole flock will dart into the air at an observer's feet, only to disappear again when they land on bare ground a few hundred yards away.

552 **Chestnut-collared Longspur**
(*Calcarius ornatus*)
Grosbeaks, Buntings, Finches, Sparrows (Fringillidae)

Description: 5½–6½" (14–16 cm). Sparrow-sized. Similar to the Lapland Longspur, but breeding male has *wholly black underparts* and some white on its face. Tail of female and winter male similar to that of Lapland Longspur but with *more white at sides*.

Voice: Soft, sweet, and tumbling, somewhat

like the Western Meadowlark.

Habitat: Dry elevated prairies and short-grass plains.

Nesting: 3–5 pale green eggs spotted with brown and lavender in a grass-lined hollow under a clump of grass.

Range: Alberta and Manitoba south to Minnesota and Wyoming. Winters from Colorado and Kansas south to Texas and northern Mexico.

The upland prairies favored for nesting have been extensively planted in wheat, so these longspurs are much less numerous than formerly. They need only a small area, however, and often several pairs will crowd into a patch of land or even the narrow strips of unplowed grassland along highways. Here the males can be seen singing from the tops of fence posts, rocks, or tall weed stalks.

553 McCown's Longspur
(*Calcarius mccownii*)
Grosbeaks, Buntings, Finches, Sparrows (Fringillidae)

Description: 5¾–6″ (14–16 cm). Sparrow-sized. Breeding male streaked above with black crown, whitish face, and black mustache; gray below with a bold black band across breast. Female and winter male duller and more streaked; best identified by tail pattern, which is largely white with central pair of tail feathers black and with narrow black band at tip.

Voice: Dry rattle; also a clear sweet warble given during a fluttering flight with wings raised high over back.

Habitat: Arid plains.

Nesting: 3 or 4 pale green eggs spotted with dark brown and black in a hollow scrape lined with fine grass and hair on open ground.

Range: Alberta, western Manitoba, and

southwestern Manitoba south to the Dakotas, Wyoming, and Colorado. Winters from Nebraska and Colorado south to northern Mexico.

This longspur nests in higher and more arid short-grass plains than does the Chestnut-collared Longspur, and so has been less affected by plowing of the prairie. They so dislike moisture that in wet seasons they may abandon areas where they normally are abundant. In summer they feed chiefly on grasshoppers, but in fall and winter, when they gather in large flocks with other longspurs and with Horned Larks, they prefer seeds. In winter plumage they can be difficult to distinguish from the other longspurs, but close up they are easily identified by their stouter bill.

554 Smith's Longspur
(*Calcarius pictus*)
Grosbeaks, Buntings, Finches, Sparrows (Fringillidae)

Description: 5¾–6½″ (15–16 cm). Sparrow-sized. Breeding male streaked dark brown and buff above, clear warm buff below; bold black-and-white head pattern. Small white wing patch most evident in flight; tail black, with white outer feathers. Females and winter males duller and without head pattern, but always much buffier than other longspurs.

Voice: Dry rattle, like running a finger along the teeth of a comb.

Habitat: Arctic tundra and forest edge; winters on open grassy plains.

Nesting: 3–5 pale brown eggs spotted with darker brown, in a grass-walled hollow lined with plant down and feathers and concealed under a clump of grass or a dwarf willow.

Range: Northern Alaska across northern

Canada to Hudson Bay. Winters from Nebraska south to Texas.

Longspur identification is difficult in the Midwest, where all four species winter, but this species, clad in warm buff the year around, can be told at a glance. At times they are found in huge flocks moving over the dry winter grasslands in search of seeds, uttering a distinctive clinking call. On the Arctic tundra they seem to prefer drier, more elevated areas than does the Lapland Longspur.

555, 567 Bobolink
(*Dolichonyx oryzivorus*)
Orioles, Blackbirds (Icteridae)

Description: 6–8" (15–20 cm). Larger than a House Sparrow. Breeding male largely black with *white rump* and back, *dull yellow nape.* Female and winter male rich buff-yellow, streaked on back and crown. *Short, finch-like bill.* Female Red-winged Blackbird is darker, less buffy, and has a longer bill.

Voice: Flight song is a series of joyous, bubbling, tumbling, gurgling phrases with each note on a different pitch. Call a soft *pink,* often heard on migration.

Habitat: Prairies and meadows; marshes during migration.

Nesting: 4–7 eggs spotted with red-brown and purple; in a poorly made but well-concealed cup of grass, stems, and rootlets placed on the ground in a field.

Range: Breeds from British Columbia, Manitoba, and Newfoundland south to Pennsylvania, Colorado, and northern California. Winters in southern South America.

The Bobolink was probably confined to the central grasslands originally, but with the settling of the Northeast it quickly spread into New England.

Now, with farms abandoned and the land returning to forest, the species is declining. Each fall, migrant Bobolinks used to gather in large numbers in southern rice fields, where their habit of eating grain earned them the name "Ricebird."

556 Horned Lark
(*Eremophila alpestris*)
Larks (Alaudidae)

Description: 7–8″ (17–20 cm). Larger than a sparrow. Brown, with *black stripe below eye, black crescent on breast, and black "horns"* (not always seen). Walks rather than hops. In flight, tail seen as black with white edges. Similar-looking pipits have brown tails and lack the face pattern.

Voice: *Ti-ti.* Song delivered in flight is a high-pitched series of tinkling notes.

Habitat: Plains, fields, airports, and beaches.

Nesting: 3–5 brown-spotted gray eggs in a hollow in the ground lined with fine grass.

Range: Arctic south to North Carolina, Missouri, coastal Texas, and northern South America. Also in Eurasia and North Africa.

The only true lark in the New World, this is one of our earliest nesting birds. Even in the northern states, nests may be found in February, when the first set of eggs is often destroyed by severe snowstorms. As many as three broods are raised each year. The species favors the most barren habitats; as soon as thick grass begins to grow in an area, the birds abandon it. In the fall they roam over the open countryside in large flocks, often in company with pipits, longspurs, and Snow Buntings.

577 Smooth-billed Ani
(Crotophaga ani)
Cuckoos (Cuculidae)

Description: 14" (35 cm). Jay-sized. Black, with a very long tail half the length of the bird. Huge bill with arched ridge.

Voice: Slurred double note with a rising inflection that has a whining, metallic quality; quite different from that of the Groove-billed Ani.

Habitat: Open agricultural country, often near cattle or other livestock; also found in scrub and thickets.

Nesting: 3–5 blue-green (often stained) eggs in a bulky stick nest in dense vegetation. Probably polygamous.

Range: Southern Florida; also from the West Indies and Mexico to South America.

These birds have some peculiar traits. Usually several females lay eggs in a single nest, deposited in layers separated more or less by leaves or grass. Up to 30 eggs have been found in one nest. Those at the bottom do not hatch. The females share incubation, often two or more simultaneously. Anis prefer open, cultivated country. They often alight on the backs of cattle to remove ticks.

582 White-necked Raven
(Corvus cryptoleucus)
Jay, Magpies, Crows (Corvidae)

Description: 19–21" (48–53 cm). Crow-sized. Similar to the Common Raven but somewhat smaller. White bases to feathers of neck and breast seldom seen. Best told by voice.

Voice: Harsh *kraak,* higher-pitched than the Common Raven's.

Habitat: Arid grasslands and mesquite; plains and deserts.

Nesting: 5–7 dull green eggs spotted and streaked with brown and purple. Nest a loose mass of thorny sticks lined with grass, moss, and bark strips and placed in an exposed tree or on a telephone pole.

Range: Central Texas, New Mexico, and Arizona south into Mexico. Winters north to the United States border.

It replaces the Common Raven at lower elevations, and in our part of its range is the only raven likely to be seen. More gregarious than its larger northern relative, many are often found at garbage dumps. The birds gather in noisy and conspicuous roosts. During the breeding season, however, they are not social, pairs nesting in widely spaced territories.

City Parks and Suburban Areas

Areas much modified by man, including lawns, gardens, parks, well-planted residential areas, as well as vacant lots, industrial areas, and urban districts. The birds treated here are all very tolerant of such disturbed habitats. During migration, these areas may be visited briefly by birds of a variety of habitats; ducks and geese may stop off on ponds and reservoirs, and warblers, vireos, orioles, flycatchers, and sparrows may frequent trees and shrubbery. In winter, finches, chickadees, nuthatches, and woodpeckers may turn up at feeders, and owls may be found in groves of pines or cedars.

322 Mourning Dove
(*Zenaida macroura*)
Pigeons, Doves (Columbidae)

Description: 12″ (30 cm). Soft, sandy buff with a long, pointed tail bordered with white.

Voice: Low, mournful (hence its name) *coo-ah, coo, coo, coo.*

Habitat: Open fields, parks, and lawns with many trees and shrubs.

Nesting: 2 white eggs in a loosely made nest of sticks and twigs in low bushes and tall trees, more rarely on the ground.

Range: Southern Alaska, British Columbia, Saskatchewan, Ontario, Quebec, and New Brunswick to Panama and the West Indies. Winters north to northern United States.

This abundant bird has benefited from man's cutting the forest and burning off the grass. It is common in rural areas in all parts of the United States, as well as city parks and, in winter, suburban feeders. In some states it is hunted as a gamebird while in others it is protected as a "songbird." Its species name *macroura* is Greek for "long-tailed." The young are fed regurgitated, partially digested food known as pigeon milk.

323 Ringed Turtle Dove
(*Streptopelia risoria*)
Pigeons, Doves (Columbidae)

Description: 12″ (30 cm). A slender, pale sandy dove with a narrow black collar on the hindneck and a rounded, not pointed, tail. Mourning Dove similar but darker with pointed tail and no collar.

Voice: Soft mellow *kooo-krooo,* rising and then falling in pitch.

Habitat: City parks, suburban areas, usually where trees are present.

Nesting: 2 white eggs in a flimsy saucer of twigs and grass on a window ledge or in a dovecote.

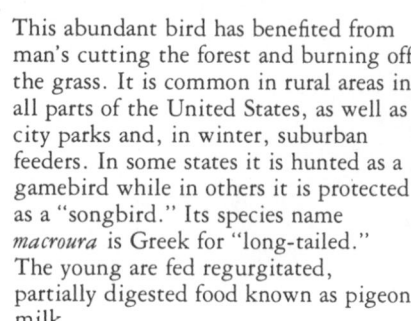

Range: Introduced and established in the vicinity of Miami and Tampa, Florida, and in many other cities in the world.

This dove has been domesticated for so long that no one is sure which wild species is its ancestor, although it is thought to be an African species. During its centuries in captivity it has become adapted to living with man, and is unsuccessful in rural areas. Even today, its pleasing call makes it a favorite cage bird.

327 Rock Dove
(*Columba livia*)
Pigeons, Doves (Columbidae)

Description: 13½″ (34 cm). Chunky, with a short, rounded tail. Generally bluish-gray with two narrow black wing bands and a broad black terminal tail band; *white rump.*
Voice: Soft, guttural cooing.
Habitat: City parks, suburban gardens, and farmland.
Nesting: 2 white eggs in a crude nest lined with sticks and debris placed on cliffs, buildings, and bridges.
Range: Native and resident in much of the temperate and subtropical regions of the Old World north of the Equator. Introduced into many other parts of the world and now widely established through much of North America.

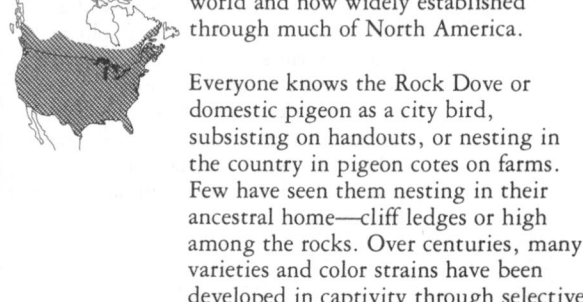

Everyone knows the Rock Dove or domestic pigeon as a city bird, subsisting on handouts, or nesting in the country in pigeon cotes on farms. Few have seen them nesting in their ancestral home—cliff ledges or high among the rocks. Over centuries, many varieties and color strains have been developed in captivity through selective breeding. Since they have been accused of carrying human diseases, there have been several attempts to eradicate them from our cities; but they are so prolific that little progress has been made toward this end.

332, 336 Purple Martin
(*Progne subis*)
Swallows (Hirundinidae)

Description: 7–8½″ (18–21 cm). Bluebird-sized. Our largest swallow. Adult male dark steel-blue. Female and immature male duller above, pale gray below. Overhead, similar in shape to Starling but flight more buoyant and gliding.

Voice: Liquid, gurgling warble. Also a penetrating *tee-tee-tee*.

Habitat: Open woodland, residential areas, and agricultural land.

Nesting: 4 or 5 white eggs in a mass of grass and other plant material placed in a natural cavity—sometimes a hole in a tree but more often in a "martin house" with many separate compartments, where the birds nest in a colony.

Range: Breeds from British Columbia, Manitoba, and Nova Scotia south to the West Indies and central Mexico. Winters in South America.

The custom of erecting a martin house to attract these beneficial birds was practiced by the early settlers and, before them, by the southern Indian tribes, who hung clusters of hollow gourds in trees near their gardens. In other areas the species nested in tall dead trees riddled with woodpecker holes, but these original colonies never reached the size—as many as 200 pairs—of colonies found in large martin houses today.

335 Chimney Swift
(*Chaetura pelagica*)
Swifts (Apodidae)

Description: 5½" (14 cm). Sparrow-sized. Stubby, brownish-gray body (appearing black in flight) with very short tail; long, narrow, curved wings.

Voice: Loud, chattering twitters.

Habitat: Breeds and roosts in chimneys; feeds entirely on the wing.

Nesting: 4 or 5 white eggs in a nest made of twigs cemented together with the bird's saliva and fastened to the inner wall of a chimney or, rarely, in a cave or hollow tree.

Range: Eastern North America, breeding from southeastern Saskatchewan, southern Manitoba, central Ontario, southern Quebec, Nova Scotia, south to the Gulf states. Winters in the upper Amazon basin.

Members of this family are among the fastest fliers in the bird world. Swifts spend all of their daylight hours on the wing and only come to rest at evening. They feed exclusively on flying insects. They drink water and bathe by dipping into the water of a pond or river as they fly over it. Since they never perch, they gather twigs in flight, snapping them off with their bill or feet as they pass. Sometimes a twig fails to break and the bird is tossed backward, only to return again. They gather in communal roosts in air shafts or large chimneys, often whirling in a huge circle as they funnel down for the night. Their winter range was unknown until recently when a few banded swifts were recovered from the Amazon Valley in Peru.

**348 Common Flicker
including "Yellow-shafted Flicker"
and "Red-shafted Flicker"**
(*Colaptes auratus*)
Woodpeckers (Picidae)

Description: 12″ (30 cm). A large brownish
woodpecker. *Brown back* with dark bars
and spots: *whitish below with black spots,
black crescent* on breast; *white rump* in
flight. Eastern birds have *red patch on
nape* (male has a black "mustache") and
yellow wing linings. Western birds lack
nape patch (males have red "mustache"
and salmon wing linings).

Voice: Loud, repeated *flicker* or *wicka-wicka-
wicka*. Also a loud *kleeer*.

Habitat: Open country with trees; parks and
rural estates.

Nesting: 6–8 white eggs in a tree cavity, power
pole, or bird house.

Range: Alaska, Manitoba, and Newfoundland
south to southern Florida, the Gulf
Coast, and southern Mexico. Also in
the West Indies.

Flickers are the only brown-backed
woodpeckers in the East. They are the
only woodpeckers in North America
that commonly feed on the ground,
searching for ants and beetle larvae on
lawns or even sidewalks. During
courtship and to proclaim their
territory, flickers hammer on dead
limbs or tin roofs. On the Great Plains
the "yellow-shafted" and "red-shafted"
forms meet; they interbreed, hybridize,
and are considered one species.

**393, 394 Northern Oriole
including "Baltimore Oriole" and
"Bullock's Oriole"**
(*Icterus galbula*)
Orioles, Blackbirds (Icteridae)

Description: 7–8½″ (18–21 cm). Eastern male,
formerly "Baltimore Oriole," has black

head, back, wings, and tail; orange breast, rump, and shoulder patch. Eastern female olive-brown with dull yellow-orange underparts and two dull white wing bars. Western male, formerly "Bullock's Oriole," is similar to eastern male but has orange cheeks and eyebrow and large white wing patch. Western female has whitish underparts.

Voice: Clear and flute-like whistled single or double notes in short, distinct phrases with much individual variation.

Habitat: Deciduous woodland and shade trees. Before its decline, the American elm was a favorite nesting site for the eastern bird.

Nesting: 4–6 grayish eggs spotted and scrawled with dark brown and black. Nest a well-woven pendant bag of plant fibers, bark, and string suspended from the tip of a branch.

Range: Breeds from British Columbia, Saskatchewan, and Nova Scotia south to Georgia, Louisiana, and northern Mexico. Winters from southern Mexico southward.

Until recently the western populations of this bird ("Bullock's Oriole") were thought to be a separate species from the eastern populations which were called the "Baltimore Oriole." When trees were planted on the Great Plains, the two forms extended their ranges and met. Despite the differences in their appearance, it was found that they interbreed freely, and most birds in the central plains are hybrids. Orioles readily accept short pieces of yarn for nesting material and apparently show no color preference.

400 American Robin
"Robin"
(*Turdus migratorius*)
Thrushes (Turdidae)

Description: 9–11" (23–28 cm). Gray above, brick-red below. Head and tail black in males, dull gray in females. Young birds are spotted below.

Voice: Song is a series of rich caroling notes, rising and falling in pitch: *Cheer-up, cheerily, Cheer-up, cheerily.*

Habitat: Towns, gardens, open woodland, and agricultural land.

Nesting: 3–5 blue-green eggs in a well-made cup of mud reinforced with grass and twigs, lined with softer grasses and placed in a tree or on a ledge or windowsill; they usually have two broods a season.

Range: Alaska, Manitoba, and Newfoundland south to the Carolinas, Arkansas, and Guatemala; occasionally breeds along the Gulf Coast. Winters north to Newfoundland, southern Ontario, and British Columbia.

Robins originally nested in forests; where they still do so they are much shyer than the Robins of the dooryard. They breed only rarely in the Deep South, where they prefer large shade trees on lawns. Although usually considered a harbinger of spring, Robins often winter in the northern states, where they frequent cedar bogs and swamps and are not usually noticed by a casual observer, except when they gather in large roosts, often containing thousands of birds. As with many birds, their normal mortality rate is about 80 percent a year.

410, 559 House Finch
(*Carpodacus mexicanus*)
Grosbeaks, Buntings, Finches,
Sparrows (Fringillidae)

Description: 5–6″ (13–15 cm). Sparrow-sized. Male
is streaked brown with bright red
breast, forehead, eyebrow, and rump.
Female lacks red; similar to female
Purple Finch but more finely streaked
and without contrasting stripes on face.

Voice: Clear warble like that of the Purple
Finch, but weaker and less musical.

Habitat: Cities and residential areas in the East;
also in desert brush in Texas and the
Far West.

Nesting: 4 or 5 pale blue eggs lightly spotted
with black in a well-made cup of grass
in a bush, thicket, natural cavity, or on
a building.

Range: This western species occurred naturally
east to Nebraska and Texas. It was
introduced in the East and is
established from Maine to the
Carolinas.

The eastern population of this species is
descended from cagebirds released near
New York City in the 1940s. For years
the birds barely survived on Long Island,
but they then spread in suburban areas.
In the late 1960s and 1970s they finally
established themselves in urban New
York, where their musical song and
bright colors add a cheerful touch. The
eating habits of these city birds are not
well known, but they probably subsist
on the berries of ornamentals and on
food put out for the more abundant
House Sparrows.

419 Mockingbird
(*Mimus polyglottos*)
Mockingbirds, Thrashers (Mimidae)

Description: 9–11″ (23–28 cm). Robin-sized. A
slender, long-tailed gray bird with

white patches on the wings and tail.

Voice: Long series of musical and grating
phrases, each repeated three or more
times; often imitates other birds. Call a
harsh *chack*.

Habitat: Residential areas, city parks, farmlands,
open country with thickets, and desert
brushland.

Nesting: 3–5 blue-green eggs, spotted with
brown, in a bulky cup of sticks and
weed stems in a bush or low tree.

Range: Breeds from southern Canada south
to the Caribbean; winters in
southern part of range.

Its beautiful song is richest on warm,
moonlit nights in spring, when the
bird may spend hours giving amazing
imitations of other species. The songs
of 36 other species were recognized
from the recording of one mockingbird
in Massachusetts. Birds in the western
part of the species' range have less
musical songs and are less imitative.
Mockingbirds are strongly territorial
and, like a number of other birds, will
attack their reflection in a window, hub
cap, or mirror, at times with such vigor
that they injure or kill themselves.
Thus the boundaries of a bird's territory
can be learned by placing a mirror at
strategic locations and noting where the
attack ceases.

420 **Gray Catbird**
"Catbird"
(*Dumetella carolinensis*)
Mockingbirds, Thrashers (Mimidae)

Description: 8–9¼" (20–23 cm). Smaller than a
Robin. A slender, long-tailed, *dark
gray* bird with a *black cap* and rusty
undertail coverts.

Voice: Long, irregular succession of musical
and mechanical notes and phrases; a
cat-like mewing. Sometimes seems to
mimic other birds.

Habitat: Thickets and brush, residential areas
and gardens.

Nesting: 4 or 5 glossy blue-green eggs in a bulky
mass of twigs, stems, and leaves lined
with finer plant material and concealed
in a dense bush or in a tangle of vines.

Range: British Columbia, Manitoba, and Nova
Scotia south to Florida, Texas, and
Washington. Winters from the Gulf
Coast and the Carolinas to Panama.

Formerly known as the "Catbird," its
name has now been changed officially to
Gray Catbird because there is an all-
black species, the Black Catbird, in
southern Mexico. It often announces its
presence by a harsh, cat-like whine
issuing from a dense tangle; the bird
responds to an imitation of this call,
popping suddenly into view for a better
look. Catbirds are largely insectivorous,
and their pleasing song has made
them welcome in suburban gardens.

429 **Dark-eyed Junco**
including "White-winged Junco,"
"Slate-colored Junco," and
"Oregon Junco"
(*Junco hyemalis*)
Grosbeaks, Buntings, Finches,
Sparrows (Fringillidae)

Description: 5–6½" (13–16 cm). Sparrow-sized.
Variable, but generally slate-gray or
gray-brown above, with white abdomen
sharply demarcated from gray of breast.
Shows white along sides of tail in
flight. Pink bill. Some birds have buff
flanks.

Voice: Trill like the Chipping Sparrow but
slower and with a more musical,
tinkling quality. Also a soft twittering.

Habitat: Coniferous or mixed forests; winters in
fields, gardens, city parks, and roadside
thickets.

Nesting: 3–5 pale green, brown-spotted eggs in
a deep, well-made cup of grass, moss,

and strips of bark well concealed on or near the ground in vegetation in a bank or on the forest floor.

Range: Alaska and Newfoundland south to mountains in Georgia and Mexico. Winters south to the Gulf Coast and northern Mexico.

Until recently the many geographical forms of this bird were considered separate species, but since they interbreed wherever their ranges meet, they are now considered one species. The eastern form, formerly called the "Slate-colored Junco," is the only one usually encountered in the eastern states. Occasionally, however, black-headed, rusty-flanked western birds, "Oregon Juncos," may also be seen, and the "White-winged Junco" from the Black Hills in South Dakota is an accidental winter visitor. Juncos are among the commonest of our winter birds, often visiting feeders.

---

435 **Blue Jay**
(*Cyanocitta cristata*)
Jays, Magpies, Crows (Corvidae)

Description: 12″ (30 cm). *Bright blue* above with much white and black in the wing and tail; white below; black facial markings; *prominent crest.*

Voice: Raucous *jay-jay,* harsh cries, and a rich variety of other calls. One is almost identical to the scream of the Red-shouldered Hawk. Also a musical *queedle-queedle.*

Habitat: Chiefly oak forest, but now also city parks and suburban yards, especially where oak trees predominate.

Nesting: 4–6 brown-spotted greenish eggs in a coarsely built nest of sticks lined with grass and well concealed in a crotch or forked branch of a tree, often a conifer.

Range: East of the Rockies, from southern Canada to the Gulf of Mexico.

Although sometimes disliked because they chase smaller birds away from feeders, Blue Jays are among our handsomest birds. They often bury seeds and acorns, and since many are never retrieved they are, in effect, tree planters. They have a violent dislike of predators, and their raucous screaming makes it easy to locate a hawk or a roosting owl. Although seen throughout the year, they are migratory and travel in large loose flocks in both spring and fall. In the East, birds from farther north replace the local population in winter.

466 Eastern Phoebe
(*Sayornis phoebe*)
Tyrant Flycatchers (Tyrannidae)

Description: 7" (17 cm). Dull olive-green without an eye-ring or wing bars. *Wags its tail.*

Voice: Clear *phoe-be,* repeated many times; the second syllable is alternately higher or lower than the first. Distinctive, short *chip.*

Habitat: Open woodland near streams; cliffs, bridges, and buildings with ledges.

Nesting: 4 or 5 white eggs in a mud-and-grass nest lined with moss and hair. The nest is attached to ledges of buildings, bridges, cliffs, wells, and quarries; also under roots of fallen trees.

Range: Breeds in Canada and the United States east of the Rockies, south to the northern limits of the Gulf states. Winters from Virginia and the Gulf Coast south to Mexico.

The Phoebe arrives early in spring and departs late in fall, sometimes even staying through the winter in the northern states. In the absence of insects its winter food is berries. Phoebes are extraordinarily tame at the nest. It was probably the first bird ever banded: Audubon marked one with a

silver wire on the leg in 1840 and
recorded its return the following year.

---

479 **Ruby-throated Hummingbird**
(*Archilochus colubris*)
Hummingbirds (Trochilidae)

Description: 3½″ (9 cm). Tiny. Metallic green
above, white below; male has a *brilliant
red throat*. Needle-like bill.

Voice: Mouse-like twittering squeak. In flight
they make humming sounds with their
wings, which accounts for their name.

Habitat: Suburban gardens, parks, and
woodlands.

Nesting: 2 white eggs the size of large peas in a
woven nest of plant down held together
with spider silk. The nest, about 2
inches in diameter, is covered with
lichens and is saddled to the branch of a
tree, usually in a forest clearing.

Range: The only hummingbird breeding east of
the Mississippi River. Breeds from
southern Canada to the Gulf Coast.
Winters chiefly from Mexico to Panama
and north to the immediate Gulf states.

These smallest of all birds are
particularly attracted to tubular red
flowers such as salvia and trumpet
creeper, as well as bee balm, petunia,
jewelweed, and thistle. Hummers are
also attracted to artificial feeders—red
glass tubes filled with a mixture of
honey and sugar water. With their
remarkable powers of flight they are the
only birds that can fly backwards as
well as hover in one spot like an insect.
They are constantly in motion,
perching on twigs or wires only briefly
to rest and to survey their
surroundings, or when they are at the
nest. During courtship the female sits
quietly on a perch while the male
displays in a pendulum dance,
swinging in a wide arc and buzzing
loudly with each dip.

480 Rufous Hummingbird
(Selasphorus rufus)
Hummingbirds (Trochilidae)

Description: 3½–4" (9–10 cm). Male has bright rufous upperparts and flanks and an iridescent orange-red throat. Female green above, with a rufous tinge on rump and flanks, and with much rufous in the tail. Female Ruby-throated Hummingbird is similar but lacks rufous on rump and flanks.

Voice: An abrupt, high-pitched *zeee;* various thin, squealing notes.

Habitat: Mountain meadows, forest edges; in migration and winter often in gardens with hummingbird feeding stations.

Nesting: 2 white eggs in a lichen-covered cup of plant down and spider web, attached to a horizontal branch.

Range: Southeastern Alaska, British Columbia, southwestern Alberta, and western Montana south to Washington, Oregon, Idaho and northern California. Winters mainly in Mexico. Occurs in small numbers along the Gulf Coast during migration and winter, and casually in the Carolinas.

This species is known in eastern North America mainly as a scarce migrant and winter visitor to Louisiana and Texas. While in that area it feeds chiefly on the flowers of hibiscus and salvia, which often bloom all winter long. A few birds generally spend the winter, but may disappear abruptly when the first severe cold spell arrives; it is not known whether these birds succumb to the cold or quickly move farther south.

484 Monk Parakeet
(Myiopsitta monachus)
Parrots (Psittacidae)

Description: 11" (28 cm). Bright green above and gray below with scalloping on the throat; primaries dark blue; tail long and pointed.

Voice: Loud, harsh, screeching *eeeh-eeeh*.

Habitat: City parks, suburban yards, and semi-open country.

Range: Introduced locally in the United States. Native to southern South America.

Nesting: 5 or 6 white eggs in a huge, bulky stick nest placed in a tree or on top of a power pole, or attached to a building wall. The nest is domed and has entrances to the egg chambers on the sides and bottom.

This noisy but attractive parrot was first reported wild in the late 1960s, presumably having escaped from a shipment at New York's Kennedy Airport. Since that time it has spread to surrounding regions. Its huge stick nests, used both for breeding and roosting, are conspicuous and may contain from one to as many as six pairs of birds. Because of its fondness for fruits and grain, the Monk Parakeet is now feared as a potential pest and is being controlled by destruction of its nests.

486 House Wren
(*Troglodytes aedon*)
Wrens (Troglodytidae)

Description: 4½–5¼″ (11–13 cm). A tiny bird with a short tail that is often held cocked over the back. Dusky brown above, paler below, with no distinctive markings. Similar Winter Wren is smaller, darker, with a shorter tail and a pale eyebrow.

Voice: A gurgling, bubbling, exuberant song, first rising, then falling.

Habitat: Residential areas, city parks, farmlands, and woodland edges.

Nesting: 5–8 white eggs, thickly speckled with brown, in a cup lined with feathers and other soft material contained within a

mass of sticks and grass, which is placed in a natural cavity or bird box.

Range: British Columbia, Ontario, and Maine south to the Carolinas, Missouri, and northern Mexico. Winters north to South Carolina, the Gulf Coast, and southern California.

This wren often nests in odd places such as mailboxes, flower pots, and even the pockets of coats on clotheslines. It is a favorite with people who put out bird boxes but has the distressing habit of piercing the eggs of other birds in its area. If wrens return in spring to find an old nest still in place, they usually remove it stick by stick, then proceed to rebuild, often using the material they've just discarded. Outside the breeding season it is shy, much less in evidence than when it is singing during the breeding season.

---

494 Brown Thrasher
(*Toxostoma rufum*)
Mockingbirds, Thrashers (Mimidae)

Description: 11½" (29 cm). Blue Jay-sized. Rufous-brown above, white below *with dark brown streaks*. Curved bill, long tail.

Voice: A variety of musical phrases, each repeated twice. The similar-sounding Mockingbird usually repeats each phrase three or more times. Call is a sharp *smack!*

Habitat: Thickets, fields with scrub, and woodland borders.

Nesting: 4 or 5 pale blue, brown-dotted eggs in a large, coarsely built nest of twigs, leaves, and rootlets lined with grass; usually near the ground in a dense, often thorny bush.

Range: Alberta, Manitoba, Ontario, and northern New England south to the Gulf Coast and Florida. Winters in the southern part of the breeding range.

Brown Thrashers may be confused with thrushes but are larger, have longer tails, and are streaked (not spotted) below. They belong to the same family as the Mockingbird, but, unlike that species, are retiring and secretive. They often feed on the ground, scattering dead leaves with their beaks as they search for insects.

---

506 Cedar Waxwing
(*Bombycilla cedrorum*)
Waxwings (Bombycillidae)

Description: 6½–8″ (16–20 cm). Smaller than a Robin. A *sleek, crested, brown* bird with a black mask, yellow tips on the tail feathers, hard red wax-like tips on the secondary wing feathers. Almost always seen in flocks.

Voice: Thin lisp, *tseee.*

Habitat: Open woodlands, orchards, and residential areas.

Nesting: 4–6 blue-gray eggs spotted with dark brown and black placed in a bulky cup of twigs and grass in a tree in the open.

Range: Breeds from British Columbia and Cape Breton Island south to Georgia, Arkansas, and California. Winters from New England and British Columbia to Panama and the Greater Antilles.

Waxwings spend most of the year in flocks whose movements may be quite erratic. Hundreds will suddenly appear in an area to exploit a crop of berries, only to vanish when that crop is exhausted. Since the young are fed to some extent on small fruits, waxwings tend to nest late in the summer when there is a good supply of berries. Adults store food for the young in their crop, a pouch located in their throat, and may regurgitate as many as thirty choke cherries, one at a time, into the gaping mouths. In summer insects are also taken, the birds hawking for them like flycatchers. These social birds have the amusing habit of passing berries or even apple blossoms from one bird to the next down a long row sitting on a branch, until one bird eats the food.

516, 571 Brown-headed Cowbird
(*Molothrus ater*)
Orioles, Blackbirds (Icteridae)

Description: 6–8″ (15–20 cm). Male black with glossy brown head; female plain gray. Both have a finch-like bill.

Voice: Squeaky gurgle. Call is *check* or a rattle.

Habitat: Agricultural land, fields, woodland edges, and suburban areas.

Nesting: 4 or 5 white eggs, lightly speckled with brown, laid one at a time in the nests of other songbirds.

Range: British Columbia, central Saskatchewan, central Ontario, Quebec, and Newfoundland south to Virginia, Louisiana, and northern Mexico. Winters regularly north to Maryland, Texas, and California.

This species and the Bronzed Cowbird are the only North American songbirds that are brood parasites, laying their eggs in the nests of other birds and leaving them to the care of foster parents. Unlike parasitic Old World cuckoos, which lay eggs closely resembling those of a host species, cowbirds lay eggs in the nests of over 200 other species, most smaller than themselves. Some host species eject the unwanted egg, others lay down a new nest lining over it, but most rear the young cowbird as one of their own. It has been suggested that cowbirds became parasitic because they followed roving herds of bison and had no time to stop to nest. The young cowbird grows quickly at the expense of the young of the host, taking most of the food or pushing them out of the nest.

524 Eurasian Tree Sparrow
(*Passer montanus*)
Weaver Finches (Ploceidae)

Description: 6″ (15 cm). Streaked brown above, dull white below. *Crown chocolate brown,* throat black, *cheek white with prominent black spot.* Sexes alike. The male House Sparrow is similar, but has a gray crown and lacks the black spot on the cheek.

Voice: Loud chirping, similar to that of the House Sparrow.

Habitat: City parks, suburbs, and farmland.

Nesting: 5 brown-spotted buff eggs in a tree cavity, bird box, or hole in a wall.

Range: Introduced around St. Louis, Missouri, in 1870. Native to Europe and much of Asia.

This introduced species differs from its relative, the House Sparrow, in that the sexes are alike. It is much less aggressive and quarrelsome; and it is more gregarious, often assembling in larger flocks. Altogether, it is a more attractive bird, both in appearance and behavior. These weavers sometimes visit grainfields and feed on corn, oats, and wheat, but they also consume many injurious weed seeds and, to a lesser extent, insects.

525, 526 House Sparrow
(*Passer domesticus*)
Weaver Finches (Ploceidae)

Description: 5–6½″ (13–16 cm). Male has *black throat,* white cheeks, and chestnut nape; gray crown and rump. Female and young are streaked dull brown above, dingy white below, with pale eyebrow.

Voice: Shrill, monotonous, noisy chirping.

Habitat: Cities, towns, and agricultural areas.

Nesting: 5 or 6 white eggs lightly speckled with brown in a loose mass of grass, feathers, strips of paper, string, and similar debris placed in a man-made or natural cavity. Two to three broods a season. Sometimes builds a globular nest in a tree.

Range: Introduced and now found throughout temperate North America. Native to Eurasia and North Africa, and introduced on all continents and on many islands.

Wherever this species occurs it is intimately associated with man, as its scientific name *domesticus* suggests. The entire North American population is descended from a few birds released in Central Park, New York City, in 1850. These birds found an unoccupied niche—the many towns and farms of the settled parts of the country—and quickly multiplied. As so often happens, introduced species can become a problem, and the House Sparrow is no exception. Because they compete for food and nest sites, some native species have suffered. Although they consume insects and weed seeds, they may do considerable damage to crops.

530 Chipping Sparrow
(*Spizella passerina*)
Grosbeaks, Buntings, Finches, Sparrows (Fringillidae)

Description: 5–5½" (13–14 cm). A small sparrow. Upperparts are brown streaked with black; underparts, sides of face, and rump are gray; *chestnut crown; white eyebrow* with thin black line through eye. Young birds have streaked crown, buff eyebrow, and duller underparts.
Voice: Thin musical trill, all on one note like a sewing machine.
Habitat: Grassy woodland edges, gardens, city parks, brushy pastures, and lawns.
Nesting: 3–5 pale blue eggs lightly spotted with brown in a solid cup of grass and stems, almost always lined with hair, placed in

shrubbery or in a tangle of vines.

Range: Breeds from the Yukon, Manitoba, and Newfoundland south to Florida, Nicaragua, and Baja California. Winters from California, Tennessee, and Maryland southward.

The bird's habit of lining its nest with hair has earned it the name "Hairbird." They formerly utilized horsehair, but with the decline in the use of horses they take any hair available and will even pluck strands from the coat of a sleeping dog. Originally an inhabitant of natural clearings and brushy forest borders, they are now found in gardens and suburban areas and have become a familiar songbird. During most of the year they feed on the ground, but in the breeding season males always sing from an elevated perch. Their food consists mainly of seeds, but in summer the adults and the young feed on insects.

542 **Song Sparrow**
(*Melospiza melodia*)
Grosbeaks, Buntings, Finches, Sparrows (Fringillidae)

Description: 5–7" (13–17 cm). A common sparrow with heavily streaked underparts and a *large central spot on breast. Pumps its tail in flight.*

Voice: 3 short notes followed by a varied trill, sometimes interpreted as *Madge-Madge-Madge, put-on-your-tea-kettle-ettle-ettle.*

Habitat: Thickets, pastures, undergrowth in gardens, and city parks.

Nesting: 3–5 pale green, brown-spotted eggs in a well-made cup of grass and leaves, often lined with hair, concealed in weeds on the ground or in a low bush.

Range: Aleutians, Alaska and Newfoundland south to the Carolinas, North Dakota, and Mexico. Winters from southern Canada to the Gulf Coast and Mexico.

Probably the best known of our native sparrows, it is found almost everywhere in North America. Over its vast range the species shows a great deal of geographical variation. In Alaska and the Aleutian Islands the birds are large, dark, and long-billed; it is hard to believe they are the same species as the familiar bird of our lawns and parks.

565 Starling
(*Sturnus vulgaris*)
Starlings (Sturnidae)

Description: 7½–8½" (19–21 cm). Smaller than a Robin. A short-tailed, chunky, iridescent black bird; long, pointed bill, yellow in summer and dark in winter. Plumage flecked with white in winter.

Voice: A series of discordant, musical, squeaky, and rasping notes; often imitates other birds. Call a descending *whee-ee.*

Habitat: Cities, suburban areas, farmlands, and ranches.

Nesting: 4–6 pale blue eggs in a mass of twigs, grass, and trash lined with finer plant material and feathers placed in a tree or building cavity.

Range: Introduced. Occurs from Alaska and Quebec south to the Gulf Coast and northern Mexico. Native to Eurasia, and introduced also in South Africa, Australia, New Zealand, and on certain oceanic islands.

Conditioned by centuries of living in settled areas in Europe, it easily adapted to American cities when 100 birds were liberated in Central Park, New York City, in 1890. Since then it has spread over most of the continent. Its large roosts are often located on buildings and may contain tens of thousands of birds. These congregations create much noise, foul the area, and

have proved difficult to drive away.
Starlings are aggressive birds and
compete with native species for nest
cavities and food. There has been much
debate regarding their economic value,
but their consumption of insects seems
to tip the balance in their favor.

572, 573 Common Grackle
(*Quiscalus quiscula*)
Orioles, Blackbirds (Icteridae)

Description: 12″ (30 cm). Blue Jay-sized. *Long
wedge-shaped tail* displaying a
longitudinal ridge or keel when in
flight. Appears all black at a distance
but is actually highly iridescent, with
colors varying from blue to purple to
green to bronze, depending on the
light. Bright yellow eyes.

Voice: Clucks. High-pitched, rising screech
like a rusty hinge.

Habitat: Lawns, parks, fields, open woodland.

Nesting: 5 pale blue eggs with black scrawls in a
bulky stick nest lined with grass,
placed anywhere from low in a bush to
high in a tree. Partly in colonies,
breeding most often in tall evergreens.

Range: Southern Canada to the Gulf states east
of the Rockies.

These familiar birds arrive from the
South early in spring and depart late in
fall. In some northern areas they
congregate by the thousands during
migration as well as in winter roosts.
Their diet is extremely varied,
including insects, crayfish, frogs, mice,
nestling birds, and eggs as well as
grains and wild fruits. At feeders they
are especially attracted to cracked corn.
They are most numerous near dwellings
and are even found raiding litter
baskets at public beaches.

579 Common Crow
(*Corvus brachyrhynchos*)
Jays, Magpies, Crows (Corvidae)

Description: 17–21" (43–53 cm). Stocky black bird with a stout bill and a fan-shaped tail. The smaller Fish Crow has a higher-pitched voice; the larger Raven has a wedge-shaped tail.

Voice: Familiar *caw-caw* or *caa-caa*.

Habitat: Woodlands, farmland, and suburban areas.

Nesting: 4–6 dull green eggs, spotted with dark brown, in a large mass of twigs and sticks lined with feathers, grass, and rootlets and placed in a tree.

Range: Breeds from British Columbia and Newfoundland south to Florida, the Gulf Coast, and northern Mexico. Winters north to southern Canada.

Every continent except South America has at least one familiar roadside crow, and this is the species in North America. It is almost impossible to go into the countryside without seeing these birds along highways or flying overhead. Intelligent, wary, virtually omnivorous, and with a high reproductive capacity, the Common Crow is undoubtedly much more numerous than it was before the arrival of settlers. They may gather in roosts of over half a million birds and are so abundant that even an ardent defender of birds might not deny that they are destructive to crops and should be controlled, although they consume enormous amounts of grasshoppers, cutworms, and other harmful insects. Crows make interesting pets if obtained while quite young, learning to mimic the human voice. They often carry off and hide bright objects.

Thickets and Second Growth

Partly open country with scattered small trees, bushes, and shrubs. Such habitat often develops on land that has been cleared of forest, and may follow a grassland stage. Second growth generally consists of trees that do *not* form a closed canopy of foliage and that do allow sunlight to filter through, so that there is a richer understory of bushes and herbaceous vegetation than in mature forest.

In addition to the birds treated in this section one may find birds of Deciduous Forests, especially where these two habitats are adjacent to one another.

357   Yellow Warbler
(*Dendroica petechia*)
Wood Warblers (Parulidae)

Description: 4½–5″ (11–13 cm). Bright yellow
with a light olive-green tinge on back.
Male has fine rusty streaks on breast.
The only largely yellow warbler with
yellow (not white) *spots in the tail.*

Voice: Bright and musical *sweet-sweet-sweet,
sweeter-than-sweet.*

Habitat: Moist thickets, especially along streams
and in swampy areas; gardens.

Nesting: 4 or 5 pale blue eggs thickly spotted
with brown, in a well-made cup of
bark, plant fibers, and down placed in
an upright fork in a small sapling.

Range: Breeds from Alaska, northern Quebec,
and Newfoundland south to the
Carolinas, Missouri, and Texas, and
through Central America and the West
Indies to northern South America.
Winters north to southern Mexico.

This is one of the most widespread of
our warblers, showing great
geographical variation. In the tropical
parts of its breeding range it nests
mainly in mangrove swamps, and there
it may have a chestnut head or crown
patch. In temperate North America it
is one of the principal victims of the
cowbird, which lays its eggs in the nests
of other birds. The warbler often
responds to the unwanted egg by
burying it, along with some of its own
eggs, under a new nest lining.
Occasionally a nest is found with up
to six layers, each containing one or
more cowbird eggs.

358   Wilson's Warbler
(*Wilsonia pusilla*)
Wood Warblers (Parulidae)

Description: 4½–5″ (11–13 cm). Adult male olive-
green above and yellow below with *black*

crown patch. Females and young males lack the black crown and may be distinguished from other olive-green warblers with yellow underparts by their lack of wing bars, streaks, tail spots, or other markings.

Voice: Rapid, staccato series of *chips,* dropping in pitch at the end.

Habitat: Moist thickets in woodland and along streams; alder and willow thickets and bogs.

Nesting: 4 or 5 brown-spotted white eggs in a bulky mass of leaves, rootlets, and moss lined with hair and fine plant materials, concealed on the ground in a dense clump of weeds or sedge.

Range: Breeds from Alaska and Newfoundland south to northern New England, Minnesota, and, in the western mountains, to southern California. Winters in Mexico and Central America.

Seen briefly on migration, Wilson's Warbler is seldom found more than a dozen feet from the ground. It is an active bird and like a flycatcher spends much time darting after small flying insects. It was named for the great Scottish-American ornithologist and artist, Alexander Wilson (1766–1813).

359 Yellow-breasted Chat
(*Icteria virens*)
Wood Warblers (Parulidae)

Description: 6½–7½" (16–19 cm). Larger than a sparrow. Olive-green above with bright yellow breast and white abdomen, *stout black bill,* black face mask bordered above and below with white; *white spectacles.* Tail long.

Voice: Series of widely spaced croaks, whistles, and short repeated phrases, very unlike a typical warbler's song. Often sings at night. At times it performs a display-flight, flopping awkwardly up and down with legs dangling while singing.

Habitat: Dense thickets and brush, often with thorns; streamside tangles and dry brushy hillsides.

Nesting: 4 or 5 brown-spotted white eggs in a bulky mass of bark, grass, and leaves, lined with finer grass, concealed in a dense bush.

Range: British Columbia, Ontario, and Massachusetts south to Florida, the Gulf Coast, and northern Mexico. Winters in Mexico and Central America.

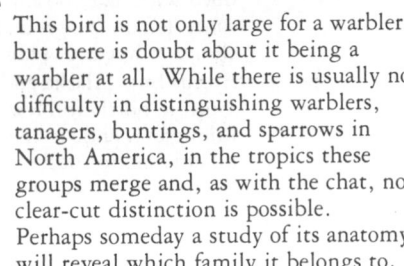

This bird is not only large for a warbler but there is doubt about it being a warbler at all. While there is usually no difficulty in distinguishing warblers, tanagers, buntings, and sparrows in North America, in the tropics these groups merge and, as with the chat, no clear-cut distinction is possible. Perhaps someday a study of its anatomy will reveal which family it belongs to.

361 Blue-winged Warbler
(*Vermivora pinus*)
Wood Warblers (Parulidae)

Description: 4½″ (11 cm). Sexes similar, *mostly bright yellow with blue-gray wings and white wing bars;* back and tail greenish.

Voice: Insect-like buzzy song, which sounds like a tired sigh, *seeee-bzzzz,* the "bzzz" pitched lower.

Habitat: Abandoned fields and pastures grown up to saplings; forest clearings and edges with clumps of catbrier, blackberry, and various bushes and young trees.

Nesting: 5 brown-dotted white eggs in a grass-lined cup of dead leaves and fibers placed on or very near the ground in thick undergrowth.

Range: From Nebraska, central Iowa, southern Wisconsin, southern Ontario and central New England south through

east-central and Atlantic Coast states to South Carolina. Winters from Mexico to Panama.

This warbler perches motionless for minutes at a time when uttering its song. It frequently hybridizes with its close relative the Golden-winged Warbler.

363 Prairie Warbler
(*Dendroica discolor*)
Wood Warblers (Parulidae)

Description: 5" (13 cm). Olive above, *bright yellow below with black spots and streaks along sides; male has chestnut streaks on back.* Wags its tail vigorously.

Voice: Buzzy *zee-zee-zee,* up to 10 rapidly ascending notes.

Habitat: Not found on prairies. In the North, mixed pine-oak barrens, old pastures, and on hillsides with scattered red cedars; in the South in open scrub; in extreme southern Florida in mangrove swamps.

Nesting: 4 brown-spotted white eggs in a nest of grass and leaves lined with hair and feathers, usually set low in a bush or a small tree.

Range: South Dakota, Wisconsin, Ontario, and central New England south to Oklahoma, the Gulf Coast, and Florida. Winters in southern Florida, the West Indies and Central America.

This species avoids thick woods and has benefited greatly from the cutting and burning of the forests, which favors the younger seedlings and smaller bushes that sprout after fires. Like the Palm Warbler, it ranges low, rarely ascending higher than 10 feet.

371 Common Yellowthroat
"Yellowthroat"
(*Geothlypis trichas*)
Wood Warblers (Parulidae)

Description: 4½–6″ (11–14 cm). Olive-brown above, *bright yellow on throat and upper breast.* Male has *bold black face mask,* bordered above with white. Females and young males lack the face mask but may be recognized by the bright yellow throat and wren-like behavior.

Voice: Loud, fast *witchity-witchity-witchity-witchity-wit* or *which-is-it, which-is-it, which-is-it.* Call a sharp *chip.*

Habitat: Moist thickets and grassy marshes.

Nesting: 3–5 white eggs with brown and black spots in a loose mass of grass, sedge, and bark lined with rootlets, hair, and fine grass and concealed on or near the ground in a dense clump of weeds or grass.

Range: Breeds from Alaska, Ontario, and Newfoundland south to Florida, the Gulf Coast, and Mexico. Winters regularly north to the Carolinas, Louisiana, and central California.

A small bird with a yellow throat, skulking in the grass or weeds of a marshy spot, is almost certainly a Common Yellowthroat. Its cheerful song is well known. At the height of the breeding season, the males perform an attractive flight display, mounting into the air while uttering a jumble of high-pitched notes, then bouncing back into the grass while giving the usual song. It is the northernmost member of a group of yellowthroat species that occurs as far south as Argentina. Until recently this species was called simply "Yellowthroat."

373 Nashville Warbler
(*Vermivora ruficapilla*)
Wood Warblers (Parulidae)

Description: 4–5" (10–13 cm). Olive-green above, bright yellow below, with *top and sides of head gray, narrow white eye-ring,* and inconspicuous patch of rust on the crown. Differs from the Mourning Warbler in having a *yellow throat,* not gray or black.

Voice: Loud, ringing *chip-chip-chip-chip chipper-chipper-chipper-chipper.*

Habitat: Woodland edges; thickets in open mixed forest or brushy borders of swamps.

Nesting: 4 or 5 white eggs speckled with brown in a cup of grasses, leaves, and roots lined with pine needles and fine grass; concealed on the ground in the base of a bush or a tussock of grass.

Range: Breeds from British Columbia, Manitoba, Quebec, and Nova Scotia south to Connecticut, Maryland, West Virginia, Michigan, Minnesota, Utah, and central California. Winters from northern Mexico southward to Guatemala.

This warbler has benefited from the arrival of settlers and the clearing of forests. It breeds most successfully in brushy, overgrown pastures, a habitat that has become more widespread with the decline of farming in the Northeast. As these pastures become second-growth woodland and the ground loses its cover of brush, the Nashville Warbler will probably become less abundant.

377 Chestnut-sided Warbler
(*Dendroica pensylvanica*)
Wood Warblers (Parulidae)

Description: 5" (13 cm). Sexes similar: yellow-green crown; *long, thin chestnut line on sides;*

white underparts, streaked back.
Immatures uniform yellow-green above,
dull whitish below, with white eye-ring
and yellow wing bars.

Voice: Rich and musical with an emphatic
ending, sometimes interpreted as *very
very pleased to MEET-CHA!*

Habitat: Young, open, second-growth woodland
and scrub.

Nesting: 4 brown-spotted white eggs in a grass-
and-bark nest lined with hair and
rootlets, only a few feet up in a small
tree or bush.

Range: Breeds from southern Canada to east-
central United States, south in the
Appalachian Mountains. Winters from
Nicaragua to Panama.

This attractive bird was rare in the days
of Audubon and Wilson, who seldom
saw it and knew little about its habits.
It has increased tremendously as
abandoned pastures in the northern
states have grown up in dense thickets,
a vast new habitat unavailable when the
land was clothed in virgin forest.

378 Golden-winged Warbler
(*Vermivora chrysoptera*)
Wood Warblers (Parulidae)

Description: 4½" (11 cm). Sexes similar: gray above,
white below, with *black mask* and throat
with white eyebrow and mustache; *yellow
crown and wing patch.*

Voice: Slow, drawled, insect-like song
resembling that of the Blue-wing but
longer, *seee buzzz, buzz,* with the first
note higher.

Habitat: Abandoned fields and pastures grown
up to saplings but usually in moister
situations.

Nesting: 5 white purplish-spotted eggs in a cup
of dead leaves and fibers set on or near
the ground in thick vegetation.

Range: Breeds from Minnesota and New
Hampshire south to New Jersey and

Iowa, and in the mountains to Georgia. Winters from southern Mexico to northern South America.

Where the breeding ranges of this species and the Blue-winged Warbler overlap, the two frequently hybridize; the offspring of these crosses show various combinations of the characters of the parent species and have been called "Lawrence's Warbler" and "Brewster's Warbler." The fact that these two species interbreed shows that they are quite closely related, and suggests that the rather striking differences between them have evolved during the last few tens of thousands of years.

382, 402 American Redstart
(*Setophaga ruticilla*)
Wood Warblers (Parulidae)

Description: 4½–5½" (11–14 cm). Male is black with bright orange patches on wings and tail; white belly. Females and young birds dull olive-brown above, white below, with yellow wing and tail patches.

Voice: Five or six high-pitched notes or two-note phrases, ending with an upward or downward inflection: *chewy-chewy-chewy, chew-chew-chew.*

Habitat: Second-growth woodlands; thickets with saplings.

Nesting: 4 dull white eggs, speckled with brown, in a neat, well-made cup of grass, bark shreds, plant fibers, and spider web lined with fine grass and hair, placed in a fork in a sapling or next to the trunk of a tree.

Range: Breeds from southeastern Alaska, central Manitoba, central Quebec, and Newfoundland south to Georgia, southern Louisiana, southeastern Oklahoma, Colorado, and northern California. Winters from Mexico to South America.

This is one of the most abundant birds in North America, because its favored habitat, second-growth woodland, covers such vast areas of the continent. It has a distinctive habit of dropping down suddenly in pursuit of a flying insect, then fanning its brightly marked tail from side to side. It takes a full year for the males to acquire the black-and-orange adult plumage, so it is not unusual to find what appears to be a female singing and displaying like a male.

383 White-eyed Vireo
(*Vireo griseus*)
Vireos (Vireonidae)

Description: 5″ (13 cm). Warbler-sized. Olive-green above and white below with yellow flanks; *yellow spectacles;* white wing bars. Adult has *white eye;* immature has dark eye.

Voice: Loud, explosive series of notes: *chip-a-wheeoo-chip* or *quick give me the rain check!*

Habitat: Dense swampy thickets and hillsides with blackberry and briar tangles.

Nesting: 4 brown-dotted white eggs in a purse-shaped nest of bark strips and grass, lined with spider silk, moss, and lichens and set from three to six feet up in thick undergrowth.

Range: Nebraska, Illinois, Ohio, southeastern New York, and central New England south to southern Florida and northeastern Mexico. Winters from the Gulf states to Honduras and the northern West Indies.

While most vireos inhabit tall trees, this species is usually found in thickets, where its presence is most easily detected by its loud and distinctive song. A patient observer can usually get a good look at one by standing quietly and waiting for the bird's curiosity to bring it into view. The Brown-headed Cowbird favors this vireo's nest for its own eggs.

401, 520 Rufous-sided Towhee
(*Pipilo erythrophthalmus*)
Grosbeaks, Buntings, Finches,
Sparrows (Fringillidae)

Description: 7–9½" (17–24 cm). Male has black head and upperparts, white underparts; bright rufous patches on flanks. Female is similar, but warm brown where male is black.

Voice: Song a cheerful *drink-your-TEA*, second note lower, third note higher. Call a clear *to-wheee?*, also *chewink*.

Habitat: Thickets and brushy woodland edges.

Nesting: 4–6 white eggs lightly spotted with red-brown in a loose cup of weed stems, grass, and bark on or near the ground in dense cover.

Range: British Columbia, Saskatchewan, and Maine south to Florida, Louisiana, and Guatemala. Winters north to Maryland, Nebraska, and southern British Columbia.

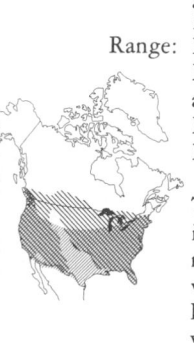

The name "Towhee," an imitation of its call note, was given in 1731 by the naturalist and bird artist Mark Catesby, who encountered it in the Carolinas. Few birds show as much geographical variation in voice; the calls of birds in the West bear little resemblance to those in the East. The birds vary greatly in appearance as well, and until recently the eastern "Red-eyed Towhee" and the western "Spotted Towhee" were thought to be distinct species. They interbreed where they come in contact, however, and are now considered the same species. Towhees often feed on the ground, scratching noisily in the dry leaves.

406, 407 Cardinal
(*Cardinalis cardinalis*)
Grosbeaks, Buntings, Finches,
Sparrows, (Fringillidae)

Description: 8–9" (20–23 cm). Male bright red with *crest,* black face, *stout red bill.* Female buff-brown tinged with red on crest, wings, and tail.

Voice: Rich *what-cheer, cheer, cheer; purty-purty-purty-purty* or *sweet-sweet-sweet-sweet.* Also a metallic *chip.*

Habitat: Woodland edges, thickets, brushy swamps, and gardens.

Nesting: 3 or 4 pale green eggs spotted with red-brown in a deep cup of twigs, leaves, and plant fibers concealed in a thicket.

Range: Resident from the Dakotas, southern Ontario, and Nova Scotia south to the Gulf Coast, and from southern Texas, Arizona, and southern California southward into Mexico.

This species, named after the red robes worn by Roman Catholic cardinals, has extended its range northeastward into southern Canada in recent decades. Cardinals are aggressive birds, and occupy territories year-round. Both sexes are accomplished songsters and may be heard at any time of year rather than just in the spring when most other birds are singing. As in most members of the finch family, seeds form a main part of the diet, although insects are taken in the breeding season. They often come to bird feeders in winter.

411 Common Redpoll
(*Carduelis flammea*)
Grosbeaks, Buntings, Finches,
Sparrows (Fringillidae)

Description: 5–5½" (13–14 cm). Smaller than a sparrow. Pale, brown-streaked, with *bright red cap* and black chin. Male has a pink breast.

Voice: Twittering trill. Call is a soft rattle.

Habitat: Tundra and dwarf arctic birch in summer; brushy pastures, open thickets, and weedy fields in winter.

Nesting: 4–6 pale green eggs, spotted with red-brown, in a well-made cup of grass, moss, and twigs lined with plant down and placed in a low willow or birch.

Range: Breeds from Aleutians west to Unalaska Island and Alaska and northern Quebec south to Newfoundland, Magdalen Islands, and British Columbia. Winters south to the Carolinas, Oklahoma, and California. Also in northern Eurasia.

A stand of winter weeds visited by a flock of these energetic little birds is a scene of feverish activity as they tear dried flower stalks apart and rush to the ground to pick up the seeds. They spend much time on the ground, often in dense stands of weeds, and are therefore easier to overlook than the more arboreal goldfinches and siskins. They are tame and trusting, and allow close approach; unfortunately this trait causes them to fall prey to predators.

Hoary Redpoll
(*Carduelis hornemanni*)
Grosbeaks, Buntings, Finches, Sparrows (Fringillidae)

Description: 4½–5½″ (11–14 cm). Smaller than a sparrow. Brown-streaked, with a *red cap*. Male has a pale pink breast. Similar to the Common Redpoll but slightly paler, with a smaller bill and an unstreaked rump and undertail coverts.

Voice: Series of metallic *chips* given in flight; soft twittering calls when feeding on the ground. The calls are sharper than those of the Common Redpoll.

Habitat: Weedy pastures and roadsides in winter, tundra in summer.

Nesting:	5 or 6 pale blue eggs, lightly spotted with brown, in a feather-lined cup of grass and shreds of bark, concealed under a rock or a clump of tundra vegetation.
Range:	Along the coasts of the Arctic Ocean, wandering southward in winter to the northern United States.

The Hoary Redpoll is generally found farther north and in more open tundra than the Common Redpoll. The two species have at times been considered a single species, but they are now known to nest side by side, without interbreeding, in parts of Canada and Alaska.

437   Lazuli Bunting
(*Passerina amoena*)
Grosbeaks, Buntings, Finches,
Sparrows (Fringillidae)

Description:	5–5½" (13–14 cm). Sparrow-sized. Male bright blue with pale cinnamon breast, white belly and wing bars. Female dull brown, lighter below, with two pale wing bars. Female Indigo Bunting similar, but lacks conspicuous wing bars.
Voice:	A high-pitched, excited series of warbled phrases, the first notes usually repeated, descending the scale and ascending again at the end; similar to song of Indigo Bunting but phrases less distinct and only the first phrases repeated.
Habitat:	Dry, brushy ravines and slopes; cleared areas and weedy pastures.
Nesting:	3 or 4 pale blue eggs in a loose cup of grass and rootlets in a bush.
Range:	British Columbia, Saskatchewan, and North Dakota south through western United States to southern California, northern New Mexico, western Oklahoma, and eastern Nebraska. Winters in Mexico.

This western relative of the Indigo Bunting has increased in numbers with the cutting of western forests and their replacement by brush. The two species hybridize sparingly where their ranges overlap, but because this hybridization has not become more widespread the two birds are still considered separate species.

438, 513 Indigo Bunting
(*Passerina cyanea*)
Grosbeaks, Buntings, Finches, Sparrows (Fringillidae)

Description: 5½" (14 cm). Sparrow-sized. *Male in bright sunlight brilliant turquoise blue,* otherwise looks black; wings and tail darker. Female drab brown, paler beneath.

Voice: Rapid, excited warble, each note or phrase repeated.

Habitat: Brushy slopes, abandoned farmland, old pastures and fields grown up to scrub, woodland clearings, and forest edge adjacent to fields.

Nesting: 3 or 4 pale blue eggs in a compact woven cup of leaves and grass placed in a sapling or bush within a few feet of the ground among relatively thick vegetation.

Range: New England to the Gulf states, west to Kansas and Texas. Winters chiefly from Mexico and the West Indies south to Panama.

Indigo Buntings have no blue pigment; they are actually black, but the diffraction of light through the structure of the feathers makes them appear blue. These attractive birds are also found in rural roadside thickets and along the right-of-way of railroads, where woodland meets open areas. They are beneficial to the farmer and fruit grower, consuming many insect pests and weed seeds.

439 Blue Grosbeak
(*Guiraca caerulea*)
Grosbeaks, Buntings, Finches,
Sparrows (Fringillidae)

Description: 6–7½" (15–19 cm). Slightly larger
than a House Sparrow. Male dark blue
with *two buff wing bars* and a stout, dark
bill. Female dark buff-brown with two
buff wing bars. Indigo Bunting similar
but smaller, lacks wing bars, and is not
as rust-colored.

Voice: Sweet, jumbled warble. Also a metallic
klink.

Habitat: Brushy, moist pastures and roadside
thickets.

Nesting: 3 or 4 pale blue eggs in a loose cup of
grass, weed stems, and leaves concealed
in a clump of weeds.

Range: California, Colorado, Missouri, Illinois,
and New Jersey south to Florida, the
Gulf Coast, Mexico, and Costa Rica.
Winters in Central America.

This grosbeak is the only North
American member of a group of
tropical finches common in parts of
South America. Each fall it gathers in
large flocks and visits sorghum fields in
search of insects and seeds.

449 Bell's Vireo
(*Vireo belii*)
Vireos (Vireonidae)

Description: 4¾–5" (11–13 cm). Smaller than a
sparrow. Dull olive-gray above, whitish
below, with a faint white eye-ring and
fainter wingbars. White-eyed Vireo
similar but smaller and has white eyes.

Voice: Fast, warbled *tweedle-deedle-dum?*
Tweedle-deedle-dee! First phrase up,
second phrase down.

Habitat: Dense bottomland thickets, willow
scrub, and mesquite.

Nesting: 3–5 white eggs sparsely marked with

brown in a well-made pendant cup of plant down and bark strips, placed in a dense tree or shrub.

Range: Northern California, Colorado, the Dakotas, and Indiana south to Guatemala. Winters to Nicaragua.

Although often victimized by cowbirds, this bird raises relatively few of the brood parasites, simply abandoning a nest when a cowbird's egg is laid in it. This species was named by Audubon for John G. Bell (1812–1899), a New York taxidermist who accompanied him on his trip up the Missouri River in the 1840s.

Black-capped Vireo
(*Vireo atricapillus*)
Vireos (Vireonidae)

Description: 4½–4¾" (11–12 cm). Smaller than a sparrow. Olive-green above, white below, *crown and sides of head glossy black,* white "spectacles." Female similar, but crown and sides of head slate-gray.

Voice: Harsh and varied phrases, sometimes musical.

Habitat: Dense oak scrub and juniper thickets.

Nesting: 4 unspotted white eggs in a well-made pendant cup of plant fibers and bark strips decorated with lichens, concealed in a shrub or bush.

Range: Breeds from Kansas south through Oklahoma to central Texas. Winters in Mexico.

This little vireo, with its restricted range, differs from most vireos in being rather nervous and active—more like a warbler in its behavior. It is a tireless singer but is often difficult to find in the dense oak scrub. It has a titmouse-like habit of hanging upside-down while foraging in twigs.

456 Orange-crowned Warbler
(*Vermivora celata*)
Wood Warblers (Parulidae)

Description: 4½–5½" (11–14 cm). Smaller than a
sparrow. Dark olive-green, with vague
streaking and yellow tinge on the
breast. *No wing bars or eyebrows.*
Autumn immatures differ from young
Yellow Warblers in that they lack
yellow spots in the tail and are faintly
streaked.

Voice: High, sweet trill like that of the
Chipping Sparrow's musical call.

Habitat: Thickets and brushy woodlands.

Nesting: 4 or 5 white eggs with red-brown spots
in a cup of grass and bark fibers lined
with feathers and finer grass; concealed
on the ground under a bush or close to
the ground in a low thicket.

Range: Alaska, Manitoba east to Quebec and
Labrador south to Texas and northern
Mexico. Winters from South Carolina,
Arkansas, and California to Guatemala.

While the Orange-crown is a common
bird in the West and in winter along
the Gulf Coast, in most of the East it is
a rather rare migrant. It is slightly
more numerous in the fall, when the
birds—mostly immatures—show a
fondness for stands of goldenrod and
generally forage close to the ground.

462 Willow Flycatcher
"Traill's Flycatcher"
(*Empidonax traillii*)
Tyrant Flycatchers (Tyrannidae)

Description: 6" (15 cm). Sparrow-sized. Olive-green
with a whitish throat. Distinguishable
from Alder Flycatcher only by voice and
breeding habitat (see below).

Voice: A wheezy *fitz-bew* or *pit-speer;* the song
of the Alder Flycatcher is a burry *fee-
bee-o,* descending more abruptly in
pitch.

Habitat: Swampy thickets, upland pastures, and old abandoned orchards; Alder Flycatchers occur along wooded lake shores and streams.

Nesting: 3 or 4 creamy white eggs with fine brown speckling, in a neat, compact cup of plant down and fibers placed in a low bush or sapling.

Range: Breeds from southern British Columbia, Alberta, North Dakota, Western New York, and Maine south to Virginia, Arkansas, and California. Winters in South America.

The Willow and Alder Flycatchers are so similar in appearance that it is only within the last two decades that it has been realized that they are two distinct species. Until then they were together called "Traill's Flycatcher." Both species breed in the northeastern United States, but north of the Great Lakes and Maine only the Alder Flycatcher occurs. The name *Empidonax* is from the Greek and means "gnat-tyrant," an allusion to the favorite food of these birds; the name *traillii* honors Thomas S. Traill (1781–1862), a distinguished Scottish naturalist and patron of Audubon.

Alder Flycatcher
"Traill's Flycatcher"
(*Empidonax alnorum*)
Tyrant Flycatchers (Tyrannidae)

Description: 5–6" (13–15 cm). Smaller than a House Sparrow. Dull gray-green above, whitish below, with two dull white wing bars and a narrow white eye-ring. Indistinguishable in appearance from the Willow Flycatcher; best identified by voice and breeding habitat.

Voice: A burry *fee-bee-o*, rather different from the wheezy *fitz-bew!* of the Willow Flycatcher.

Habitat: Alder swamps, streamside and lakeside

thickets, and second growth.

Nesting: 3 or 4 white eggs finely speckled with brown, in a loose cup of grass with little or no plant down (like the Willow Flycatcher), placed in a low bush or sapling.

Range: Alaska, Manitoba, and central Quebec south to southern New England, New York, Ohio, Minnesota, and British Columbia. Winters in Central and South America.

This species in general has a more northerly distribution than its close relative the Willow Flycatcher. Although the habitats of the two species differ, in a few places where their ranges meet the two can be heard singing in the same general area. It was in such an area in upstate New York that the small but constant differences between these birds were first noticed; research carried on in the 1950s and 1960s showed that they were two distinct species. Previously the Willow and Alder flycatchers had been called "Traill's Flycatcher."

476, 477 Painted Bunting
(*Passerina ciris*)
Grosbeaks, Buntings, Finches, Sparrows, (Fringillidae)

Description: 5½" (14 cm). Sparrow-sized. Perhaps our most brilliant bird: male has bright red underparts and rump, green back, purple head, and red eye-ring; female is bright green all over, lighter below.

Voice: Loud, clear, and variable song consisting of a series of high-pitched musical notes reminiscent of the Indigo Bunting; the call is a sharp, metallic *tsick*.

Habitat: Brushy tangles, hedgerows, briar patches, woodland edges, and swampy thickets.

Nesting: 3 or 4 white eggs marked with reddish-

brown dots in a cup of compactly
woven grass stems, rootlets, and bark
strips, lined with moss and hair, placed
near the ground in the fork of a bush or
small tree.

Range: Missouri and North Carolina south to
the southeastern states and west to New
Mexico and Oklahoma. Winters from
the Gulf states south to the Bahamas
and Cuba, and through Mexico to
Panama.

This gaudy finch is one of the most
beautiful birds in North America. Its
brilliant plumage made it a popular
cagebird until it came under federal
protection, and it is still sold in the
markets of Mexico and the West Indies.
Despite its vivid coloration, however, it
is often difficult to see as it skulks
among dense thickets, although in
Florida, at least, it often comes to
feeding stations. Its other well-known
name is "Nonpareil," meaning "without
equal." This species is common in parts
of the Deep South and raises as many as
three broods. The female is one of the
few truly green birds in North
America.

---

489 Carolina Wren
(*Thryothorus ludovicianus*)
Wrens (Troglodytidae)

Description: 5½" (14 cm). Rich brown above, buff
below; *conspicuous white line above and
behind eye.*

Voice: Loud whistled *tweedle-tweedle-tweedle* or
TEA-kettle, TEA-kettle, TEA-kettle tea
which is sung all day long in all
seasons.

Habitat: Woodland thickets, ravines, and rocky
slopes covered with brush.

Nesting: 5 brown-spotted whitish eggs in a
feather-lined domed stick nest with an
entrance on the side; placed in stone
walls, hollow tree stumps, tin cans,

mail boxes, birdhouses, and even coat pockets on clotheslines.

Range: Chiefly southeastern United States north to the central portions of Wisconsin, Michigan, and New York, and southern New England.

These wrens do not migrate. At the northern edge of their range they increase in mild years, but a severe cold season with heavy snows will decimate their numbers. They live in thickets and swamps, frequenting brush piles and old wooden buildings.

490 Bewick's Wren
(*Thryomanes bewickii*)
Wrens (Troglodytidae)

Description: 5½″ (14 cm). Gray-brown above, white below, with a long fan-shaped tail tipped with white. Sexes similar.

Voice: Loud, melodious song with the usual bubbly wren-like warble, also reminiscent of a Song Sparrow.

Habitat: Thickets, brush piles, and hedgerows in farming country; also open woodland and scrubby areas, often near streams.

Nesting: 5–7 brown-spotted white eggs in a stick nest lined with leaves, grass, and feathers. The nest may be found in almost any cavity, including woodpecker holes, tin cans, coat pockets or sleeves, baskets, tool sheds, and brush piles.

Range: Locally from western United States to east of the Appalachian Mountains, but absent from the Atlantic Coast; south to the Gulf of Mexico and central Mexico.

Bewick's Wren is named for Thomas Bewick, (1753–1828), an English ornithologist and engraver. Although this species resembles the somewhat larger Carolina Wren, it has an entirely different song and, at close range, shows white in the outer tail feathers. Bewick's Wren lives in similar surroundings but generally prefers drier situations.

521 Black-billed Cuckoo
(*Coccyzus erythropthalmus*)
Cuckoos (Cuculidae)

Description: 12" (30 cm). Very similar to Yellow-billed Cuckoo—brown above, white below—but *bill entirely black,* wings brown, and much less white at tips of tail feathers. Narrow red eye-ring.

Voice: A series of *cu-cu-cu-cu* notes in groups of two to five. All of them on the same pitch.

Habitat: Similar to the Yellow-billed Cuckoo: moist thickets in low, overgrown pastures and orchards, but occurs in thicker undergrowth and in sparse woodland.

Nesting: 2 or 4 blue-green eggs in a flimsy, shallow nest of twigs lined with grass and plant down. The nest is low to the ground in a dense thicket or thorn bush.

Range: Southern Canada to South Carolina, Tennessee, and Kansas. Winters in northwestern South America.

Both eastern cuckoos are adept at hiding and skulking in dense vegetation, and are more often heard than seen. Their loud notes, repeated over and over again, are reminiscent of those of grebes and doves, but deeper in tone and more repetitive. When tracked down, they slip away to another location and repeat the call. Cuckoos are extremely beneficial to the farmer and horticulturist, consuming enormous quantities of destructive hairy caterpillars, especially tent caterpillars and gypsy moth larvae. They are most numerous in years of tent caterpillar infestations.

522 Yellow-billed Cuckoo
(*Coccyzus americanus*)
Cuckoos (Cuculidae)

Description: 10½–12½" (26–32 cm). Jay-sized.
Slender, long-tailed bird, brown above
and white below, with *large white spots
on underside of tail and a flash of rufous in
wings.* Bill slightly curved with yellow
lower mandible. Black-billed Cuckoo is
similar but has very little rufous in
wings and smaller white spots on tail.

Voice: Rapid, rattling *ka-ka-ka-ka-ka-ka-kow-
kow-kowp, kowp, kowp, kowp,* becoming
slower at the end.

Habitat: Moist thickets, willows, overgrown
pastures, and orchards.

Nesting: 2–4 pale blue-green eggs in a flimsy
saucer of twigs placed in a bush or
small sapling.

Range: Breeds from British Columbia,
Minnesota, and Maine south to Mexico
and the West Indies. Winters in South
America.

This bird's tendency to utter its
distinctive call at the approach of a
storm has earned it the name "Rain
Crow." Both the Yellow-billed and
Black-billed Cuckoos are fond of hairy
caterpillars, and during outbreaks of
tent caterpillars are valuable in keeping
these insects in check. Usually shy and
elusive, these birds are easy to overlook.

529 Harris' Sparrow
(*Zonotrichia querula*)
Grosbeaks, Buntings, Finches,
Sparrows (Fringillidae)

Description: 7½" (19 cm). Adult has *black crown,
throat, and chest;* pink bill; gray face;
brown back, wings, and tail; and *white
abdomen with spotted or streaked sides.*
Immatures have buff faces and lack
solid black crown, throat, and breast.

Voice: Series of clear, high notes followed by

another series, each on a different pitch.

Habitat: Breeds in mossy bogs and scrub forests, migrates through the prairie regions, and winters in dense river-bottom thickets, woodland borders, clearings, and brush piles.

Nesting: 3–5 pale green, brown-blotched eggs in a plant fiber and leaf nest lined with grass, placed on the ground at the base of a bush or in a stunted spruce tree.

Range: Breeds in northern Canada west of Hudson Bay south to northern Manitoba. Winters in interior from Iowa and Nebraska south to Texas and Louisiana.

These large, handsome sparrows are favorites at eastern feeders since they rarely stray so far from their normal Midwestern range. They vigorously scratch in the leaves and soil for food, and eat weed seeds, flower buds and blossoms, small fruits such as berries, and a great variety of insects, spiders, and snails. They were named by Audubon for Edward Harris (1799–1863), companion on his western trip in 1843.

539 **White-throated Sparrow**
(*Zonotrichia albicollis*)
Grosbeaks, Buntings, Finches, Sparrows (Fringillidae)

Description: 6–7" (15–17 cm). Upperparts streaked, underparts clear gray. *Head has black-and-white stripes; sharply defined white throat patch; dark bill.* Females and young birds are duller. White-crowned Sparrow is similar but lacks the white throat patch and is slimmer, with a pink bill.

Voice: Song a clear, whistled *Poor Sam Peabody, Peabody, Peabody,* or *Sweet Sweet Canada, Canada, Canada.* The latter rendition is perhaps more appropriate, since most of these birds breed in Canada.

Habitat: Brushy undergrowth in coniferous woodland. Winters in brush woodland, pastures, and suburban areas.

Nesting: 4 or 5 pale green eggs heavily spotted with brown in a cup of grass, rootlets, and moss on or near the ground in forest undergrowth.

Range: Mackenzie, central Quebec, and Newfoundland south to Pennsylvania, Wisconsin, and North Dakota. Winters south to the Gulf Coast and northern Mexico.

This very common sparrow is known as a winter visitor and a migrant. During the colder months every hedgerow and thicket seems to be filled with White-throats, and on warm days one can readily hear their plaintive song. When evening comes and they gather to roost in dense thickets, their silvery flocking call is almost as evocative as their song.

---

540 **White-crowned Sparrow**
(*Zonotrichia leucophrys*)
Grosbeaks, Buntings, Finches, Sparrows (Fringillidae)

Description: 6–7½" (15–19 cm). Larger and longer-tailed than a House Sparrow. *Crown has bold black-and-white stripes.* Upperparts streaked, underparts clear pearly gray. *Pink bill.* Young birds similar, but crown stripes buff and dark brown, underparts washed with dull buff. Similar to White-throated Sparrow but more slender without white throat, and generally with a more erect posture.

Voice: Short series of clear whistles followed by buzzy notes.

Habitat: Nests in dense brush, especially where near open grassland; winters in open woods and gardens.

Nesting: 3–5 pale green eggs thickly spotted with brown in a bulky cup of bark strips, grass, and twigs lined with grass and hair, on or near the ground.

Range: Alaska and Manitoba east to Labrador and Newfoundland, and south in the western mountains to northern New Mexico and central California. Winters north to New Jersey and southern British Columbia.

The handsome White-crown is a favorite not only of bird-watchers but of laboratory scientists: much of what we know about the physiology of bird migration has been learned from laboratory experiments with this species. In the East, these birds are much less numerous than White-throated Sparrows, but flocks of White-throats often contain a few of these slender, elegant birds. Much of their feeding is done on the ground but, like White-throats, they will respond to a squeaking noise by an observer by popping up to the top of a bush.

543 Fox Sparrow
(*Passerella iliaca*)
Grosbeaks, Buntings, Finches, Sparrows (Fringillidae)

Description: 6½–7½" (16–19 cm). Larger and heavier than a House Sparrow. Boldly striped with *rich rufous above;* underparts white, heavily spotted with rufous. Sides of head gray with rufous stripes. *Tail bright rufous.*

Voice: Loud, short, melodious warble.

Habitat: Coniferous forest undergrowth in summer; dense woodland thickets, weedy pastures, and brushy roadsides in winter.

Nesting: 4 or 5 pale green eggs densely spotted with red-brown in a thick-walled cup of leaves in grass and moss, concealed in vegetation on or near the ground.

Range: Breeds from Unalaska Island in the Aleutians, Alaska and northern Quebec south to New Brunswick, Colorado,

southern California. Winters south to the Gulf Coast and northern Mexico.

Away from the breeding grounds, Fox Sparrows are most conspicuous during spring migration, when one frequently hears their rich, melodious song coming from brushy thickets and roadsides. They scratch in leaves for food and often make so much noise that one expects to find a larger animal. Western birds tend to be more dusky brown or slaty and bear little resemblance to the "fox-colored" eastern birds.

Bachman's Sparrow
(*Aimophila aestivalis*)
Grosbeaks, Buntings, Finches,
Sparrows (Fringillidae)

Description: 6″ (15 cm). A dull-colored, nondescript bird, streaked above, plain below with a *buff breast*.

Voice: Clear, sweet whistle followed by a trill on a different pitch.

Habitat: Dry open pine or oak woods with a scattering of scrub; overgrown weedy fields and pastures.

Nesting: 4 white eggs in a domed nest made of plant fibers and placed on the ground in a grass clump or at the base of a bush or palmetto; entrance on the side.

Range: Southeastern United States, breeding north to Illinois, Indiana, Ohio, and Pennsylvania, but very local. Winters chiefly in the south Atlantic and Gulf states.

In the southern parts of its range, its older name, "Pine-woods Sparrow," is more appropriate since it dwells in open stretches of pines with grass and scattered shrubs for ground cover. Farther north it is also commonly found in abandoned fields and pastures. It spends much of the time feeding on the

ground, where it is hard to see except when it mounts a bush or weed stalk to sing. Like many other sparrows, it feeds on insects such as crickets and beetles, and on seeds of grasses and sedges. It was named by Audubon for his close friend, Dr. John Bachman (1790–1874), who discovered the species in South Carolina.

Texas Thickets and Second Growth

A very limited region in southern Texas, near the Rio Grande. It may be moist and have dense thickets and subtropical woodland, or dry, with an impenetrable growth of mesquite and other thorny trees and shrubs, or with a sparse growth of cactus. Also included here are the juniper woodlands of the Edwards Plateau.

250 Jaçana
(*Jacana spinosa*)
Jaçanas (Jacanidae)

Description: 8–9" (20–23 cm). Robin-sized. Head and neck black, body and wings dark rufous. *Large pale green wing patches visible in flight and a bright yellow frontal shield.* Very long toes.

Voice: Various high-pitched squeaking and bickering notes.

Habitat: Ponds with heavy growth of lily pads and other floating vegetation.

Nesting: 4 pale buff eggs thickly scrawled with black, in a loose cup of leaves and stems placed in the open on floating vegetation.

Range: Resident from northern Mexico south to Panama. Casual in southern Texas.

These birds, with their strikingly long toes, are adept at balancing on floating plants and are therefore able to exploit a habitat available to few other birds. They are quarrelsome and often engage in combat with one another, using sharp spurs on the bend of the wing. Females are somewhat larger than males, and defend a large territory in which several males build nests and care for the eggs and young.

---

258 Scaled Quail
(*Callipela squamata*)
Quail, Partridges, Pheasants
(Phasianidae)

Description: 10–12" (25–30 cm). A stocky, grayish quail, finely barred with black on back and underparts, and a conspicuous *white crest.*

Voice: A barking *chekar;* various soft clucking notes.

Habitat: Dry grasslands and brushy deserts.

Nesting: About 14 pale buff eggs, evenly spotted with reddish-brown, in a grass-lined hollow in dry grasslands.

Range: Arizona, Colorado, western Kansas, and western Oklahoma south to central Mexico.

These modestly plumaged quail, often called "Cottontops" by hunters, are characteristic birds of the drier desert areas of the Southwest. Their numbers fluctuate markedly from year to year, because the birds are sensitive to drought and heavy rains. They spend most of the year in small flocks, which break up into pairs at the beginning of the breeding season.

272 Chachalaca
(*Ortalis vetula*)
Chachalacas (Cracidae)

Description: 18–21" (46–53 cm). W. 26" (0.7 m). Crow-sized. Olive-brown body; long iridescent green tail tipped with white. Has a slight crest, and bare pinkish-red skin at side of throat.

Voice: Loud, ringing *cha-cha-lac,* often in chorus at dawn and dusk. The female's call has been described as *keep-it-up,* answered by the lower-pitched male's *cut-it-out.*

Habitat: Open woodland, clearings, and thickets.

Nesting: 3 dull white eggs in stick nest lined with leaves and moss, usually on a low tree limb.

Range: Extreme southern Texas to Nicaragua.

These noisy, gregarious birds are a feature of the Rio Grande delta, and are locally common in the Santa Ana Wildlife Refuge where they are fed by tourists and have become remarkably tame. Although primarily arboreal in habits, they often come to the ground to feed on leaves, buds, berries, nuts, and tidbits from human sources. Where they are not protected, they are hunted as game.

276 Pauraque
(*Nyctidromus albicollis*)
Nightjars (Caprimulgidae)

Description: 12″ (30 cm). Larger than the Whip-poor-will. Mottled brown. Brown body; wings and tail show white bands in flight, especially conspicuous in the male. Identified mainly by voice.

Voice: A burry *pur-WHEEER,* slurred downward and uttered at night.

Habitat: Semi-open scrub country with thickets, and in light woodland clearings.

Nesting: 2 pinkish-buff, brown-blotched eggs on bare ground near a bush or a tree.

Range: Extreme southern Texas south through Mexico and Central America to southern South America.

These birds are virtually impossible to see on the ground in daylight because they match dead leaves and twigs almost perfectly. But when the Pauraque is flushed from the side of the road by car headlights, the white wing patch, like that of a nighthawk, may be seen distinctly, and the eyes shine a brilliant red. Like other nightjars, Pauraques have an enormously wide gape that enables them to catch large moths, beetles, crickets, and fireflies on the wing at night.

287 Elf Owl
(*Microthene whitneyi*)
True Owls (Strigidae)

Description: 5½″ (14 cm). Sparrow-sized. Short tail, no ear tufts, yellow eyes; buff with indistinct dark streaks.

Voice: Rapid series of high-pitched notes, higher in the middle.

Habitat: Desert, dry open woodland, and streamside thickets with trees.

Nesting: 3 white eggs in deserted woodpecker holes in cacti, oaks, pines, and other trees.

Range: Southwestern United States from
southern Texas to southeastern
California and south to central Mexico.

When captured, this tiny owl feigns
death until sure that all danger has
passed. It feeds almost exclusively on
insects, catching them in the air or on
the ground, but also takes mice and
lizards.

---

311 **Harris' Hawk**
(*Parabuteo unicinctus*)
Hawks, Eagles (Accipitridae)

Description: 18–30″ (46–76 cm). W. 43″ (1.1 m).
Crow-sized. Brown and black, with a
black-and-white tail and rich chestnut
shoulders and thighs.
Voice: A low, harsh scream.
Habitat: Semi-arid regions in scrub with
mesquite, cacti, and yucca.
Nesting: 2–4 dull white eggs faintly spotted
with brown in a stick nest lined with
grass usually placed low in scrubby
brush, cacti, or small trees.
Range: Common in southern Texas and local
westward to southeastern California; to
southern South America.

This strikingly marked hawk, normally
tame and fearless, is often seen perched
on a telephone or power pole along the
highways of southern Texas, or leisurely
flying along scanning the ground for
rabbits, quail, lizards, or snakes. It is
occasionally observed on the ground
feasting on carrion with vultures and
caracaras.

321 White-winged Dove
(*Zenaida asiatica*)
Pigeons, Doves (Columbidae)

Description: 12″ (30 cm). A brownish-gray dove
with blackish wings that have a *broad
diagonal white bar;* tail has *whitish
corners,* noticeable in flight.

Voice: Drawn-out *hooo-hooo-ho-hooo* or *who-
cooks-for-you.*

Habitat: Open arid country with dense thickets
of shrubs and low trees.

Nesting: 2 cream-buff eggs in a crude, frail,
platform of loose twigs in low bushes.

Range: Breeds in the West Indies and from
southwestern United States and
southern Florida to Panama and from
Ecuador to Chile. Winters south of the
United States.

In some areas these doves nest in huge
colonies covering many acres. When
the birds rise, flashing their
conspicuous white wing patches, they
are a handsome sight.

324 White-fronted Dove
(*Leptotila verreauxi*)
Pigeons, Doves (Columbidae)

Description: 12″ (30 cm). Brown with whitish
forehead, belly, and tail tips; wing
linings chestnut.

Voice: Deep, drawn-out, descending *coo,* lower-
pitched than most of our pigeons.

Habitat: Dense, moist woodland and thickets.

Nesting: 2 white eggs in a stick nest lined with
plant fibers in a dense bush, vine, or
tree.

Range: Southernmost Texas (just north of the
lower Rio Grande Valley) to southern
South America.

Uncommon and local along the
Mexican border, it is primarily a forest
species with a wide vertical range,
feeding mostly on the ground but also

flying to the tops of tall trees. When flushed, the bird makes a whistling sound with its sickle-shaped outermost primaries. It feeds on various seeds and nuts, and occasionally on small fruits such as wild figs, palm fruit, and various berries.

326 Inca Dove
(*Scardafella inca*)
Pigeons, Doves (Columbidae)

Description: 8″ (20 cm). Bluebird-sized. *Scaly gray body* with contrasting *chestnut in the wings. Long, white-edged tail.*
Voice: *Coo-coo* or *no-hope.*
Habitat: Semi-arid country with cactus and mesquite thickets; also parks, yards, and ranches.
Nesting: 2 white eggs in a frail nest usually of small twigs placed low in a tree or a bush.
Range: Arizona, New Mexico, and southern parts of Texas, to Costa Rica.

This tiny bird is much like a Ground Dove except for its long, pointed tail. Perhaps because both of these species are too small to be considered game, they show little fear of man; the Inca Dove is so tame it nests in city parks and suburban gardens.

Red-billed Pigeon
(*Columba flavirostris*)
Pigeons, Doves (Columbidae)

Description: 14″ (35 cm). A large pigeon, deep maroon and gray, without distinctive markings; looks blackish at a distance.
Voice: Loud, high-pitched, clear *coo's.*
Habitat: Thick forest and woodland borders, often near water.
Nesting: 1 white egg in a grass- or fiber-lined stick nest in a bush or tree.

Range: Southernmost Texas (lower Rio Grande Valley) to Costa Rica.

It is found in the densely wooded bottomlands near the Mexican border and occasionally in more open country around clearings in the forest, or in groves of large trees along rivers. It feeds extensively in the crowns of tall trees on wild figs and other fruits, as well as on various nuts and seeds. Like many other pigeons, it makes a series of cooing calls and a loud clapping noise with its wings as it rises in flight.

Cave Swallow
(*Petrochelidon fulva*)
Swallows (Hirundinidae)

Description: 5½″ (14 cm). A stocky swallow with a square tail, steel-blue upperparts, *pale buff rump* and underparts, and chestnut forehead. The more widespread Cliff Swallow is similar, but has a chestnut throat and white forehead.
Voice: Series of squeaks, twitters, and warbles.
Habitat: Chiefly open country near caves and cliffs.
Nesting: 4 brown-spotted pinkish eggs in a mud nest lined with grass, roots, and feathers, attached to cliff walls, caves, and occasionally to bridges and old buildings.
Range: Southern Texas and southeastern New Mexico south through Mexico; Greater Antilles of the West Indies; isolated populations in Ecuador and Peru.

This bird is extremely local north of the Mexican border and relatively few nest within the United States. Most nests are in inaccessible places, plastered to walls far inside remote caves and crevices. Like all swallows, they catch their insect prey on the wing.

345 Ladder-backed Woodpecker
(*Picoides scalaris*)
Woodpeckers (Picidae)

Description: 7″ (17 cm). Barred black-and-white back, strong *black-and-white facial pattern forming a triangle;* male has red cap, female has black cap.

Voice: Loud rattling call similar to that of the Hairy Woodpecker; also a harsh single or double note.

Habitat: Arid areas with thickets and trees.

Nesting: 4 or 5 white eggs in holes of trees, cacti, poles, and posts.

Range: Southwestern United States from California, Nevada, Utah, Colorado, and Texas south through Mexico to Honduras.

Within its range, it is the only small woodpecker so marked. The most numerous of its family in Texas, it replaces the Downy in more arid sections. Familiar and trusting, it frequents ranches, village yards, and parks. It is closely related to Nuttall's Woodpecker of California.

350 Golden-fronted Woodpecker
(*Melanerpes aurifrons*)
Woodpeckers (Picidae)

Description: 9½″ (24 cm). Robin-sized. Both sexes have black-and-white barring above and are buff below like the Red-bellied Woodpecker, but male has red restricted to cap, an orange nape, and yellow forecrown; female lacks red but has orange nape.

Voice: Loud *churrrr.* Call a burry *chuck-chuck-chuck.*

Habitat: Open woods in dry country and river bottoms with trees.

Nesting: 4 or 5 white eggs in holes in mesquite trees, poles, and posts.

Range: Resident from Oklahoma and Texas south to Costa Rica.

This familiar woodpecker is common in parks and shade trees of Texas towns and cities. A southwestern species, it is a close relative of and resembles the Red-bellied Woodpecker found mainly in the Southeast. The species name *aurifrons* is Latin for gold-fronted.

381 Verdin
(*Auriparus flaviceps*)
Titmice (Paridae)

Description: 4–4½″ (10–11 cm). Smaller than a House Sparrow. Dull gray with a *yellowish head* and *rufous bend of wing.*
Voice: A thin *tsilip!,* frequently repeated.
Habitat: Brushy desert; mesquite thickets.
Nesting: 4 or 5 pale bluish-green eggs, spotted with brown, in a globular mass of thorny twigs lined with feathers and soft grass and placed in a bush.
Range: California, Utah, and south central Texas southward to northern Mexico.

These tiny desert birds are rarely seen to drink, and are thought to obtain moisture from insect food. They occur in very arid areas, often far from water, and seem to require only brushy vegetation and a source of food. The well-insulated nest no doubt protects the eggs and young from intense heat.

387 Black-headed Oriole
(*Icterus graduacauda*)
Orioles, Blackbirds (Icteridae)

Description: 9″ (23 cm). Robin-sized. Male *greenish-yellow with black head,* wings, and tail. Females are slightly duller and smaller. Immatures lack the black head.
Voice: Three-syllable warble—one of the most melodious, sweetest songs of any oriole.
Habitat: Wet thickets in woodland, openings in the forest, and tangles near water.

Nesting: 4 whitish eggs with black scrawls, in a woven partly hanging nest made of fresh green grass. Nests are often found in mesquite, less often in hackberry, ebony, persimmon, and other trees.

Range: Southern Texas to northern Guatemala.

This oriole appears to be the least known of the family in the United States, probably due to its retiring habits. It keeps well within the foliage and under the forest canopy. It feeds extensively on wild fruits, especially hackberries. Both in Texas and Mexico these birds travel in pairs, even outside the nesting season.

390 Kiskadee Flycatcher
(*Pitangus sulphuratus*)
Tyrant Flycatchers (Tyrannidae)

Description: 10½" (26 cm). Robin-sized. Broad black bill; *black-and-white striped head;* olive-brown back; underparts bright yellow; rufous wings and tail conspicuous in flight.

Voice: Loud, piercing *kis-ka-dee;* also an incessant, shrill chattering.

Habitat: Rivers, streams, and lakes bordered with dense vegetation; also in more open country and in parks in most of its range.

Nesting: 4 creamy white, brown-spotted eggs in a bulky, domed stick nest with the entrance at the side, often in a thorn tree or bush.

Range: Extreme southern Texas (lower Rio Grande Valley) to South America.

This large and striking bird, also called the Derby Flycatcher, is numerous throughout Latin America. In addition to insects, it eats small fruits and even fishes, diving straight into the water like a kingfisher, although not as deeply. Its bulky stick nest is a conspicuous landmark.

Yellow-green Vireo
(*Vireo flavoviridis*)
Vireos (Vireonidae)

Description: 6–7" (15–17 cm). Sparrow-sized. Olive-green above, paler below, with a yellowish tinge on the back, flanks, and undertail coverts; crown dull gray, eyebrow whitish. Eye red. Similar to Red-eyed Vireo but without black borders to whitish eyebrow.

Voice: A series of deliberate, musical phrases, more widely spaced than in the song of Red-eyed Vireo.

Habitat: Streamside thickets and woodlands.

Nesting: 3 or 4 white eggs lightly spotted with brown, in a pendant cup of plant fibers and bark strips, bound together with spider web and suspended from a forked branch in a bush or small sapling.

Range: Rio Grande Valley (rare) south through Mexico and Central America to Bolivia and Brazil.

The Yellow-green Vireo is one of the tropical members of the group of species that includes our familiar Red-eyed Vireo. Like the Red-eye, this bird obtains its food by searching rather carefully in the foliage of trees, without the more active motions of warblers. Its song is repeated monotonously throughout the day.

Golden-cheeked Warbler
(*Dendroica chrysoparia*)
Wood Warblers (Parulidae)

Description: 4½–5" (11–13 cm). Male black, with two white wing bars, white belly, and *conspicuous yellow sides of face.* Female similar, but back olive-green.

Voice: A buzzy *bzzzz seewee seewee.*

Habitat: Rocky hillsides clothed with juniper.

Nesting: 4 white eggs finely dotted with brown, in a cup of bark strips, grass, and cobweb, in a juniper.

Range: South central Texas; winters in Mexico, Guatemala, Honduras, and Nicaragua.

This relative of the Black-throated Green Warbler of the East breeds only in Texas in juniper woodlands on the Edwards Plateau and in a small area near Dallas. Even in this restricted range the birds are localized, and the small population is being steadily reduced by habitat destruction and the depredations of cowbirds.

397 Lichtenstein's Oriole
(*Icterus gularis*)
Orioles, Blackbirds (Icteridae)

Description: 9" (23 cm). Robin-sized. Bright orange-yellow with black face and throat, upper back, wings, and tail. Similar to the Hooded Oriole, but larger, with a heavier bill and *orange-yellow shoulders.* Male and female look alike.

Voice: Series of loud whistles and harsh chatters.

Habitat: Forest and scattered groves of tall trees, especially near water.

Nesting: 3 or 4 whitish, purple-streaked eggs, often in a two-foot-long cylindrical or bag-shaped nest woven of tough fibers and suspended from a branch.

Range: Extreme southern Texas (but rare there) to northern Nicaragua.

The best places to see this very local species north of the Mexican border are the Brownsville region and the Santa Ana Wildlife Refuge. Although mainly found in the dense foliage of tall forest trees, it builds a conspicuous nest suspended far out on a slender, drooping limb, where it is safe from most predators. It varies a diet of insects and spiders with fruits such as figs and berries.

398 Hooded Oriole
(*Icterus cucullatus*)
Orioles, Blackbirds (Icteridae)

Description: 7–7¾" (17–19 cm). Male *orange,* with black wings crossed with two white bars, black tail, and *black throat and upper breast.* Bill thin and curved; tail long and graduated. Female olive-gray above, olive-yellow below, with two white wing bars. Yearling male looks like female but has black throat.

Voice: Series of whistles, chatters, and warbles.

Habitat: Originally streamside growth, but has adapted to tree plantations, city parks, and suburbs with palm or eucalyptus trees and shrubbery.

Nesting: 3–5 white eggs blotched with dark brown and purple, in a basket of plant fibers with entrance at the top, hanging from palm fronds or the branches of eucalyptus or other trees.

Range: Central California, Nevada, central Arizona, southern New Mexico and southern Texas south throughout Mexico to Guatemala and Belize.

Probably the commonest breeding oriole in southern Texas. These trusting birds often visit ranches and suburban areas for food. They are largely insectivorous but take fruit when it is available. This species is heavily parasitized by the Bronzed Cowbird. Most Hooded Oriole nests contain one or more eggs of this brood parasite.

405 Pyrrhuloxia
(*Cardinalis sinatus*)
Grosbeaks, Buntings, Finches, Sparrows (Fringillidae)

Description: 7½–8½" (19–21 cm). Smaller than a Robin. Male is gray, with rose-red breast, crest, wings, and tail. Female is similar but paler and lacks red on the breast. Stubby parrot-like *yellow bill*.

Voice: A series of whistled notes, otherwise similar to Cardinal but thinner and shorter.

Habitat: Desert brush, especially along stream beds.

Nesting: 3 or 4 white eggs lightly speckled with brown in a loosely built cup of grass, twigs, and bark strips concealed in dense, thorny bush.

Range: Central Baja California, Arizona, southern New Mexico, and southern Texas south to central Mexico.

Also called the "Gray Cardinal," it is similar to the Cardinal in most respects except that it is often found in flocks after the breeding season. These birds are partial to mesquite thickets and use their strong bills to crush the mesquite beans. Although shy and difficult to detect in their dense habitat, they respond to squeaking noises made by an observer.

415, 512 **Vermilion Flycatcher**
(*Pyrocephalus rubinus*)
Tyrant Flycatchers (Tyrannidae)

Description: 6″ (15 cm). Male *brilliant scarlet* with dark brown back, wings, and tail; female similar to male above but *white below with dark streaks*.

Voice: Call is *peet-peet* or *peet-a-weet*. Also has a soft, tinkling flight song.

Habitat: Trees and shrubs in open river bottoms and along roadsides.

Nesting: 3 creamy white eggs with dark brown spots in a well-made nest of fibers, feathers, and spider web lined with bits of lichen, placed on a horizontal branch.

Range: From southwestern United States east to Texas and south to Honduras; western South America; the Galapagos Islands.

This species is unusual among flycatchers in that the sexes are differently colored. In southern Texas it is conspicuous and tame, often nesting near houses and farmyards. The bright colors of the male have earned it the Spanish name *brasita de fuego,* "little coal of fire."

430 Rose-throated Becard
(*Platypsaris aglaiae*)
Cotingas (Cotingidae)

Description: 6½" (16 cm). Sparrow-sized. Male gray above with black cap and pale rose-red throat; whitish below. Female brown, paler below, and with a dusky grayish cap.

Voice: A high-pitched whistle, *seeeeooo;* various chattering notes.

Habitat: Thick woodland along streams; wooded canyons.

Nesting: 4 or 5 white eggs spotted with brown, in a cavity in a globular nest of grass and plant fibers, suspended from the tip of a drooping branch.

Range: Southeastern Arizona and the Rio Grande Valley in Texas south to Costa Rica.

This quiet, unobtrusive bird spends most of its time foraging in tall trees and is therefore difficult to find. It is adept at catching flying insects like a flycatcher, and also feeds on berries. It is the only North American member of the cotinga family, a large and very colorful group of birds confined to the American tropics. The northern limit of its range is just within our borders, and it is nowhere common in our area.

431 "Black-crested Titmouse"
(*Parus atricristatus*)
Titmice (Paridae)

Description: 5–6" (13–15 cm). Sparrow-sized. Gray above, whitish below, with pale rusty flanks and a slender *black crest*. The Tufted Titmouse is similar, but has a gray crest and only the forehead black.

Voice: A variety of squeaking and chattering notes, indistinguishable from those of the Tufted Titmouse.

Habitat: Riverbottom woodlands, groves, and well-planted gardens.

Nesting: 4–7 white eggs, spotted with brown, in a natural tree cavity or bird box, lined with soft plant material.

Range: Southwestern Oklahoma and Texas south to central Mexico.

This southwestern bird is the local representative of the Tufted Titmouse of the East. Where the ranges of the two come in contact, the birds hybridize freely; very probably they are representatives of a single, variable species. In all respects the ecology and behavior of the two birds are alike.

Varied Bunting
(*Passerina versicolor*)
Grosbeaks, Buntings, Finches, Sparrows (Fringillidae)

Description: 4½–5½" (11–14 cm). Sparrow-sized. Male dark purple-blue, with a dull red patch on the nape; looks all black at a distance. Female dull gray *without distinctive markings*. Female Indigo Bunting is browner, with a suggestion of wing bars.

Voice: A series of sweet notes, similar to Indigo Bunting but thinner.

Habitat: Dense desert brush, especially along stream beds.

Nesting: 3 or 4 pale blue eggs in a deep cup of grass, twigs, and bark strips placed in a dense thicket.

Range: Resident from Arizona and southern
Texas south into Mexico.

This primarily Mexican species reaches
the southernmost parts of the United
States. It is unevenly distributed and
inconspicuous, so that very little is
known about it. The birds spend most
of their time concealed in dense desert
brush, coming into view only when the
male sings from the top of a bush. They
probably feed primarily on weed seeds.

Tropical Parula
"Olive-backed Warbler"
(*Parula pitiayumi*)
Wood Warblers (Parulidae)

Description: 4–5″ (10–13 cm). A small bluish-
backed warbler with a bright yellow
breast, two white wing bars, and a patch
of olive-green in the middle of the
back. The Northern Parula is similar
but male has a dark breast band.

Voice: A buzzy, ascending trill, *zzzzzzzzzz-up*.

Habitat: Riverbottom woodlands and thickets.

Nesting: 3 or 4 white eggs spotted with brown,
in a cup built into a mass of hanging
moss, usually along a stream.

Range: Rio Grande Valley (rare) and northern
Mexico south to Brazil and Argentina.

This species has become quite scarce
along the Rio Grande, the only part of
the United States in which it nests,
due to parasitism by cowbirds, the
disappearance of Spanish moss, and the
use of pesticides. During a period in the
1960s it apparently did not nest at all,
but now a few pairs breed in certain
tracts of riverbottom woods.

468 Tropical Kingbird
(*Tyrannus melancholicus*)
Tyrant Flycatchers (Tyrannidae)

Description: 8½" (21 cm). Bright yellow underparts,
olive back, and dark patch through eye.
Slightly forked brown tail without white.

Voice: Incessant high-pitched, rapid chatter.
Its call is a loud *queer-a-chi-queer.*

Habitat: Open country around farmland, lake
and river shores, thickets, and isolated
groves of tall trees.

Nesting: 3 or 4 pinkish, brown-spotted eggs in a
stick nest lined with grass and moss in
a tree.

Range: Southeastern Arizona, Sonora in Mexico,
and extreme southern Texas (lower Rio
Grande Valley) south to Bolivia and
Argentina.

The most brightly colored kingbird to
visit the United States, it is also very
local, being restricted to southern Texas
and southeastern Arizona. In winter it
moves southward into Mexico. It
prefers to nest in chaparral thickets, the
wilder areas, in isolated trees around
ranches, and along rivers. Like its
relatives, it is noisy and aggressive,
feeding mostly on flying insects.

471 Wied's Crested Flycatcher
(*Myiarchus tyrannulus*)
Tyrant Flycatchers (Tyrannidae)

Description: 9½" (24 cm). A large flycatcher, olive
above and yellow below, with
cinnamon wings and tail. The Great
Crested Flycatcher has brighter
underparts and a brown, not blackish,
lower mandible; best distinguished by
voice.

Voice: A burry *purreeeer;* a sharp *wit!* or *whit!,*
very different from Great Crested
Flycatcher's loud *wheeep!*

Habitat: Arid lands in areas with cacti or large
trees.

Nesting: 3–5 creamy white brown-spotted eggs in a nest lined with feathers, fibers, and hairs, placed in a tree cavity, in cacti, or on fence posts.

Range: Southwestern United States east to southern Texas; also from Mexico to South America.

This species (sometimes more aptly known as the "Brown-crested Flycatcher") replaces the Great Crested Flycatcher in arid country. This bird was named for Prince Maximilian of Wied, a German naturalist and traveler in early 19th century America.

472 Ash-throated Flycatcher
(*Myiarchus cinerascens*)
Tyrant Flycatchers (Tyrannidae)

Description: 8″ (20 cm). Dull olive above, yellowish below; like Wied's Crested Flycatcher and the Great Crested Flycatcher, but smaller and less colorful; back browner, throat paler.

Voice: *Purreeeer,* similar to call of Wied's Crested Flycatcher but softer. Also a soft *Pwit.*

Habitat: Deserts with cactus and mesquite thickets; also dry woods.

Nesting: 4 or 5 creamy white, brown-spotted eggs in a nest lined with vegetable fibers in a tree or a cactus hole.

Range: Washington and Colorado south to southwestern United States, east to Texas, and south to Guatemala.

It lives in the hottest, driest parts of the West, but farther north is also found in dry, shady, open woodland. All flycatchers in the genus *Myiarchus* look alike. They may be identified according to the habitats and, where habitats overlap, by their voice.

Beardless Flycatcher
(*Camptostoma imberbe*)
Tyrant Flycatchers (Tyrannidae)

Description: 4″ (10 cm). Nondescript, dull-colored bird with a tiny bill. Olive-gray above with pale buff wing bars; whitish below with dusky throat and breast.

Voice: A thin *tee-tee-tee-tee-tee,* loudest in the middle. Also three long notes followed by a trill.

Habitat: Low thorn scrub, especially mesquite thickets and woodland borders.

Nesting: 2 or 3 white, brown-speckled eggs in a globular nest of plant fibers with a side entrance.

Range: Extreme southern portions of Texas and Arizona south through Mexico and Central America to northwestern Costa Rica.

This tiny bird, the smallest flycatcher in the United States, lacks the stout bristles at the base of the bill present in most members of its family; hence its name. Instead of flycatching on the wing, it looks and acts like a kinglet or small vireo, hopping among twigs and branches in search of insects.

478 Olive Sparrow
(*Arremonops rufivirgatus*)
Grosbeaks, Buntings, Finches, Sparrows (Fringillidae)

Description: 5¾″ (14 cm). Unstreaked, dull olive-green, with *brown head stripes,* buff breast, and whitish belly; no wing bars; rather like a small edition of the Green-tailed Towhee.

Voice: Series of musical *chips,* becoming more rapid at the end.

Habitat: Brushy areas, woodland borders and clearings, and overgrown fields.

Nesting: 4 white eggs in a domed nest made of twigs, grass, and leaves, placed low in a shrub or a cactus.

Range: Southern Texas and Mexico to Nicaragua and Costa Rica.

Flitting from shrub to shrub and crawling about the undergrowth, this unobtrusive, drab little finch is seldom out in the open. Nevertheless it is not shy, and when it sings from an exposed perch or engages in nesting activities it may be readily observed. It feeds on seeds, small larvae, and grubs.

---

481 Buff-bellied Hummingbird
(*Amazilia yucatanensis*)
Hummingbirds (Trochilidae)

Description: 4½" (11 cm). Green above with glittering green throat, brown tail, and *tawny or rich buff belly. Bill long and thin, bright orange-red with black tip.*
Voice: Shrill and squeaky.
Habitat: Woodland borders and thickets.
Nesting: 2 white eggs in woven nest of plant fibers decorated with lichens. Nest is saddled to the limb of a tree or in a shrub.

Range: Southernmost Texas (lower Rio Grande Valley) south through Mexico to Guatemala and Belize (British Honduras).

This mainly Mexican species may be found among the dense tangled thickets and vines in light, open woodland. It also comes to feed on the flowers in nearby gardens. Unlike most other hummers north of Mexico, the sexes are alike in color. It usually leaves the Rio Grande area in winter and retires southward into adjacent Tamaulipas, Mexico, until the following spring.

483 Green Jay
(Cyanocorax yncas)
Jays, Magpies, Crows (Corvidae)

Description: 12″ (30 cm). Strikingly colored with *bright green body and tail* with yellow on the sides; *brilliant blue crown and cheeks;* rest of head, throat, and breast black.

Voice: Variety of jay-like calls. Also a deep rattle.

Habitat: Dry thickets and open forest with thick undergrowth; sometimes in more open country around ranch houses.

Nesting: 4 brown-spotted, grayish eggs in a loosely made stick nest of thorns lined with rootlets or grass and placed in a bush or a small tree.

Range: Southernmost Texas (Rio Grande delta) south through Mexico to Honduras; then from Columbia and Venezuela to Brazil and Bolivia.

In winter months and when not nesting, these inhabitants of dense thickets visit more open country, even near ranches and smaller towns. Like most jays, they are omnivorous, taking fruits, seeds, insects, and even corn. At times they visit feeders for meat scraps.

491 Canyon Wren
(Catherpes mexicanus)
Wrens (Troglodytidae)

Description: 5½–6″ (14–15 cm). Sparrow-sized. Dark rusty above and below, conspicuous *white throat and upper breast.*

Voice: A high, clear series of descending notes; *tee-tee-tee-tee-tew-tew-tew-tew.*

Habitat: Rocky canyons and cliffs; old stone buildings.

Nesting: 4–6 white eggs lightly speckled with reddish brown, in a shallow cup of feathers, plant down, and moss in a crevice among rocks or, occasionally in a building.

Range: Resident from British Columbia,

Montana, and western South Dakota south through western Oklahoma and central Texas to southern Baja California and southern Mexico.

Like most wrens, this bird is quite secretive, and often when one can plainly hear its musical song reverberating from the walls of a canyon, it takes a long and patient search to spot the singer, perched high up on a ledge or quietly picking its way through a clump of brush.

492 Rock Wren
(*Salpinctes obsoletus*)
Wrens (Troglodytidae)

Description: 5–6½″ (13–16 cm). A sparrow-sized wren, pale grayish-brown with a finely streaked breast. Whitish or pale buff tips to the outer tail feathers.

Voice: A dry trill; a rhythmic series of musical notes; *chewee, chewee, chewee, chewee.*

Habitat: Rock-strewn slopes, canyons, cliffs, and dams, in arid country.

Nesting: 4–6 white eggs, lightly speckled with pale brown, in a shallow nest of plant fibers and roots, lined with feathers and placed in a crevice among rocks or in a hollow stump.

Range: British Columbia, Saskatchewan, and North Dakota south to the mountains of Costa Rica. Winters from California and Texas southward.

This species is found in much the same habitat as its relative the Canyon Wren but is more partial to rocky slopes, while the Canyon Wren favors sheer cliffs. The Rock Wren has the unusual habit of laying down a path of small pebbles in front of its nest; this little "pavement" often simplifies an observer's effort to locate a nest.

493 Cactus Wren
(*Campylorhynchus brunneicapillus*)
Wrens (Troglodytidae)

Description: 7–8¼" (18–21 cm). A Robin-sized wren with spotted underparts, white eyebrows, rusty crown, and white spots on the outer tail feathers.

Voice: Rapid, mechanical *chug-chug-chug-chug-chug*.

Habitat: Arid desert thickets and cacti.

Nesting: 4 or 5 buff eggs heavily speckled with brown. The nest is a mass of fine grass and straw with a side entrance lined with feathers and hair, placed in the top of a thorny desert shrub or cactus.

Range: Southern California, southern Nevada, Utah, and western Texas south to Central America.

It is easy to spot an area inhabited by Cactus Wrens because, like other members of the family, they build many "dummy" nests, which are never used for breeding but serve only as roosts. These are usually guarded by sharp spines; indeed, it is difficult to understand how the birds can use them without being impaled. Although their grating song is hardly musical, it is a most evocative sound to those who love the desert.

495 Long-billed Thrasher
(*Toxostoma longirostre*)
Mockingbirds, Thrashers (Mimidae)

Description: 11" (28 cm). Jay-sized. Gray cheeks and blackish breast streaks. Similar to the Brown Thrasher, but darker and grayer with a longer bill.

Voice: Varied series of paired phrases. Similar to the Brown Thrasher although the call notes are pitched higher.

Habitat: Dense tangles and thickets in both open country and wooded areas and in both moist and dry regions.

Nesting: 3 or 4 pale blue, brown-dotted eggs in a nest of twigs and leaves lined with rootlets and placed in a dense thorn bush or cactus.

Range: South-central Texas south through eastern Mexico to Veracruz.

This close relative of the Brown Thrasher is equally at home in dense mesquite thickets in the driest regions and in heavy bottomland forests near the Rio Grande. Many nests have been found, but details of the Long-bill's habits remain relatively unknown. They feed extensively on insects, supplemented by fruits.

---

496 Curve-billed Thrasher
(*Toxostoma curvirostre*)
Mockingbirds, Thrashers (Mimidae)

Description: 9½–11½″ (24–29 cm). Drab, pale brown, with a long tail and *strongly decurved bill.* Breast faintly spotted; eyes red.

Voice: Sharp, whistled *whit-WHEET!* Song a rapid series of musical notes and phrases.

Habitat: Arid desert brushland and cactus.

Nesting: 4 pale blue-green eggs, finely speckled with brown in a bulky cup of twigs and rootlets, placed in a dense thorny desert shrub or in a branching clump of cactus.

Range: Resident from northwestern and central Arizona, New Mexico, and western Oklahoma to southern Mexico.

The most characteristic dawn sound in Texas brushland—or indeed wherever this bird occurs—is its sharp call, which sounds much like a human whistling to attract attention. Like the Cactus Wren, it builds nests that are conspicuous but hard to reach because they are placed in the center of dense, thorny desert vegetation. The curved

bill is used to toss dead leaves aside in
search of insects on the ground.

---

497 **Sage Thrasher**
(*Oreoscoptes montanus*)
Mockingbirds, Thrashers (Mimidae)

Description: 8½" (21 cm). Brown-gray above, buff
below with conspicuous black streaks;
bill strongly curved; tail relatively short
with white patches in the corners; two
white wing bars.

Voice: Continuous sweet warble without the
broken-up phrases of the more familiar
Brown Thrasher. The common call
note is a deep clucking sound.

Habitat: Dry sagebrush plains and arid areas
as in rocky canyons; winters in dense
thickets and lowland scrub.

Nesting: 4 or 5 brown-blotched blue-green eggs
in a stick nest lined with rootlets and
grass, often with fur or feathers, placed
in a bush, usually with thorns.

Range: Breeds from southern British Columbia,
central Idaho, and southern Montana
south to southern California, southern
Nevada, New Mexico, and western
Oklahoma. Winters chiefly in the
southwestern states to northern Mexico.

This arid-country thrasher feeds to a
large extent on insects, but also on
small fruits such as berries. It seems to
be a cross between a thrasher and a
mockingbird. The flicking of its tail
and its general appearance, except for
the streaked underparts, recall a
mocker, but its generally terrestrial
habits, and particularly its habit of
diving into a bush for cover when
alarmed, remind one of a thrasher.
On its breeding grounds the Sage
Thrasher is wary and difficult to
approach, but when visiting gardens
and city parks during the migrations it
is much tamer.

White-collared Seedeater
(*Sporophila torqueola*)
Grosbeaks, Buntings, Finches,
Sparrows (Fringillidae)

Description: 4″ (10 cm). Male black above, pale buff
to white below; *whitish half-collar on
nape and black band across chest.* Female
dull brown above, tawny below. Both
sexes have double wing bars. Bill thick
and stubby.

Voice: Several high notes followed by a series
of lower notes.

Habitat: Weedy or open fields grown up to
scrub, roadsides, and agricultural lands
generally.

Nesting: 4 or 5 blue-green, brown-spotted eggs
in a nest of rootlets and grasses lined
with hair, placed in a small shrub or
vine.

Range: Extreme southern Texas south to Costa
Rica.

Although tame, these tiny thick-billed
finches feed close to the ground among
tall grasses and can be clearly seen only
when they sing on top of a stalk or
fence post. They are nonmigratory,
although some post-breeding
wandering may occur, especially among
younger birds. As their name indicates,
they are avid consumers of seeds.

528 **Black-throated Sparrow**
(*Amphispiza bilineata*)
Grosbeaks, Buntings, Finches,
Sparrows (Fringillidae)

Description: 5¼″ (13 cm). Sexes look alike—gray
above, white below, with striking black
throat and breast; two conspicuous
white stripes on the side of the head,
one above and the other below the eye.

Voice: Two clear notes followed by a buzzy
trill.

Habitat: Desert with cactus, mesquite, and

creosote bush, and also sagebrush; often found where it is rocky.

Nesting: 4 white eggs in a loosely built nest of bark strips, grass, and stems lined with wool, hair, or feathers and placed in a thorny bush.

Range: Chiefly arid southwestern states, but north to southwestern Wyoming and Colorado, south to northern Mexico, and east to the western portions of Oklahoma and Texas.

This handsome sparrow of the arid Southwest is well named. Its alternate name, "Desert Sparrow," is also appropriate, for despite its vivid markings, it is often difficult to detect among the rocks and scrub, especially when not moving about. However, it may be observed when it mounts a bush or rock to sing its pleasant song. It can go for long periods without water, obtaining the necessary moisture from the plants and insects that are its principal diet during the summer months.

Botteri's Sparrow
(*Aimophila botterii*)
Grosbeaks, Buntings, Finches, Sparrows (Fringillidae)

Description: 5–6½″ (13–16 cm). Streaked with warm brown above, plain buff below. Similar to Grasshopper Sparrow, but streaks on back less contrasting and *crown without central stripe.* Similar to Cassin's Sparrow but browner, not as gray.

Voice: 3 or 4 notes followed by a trill that is loudest in the middle.

Habitat: Brushy coastal prairie in Texas; arid desert grassland elsewhere.

Nesting: 3–5 white eggs, usually unmarked, in a cup of grass concealed on the ground.

Range: Arizona and Southern Texas to southern Mexico.

Lacking distinctive field marks, this rare bird is best identified by its range and song. Unless singing, it is so shy and inconspicuous that its movements outside the breeding season are virtually unknown. Most are said to withdraw into Mexico for the winter, but occasionally one is seen in Texas, and perhaps many remain on the breeding grounds all year. Because of heavy grazing in their tall-grass prairie habitat, the birds are now less numerous.

---

576 Great-tailed Grackle
(*Quiscalus mexicanus*)
Orioles, Blackbirds (Icteridae)

Description: Males 16–17" (40–43 cm); females 12–13" (30–33 cm). Tail very long and keel-shaped. Male black, *iridescent purple on back and breast.* Female smaller, brown with a pale breast. *Eyes always yellow.* Common Grackle is smaller; female lacks pale breast. Boat-tailed Grackle of salt marshes is very similar but males are iridescent blue or blue-green and often have brown eyes. Best distinguished by their calls.

Voice: Variety of whistles, clucks, and hissing notes.

Habitat: Farmlands with scattered trees and thickets.

Nesting: 3 or 4 pale blue eggs spotted and scrawled with brown and purple, placed in a bulky nest of sticks, grass, and mud in a tree. In loose colonies.

Range: Western Louisiana, Texas, and Arizona south to northern South America.

Where Great-tails and Boat-tails occur together, the Great-tail tends to avoid salt marshes, the chief habitat of the Boat-tail. Occasionally, however, the two may nest very near one another, and the species have been known to hybridize on rare occasions. The Great-tail seems to be extending its range eastward but has not yet reached Florida.

578 Groove-billed Ani
(*Crotophaga sulcirostris*)
Cuckoos (Cuculidae)

Description: 12″ (30 cm). Jay-sized. Black with a very long tail half the length of the bird. Huge bill with arched ridge and narrow grooves. Flight loose and floppy; travels in small flocks. Smooth-billed Ani lacks grooves on bill and does not occur in Texas.

Voice: Soft, liquid, gurgling notes and, if alarmed, rather loud, harsh calls. Also a rollicking *wee-cup*.

Habitat: Arid agricultural land especially where there are cattle.

Nesting: 3 or 4 pale blue eggs in a huge stick nest, often situated in thorn growth.

Range: Northern Mexico and the lower Rio Grande Valley south through Central America to the Guianas and Peru.

In flight, both species flap their wings loosely, alternating with short glides. The long tail, which appears to be on a hinge, wiggles up and down and from side to side like a pendulum and looks as though it might drop off. Both Anis feed largely on a mixed diet of insects, seeds, and fruits. In the United States their ranges do not overlap.

Mexican Crow
(*Corvus imparatus*)
Jays, Magpies, Crows (Corvidae)

Description: 15″ (38 cm). A small crow, all black including bill and feet. White-necked Raven is larger and has a wedge-shaped tail; Common Crow is slightly larger and is best distinguished by voice.

Voice: A soft, croaking *gar-lic,* very different from the familiar *caw, caw* of the Common Crow.

Habitat: Arid open country, but with thickets and brush such as mesquite; also ranches and farms, as well as along woodland streams.

Nesting: 4 or 5 greenish eggs blotched with brown; in a stick nest lined with leaves, grasses, or reeds, and set in a low bush or tree.

Range: Chiefly northwestern Mexico, occurring regularly in small numbers in southernmost Texas, especially around Brownsville where it frequents the town dump along with flocks of gulls.

This relatively little-known species occurs, like most crows, in flocks and feeds on a great variety of items, including seeds, grains, fruits, meat, carrion, and insects. Unknown north of the Mexican border before the 1960s, it has in recent years become a regular visitor to the Brownsville region.

Deciduous Forests

Forests made up chiefly of trees that shed their leaves seasonally, usually in the fall after killing frosts. The main trees here are oaks, maples, hickories, elms, and locusts.

In addition to the birds treated here, one may occasionally find some of the birds of Coniferous Forests.

256 American Woodcock
(Philohela minor)
Woodcocks (Scolopacidae)

Description: 11″ (28 cm). Quail-sized. Very stocky, with rounded wings and long bill. Rufous below, "dead leaf" pattern above. Large bulging eyes.

Voice: Loud, buzzy *beep* similar to the call of a nighthawk and often repeated about every two seconds.

Habitat: Moist woodland and thickets near open fields.

Nesting: 4 brown-spotted buff eggs among dead leaves or under bushes.

Range: Eastern North America from southern Canada to the Gulf states. Winters chiefly in the South.

The Woodcock is seldom seen, for its protective coloring renders it virtually invisible. When flushed from underfoot, it zigzags off through the brush with a whistling of wings. Those fortunate enough to live near their breeding grounds may see woodcocks perform their courtship flight in early spring each year. In these spectacular aerial displays the male spirals up to a considerable height, circles, then plummets down to earth, calling as he descends. Woodcocks subsist chiefly on earthworms, which they extract with their long bills; the tip of the upper mandible is flexible so that they can grasp a worm while probing in mud without opening the bill. Insect larvae are also eaten, and occasionally vegetable matter.

268 Ruffed Grouse
(Bonasa umbellus)
Grouse (Tetraonidae)

Description: 16–19″ (40–48 cm). A brown chicken-like bird with a fan-shaped, black-banded tail and black "ruffs" on the sides of the neck.

Voice: Female gives soft hen-like clucks. In spring the male often sits on a log and beats the air with its wings, creating a drumming sound that increases rapidly in tempo.

Habitat: Deciduous forests, especially those with scattered clearings; abandoned farmlands and overgrown pastures.

Nesting: 8–11 pinkish-buff eggs, plain or spotted with dull brown, in a shallow depression lined with leaves and concealed under bushes.

Range: Breeds from Alaska and northern Canada south to the Carolinas, South Dakota, and California, and in the Appalachians to Georgia.

One of the most highly esteemed gamebirds in North America, it is taken annually in large numbers. However, as long as suitable habitat exists, it seems able to withstand this pressure. Although large numbers of eggs are laid, young grouse have many enemies and few of the young reach maturity. In winter, the grouse grow comb-like rows of bristles on their toes, which serve as snowshoes.

269, 273 **Turkey**
(*Meleagris gallopavo*)
Turkeys (Meleagrididae)

Description: Males 48″ (122 cm); females 36″ (91 cm). Similar to the domestic turkey but more slender; tail tipped with chestnut, not white.

Voice: Familiar *gobble* of the domestic bird. Also a number of clucks and yelps.

Habitat: Open woodlands and forests with scattered natural or man-made clearings.

Nesting: 10–15 buff eggs, lightly spotted with brown and black, in a shallow leaf-lined depression concealed in vegetation on the forest floor.

Range: Locally common from Wyoming, Illinois, and New York to Mexico and the Gulf Coast. Formerly more widespread and abundant.

No bird is more distinctively American than the "Wild Turkey." The species was even suggested as our national bird by Benjamin Franklin, who pointed out that the Bald Eagle is principally a carrion feeder. For a time, intense hunting seemed to be driving the Turkey to extinction, but with habitat management, controlled hunting seasons, and careful reintroductions, it has again become fairly common in many parts of its former range. Although well known to the American Indians and widely used by them as food, certain tribes considered these birds stupid and cowardly and did not eat them for fear of acquiring these characteristics. Turkeys often roost over water because of the added protection that this offers. They are polygamous, and the male gobbles and struts with fanned tail to attract and hold his harem. They are swift runners.

277 Whip-poor-will
(*Caprimulgus vociferus*)
Nightjars (Caprimulgidae)

Description: 10″ (25 cm). Jay-sized. A leaf-brown, strictly nocturnal bird with a *black* throat. In flight, male has *white outer tail feathers,* female's are brown.

Voice: A loud, rhythmic *whip-poor-will,* repeated over and over, at night.

Habitat: Dry open woodland near fields.

Nesting: 2 white eggs, scrawled with gray and brown, placed on the ground among dead leaves.

Range: Southern Canada to southern United States, and in the mountains as far south as Mexico. Winters from the Gulf of Mexico to Honduras.

It is rarely seen because it sleeps by day on the forest floor, its coloration matching the dead leaves. At night its eyes reflect ruby red in car headlights. It feeds exclusively on moths and other night insects caught on the wing.

278 Chuck-will's-widow
(*Caprimulgus carolinensis*)
Nightjars (Caprimulgidae)

Description: 12" (30 cm). Pigeon-sized. Larger than the Whip-poor-will. Buff-brown body, *brown* throat.

Voice: *Chuck-will's-wid-ow,* repeated over and over, the *chuck* deep and low, the rest of the call whistled. Also utters a frog-like croak when flying.

Habitat: Open woodland and clearings near agricultural country.

Nesting: 2 creamy white eggs with purple and brown markings on bare ground or dead leaves.

Range: Kansas, Indiana, and Long Island south to the Gulf states. Winters chiefly in the West Indies and from Mexico to northern South America.

It is nocturnal and rarely seen during the day. When flushed it flies off a short distance, then drops to the ground again. "Chucks" hunt low to the ground, catching flying insects such as moths, beetles, and winged ants and termites. They have occasionally been reported to take warblers and sparrows.

279, 280 Screech Owl
(*Otus asio*)
True Owls (Strigidae)

Description: 10″ (25 cm). A *small,* mottled owl with prominent *ear tufts;* eyes yellow. Both rufous and gray color phases occur, as well as brownish intermediates.

Voice: A tremulous, descending wail; soft purrs and trills.

Habitat: Open deciduous woods, wood lots, suburban areas, lakeshores, old orchards.

Nesting: 3–8 white eggs placed without a nest lining in a cavity in a tree or in a bird box.

Range: Southeastern Alaska, British Columbia, Manitoba, and northern New England south to the Gulf Coast and Mexico.

Screech Owls are fearless in defense of their nests and will often strike an unsuspecting human on the head as he passes nearby at night. When discovered during the day, they often freeze in an upright position, depending on their cryptic coloration to escape detection. The two color phases, which vary in proportion geographically, are not based on age, sex, or season.

285 Barred Owl
(*Strix varia*)
True Owls (Strigidae)

Description: 20″ (51 cm). W. 44″ (1.1 m). A large, stocky owl, gray-brown with cross-barring on the neck and breast and streaks on the belly; *no ear-tufts.*

Voice: A loud, barking *hoo, hoo, hoo, hoo, hoo, hoo-hooo-aw!;* a variety of other barking calls and screams.

Habitat: Low, wet woods and swamp forest.

Nesting: 2–4 white eggs, in an unlined cavity in a hollow tree or (rarely) an abandoned building; sometimes in an abandoned crow's nest.

Range: East of the Rockies from central Canada to the Gulf of Mexico and in mountains as far south as Honduras.

This owl is seen only by those who seek it out in its dark retreat, usually a thick grove of trees in lowland forest. There it rests quietly during the day, coming out at night to feed on rodents, birds, frogs, and crayfish. If disturbed, it will fly easily from one grove of trees to another.

289 Saw-whet Owl
(*Aegolius acadicus*)
True Owls (Strigidae)

Description: 7″ (17 cm). Very small, earless, yellow-eyed owl; brown above, streaked with white and rufous below.

Voice: Usually silent; in late winter and spring utters a monotonous series of whistles.

Habitat: Low, moist, coniferous woodland; in winter in evergreen thickets in parks, yards, estates; also isolated pines.

Nesting: 5 or 6 white eggs placed without a nest lining in a deserted woodpecker hole or natural cavity.

Range: Southern Alaska, Manitoba, and Nova Scotia south to Connecticut, Maryland, Kansas, New Mexico, California, and southern Mexico. Winters south to Guatemala and the Gulf Coast.

Saw-whet Owls are almost entirely nocturnal, spending the day roosting quietly in dense foliage. At such times they are extraordinarily tame and may be approached closely or even handled. At night this tiny owl becomes a rapacious hunter, preying on mice and other small rodents.

293 Cooper's Hawk
(*Accipiter cooperii*)
Hawks, Eagles (Accipitridae)

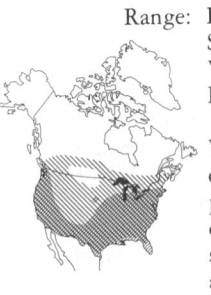

Description: 14–20″ (35–51 cm). W. 28″ (0.7 m).
Crow-sized hawk with long tail and
short, rounded wings. Slate gray above,
finely rust-barred below. Similar to the
more common Sharp-shinned Hawk but
larger, with *tail rounded at tip* (tail of
Sharp-shin is square).

Voice: Loud *cack-cack-cack-cack*. Also a
scream.

Habitat: Deciduous and, less often, coniferous
forests, especially where these are
interrupted by meadows and clearings.

Nesting: 4 dull white, brown-spotted or plain
eggs on a bulky platform of sticks and
twigs, usually more than 20 feet
aboveground.

Range: British Columbia, Ontario, and Nova
Scotia south to Florida and Costa Rica.
Winters north to southern New
England and British Columbia.

While many people know of the decline
of the Peregrine Falcon due to
pesticides, few are aware that the once-
common Cooper's Hawk has suffered a
similar fate and is now gone from large
areas of the eastern deciduous forest.
The larger Goshawk is taking over at
the northern limit of this forest, where
it borders on spruce and firs. As with
many other hawks, the females are
larger than the males; some small males
are difficult to distinguish from the
smaller Sharp-shinned Hawk. Even
experienced bird-watchers are often
unable to identify hawks in this size
range. When it is in pursuit of prey
its flight is swift and dashing, and its
long tail makes it highly maneuverable.
Otherwise it alternately flaps and glides
like others of the same genus.

297 Broad-winged Hawk
(*Buteo platypterus*)
Hawks, Eagles (Accipitridae)

Description: 13–15" (33–38 cm). W. 33" (0.8 m).
Crow-sized. Adult brown above, barred
with rusty below, with *broad black-and-
white tail bands;* immatures similar but
streaked below, with tail bands less
distinct.

Voice: Thin, unhawklike whistle, *pweeeeee.*

Habitat: Chiefly deciduous woodland.

Nesting: 3 or 4 white eggs with irregular small
and large spots, in a stick nest lined
with green leaves set in the crotch of a
tree.

Range: Breeds from southern Canada south
nearly throughout the eastern United
States. Winters in tropical South
America.

This hawk is best known for its
spectacular migrations; thousands of
birds fly by, with single flocks of up to
several hundred individuals. During
breeding, this hawk is secretive or,
rather, unobtrusive. It lives mainly in
the woods, beneath the canopy or
hidden among the foliage. Often one is
made aware of it only through its call.
Its food consists mainly of snakes,
mice, frogs, and insects. Great numbers
migrate along the eastern ridges in
mid-September; over 19,000 were
counted in one day as they passed over
the lookout at Hawk Mountain,
Pennsylvania.

298 Red-shouldered Hawk
(*Buteo lineatus*)
Hawks, Eagles (Accipitridae)

Description: 16–24" (40–61 cm). W. 40" (1 m).
Large, long-winged hawk with rust-
barred underparts, *reddish shoulders, a
narrowly banded tail,* and a translucent
area near the tip of the wing, visible

from below. Young birds are streaked below and are best distinguished from young Red-tailed Hawks by their somewhat smaller size; narrower tail; and longer, narrower wings.

Voice: Shrill scream, *kee-yeeer,* with a downward inflection.

Habitat: Deciduous woodlands, especially where there is standing water.

Nesting: 2 or 3 brown-spotted white eggs in a large mass of leaves and twigs placed 20 to 60 feet up in a forest tree.

Range: Minnesota and New Brunswick south to the Gulf Coast, and on the Pacific Coast from northern California to Baja California. Winters north to southern New England and the Ohio Valley.

This hawk generally avoids the upland forests inhabited by the Red-tailed Hawk, and is more often found in lowlands, especially swampy woods and bogs. There it hunts by sitting quietly on a low perch, dropping down to capture snakes and frogs. It also eats insects and small mammals.

---

300 **Red-tailed Hawk**
including "Harlan's Hawk"
(*Buteo jamaicensis*)
Hawks, Eagles (Accipitridae)

Description: 18–25″ (46–63 cm). W. 48″ (1.2 m). Large, stocky hawk with a whitish breast and a *rust-colored tail.* Young birds are duller, more streaked, and lack the rust-colored tail of the adult; they are distinguished from the Red-shouldered and Swainson's Hawk by their stocky build, and broad, more rounded wings. This species is quite variable in color, especially in the western part of its range; occasional blackish individuals occur but usually retain the rust-colored tail.

Voice: High-pitched descending scream with a hoarse quality.

Habitat: Mainly deciduous forest and adjacent open country; habitat more variable in the West.

Nesting: 2 or 3 brown-spotted white eggs in a substantial structure of sticks, lined with shreds of bark and bits of fresh green vegetation, placed in a tall tree or on a rocky ledge.

Range: Alaska and Nova Scotia south to Panama. Winters north to British Columbia and the Maritime Provinces.

The most common and widespread American member of the genus *Buteo,* which includes the Red-shouldered, Swainson's, and Broad-winged Hawks, among others. Like other hawks of this group, it soars over open country in search of its prey, but just as often perches in a tree at the edge of a meadow, watching for the slightest movement in the grass below. The Red-tail rarely takes poultry, feeding mainly on small rodents. Certain western birds, with dark brown, faintly banded tails were formerly considered a separate species that was called "Harlan's Hawk."

304 Mississippi Kite
(*Ictinia mississipiensis*)
Hawks, Eagles (Accipitridae)

Description: 12–14″ (30–35 cm). W. 36″ (0.9 m). Adult gray above and pale gray below with lighter gray head and black tail; immature streaked below, with banded tail. Narrow, pointed wings.

Voice: Two or three high clear whistles, but seldom heard.

Habitat: Open woodland and mixed scrub near water.

Nesting: 2 or 3 white eggs in a stick nest placed in large or small trees.

Range: Southeastern and south-central United States, but extremely local. Winters to southern South America.

This graceful, buoyant kite is a marvelous flier and spends hours in the air. It is quite gregarious, often seen in flocks and even nesting in loose colonies. Although chiefly insectivorous, feeding largely on grasshoppers and dragonflies, it occasionally takes small snakes and frogs. Its numbers have decreased considerably in recent years.

308 Golden Eagle
(*Aquila chrysaetos*)
Hawks, Eagles (Accipitridae)

Description: 30–41" (76–104 cm). W. 78" (2 m). Large, all-dark eagle with a pale golden nape. Bill smaller and darker than that of the Bald Eagle. Young birds have a two-toned tail—white at the base and black at the tip—and white patches on the undersides of the wings.
Voice: A high-pitched *kee-kee-kee;* also a high scream or squeal, but usually silent.
Habitat: Mainly deciduous mountain forests in the East; habitat more variable in the West. In any habitat during migration.
Nesting: 2 or 3 whitish eggs, unmarked or lightly speckled with dark brown, in a large mass of sticks on a rocky ledge or in a tall tree.
Range: Eastern Aleutians, Alaska and northern Canada south to New York, northern New England, Nebraska, and central Mexico, and in the Appalachians to North Carolina. Also found in Eurasia.

Although widespread in the Northern Hemisphere, the Golden Eagle has probably never been numerous in eastern North America and, after long persecution, only a very few breeding pairs now survive. In recent years a few nests have been found, and some have produced young, but it is unlikely that

the species will ever be more than a
rarity in the eastern part of its range.

317 Turkey Vulture
(*Cathartes aura*)
New World Vultures (Cathartidae)

Description: 25–32″ (63–81 cm). W. 72″ (1.8 m).
Eagle-sized, blackish bird usually seen
soaring over the countryside. Long
wings are narrower than those of the
Black Vulture, with silvery linings;
held upward in a wide, shallow "V."
Tail long; head small, bare, and
reddish. In flight it flaps its wings less
frequently than the Black Vulture, and
rolls and sways from side to side.

Voice: Usually silent. When feeding or at the
nest, it hisses or grunts.

Habitat: Mainly deciduous forests and
woodlands; often seen over adjacent
farmland.

Nesting: 2 whitish eggs, heavily marked with
dark brown, placed without nest or
lining in a crevice in rocks, in a hollow
tree, or in a fallen hollow log.

Range: Southern British Columbia, Minnesota,
and New Hampshire to southern South
America and the subantarctic Falkland
Islands. Winters north to California
and southern New England.

This is the commonest and most
widespread of New World vultures, a
group that includes the great condors of
California and the Andes. The family is
known from fossils dating back millions
of years, not only in the Americas but
also in Europe, where these birds no
longer occur. Evidence indicates that
unlike the Old World Vultures, the
New World forms are not related tc
hawks and eagles but are descended
from another, still unidentified group
of birds. Turkey Vultures are
scavengers and in some areas are

valuable for their removal of garbage and disease-causing carrion. At night they often gather in large roosts.

---

318 Black Vulture
(Coragyps atratus)
New World Vultures (Cathartidae)

Description: 22–24″ (56–61 cm). W. 54″ (1.4 m). Black with white patches near wing tips, conspicuous in flight; head bare, grayish; feet extend beyond the short tail. Flaps its wings more often and more rapidly than the Turkey Vulture.

Voice: Hisses or grunts, seldom heard.

Habitat: Open country wherever carrion is present, but breeds in light woodlands and thickets.

Nesting: 2 eggs on the ground, under bushes, in hollow logs or trees, under large rocks, or even in caves.

Range: Kansas, Indiana, and Pennsylvania south to eastern and southern United States. South to southern South America.

Black Vultures are scavengers in many parts of the South, not only feeding on carrion but also taking weak, sick, or unprotected young birds and mammals. They are smaller but more aggressive than Turkey Vultures and drive the latter from a carcass. Both species are often found perched in trees, on fence posts, and on the ground, or flying high overhead, especially on windy days, taking advantage of thermals or updrafts. After much debate, it has been determined that while Turkey Vultures can locate carrion by smell, Black Vultures cannot. They depend on their vision to find food.

337, 339 Downy Woodpecker
(*Picoides pubescens*)
Woodpeckers (Picidae)

Description: 6" (15 cm). Sparrow-sized. Black and white, with a small red patch on the nape in males. Similar to the Hairy Woodpecker, but smaller and with a short, stubby bill.

Voice: Dull-sounding *pik*. Also a descending rattle.

Habitat: Wood lots, parks, and gardens; suet feeders in winter.

Nesting: 4 or 5 white eggs in a tree hole.

Range: From Alaska and Canada to southern United States.

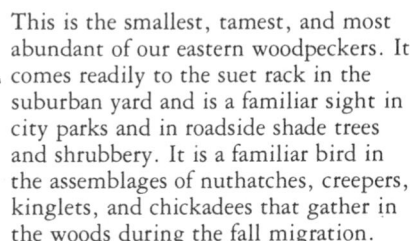

This is the smallest, tamest, and most abundant of our eastern woodpeckers. It comes readily to the suet rack in the suburban yard and is a familiar sight in city parks and in roadside shade trees and shrubbery. It is a familiar bird in the assemblages of nuthatches, creepers, kinglets, and chickadees that gather in the woods during the fall migration.

338, 340 Hairy Woodpecker
(*Picoides villosus*)
Woodpeckers (Picidae)

Description: 9" (23 cm). Robin-sized. Black and white with an *unspotted white back and long bill;* male has red head patch. Like all woodpeckers it has an undulating flight.

Voice: Call note, a sharp, distinctive *peek,* is louder than that of the Downy.

Habitat: Deciduous forest; more widespread in winter and migration.

Nesting: 4 white eggs in a tree hole.

Range: From Alaska and Canada to the Gulf of Mexico, the mountains of Panama, and the Bahamas.

The Hairy Woodpecker is more a forest bird and is shyer than its smaller

relative, the Downy Woodpecker. Thus the two species, found commonly from coast to coast, do not compete with each other. The Hairy Woodpecker is one of the most beneficial birds, saving both forest and fruit trees by destroying many harmful insects such as wood-boring beetles (which it extracts from holes with its barbed tongue). Like other woodpeckers, it hammers on a dead limb as part of its courtship ceremony and to proclaim its territory.

346 Yellow-bellied Sapsucker
(*Sphyrapicus varius*)
Woodpeckers (Picidae)

Description: 8½" (21 cm). A furtive woodpecker mottled with off-white and black; male has *red crown and throat;* female has only a red crown. Both sexes dull yellowish below. Immatures sooty brown. In all plumages the distinctive mark is a *conspicuous white wing stripe,* visible both at rest and in flight.

Voice: Mewing notes.

Habitat: Young, open deciduous or mixed forest with clearings; in migration, in parks, yards, gardens.

Nesting: 5 or 6 white eggs in a tree cavity excavated by the birds.

Range: Alaska and Canada to the mountains of Virginia and California. Winters south to Panama and the West Indies.

This species, at least on migration, is the quietest of the woodpeckers; aside from a few squeaks and whines, it is mainly silent. It is also the least conspicuous, hitching around to the opposite side of the tree trunk when approached. Sapsuckers get their name from the habit of boring holes into the cambium layer or inner bark, letting the sap exude and run down the trunk. The birds wipe up or suck the oozing sap with their brush-like tongues. They

return again and again to the same tree
and also consume the insects attracted
to it. Unfortunately, sapsucker holes
damage trees and sometimes provide
points of entry for fungus and other tree
diseases.

349 Red-bellied Woodpecker
(*Centurus carolinus*)
Woodpeckers (Picidae)

Description: 10″ (25 cm). Robin-sized. *Barred black
and white* above; pale buff below; sexes
similar except that male has red crown
and nape, female has red nape only.
A red patch on the lower abdomen is
seldom visible in the field.

Voice: *Chuck-chuck-chuck,* descending in pitch.
Also a loud, oft repeated *churrrr.*

Habitat: Open and swamp woodland; comes into
parks during migration and to feeders
in winter.

Nesting: 4 or 5 white eggs in a tree cavity, often
at the edge of woodland.

Range: Chiefly southeastern United States west
to Texas, ranging north to Minnesota,
Michigan, and Connecticut.

The common woodpecker over much of
the South, it is scarcer farther north but
has expanded its breeding range in
recent years to New York and southern
New England. Like most woodpeckers,
the "Zebraback" is beneficial,
consuming vast numbers of wood-
boring beetles as well as grasshoppers,
ants, and other insect pests. It also
feeds on acorns, beechnuts, and wild
fruits. It is one of the woodpeckers that
habitually stores food.

352 Pileated Woodpecker
(*Dryocopus pileatus*)
Woodpeckers (Picidae)

Description: 17″ (43 cm). Crow-sized. Black with white neck stripes, conspicuous white wing linings, and a prominent *red crest.*
Voice: Call flicker-like, but louder, deeper, and more *cuk-cuk-cuk-cuk-cuk,* rising and then falling in pitch.
Habitat: Dense forest and borders.
Nesting: 4 white eggs in a tree cavity.
Range: Breeds from southern Canada to the Gulf states and the mountains of the western United States.

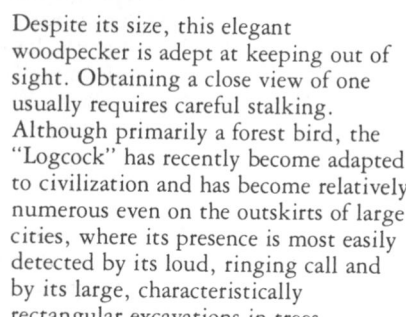

Despite its size, this elegant woodpecker is adept at keeping out of sight. Obtaining a close view of one usually requires careful stalking. Although primarily a forest bird, the "Logcock" has recently become adapted to civilization and has become relatively numerous even on the outskirts of large cities, where its presence is most easily detected by its loud, ringing call and by its large, characteristically rectangular excavations in trees.

354 White-breasted Nuthatch
(*Sitta carolinensis*)
Nuthatches (Sittidae)

Description: 5–6″ (13–15 cm). Sparrow-sized. Blue-gray above, underparts and face white, crown black. Usually seen creeping on tree trunks, often downward headfirst.
Voice: Nasal *yank-yank.* Song is a series of low whistled notes.
Habitat: Deciduous and mixed forest.
Nesting: 5 or 6 white eggs, lightly speckled with red-brown, in a cup of twigs and grass lined with feathers and hair in a natural cavity, bird box, or hole excavated by the birds themselves.
Range: British Columbia, Ontario, and Nova

Scotia south to Florida, the Gulf Coast, and Mexico.

This common nuthatch of the eastern United States is generally sedentary, but sometimes in the fall it turns up along the outer beaches, indicating that a migration is taking place. Pairs seem to remain together year-round, for the species may be found in twos even in the dead of winter. Although they often join mixed flocks of chickadees, woodpeckers, and kinglets roaming the winter woods, they tend to remain in their territories. White-breasted Nuthatches are familiar visitors to bird feeders.

355 Brown Creeper
(*Certhia familiaris*)
Creepers (Certhiidae)

Description: 5–5¾" (13–14 cm). Smaller than a sparrow. A slender, streaked, brown bird usually seen creeping up tree trunks, using its stiff tail for support.

Voice: High-pitched, lisping *tsee;* song a thin, descending warble.

Habitat: Deciduous and mixed woodlands.

Nesting: 6 or 7 white eggs, lightly speckled with brown, in a cup of bark shreds, feathers, sticks, and moss usually placed against a tree trunk behind a peeling slab of bark.

Range: Breeds from Alaska, Ontario, and Newfoundland south to Nicaragua. Winters south to the Gulf Coast and Florida. Also in Eurasia.

This inconspicuous bird is most often detected by its soft, lisping call as it works its way up a tree trunk, probing the bark for insects. In late winter and spring one may sometimes hear its song—a thin, musical warble. Unlike the nuthatch it only moves up a tree trunk; having reached the top, it will fly down to the base of another tree and repeat its spiral ascent.

360 Prothonotary Warbler
(*Protonotaria citrea*)
Wood Warblers (Parulidae)

Description: 5½" (14 cm). Male *golden-orange with blue-gray wings;* no wing bars; large white spots in tail. Female similar but duller.

Voice: Song is a ringing *sweet-sweet-sweet-sweet-sweet-sweet-sweet*. Also a canary-like flight song. Call is a loud, metallic *chip*.

Habitat: Wooded swamps, flooded bottomland forest, and streams with dead trees.

Nesting: 6 creamy white, purple-spotted eggs in a tree cavity, hole in a stump, birdhouse, or other man-made object such as a mailbox. The hole is stuffed with mosses to form a nest cup.

Range: Mainly in the southeastern states north to Minnesota, Michigan, and New York. Winters from southern Mexico to northern South America.

This is one of the characteristic birds of the southern swamplands, where its bright plumage is conspicuous in the gloomy, cypress-lined bayous. It is unusual among warblers in that it nests in holes in trees; this may be an adaptation to a habitat where such holes are numerous but where dense bushes—the usual warbler nesting site—are scarce.

362 Yellow-throated Vireo
(*Vireo flavifrons*)
Vireos (Vireonidae)

Description: 6" (15 cm). Sparrow-sized. *Bright yellow throat, breast, and "spectacles"; two conspicuous white wing bars,* olive-green head and back, gray rump, white belly.

Voice: Similar to the song of the Red-eyed and Solitary vireos, but huskier and lower in pitch.

Habitat: Tall deciduous trees at the edge of forests, along streams, roadsides, orchards, parks, and estates.

Nesting: 4 brown-blotched pinkish eggs in a cup-shaped nest of lichens, mosses, and grasses decorated and lined with spider-web silk and egg cases, set in a forked branch well up in a tree.

Range: Minnesota, Ontario, and southern New England south to the Gulf states. Winters from southern Mexico to northern South America.

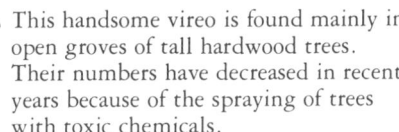

This handsome vireo is found mainly in open groves of tall hardwood trees. Their numbers have decreased in recent years because of the spraying of trees with toxic chemicals.

---

369 Hooded Warbler
(*Wilsonia citrina*)
Wood Warblers (Parulidae)

Description: 5½" (14 cm). Olive above, yellow below. Male has yellow face and *black hood,* female similar but lacks hood. Both sexes have *white tail spots.*

Voice: Clear, ringing, "flirtatious" *tawee-tawee-tawee-tee-o.*

Habitat: Mature, moist forest with luxuriant undergrowth, especially in ravines; also in wooded swamps.

Nesting: 3 or 4 creamy white, brown-spotted eggs in a grass-lined nest of dead leaves and plant fibers placed low in a small tree or shrub.

Range: Southern portions of the northern states to the Gulf states. Winters from Mexico to Panama.

The male is one of the most handsome in the family and, unlike many others, has a loud, penetrating, and very

melodious song. Even the female, which is much less strikingly patterned and colored, has conspicuous white tail spots and flirts its tail—like the male—by flashing the white tail patches as she moves about. This species usually ranges at a low level, rarely ten feet aboveground. Like most members of the family, it is adept at flycatching.

370 Kentucky Warbler
(*Oporornis formosus*)
Wood Warblers (Parulidae)

Description: 5½" (14 cm). Sparrow-sized. Sexes similar; olive-green above, bright yellow below; *black forecrown, lores* (between eyes and upper edge of bill), *and sides of throat; bright yellow spectacles.* No wing bars.

Voice: Loud, penetrating, rich *tur-dle, tur-dle,* etc., reminiscent of the song of the Carolina Wren.

Habitat: Low, moist, rich woodland with luxuriant undergrowth; often in ravines.

Nesting: 4 or 5 brown-spotted white eggs in a nest of dead leaves lined with grass, hair, and rootlets, placed on or near the ground.

Range: Iowa, Indiana, Pennsylvania, and New Jersey south to southeastern United States. Winters from southern Mexico to northwestern South America.

Named for the state where it was discovered in 1811 by Alexander Wilson, father of American ornithology, it is actually no more common in Kentucky than elsewhere in its range. Usually heard before it is seen, this rather secretive warbler remains hidden, especially in thickly vegetated ravines with streams running through them.

372 Mourning Warbler
(*Oporornis philadelphia*)
Wood Warblers (Parulidae)

Description: 5½" (14 cm). Similar to the
Connecticut Warbler—olive above and
yellow below with a gray hood—but
lacks eye-ring. Male has *black patch
below throat;* female has gray throat.

Voice: Loud, ringing, musical song: *teedle-
teedle, turtle-turtle,* the last pair of notes
lower.

Habitat: Dense thickets of blackberries and
briars in forest clearings; also in wet
woods with thick undergrowth.

Nesting: 4 brown-spotted white eggs in a nest of
fibers and leaves, lined with grass and
hair, on or near the ground.

Range: Alberta and North Dakota to southern
Canada and south to the northern
United States. Winters from Nicaragua
to northwestern South America.

This warbler supposedly gets its
vernacular name from the black
crepe-like patch on the breast of the
male, which suggests a symbol of
mourning. The scientific species name,
philadelphia, derives from the city where
Alexander Wilson discovered this
warbler in 1810. It is actually less
common in Philadelphia than in many
other places. Like other warblers of the
genus *Oporornis,* it inhabits dense,
overgrown areas with thick
undergrowth, and is often heard before
it is seen.

Bachman's Warbler
(*Vermivora bachmanii*)
Wood Warblers (Parulidae)

Description: 4½" (11 cm). Male is olive-green above
and bright yellow below, with yellow
forehead and cheeks; *black cap and large
throat patch.* Female has gray cap, lacks
the black throat, and is duller in color.

Voice: Its buzzy song is a cross between that of the Worm-eating and Parula warblers.

Habitat: Densely wooded swamps and wet thickets in heavy forest.

Nesting: 3 or 4 white eggs in a nest made of plant stems and leaves, lined with fine fibers, and placed low in shrubs and vines.

Range: Very local and rare, breeding in southeastern United States, chiefly in South Carolina, Alabama, Arkansas, and Missouri. Winters in Cuba and the nearby Isle of Pines.

By far the rarest and least known of North American warblers, inhabiting impenetrable swamps, it is more often heard than seen. For the past 25 years it has been something of a mystery. It has been placed on the endangered list and may be close to extinction. This warbler was named for Dr. John Bachman (1790–1874), friend and associate of Audubon.

388, 396   Orchard Oriole
(*Icterus spurius*)
Orioles, Blackbirds (Icteridae)

Description: 7″ (18 cm). Bluebird-sized. Adult male has *chestnut body* and *black head, back, wings, and tail;* female yellow-green; immature male like female but has *black throat.*

Voice: A rapid musical warble, somewhat like that of the Purple Finch but not as rich in quality.

Habitat: Orchards, shade trees in parks and gardens, and scattered trees along lakes and streams.

Nesting: 4–6 whitish eggs with purple scrawls, in a woven pouch-shaped nest of vegetable fibers and grass, suspended from the forked branch of a tree or bush.

Range: Breeds chiefly in southern portions of Minnesota, Wisconsin, Michigan, New York, and central New England south

to southern United States and west to
the Dakotas, Nebraska, Colorado, and
Texas; also in northeastern Mexico.
Winters from southern Mexico to
northern South America.

Southeastern Louisiana seems to be the
heart of this oriole's nesting country
since the highest densities have been
recorded there. At one locality there
were nearly 20 nests in a single live oak
and at another locality 114 nests on a
seven-acre tract, with 80 in oaks.

399, 562 Black-headed Grosbeak
(*Pheucticus melanocephalus*)
Grosbeaks, Buntings, Finches,
Sparrows (Fringillidae)

Description: 7½" (19 cm). Starling-sized. Heavy
pinkish-white bill. Male has black
head; black wings and tail have
conspicuous white patches; tawny-
orange breast, yellow belly, and tawny
back with black streaking. Female has
white eyebrows and pale buff underparts;
breast very finely streaked.

Voice: Rich warble similar to that of a Robin
but softer, sweeter, and faster. Call
note is an emphatic, sharp *tick,* slightly
metallic in tone.

Habitat: Open, deciduous woodland near water,
such as river bottoms, lakeshores, and
swampy places with a mixture of trees
and shrubs.

Nesting: 3 or 4 greenish eggs, spotted with
brown, in a loosely built stick nest
lined with rootlets, grasses, and leaves
and placed among the dense foliage of
an outer tree limb.

Range: Western North America, breeding from
extreme southern Canada to the
mountains of Mexico; winters in
Mexico.

Like the Rose-breasted Grosbeak, the
males, despite their bright colors, share

incubation with the females. However, they are not conspicuously marked above; the brightest coloration is on the breast and belly, which would be concealed as they incubate. Their food is quite varied. Heavy seeds are easily cracked open with their huge beaks, and, although sometimes a problem in fruit orchards, Black-headed Grosbeaks also consume potato beetles and other harmful insects and are highly valuable to the farmer.

408, 561   Rose-breasted Grosbeak
(*Pheucticus ludovicianus*)
Grosbeaks, Buntings, Finches,
Sparrows (Fringillidae)

Description: 8″ (20 cm). Starling-sized. Sexes very different; male black and white with a conspicuous *rose-red patch on breast and underwings.* Female heavily streaked brown on white above and below; prominent white eyebrow.

Voice: Its distinctive call note is a sharp, penetrating, metallic "clink." Song is like that of a Robin but softer and more melodious.

Habitat: Moist woodland adjacent to open fields with tall shrubs; also old and overgrown orchards.

Nesting: 4 or 5 purple-spotted whitish eggs in a loosely made nest of twigs, grass, and plant fibers set in a low branch of a tree.

Range: Southern Canada to the central United States, and in mountains as far south as northern Georgia. Winters from Mexico to northern South America.

This handsome grosbeak is one of the most conspicuous birds before the foliage comes into full leaf in early May. It is beneficial to the farmer, consuming many potato beetles and larvae as well as weed seeds, wild fruits, and buds.

416, 474 Scarlet Tanager
(*Piranga olivacea*)
Tanagers (Thraupidae)

Description: 7½″ (19 cm). Male in breeding
plumage *brilliant scarlet with black
wings and tail*. Female and male in
nonbreeding plumage olive-green;
male has black wings.

Voice: Call note an emphatic, nasal *chip-bang;*
song a burry repetitive warble,
somewhat like that of a Robin.

Habitat: Chiefly mature woodland, especially
oak and pine.

Nesting: 3 or 4 greenish, brown-spotted eggs in
a shallow nest of twigs and stems lined
with grass and placed on a horizontal
branch.

Range: Breeds from extreme southeastern
Canada to the east-central United
States. Winters from Colombia to
Bolivia.

The brilliantly colored male Scarlet
Tanager gleams in the sunlight but is
often difficult to see in thick foliage,
especially if it is motionless or moving
slowly from branch to branch high up
in the tree canopy. Only when perched
on a dead tree limb or feeding on the
ground during a cold, rainy spell is it
conspicuous. During late summer or
early autumn some of the males may
show a patchwork plumage of red and
green as they undergo a mòlt to olive-
green, except for wings and tail, which
remain black.

417, 473 Summer Tanager
(*Piranga rubra*)
Tanagers (Thraupidae)

Description: 7–8″ (17–20 cm). Smaller than a
Robin. Male solid rose-red with a *yellow
bill*. Female pale olive-green above, dull
yellow below. The male Cardinal has a
black face, conical red bill, and crest;

the male Scarlet Tanager has black wings and tail.

Voice: Distinctive rattling *chick-tucky-TUCK*. Its song is like a Robin's but softer and sweeter, not as hoarse as the Scarlet Tanager.

Habitat: Open woodlands and shade trees.

Nesting: 3 or 4 blue-green eggs, spotted with brown, in a shallow, flimsy cup near the end of a horizontal branch, 10–20 feet (3–6 meters) aboveground.

Range: Breeds from southern California, Wisconsin, and Delaware south to the Gulf Coast and northern Mexico. Winters north to southern Mexico.

Each major forest region of North America has its species of tanager; this one is found in dry oak and mixed forests of the southern states. Despite their bright colors, the males are difficult to detect in the dense foliage. A major part of the diet during the summer consists of flying insects captured in the air. On their breeding grounds the birds are most easily located by their calls, which they utter persistently throughout the day.

427 Carolina Chickadee
(*Parus carolinensis*)
Chickadees (Paridae)

Description: 4–5″ (10–13 cm). Gray above, white below, with black cap and throat, white cheeks. Similar to the more northern Black-capped Chickadee, but feathers of the folded wing usually show less white edging. Best identified by voice and range.

Voice: *Chickadee-dee-dee-dee,* higher-pitched and faster than the Black-cap; song a double whistled *see-dee, see-dee,* with a downward inflection, rather than the single two-noted song of the Black-cap.

Habitat: Deciduous woodlands and residential areas.

Nesting: 6–8 white eggs, lightly speckled with brown, placed in a cavity in a rotten stub or birdhouse lined with feathers, grass, and plant down.

Range: Resident from central New Jersey, Ohio, Missouri, and Oklahoma south to Florida and Texas.

So similar are the Carolina and Black-capped Chickadees that Audubon did not realize until 1834 that they were different species—over a century after "the" chickadee had been discovered by Europeans. The two species have much the same needs and thus compete and cannot coexist during the breeding season; instead, they replace each other geographically. Like its northern relative, the Carolina Chickadee is a familiar visitor to feeders and is a regular member of the mixed flocks of small birds that roam the winter woods.

428 Black-capped Chickadee
(*Parus atricapillus*)
Chickadees (Paridae)

Description: 4¾–5¾" (12–14 cm). Black cap and throat, white cheeks, gray back, dull white underparts. Wing feathers narrowly and indistinctly edged with white.

Voice: Buzzy *chick-a-dee-dee-dee;* clear, whistled *fee-bee,* the second note lower and often doubled.

Habitat: Deciduous and mixed forests, and open woodlands; suburban areas in winter.

Nesting: 6–8 brown-speckled white eggs in a cup of grass, fur, plant down, feathers, and moss, placed in a hole in a rotten stub excavated by the birds, or in a natural cavity or bird box.

Range: Breeds from Alaska and Newfoundland south to northern New Jersey, Missouri, and northern California. Winters south to Maryland and Texas.

Flocks of this tame and inquisitive bird spend the winter making the rounds of feeders in a neighborhood, often appearing at each feeder with striking regularity. Chickadees form the nucleus of mixed flocks of woodpeckers, nuthatches, creepers, and kinglets that move through the winter woods. Occasionally they move south in very large numbers, many thousands passing through even our largest cities. In spring chickadees disband and move into the woods to nest. They often feed upside down clinging to the underside of twigs and branches in their search for insect eggs and larvae. They are easily tamed and they soon learn to feed from the hand.

432 Tufted Titmouse
including "Black-crested Titmouse"
(*Parus bicolor*)
Titmice (Paridae)

Description: 6" (15 cm). Sparrow-sized. Gray above and white below, with *rust-colored sides; conspicuous crest*. The crest is black in Texas birds and gray elsewhere.

Voice: Its commonest call, sung year-round and carrying a considerable distance, is a whistled series of four to eight notes sounding like *Peter-Peter* repeated over and over.

Habitat: Swampy or moist woodland and shade trees in villages and city parks; in winter, at feeders.

Nesting: 5 or 6 brown-dotted white eggs in a tree cavity or a bird box stuffed with leaves and moss.

Range: Central portions of Wisconsin, Michigan, and Maine south to Florida, the Gulf Coast, Texas, and northern Mexico.

Titmice are social birds and, especially in winter, join with small mixed flocks of chickadees, nuthatches, kinglets,

creepers, and the smaller woodpeckers. Although a frequent visitor at feeders, it is not as tame or confiding as the chickadees. It often clings to the bark of trees and turns upside down to pick spiders and insects from the underside of a twig or leaf. The "Black-crested Titmouse" of Texas was until recently considered a separate species.

443 Blue-gray Gnatcatcher
(*Polioptila caerulea*)
Old World Warblers (Sylviidae)

Description: 4½–5" (11–13 cm). Smaller than a sparrow. Tiny, slender, long-tailed bird, blue-gray above and white below, with white eye-ring and white-bordered black tail. Resembles a miniature mockingbird.

Voice: Song is a thin, musical warble. Call note is a distinctive *pzzzz* with a nasal quality.

Habitat: Open, moist woodlands and brushy streamside thickets.

Nesting: 4 or 5 pale blue, brown-spotted eggs in a small, beautifully made cup of plant down and spider web, decorated with flakes of lichen and fastened to a horizontal branch at almost any height aboveground.

Range: Breeds from northern California, Colorado, central Minnesota, southern Ontario, and New Hampshire south to the Bahamas, the Gulf Coast, and Guatemala. Winters north to the Carolinas, the Gulf Coast, and southern California.

Several species of gnatcatchers are found throughout the warmer parts of the Americas. All of them build exquisite nests, which are exceedingly difficult to find unless the adults are feeding their young; the parents are quite noisy and conspicuous, and seem to ignore intruders. These birds are extremely

active, constantly flitting about
through the treetops. This species
apparently feeds exclusively on insects.

444, 445 Cerulean Warbler
(*Dendroica cerulea*)
Wood Warblers (Parulidae)

Description: 4½" (11 cm). Male has a *sky-blue head
and back; black band across white breast.*
Female is dull olive above and buff
below, and lacks the breast band.

Voice: Series of short, warbled notes followed
by a higher-pitched buzz.

Habitat: Open woodland, often near streams and
rivers.

Nesting: 4 brown-spotted whitish eggs in a nest
of plant fibers lined with grass, moss,
and hair placed high in a deciduous
tree, generally near the end of a branch.

Range: New York and the Great Lakes states
south to central and southeastern
United States. Winters in northern and
western South America south to
Bolivia.

This species has a discontinuous range,
occurring here and there in rather loose
colonies. It is usually found high in the
treetops, where it is difficult to see in
the thick foliage.

453 Red-eyed Vireo
(*Vireo olivaceus*)
Vireos (Vireonidae)

Description: 5½–6½" (14–16 cm). Sparrow-sized.
Olive-green above, whitish below, with
a *narrow white eyebrow bordered above with
black. Gray crown; red eye;* no wing
bars. Warbling Vireo is similar but
lacks the gray crown and black border
over white eyebrow.

Voice: Series of short, musical, Robin-like
phrases endlessly repeated; like that of

the Solitary Vireo but faster and not so musical.

Habitat: Deciduous forest, and shade trees in residential areas.

Nesting: 3 or 4 white eggs sparsely marked with dark brown, in a thin-walled pendant cup of bark strips and plant fibers, decorated with lichen and attached to a forked twig.

Range: Breeds from British Columbia, Ontario, and the Gulf of St. Lawrence south to Florida, southern Texas, Colorado, and Oregon. Winters in South America.

This vireo is one of the most abundant birds in eastern North America. Its principal habitat, the vast broad-leaved forests, supports millions of them, often one pair per acre. A persistent singer during the breeding season, it utters its endless series of short phrases from dawn till dusk, even on the hottest days when other birds are silent, and may even sing while grappling with the large insects it captures.

454 Warbling Vireo
(*Vireo gilvus*)
Vireos (Vireonidae)

Description: 5–6" (13–15 cm). Sparrow-sized. Similar to the Red-eyed Vireo—olive-green above, whitish below with no wing bars—but lacks the bold face pattern, having only a narrow white eyebrow. The Philadelphia Vireo is also similar but has a yellow tinge to the underparts and a dark spot between the eye and the base of the bill.

Voice: Drowsy warbling, like the song of the Purple Finch but slower.

Habitat: Deciduous woodland, especially near streams; in isolated groves and shade trees.

Nesting: 3 or 4 brown-spotted white eggs in a well-made pendant cup of bark strips and plant down fastened to a forked twig, usually near the top of a tall tree.

Range: Breeds from British Columbia, Manitoba, and New Brunswick south to the Carolinas, Louisiana, and northern Mexico. Winters in Central America.

The best place to look for this modestly plumaged vireo is in a grove of tall shade trees on the bank of a stream. Here, in the breeding season, one may hear its quiet song, and after a careful search, spot it moving deliberately through the treetop foliage in pursuit of insects. Although still common in many areas, it has decreased considerably because of the spraying of elms—its favorite tree for nesting.

461 Acadian Flycatcher
(*Empidonax virescens*)
Tyrant Flycatchers (Tyrannidae)

Description: 6″ (15 cm). Olive-green above, yellowish below. Identified chiefly by voice and habitat.

Voice: Emphatic two-noted *flee-see* with the second syllable higher in pitch, uttered on the breeding grounds and, rarely, on migration.

Habitat: Beech-maple or hemlock forest, usually under the canopy but also in clearings; often in wooded ravines.

Nesting: 3 or 4 brown-spotted buff eggs in a woven nest of plant fibers in a bush or tree, sometimes over a stream.

Range: The Great Lakes, southeastern Pennsylvania, and southern New England south to eastern United States. Winters from Panama to Ecuador and Venezuela.

The Acadian Flycatcher and its relatives in the genus *Empidonax* are difficult to distinguish, but in much of the South, the Acadian is the only breeding

species; between June and August, any
Empidonax seen in the lowlands south of
New Jersey and Missouri can safely be
called an Acadian.

---

464 **Least Flycatcher**
(*Empidonax minimus*)
Tyrant Flycatchers (Tyrannidae)

Description: 5¼″ (13 cm). Dull olive-gray above,
whitish below with two whitish wing
bars and white eye-ring. Distinguished
by voice.

Voice: Dry, insect-like *che-BEC,* snapped out
and accented on the second syllable,
and uttered incessantly through the
hottest days of summer.

Habitat: Widely distributed in open country,
nesting in shade trees, orchards,
villages, city parks, rural roadsides, and
woodland borders.

Nesting: 4 creamy white eggs in a finely woven,
cup-shaped nest made of vegetable
fibers and lined with grass and feathers,
firmly wedged in the fork or crotch of a
tree.

Range: Southern Canada south to central
United States, and in the mountains to
northern Georgia.

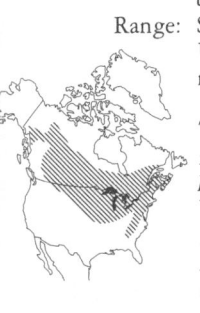

The Least Flycatcher is perhaps the
most familiar member of the difficult
Empidonax group; it is a characteristic
bird of large shade trees; its presence
is most easily detected by its call note.
An incubating bird is surprisingly tame
and will often allow itself to be touched
or even lifted off the nest.

465 Eastern Wood Pewee
(*Contopus virens*)
Tyrant Flycatchers (Tyrannidae)

Description: 6½″ (16 cm). Dull olive-gray with two whitish wing bars, no eye-ring.

Voice: A plaintive *pee-ah-weee* or *pee-weee,* rising on the last note.

Habitat: Forest, open woodland, orchards, and shade trees in parks and along roadsides.

Nesting: 3 or 4 creamy white, brown-dotted eggs in finely woven, cup-shaped nest made of vegetable fiber and covered with lichens. The nest is saddled on a horizontal limb and blends in with the branches; the lichen-covered cups look like knots, fungi, or part of the limb itself.

Range: Southeastern Canada to the Gulf of Mexico. Winters from Costa Rica to northwestern South America.

Pewees are more often heard than seen because of their dull coloration and because they frequent the dense upper canopy of the forest.

Western Wood Pewee
(*Contopus sordidulus*)
Tyrant Flycatchers (Tyrannidae)

Description: 6½″ (17 cm). A sparrow-sized flycatcher, dull olive-gray above, slightly paler below, with two whitish wing bars. The Eastern Wood Pewee extremely similar, but is slightly darker below; the two species are best distinguished by voice.

Voice: A harsh, nasal *pee-eeer,* very different from the sweet *peee-ah weee* of the Eastern Wood Pewee.

Habitat: Open woodland and woodland edges; orchards.

Nesting: 3 or 4 white eggs, spotted with brown, in a shallow saucer of grass fastened to a horizontal branch.

Range: Eastern Alaska, Mackenzie, and
Manitoba south through the western
United States to Guatemala; winters in
northern South America.

This species is generally found in more
open, park-like woodland than the
Eastern Wood Pewee, and is thus more
readily observed. In a few areas along
the western edge of the Great Plains the
two pewees occur together without
interbreeding—conclusive evidence that
despite their great similarity, they are
distinct species.

469 Great Crested Flycatcher
(*Myiarchus crinitus*)
Tyrant Flycatchers (Tyrannidae)

Description: 9″ (23 cm). Robin-sized. Brown above,
gray throat, yellow belly, *rufous wings
and tail*. Slightly crested.

Voice: Its best known call is a loud, ringing,
whistled, slightly buzzy *wheep*,
sometimes repeated. Also a raucous
whit-whit-whit-whit.

Habitat: Open forest, orchards, and large trees
in farm country.

Nesting: 5 or 6 creamy white, brown-spotted
eggs in tree cavities or bird boxes. The
bulky nest is lined with all sorts of
trash—cellophane, snakeskins, string,
rags, etc.

Range: Southern Canada to the Gulf of Mexico.
Winters mainly from southern Mexico
to Colombia.

This species is to the woodland what
the Kingbird is to open country. It is
noisy, aggressive, and even more
colorful. Living mostly under the forest
canopy, however, it is much more often
heard than seen, and is much less in
evidence than its black-and-white
relative. A mystifying habit is its
occasional use of shed snakeskins in its
nest lining. Whether this is intended to

frighten off predators or merely
decorate the nest is not known. It is the
only eastern flycatcher that nests in
holes.

499 **Veery**
(*Catharus fuscescens*)
Thrushes (Turdidae)

Description: 6½–7¼″ (16–18 cm). Smaller than a
Robin. Uniform cinnamon-brown
above, with faint spotting on the upper
breast. Our only spotted thrush with
the *upperparts uniformly cinnamon*.

Voice: Rich, downward spiral with an ethereal
quality. Call note a descending *whew*
with a vibrant tone.

Habitat: Moist deciduous woodlands; willow
thickets along streams in the West.

Nesting: 4 blue-green eggs in a bulky cup of
moss, plant fibers, and leaves placed on
the ground in a clump of grass or ferns,
or a few feet aboveground in a shrub.

Range: Breeds from British Columbia and
Newfoundland south to New Jersey,
Indiana, and, in the mountains, to
Georgia, New Mexico, and Oregon.
Winters in South America.

The beautiful song of the Veery sounds
best at dusk, as it echoes through the
deepening gloom of the forest. The bird
is rather difficult to see, but it can be
lured into view by an imitation of the
squeaking of a bird in distress. Its diet
is evenly divided between insects
obtained on the ground and fruit.

500 **Wood Thrush**
(*Hylocichla mustelina*)
Thrushes (Turdidae)

Description: 8″ (20 cm). Robin-sized. Brown above,
bright rusty on head, and *white below with
large blackish spots.*

Other brown thrushes have finer spotting on the breast.

Voice: A series of rich, melodious, flute-like phrases; a sharp *pit-pit-pit-pit*.

Habitat: Moist, deciduous woodlands with a thick understory; also well-planted parks and gardens.

Nesting: 4 greenish-blue eggs in a cup of grass and twigs, reinforced with mud and lined with fine grass and rootlets, placed in a bush or sapling.

Range: Manitoba, Ontario, and Nova Scotia south to Florida and the Gulf of Mexico. Winters mainly from Mexico to Panama, but a few winter in Texas and southern Florida.

This is the most familiar of our spotted brown thrushes, and the only one that nests regularly in the vicinity of houses. The Wood Thrush has one of the most beautiful songs of any North American bird; Thoreau wrote of it: "Whenever a man hears it he is young, and Nature is in her spring; wherever he hears it, it is a new world and a free country, and the gates of heaven are not shut against him."

503 Ovenbird
(*Seiurus aurocapillus*)
Wood Warblers (Parulidae)

Description: 6″ (15 cm). Sparrow-sized. Thrush-like warbler, olive-brown above, white below with dark streaks; conspicuous eye-ring; *orange-brown crown bordered with black stripes;* pinkish legs.

Voice: Loud staccato song—*teacher, teacher, teacher*—with geographical variation in emphasis. Flight song, often uttered at night, is a bubbling and exuberant series of jumbled notes ending with the familiar *teacher, teacher.*

Habitat: Mature, dry forest with little undergrowth.

Nesting: 4 or 5 brown-spotted white eggs in a

domed or oven-shaped grass-lined nest of dead leaves and plant fibers, placed on the ground, with a side entrance.

Range: Breeds from central Canada to the northern Gulf states. Winters from the Gulf of Mexico to northern South America.

This warbler gets its name from its peculiar ground nest, which resembles a miniature Dutch oven. A male frequently has more than one mate, and as many as three in one instance; it has also been observed that two males, as well as the female, feed the young.

---

504 Louisiana Waterthrush
(*Seiurus motacilla*)
Wood Warblers (Parulidae)

Description: 6½" (16 cm). Sparrow-sized. Dark olive brown above, white and streaked below. *Frequently bobs tail.* Similar to Northern Waterthrush but *throat unstreaked* and *eyebrow white.*

Voice: Song is three clear notes followed by a descending jumble.

Habitat: Prefers swift-moving brooks on hillsides and, where the Northern Waterthrush is absent, occurs in river swamps and along sluggish streams.

Nesting: 5 brown-blotched white eggs in a grass-lined nest of dead leaves and moss set under the overhang of a stream bank, in a stump cavity, or among exposed tree roots.

Range: Minnesota, Ontario and central New England, south to Georgia and Texas. Winters from Mexico and the West Indies to northern South America.

This bird is very similar to the Northern Waterthrush; they were confused by early American ornithologists. During spring migration the Louisiana Waterthrush arrives much earlier than the Northern.

Where the two species breed together, the Northern prefers bogs and swamps while the Louisiana prefers rushing streams and clear brooks.

505 Northern Waterthrush
(*Seiurus noveboracensis*)
Wood Warblers (Parulidae)

Description: 6″ (15 cm). Sparrow-sized. Olive-brown above, pale yellowish below with black streaks; *yellowish-white line over eye* and *streaked throat.*

Voice: Song *chee-chee-chee, chip-chip-chip-chew-chew-chew,* loud and ringing, speeding up at the end. Call a sharp *klink.*

Habitat: Cool bogs, wooded swamps, and lake shores in the breeding season; almost any wooded habitat in migration.

Nesting: 4 or 5 creamy white eggs with brown blotches in a nest of moss set in a bank, at the base of a trunk, or among the roots of an overturned tree.

Range: Breeds from Alaska and Canada to northern United States. Winters from Mexico and the West Indies to northern South America.

This warbler is called a waterthrush because of its superficial resemblance to a thrush and its fondness for water. Like its relative the Ovenbird, it walks rather than hops. This species is among the first to move south during the fall migration and southern migrants are regularly reported by the middle of July or earlier. One individual banded on a southbound flight on Long Island was recovered the following winter in Venezuela and, remarkably, was trapped one year later in Venezuela at the same locality.

509 Worm-eating Warbler
(*Helmitheros vermivorus*)
Wood Warblers (Parulidae)

Description: 5½" (14 cm). Sparrow-sized. Plain brownish above and below, with conspicuous *dark and light crown stripes*. Sexes look alike.

Voice: Song like that of Chipping Sparrow but faster, buzzy, and more insect-like.

Habitat: Chiefly dry wooded hillsides.

Nesting: 4 or 5 brown-spotted white eggs in a ground nest of dead leaves lined with moss.

Range: Breeds from Iowa, Ohio, New York, and Massachusetts south to the southeastern states. Winters in the northern West Indies and from Mexico to Panama.

The Worm-eating Warbler spends much of its time on or near the ground, quietly searching for its insect prey in the leaf litter and low vegetation. A singing male, however, often perches rather high up in a forest tree, where its habit of sitting motionless for long periods of time makes it very difficult to spot. The name "Worm-eating" reflects the bird's fondness for the small larvae of moths.

Swainson's Warbler
(*Limnothlypis swainsonii*)
Wood Warblers (Parulidae)

Description: 5" (13 cm). A plain warbler, olive-brown above and whitish beneath, with a rufous cap and a whitish line over each eye.

Voice: Three or four clear notes followed by several rapid descending notes, described as *whee-whee-whee-whip-poor-will.*

Habitat: Wooded swamps and southern canebrakes; also rhododendron thickets in the mountains.

Nesting: 3 bluish-white eggs in a loose, bulky nest of vegetable fibers, rootlets, and dead leaves placed in a dense bush or vine.

Range: Southern portions of Illinois, Indiana, Ohio, and Maryland south to southeastern United States. Winters in Cuba, Jamaica, and Yucatán south to Honduras.

This dull-colored warbler is shy and retiring, dwelling in remote, often impenetrable swamps and cane thickets. If not for its song—like that of a Hooded Warbler or a water thrush—it would frequently be overlooked. It is named after William Swainson, an early 19th century British naturalist.

564 Black-and-White Warbler
(*Mniotilta varia*)
Wood Warblers (Parulidae)

Description: 5″ (13 cm). *Black and white stripes, including crown.* Male has black throat, female's throat white.

Voice: Thin, high-pitched, monotonous *weesy-weesy-weesy-weesy* like a squeaky wheelbarrow.

Habitat: Primary and secondary forest, chiefly deciduous. In migration in parks, gardens, and lawn areas with trees and shrubs.

Nesting: 4 or 5 purple-spotted white eggs in a ground nest composed of leaves, grass, and rootlets lined with hair and fern down, set at the base of a tree, stump, or rock.

Range: Breeds from southern Canada to southern United States east of the Rockies. Winters from the southern parts of the Gulf states to northwestern South America.

This conspicuous warbler arrives in the North early in spring, usually by mid-

to late April. It is known for its habit of creeping around tree trunks and along larger branches in search of insect food in crevices in or under the bark; hence its old name, "Black-and-White Creeper." Unlike the Brown Creeper which only moves *up* a tree, and the nuthatches which only move headfirst *down* the tree, this warbler does both.

Coniferous Forests

Forests consisting mainly of cone-bearing, evergreen trees such as pines, spruces, hemlocks, and junipers. Intermixed one may find such deciduous trees as birches, willows, alder, and aspens.

In addition to the species treated here, one may also find some of the birds of Deciduous Forests, especially where the two habitats occur side by side.

263, 265 Willow Ptarmigan
(*Lagopus lagopus*)
Grouse (Tetraonidae)

Description: 15″ (38 cm). A small tundra grouse with much white in plumage. In summer, chestnut brown with white wings and belly; in winter, largely white with black outer tail feathers. Rock Ptarmigan is smaller, grayer, and has a black mark from eye to base of bill.

Voice: A growling cackle: *kuk-kuk-kuk-kuk-goback-gobackgoback.*

Habitat: Tundra; sheltered ravines and willow thickets; wanders into coniferous forests in winter.

Nesting: 7–10 red eggs, deepening in color soon after hatching, and profusely spotted with black; in a shallow scrape in tundra.

Range: Aleutians, northern Alaska, Baffin Island, and central Greenland south to Newfoundland, central Quebec, Manitoba, and British Columbia. Also in Eurasia.

During the summer, Willow Ptarmigans feed on tender leaves, buds, and berries of tundra plants, whereas in winter they subsist almost entirely on twigs of willow and alder. This winter diet gives their flesh a bitter taste.

264, 266 Rock Ptarmigan
(*Lagopus mutus*)
Grouse (Tetraonidae)

Description: 13″ (33 cm). A small tundra grouse. In winter plumage pure white with black outer tail feathers; in summer with gray-brown body, white wings and tail. *Has narrow black mark from eye to base of bill.* Willow Ptarmigan is similar but larger, chestnut rather than gray-brown, and lacks the black mark from eye to base of bill.

Voice: A hoarse croak, various mechanical crackling notes.

Habitat: Open tundra.

Nesting: 8–12 clay-colored or pinkish eggs, spotted with dark red and brown, in a grass-lined hollow in tundra.

Range: Eastern Aleutians, northern Alaska, Ellesmere Island, and northern Greenland south to Newfoundland, northern Quebec, and British Columbia. Also found in Eurasia.

Ptarmigan are unusual in that they have three different plumages each year—a largely white winter plumage, a brown breeding plumage, and an autumn plumage that resembles the breeding plumage. This species inhabits higher, more exposed tundra than the Willow Ptarmigan.

270 Spruce Grouse
(*Canachites canadensis*)
Grouse (Tetraonidae)

Description: 15–17″ (38–43 cm). Dark, chicken-like bird. Male dusky gray-brown with black throat and white-spotted sides and a chestnut-tipped tail. Female browner, underparts barred with brown.

Voice: Low hooting. Female makes clucking sounds. The drumming of this grouse consists of a noisy whirring and fluttering of the wings either from a log or in the air.

Habitat: Coniferous forests, especially those with a mixture of spruce and pine; edges of bogs.

Nesting: 8–11 buff eggs, plain or spotted with brown, in a ground hollow lined with grass and leaves concealed under low branches of a young spruce.

Range: Alaska, Manitoba, Quebec, and Nova Scotia south to New England, northern New York, Michigan, and northern Washington.

This northern grouse is extraordinarily tame and can occasionally be approached and killed with a stick; hence its local name, "fool hen." It is generally a quiet bird thinly distributed in its habitat and therefore difficult to find. Its principal foods are the needles and buds of evergreens, although insects are eaten in large quantities by young birds. Spruce Grouse are generally found singly or in small family groups, picking their way quietly over the forest floor or sitting in dense conifers.

281 Long-eared Owl
(*Asio otus*)
True Owls (Strigidae)

Description: 15" (38 cm). W. 39" (1 m). Crow-sized. *Long ear tufts close together,* heavily mottled brown, *chestnut facial disks.*
Voice: Soft low hoots, also whistles, whines, shrieks, and cat-like meows. Seldom heard except during breeding time.
Habitat: Deciduous and evergreen forests.
Nesting: 4 or 5 white eggs in the deserted nest of a crow, hawk, or squirrel.
Range: Northern Hemisphere in the temperate zone; in America from Alaska and Canada to the Gulf states and Mexico.

Although these woodland owls are gregarious in winter, they are so nocturnal and quiet that during the day up to a dozen may inhabit a dense evergreen grove without being detected. They have a tendency to roost near the trunk of a tree, and since they elongate themselves by compressing their feathers, they resemble part of the trunk itself. Only by peering intently upward can one detect the round face and telltale long ear tufts. When protecting their young they put on a spectacular display, lowering their head and fanning their

wings over their back in a threatening
attitude. A good way to locate an owl
roost is to search in pine woods for
groups of pellets—as with all owls
these regurgitated bundles of
undigested fur and bones provide an
excellent indication of their food habits.

282 Great Horned Owl
(*Bubo virginianus*)
True Owls (Strigidae)

Description: 25" (63 cm). W. 55" (1.4 m). Varying
in color from white to dark brown and
gray; mottled and streaked below,
setting off the *white throat;* prominent,
widely spaced ear tufts; yellow eyes.

Voice: Series of low, sonorous, far-carrying
hoots, *hoo, hoo-hoo, HOO HOO.* Second
and third notes shorter than the others.

Habitat: Ubiquitous, frequenting forest, desert,
open country, swamps, and even city
parks.

Nesting: 2 or 3 white eggs on the bare surface of
a cliff or cave, or even on the ground;
in the East it most often appropriates
the unused stick nest of a heron, hawk,
or crow.

Range: Wide ranging, from arctic North
America to the Straits of Magellan, but
not in the West Indies.

The largest of American "eared" owls,
it is exceeded in size only by the rare
Great Gray Owl. The Great Horned
Owl preys on a wide variety of creatures
including grouse and rabbits as well as
beetles, lizards, and frogs. It is one of
the first birds to nest, laying its eggs as
early as late January when there is still
snow on the ground.

286 Great Gray Owl
(*Strix nebulosa*)
True Owls (Strigidae)

Description: 24–33" (61–84 cm). W. 60" (1.5 m).
A huge, dusky gray, earless owl of the
north woods, with large facial disks and
distinctive black chin spot. Eyes yellow.
Barred Owl is smaller, stockier, and
browner, with dark eyes.

Voice: Very deep, booming *whoo's,* repeated
ten times or more, and gradually
descending the scale.

Habitat: Boreal coniferous forests and muskeg.

Nesting: 2–5 white eggs in a bulky nest of sticks
in a dense conifer.

Range: Alaska and Interior Canada south to
Quebec, Minnesota, Idaho, and
northern California. Wanders rarely in
winter southward into northern New
England and the Great Lakes region.
Also in Eurasia.

Like other owls of the Far North, this
species hunts during the daytime, often
watching for prey from a low perch.
Because it spends much of its time in
dense conifers, it is often overlooked.
One of the most elusive of American
birds, it was discovered in America by
Europeans before they realized that the
species also occurs in Europe.

288 Hawk-Owl
(*Surnia ulula*)
True Owls (Strigidae)

Description: 15–17" (38–43 cm). W. 33" (0.8 m).
Smaller than a crow. A *long-tailed,
day-flying owl* that behaves more like a
hawk. Barred breast; facial disks have
bold black borders.

Voice: Whistling *ki-ki-ki-ki-ki-ki,* like the call
of a kestrel.

Habitat: Clearings in boreal coniferous forests
and muskeg.

Nesting: 3–7 white eggs in a tree cavity, in an

abandoned bird's nest, or rarely on a cliff.

Range: Alaska and Labrador south to Newfoundland, Quebec, and British Columbia. May wander farther south in winter. Also in Eurasia.

The Hawk Owl is a fast-flying, diurnal bird. It may often be seen on an exposed perch at the edge of a field or clearing, on the lookout for rodents and small birds. Because it does not depend on any one source of food, it is not subject to mass movements like other northern predators.

290 Boreal Owl
(*Aegolius funereus*)
True Owls (Strigidae)

Description: 9–12" (23–30 cm). W. 24" (0.6). A rare Robin-sized owl without ear tufts. Brown with white spots above, rust-streaked below. Similar to the Saw-whet Owl but larger, with *more spotting on upperparts and forehead,* and with a *yellow bill* (Saw-whet has dark bill).
Voice: Rapid series of whistled notes.
Habitat: Boreal coniferous forest and muskeg.
Nesting: 4–6 white eggs placed in a woodpecker hole or other tree cavity or in the abandoned nest of another bird.
Range: Breeds from the limit of trees in northern Alaska, Yukon, Saskatchewan, Manitoba, Quebec, Labrador, and probably Newfoundland south to New Brunswick, Ontario, southern Manitoba, central Alberta, and northern British Columbia. Wanders rarely in winter south to New Jersey, Illinois, and Oregon. Also in Eurasia.

This small, secretive owl is considered one of the rarest winter visitors from the North. Its retiring habits cause it to be overlooked, and it is easily confused with its relative the Saw-whet

Owl. Boreals may therefore actually be more common than is presently thought. They are entirely nocturnal, spending the day concealed in dense spruce or in hollow trees. They prey mainly on rodents.

294 Sharp-shinned Hawk
(*Accipiter striatus*)
Hawks, Eagles (Accipitridae)

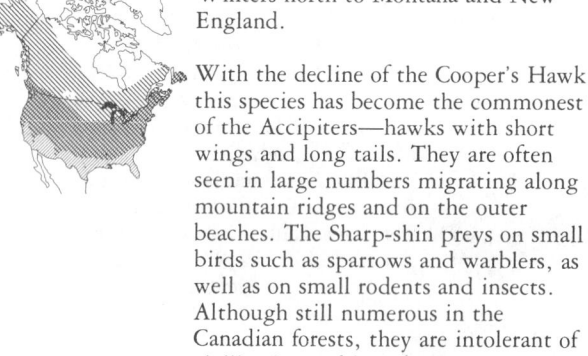

Description: 10–14″ (25–35 cm). W. 21″ (0.5 m). Jay-sized. Small, fast-flying hawk with *long tail and short, rounded wings*. Slate gray above, pale below with fine rust-barring. The larger, rarer Cooper's Hawk has rounded tail tip; Sharp-shin's is square.

Voice: Sharp *kick-kick-kick;* also a shrill squeal.

Habitat: Dense coniferous forests, less often in deciduous forests. In migration and winter it may be seen in almost any habitat.

Nesting: 4 whitish, brown-blotched eggs on a shallow, well-made platform of twigs concealed in a dense conifer.

Range: Alaska, Mackenzie, and Newfoundland south to Florida and northern Mexico. Winters north to Montana and New England.

With the decline of the Cooper's Hawk this species has become the commonest of the Accipiters—hawks with short wings and long tails. They are often seen in large numbers migrating along mountain ridges and on the outer beaches. The Sharp-shin preys on small birds such as sparrows and warblers, as well as on small rodents and insects. Although still numerous in the Canadian forests, they are intolerant of civilization and have become scarce as breeding birds in more settled areas.

296 Goshawk
(*Accipiter gentilis*)
Hawks, Eagles (Accipitridae)

Description: 20–26″ (51–66 cm). W. 42″ (1.1 m).
Larger than a crow. A heavy-bodied
hawk with a dark blue-gray back, black
crown, pale underparts finely barred
with gray, and a *conspicuous white
eyebrow*. Young bird similar but brown
above, streaked below.

Voice: Loud *kak-kak-kak-kak* when disturbed.

Habitat: Coniferous forests; also farmland,
woodland edges, and open country in
the winter.

Nesting: 3–5 very pale blue eggs in a large mass
of sticks lined with fresh sprigs of
evergreen placed in a tree.

Range: Alaska, Mackenzie, northern Quebec,
and Newfoundland south to New
England, Michigan, and New Mexico;
also southward in the Appalachians to
Maryland. Winters south to Virginia
and northern Mexico.

The Goshawk is an uncommon winter
visitor from the North; it is seldom
present in large numbers, remaining
mostly in the northern coniferous
forests unless forced to move south by a
periodic decline in the populations of
the grouse that are a staple of its diet.
The swift flight of a Goshawk chasing a
grouse has given the bird the name
"Blue Darter." It is fearless in defense
of the nest and will boldly attack
anyone who ventures too close. It has
recently begun extending its range to
the south, and now breeds in small
numbers in deciduous forests.

313 Merlin
"Pigeon Hawk"
(*Falco columbarius*)
Falcons (Falconidae)

Description: 10–14″ (25–35 cm). W. 23″ (0.6 m). Jay-sized. Slaty or brownish above; long tail boldly banded; light and streaked below; long, pointed wings. Lacks the "mustaches" of the larger Peregrine Falcon.

Voice: Usually silent. High loud cackle. Also *klee-klee-klee* like a Sparrow Hawk.

Habitat: Coniferous forests; more widespread in winter.

Nesting: 4 or 5 brown-spotted, pale, rusty eggs placed without a nest or lining in a tree cavity, on a rocky ledge, or in an abandoned crow's nest.

Range: Alaska, Mackenzie, and Labrador south to Nova Scotia, Michigan, and Oregon. Winters from British Columbia and Newfoundland (rare) to northern South America. Also breeds in northern Eurasia.

This northern species, formerly called "Pigeon Hawk," is best known as a migrant along our larger rivers and coastal marshes. It is most abundant during the migrations of the shorebirds, sparrows, warblers, and other small birds on which it feeds. This little falcon is swift and aggressive, harassing larger hawks and gulls and attacking intruders at its nest. As with other falcons, the female begins incubating as soon as the first egg is laid, so that the young hatch at intervals; when food is scarce the larger young are fed first, the smaller ones sometimes dying of starvation. Seemingly heartless, the procedure is actually advantageous since it ensures that some young will be raised successfully even in hard times.

341, 343 Black-backed Three-toed Woodpecker
(*Picoides arcticus*)
Woodpeckers (Picidae)

Description: 9″ (23 cm). Starling-sized. *Solid black back,* barred flanks, white below; male has *yellow crown* and female has solid *black crown.*

Voice: Sharp *kik.* Scolding rattle. It also hammers on dead branches.

Habitat: Coniferous forests in the boreal zone, especially where burned over, logged, or swampy.

Nesting: 4 white eggs in a cavity excavated in a tree, often rather low.

Range: Alaska and Canada to the northernmost United States and to the mountains of California in the West.

This and the Northern Three-toed Woodpecker are the most northerly of the family. Both are rather tame. The Black-backed, found only in North America, is the more southerly. It is also somewhat more numerous or, rather, less scarce, since these birds are not common anywhere. They visit dead and dying trees, scaling off bits of loose bark with vigorous sideways movements of the bill to get at the borers and beetle larvae underneath.

342, 344 Northern Three-toed Woodpecker
(*Picoides tridactylus*)
Woodpeckers (Picidae)

Description: 8½″ (21 cm). Starling-sized. Similar to the Black-backed but smaller, with shorter bill, and *back barred black-and-white.* Sexes differ as in that species.

Voice: Similar to the Black-backed but quieter.

Habitat: Same as Black-backed Three-toed Woodpecker.

Nesting: 4 white eggs in a tree hole. The nest holes of both three-toed woodpeckers are beveled on the lower side of the entrance to form a sort of doorstep for the birds.

Range: Virtually circumpolar; in America from Alaska and Canada to extreme northern United States, and in the West to the mountains of Arizona and New Mexico.

The species occurs throughout subarctic Asia and Europe as well as America. It is less numerous than the Black-backed in the southern portions of its range but extends farther south in the Rockies. It is also more sedentary, rarely moving far from its home range.

---

347 Red-cockaded Woodpecker
(*Picoides borealis*)
Woodpeckers (Picidae)

Description: 8" (20 cm). Bluebird-sized. Cap and nape black; *large white cheek patch;* back barred black-and-white; white below with black spots on the sides and flanks. Male has small red spot behind eye.

Voice: A nuthatch-like *yank-yank.* Also a rattling scold note.

Habitat: Pine forests, especially yellow and longleaf pines.

Nesting: 4 white eggs in a tree cavity, usually in a live tree with a rotting heart.

Range: Maryland and Kentucky to southeastern United States and west to eastern Texas.

The Red-cockaded Woodpecker is one of the least known of the family. Although widespread in the Southeast, it is local and restricted to pine woods. It is much less noisy and conspicuous than other woodpeckers and therefore seldom noticed. It travels in small flocks, usually in family groups of four to six. It also has the peculiar trait of digging holes in trees adjacent to its nest, allowing pine gum or resin to ooze from the holes. Such signs of pitch are evidence of its presence.

353 Red-breasted Nuthatch
(*Sitta canadensis*)
Nuthatches (Sittidae)

Description: 4½–4¾" (11–12 cm). Smaller than a sparrow. Often creeps downward headfirst on tree trunks. Upperparts blue-gray, underparts pale rusty. *Crown and line through eye black, eyebrow white.*

Voice: Tinny *yank-yank,* higher-pitched and more nasal than the call of the White-breasted Nuthatch.

Habitat: Coniferous forests; more widespread in migration and winter.

Nesting: 5 or 6 white eggs, spotted with red-brown, in a cup of twigs and grass lined with softer material and placed in a cavity in a tree. The entrance is usually smeared with pitch, presumably to discourage predators; the pitch often gets on the bird's feathers giving them a messy appearance.

Range: Alaska, Manitoba, and Newfoundland south to New Jersey, North Carolina, Colorado, and southern California. Winters south to the Gulf Coast and northern Mexico.

The principal winter food is the seeds of conifers, and in years when the seed crop fails in the North, these birds move south in large numbers. Smaller than the White-breasted Nuthatch, they tend to forage on smaller branches and twigs, seeking small insects as well as seeds. Although it accepts suet, it visits feeders less frequently than its relative.

356 **Brown-headed Nuthatch**
(*Sitta pusilla*)
Nuthatches (Sittidae)

Description: 4–5″ (10–13 cm). Smaller than a sparrow. Upperparts dull blue-gray, underparts whitish. *Crown dull brown, with a whitish spot on the nape.*

Voice: Series of high-pitched piping notes, unlike the calls of other eastern nuthatches.

Habitat: Coniferous and mixed forests.

Nesting: 5 or 6 white eggs, heavily speckled with red-brown, in a cup of bark, grass, and feathers placed in a cavity in a dead tree, fence post, or under loose bark.

Range: Resident from Delaware, Missouri, and eastern Texas south to the Bahamas, Florida, and the Gulf Coast.

The smallest of our eastern nuthatches, it spends more time among terminal branches and twigs of trees than do the other species. After breeding, these birds gather in flocks of a dozen or more and move through the woods along with woodpeckers and chickadees. They are quite agile and restless, flitting from one cluster of pine needles to another.

364 **Pine Warbler**
(*Dendroica pinus*)
Wood Warblers (Parulidae)

Description: 5½″ (14 cm). Unstreaked olive above with yellow throat and breast, faint streaking below, white belly, inconspicuous eye-stripe; two white wing bars. Female similar but duller.

Voice: Musical, somewhat melancholy trill like that of a soft, sweet Chipping Sparrow.

Habitat: Pine forests.

Nesting: 4 brown-spotted white eggs in a compact nest well concealed among

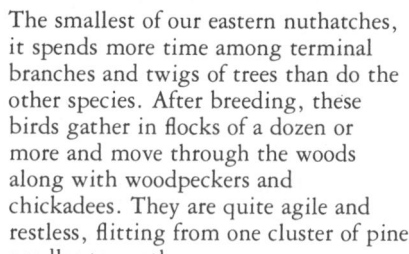

pine needles near the tip of a horizontal branch, usually higher than 20 feet.

Range: Southern Canada to the Gulf of Mexico. Winters in southern states, occasionally north to New England, and the northern West Indies.

No bird is more aptly named: it nests exclusively in pine trees, spends much of its life there, and only during migration is found in shrubbery or deciduous growth of parks and gardens. It is relatively rare and local inland in the North.

366 Magnolia Warbler
(*Dendroica magnolia*)
Wood Warblers (Parulidae)

Description: 5″ (13 cm). Male is bright yellow below with heavy black streaks, a black facial patch, and a large white wing patch. Female and immature birds are similar but duller. Broad white patches on the sides of tail in all plumages.

Voice: *Weeta-weeta-weeteo*. Call note *tslip*.

Habitat: Breeds in open stands of young spruce and fir. In migration is found almost any place where shrubbery or trees occur.

Nesting: 4 brown-spotted white eggs in a shallow twig-and-grass nest lined with rootlets.

Range: Central Canada to northeastern United States, and in the mountains south to Virginia. Winters in the West Indies and Middle America.

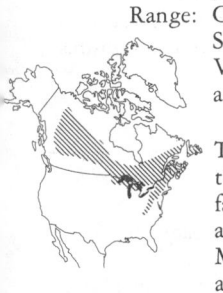

This pretty warbler got its name from the first specimen obtained by the famous ornithologist Alexander Wilson among some magnolia trees in Mississippi in the early 1800s. It actually breeds in conifer trees in the North, but the name has remained. It is one of our most numerous warblers during migrations, and on certain

spring days the trees seem to be filled
with them. They may also be found
feeding near the ground in low bushes.

---

367 Canada Warbler
(*Wilsonia canadensis*)
Wood Warblers (Parulidae)

Description: 5″ (13 cm). Solid gray above, without
wing bars, yellow below with yellow
"spectacles"; *black-spotted necklace on
breast.*

Voice: Rapid, jerky warble.

Habitat: Cool, moist woodland that is nearly
mature and has much undergrowth.

Nesting: 4 brown-spotted white eggs in a nest of
dried leaves and grass on or near the
ground at the base of a stump or in a
fern clump.

Range: Southern Canada to northern United
States east of the Rockies, and in the
eastern mountains to northern Georgia.
Winters in northwestern South
America.

This warbler received its name from its
discovery in Canada, although it is
certainly not confined to Canada, even
in the breeding season. It ordinarily
ranges at low levels, usually from the
ground to six feet up. Like several other
warblers it is adept at fly-catching,
conspicuously flitting from bush to
bush. Flying insects form a great
portion of its diet, but it also captures
spiders and insect larvae.

---

368 Cape May Warbler
(*Dendroica tigrina*)
Wood Warblers (Parulidae)

Description: 5″ (13 cm). Male in breeding plumage
is yellow below with *conspicuous chestnut
cheek patch,* white wing patch, and
heavy black streaks on underparts.

Female much duller, with greenish-yellow cheeks.

Voice: Four or more high, thin notes without change in pitch or volume: *seet-seet-seet-seet*.

Habitat: Open spruce forests; in migration, in evergreen or deciduous woodlands and often in parks, estates, or suburban yards.

Nesting: 4 brown-spotted white eggs in a bulky, compact, twig-and-moss nest lined with grass, fur, and feathers.

Range: Southern Mackenzie, Manitoba, Ontario, and Quebec south to Nova Scotia, Maine, northern New York, Michigan, and North Dakota. Winters in southern Florida and the Caribbean region.

This warbler gets its name from the fact that the first specimen was collected at Cape May, New Jersey, where it is a common migrant. During migration these birds show a curious attraction to Norway spruces.

374 Kirtland's Warbler
(*Dendroica kirtlandii*)
Wood Warblers (Parulidae)

Description: 6" (15 cm). A large warbler, gray above with black streaks; yellow below with black streaks on sides; black cheeks with conspicuous white eye-ring. Female similar but duller. *Wags its tail.*

Voice: Low-pitched, loud, bubbling, and rising at the end.

Habitat: Found only in dense stands of young jack pines.

Nesting: 4 brown-dotted white eggs in a nest composed of bark strips and vegetable fibers lined with grass and pine needles and sunk in the ground.

Range: Breeds only in north-central Michigan. Winters in the Bahamas.

This warbler is noted for its extremely limited range. During the breeding

season it is confined to dense stands of young jack pines that spring up after forest fires. Once such stands reach about 20 feet, the birds abandon them. Even in winter it inhabits low scrub, although not always pines. Recently a sanctuary has been established by the State of Michigan where controlled burning will attempt to maintain the required habitat of this rare bird.

375 Black-throated Green Warbler
(*Dendroica virens*)
Wood Warblers (Parulidae)

Description: 5″ (13 cm). Crown and upperparts olive green, *throat and sides of breast black, face yellow.* Female similar but duller.

Voice: Thin, buzzy, lazy *trees, trees, murm' ring' trees;* or faster *zee-zee-zee-zoo-zee.*

Habitat: Open stands of hemlock or pine; in migration in a variety of habitats.

Nesting: 4 or 5 white eggs, spotted with brown, in a cup of grass, moss, and plant fibers lined with hair and feathers and placed in the branches of a conifer.

Range: Northwest Territories, Ontario, and Newfoundland south to northern New Jersey, Ohio, Minnesota, and Alberta, and in the mountains to Georgia. Winters from Florida and Texas south to northern South America, and in the West Indies.

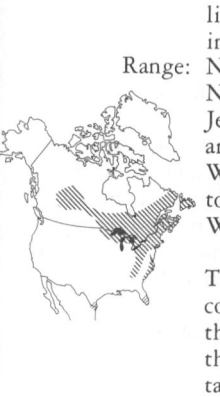

The Black-throated Green is one of the commonest warblers in migration; at this season it feeds at any height above the ground, but where the trees are tall, it spends most of its time among the highest branches. Its distinctive song is one of the easiest of warbler songs to learn.

376 Yellow-throated Warbler
(*Dendroica dominica*)
Wood Warblers (Parulidae)

Description: 5″ (13 cm). Gray, unstreaked
upperparts, *bright yellow throat,* white
belly, *black-and-white facial pattern,*
heavy black streaks on sides. Sexes
alike.

Voice: Series of clear ringing notes descending
in pitch and increasing in speed, rising
abruptly at the end: *teeew-teeew-teeew-
teew-tew-tew-twi.*

Habitat: Forests of pine, cypress, sycamore, and
oak, in both swampy places and dry
uplands.

Nesting: 4 purple-spotted greenish eggs in a nest
of grass and bark strips lined with hair
and feathers, often set in clumps of
Spanish moss or among pine needles.

Range: Southern New Jersey, Ohio, and
Illinois south to southeastern United
States and west to Missouri and Texas.
Winters chiefly in the Gulf states south
to the West Indies and Costa Rica.

This attractive warbler is usually found
in live oaks draped with Spanish moss
or in longleaf pines. It often creeps over
the branches of the trunk like a Black-
and-White Warbler. Occasionally it
may stray as far north of its usual range
as New York and New England.

379 Yellow-rumped Warbler
including "Myrtle Warbler"
and "Audubon's Warbler"
(*Dendroica coronata*)
Wood Warblers (Parulidae)

Description: 5–6″ (13–15 cm). Breeding male dull
bluish above, streaked with black;
breast and flanks blackish. *Rump yellow.*
Two white wing bars. Crown and small
area at sides of breast yellow. Eastern
birds ("Myrtle Warbler") have white
throats; western birds ("Audubon's

Warbler") have yellow throats. Females, fall males, and young are streaked gray-brown, but always have yellow rump and white spots in tail.

Voice: A thin, buzzy warble; a sharp *chek!*

Habitat: Coniferous and mixed forests; widespread during migration and winter.

Nesting: 4 or 5 white eggs, spotted and blotched with brown, in a bulky nest of twigs, rootlets, and grass lined with hair and feathers and placed in a conifer.

Range: Northern Alaska, northern Manitoba, and central Quebec south in the West to northern Mexico and in the East to Maine, Massachusetts, northern New York, and Michigan. Winters from southern part of breeding range south to Costa Rica and the West Indies.

Until recently, the eastern and western populations of the Yellow-rumped Warbler were thought to be two distinct species, respectively the "Myrtle Warbler" and "Audubon's Warbler." However, it has been found that in the narrow zone where the ranges of the two come together, the birds hybridize freely. In the East, the "Myrtle Warbler" is an abundant migrant, and the only warbler that regularly spends the winter in the northern states.

380, 404 Blackburnian Warbler
(*Dendroica fusca*)
Wood Warblers (Parulidae)

Description: 5″ (13 cm). Breeding male black and white with *vivid orange throat and large white wing patch;* female is similar but has yellow throat. Back boldly striped.

Voice: Very thin and wiry, increasing in speed and rising to the limit of hearing. *Sleet-sleet-sleet-sleet-sleet-sleeeee.* Also *tiddly-tiddly-tiddly-tiddly* at same speed and pitch.

Habitat: Most numerous in mixed forests of hemlock, spruce, and various hardwoods, usually ranging high in the trees.

Nesting: 4 brown-spotted white eggs in a twig nest lined with lichens, mosses, and hair, usually high in a large conifer.

Range: Southeastern Canada to the northeastern United States and south in the mountains to northern Georgia. Winters chiefly in northwestern South America.

Blackburnian Warblers are usually found high in trees, even during migrations, and are not readily noticed in the dense foliage unless their high-pitched song announces their presence. At times they may be detected at the ends of branches, picking at leaves for bugs or caterpillars.

384 Evening Grosbeak
(*Hesperiphona vespertina*)
Grosbeaks, Buntings, Finches, Sparrows (Fringillidae)

Description: 7½–8½" (19–21 cm). Starling-sized. Stocky finch with a very large, *pale greenish or yellowish conical bill*. Male has brown head shading to *yellow on lower back*, rump, and underparts; bright yellow forehead and eyebrow; *bold white wing patches*. Female similar but grayer.

Voice: Song a series of short, musical whistles. Call note similar to the chirp of the House Sparrow but louder and more ringing.

Habitat: Nests in coniferous forests; visits deciduous woodlands and suburban areas in winter.

Nesting: 3 or 4 pale blue-green eggs, lightly speckled with dark brown, gray, and olive, in a shallow, loose cup of twigs lined with rootlets and placed in a conifer.

Range: British Columbia and Nova Scotia
south to northern New England,
Minnesota, Mexico (in mountains), and
California. Winters south to southern
California, Texas, and South Carolina.

This grosbeak formerly bred no farther
east than Minnesota, but more food
available at bird feeders may have
enabled more birds to survive the
winter, and the species now breeds east
to the Atlantic. Like most of the
northern finches, however, these birds
are more numerous in some years than
in others. In winter they feed in flocks
mainly on the seeds of box elder or, at
feeders, on sunflower seeds. In spring
the outer coating of the bill peels off,
exposing the blue-green color beneath.

389, 475 Western Tanager
(Piranga ludoviciana)
Tanagers (Thraupidae)

Description: 6–7" (15–17 cm). Sparrow-sized. Male
bright yellow with red head and black
wings, back, and tail. *Two bold wing
bars.* Female olive-green, like other
female tanagers, but shows two light
wing bars.
Voice: Burry warbling song; also a harsh,
frequently repeated *pit-ick* or *pit-it-ick*.
Habitat: Coniferous or mixed pine-oak forests.
Nesting: 3 or 4 pale blue-green eggs, lightly
speckled, placed in a flimsy saucer of
twigs, grasses, and pine needles near
outer end of a pine or oak branch.
Range: British Columbia, Mackenzie, and
South Dakota south to western Texas
and Baja California. Rarely wanders
eastward in fall to Atlantic coastal
states.

This western relative of the Scarlet and
Summer Tanager occasionally turns up
at feeders in the East, where it is easily
recognized by its two wing bars. In the

West it spends most of its time feeding deliberately in the tops of dense forest trees, making it difficult to see despite its bright colors. It feeds on insects and, like other tanagers, supplements its diet with fruit.

403, 455 Bay-breasted Warbler
(*Dendroica castanea*)
Wood Warblers (Parulidae)

Description: 5½" (14 cm). Male in breeding plumage has chestnut cap, throat, and sides, blackish face, and a conspicuous buff patch on side of neck. Upperparts streaked. Females, fall males, and immatures are olive above, with two white wing bars; similar to fall Blackpolls but with dark legs and often some trace of chestnut on flanks.

Voice: High, thin *teesi-teesi-teesi-teesi,* without change in pitch or volume.

Habitat: Breeds in open spruce forests. During migration frequents deciduous trees as well.

Nesting: 5 white eggs with brown markings in a loosely built, hair-lined nest of twigs, grass, and needles set in a conifer as much as 50 feet aboveground.

Range: Southeastern Canada and northeastern United States. Winters in Panama and northwestern South America. Migrates by way of Mexico and Central America on the Atlantic side.

This warbler, like the Cape May and Tennessee warblers, has increased in numbers in recent years. It is a handsome bird and is eagerly sought by enthusiasts in the spring warbler waves during middle and late May.

409, 558 Purple Finch
(*Carpodacus purpureus*)
Grosbeaks, Buntings, Finches,
Sparrows (Fringillidae)

Description: 5½–6½" (14–16 cm). Sparrow-sized but with a thicker bill. *Male dull rosy-red,* more raspberry than purple, *especially on head and rump.* Female and young heavily streaked with dull brown and with *bold, pale eyebrow.* Similar to House Finch but duller, with red coloration not concentrated on crown and breast. Female House Finch more finely streaked and lacks line over the eye.

Voice: Rich musical warble. Call a distinctive *tick* as it flies.

Habitat: Mixed and coniferous woodlands; ornamental conifers in gardens.

Nesting: 4 or 5 blue-green eggs, spotted at the larger end with dark brown, in a well-made cup of grasses and twigs, often lined with hair, placed in a conifer.

Range: British Columbia, Quebec, and Newfoundland south to New Jersey, Minnesota, and Baja California. Winters from Nova Scotia and British Columbia to Florida, the Gulf Coast, and Texas.

Purple Finches are quite numerous and conspicuous in spring migration, and for a few weeks each year one can hear the rich, spirited song of the brightly colored males. In winter they visit feeding stations in large numbers, showing a fondness for sunflower seeds.

412 Red Crossbill
(*Loxia curvirostra*)
Grosbeaks, Buntings, Finches,
Sparrows (Fringillidae)

Description: 5¼–6½" (13–16 cm). Sparrow-sized. *Mandibles crossed* at tips. Male dusky brick red. Female gray tinged with dull green, brightest on rump. White-winged Crossbill has two white wing bars.

Voice: Song *chipa-chipa-chipa, chee-chee-chee-chee;* also a sharp *kip-kip-kip.*

Habitat: Coniferous forests; visits ornamental evergreens in winter.

Nesting: 3 or 4 pale blue-green eggs lightly spotted with brown in a shallow saucer of bark strips, grass, and roots lined with moss and plant down placed near the end of a conifer branch.

Range: Southern Alaska, Manitoba, Quebec, and Newfoundland south in the eastern United States to North Carolina (mountains) and Wisconsin; in the west to northern Nicaragua. Winters south to the Gulf Coast. Also in Eurasia.

These birds are sporadic visitors in winter, appearing in large numbers, then not appearing for several years. Such winter flocks often travel great distances, many of the birds that visit New England coming all the way from the Rocky Mountains. Crossbills feed exclusively on conifer seeds, the crossed mandibles enabling them to extract the seeds from the cones. Because their chosen food is available in winter, they commonly begin nesting as early as January, but they have been found nesting in every month of the year.

---

413 White-winged Crossbill
(*Loxia leucoptera*)
Grosbeaks, Buntings, Finches,
Sparrows (Fringillidae)

Description: 6–6½″ (15–16 cm). Size of a large sparrow. *Mandibles crossed* at tips. Male raspberry-pink; females grayer, without pink. Both sexes have two white wing bars.

Voice: Like the Red Crossbill but a softer *chiff-chiff-chiff.* Song is a series of sweet canary-like warbles and trills.

Habitat: Coniferous forests.

Nesting: 2–4 pale blue eggs, spotted with dark brown, laid in a shallow saucer of bark strips, grass, and roots lined with moss and plant down, placed near the end of a conifer branch.

Range: Alaska and northern Quebec south to Newfoundland and British Columbia. In winter, south to the Carolinas and Oregon. Also in northern Eurasia.

Like the Red Crossbill, these birds use their crossed mandibles to extract seeds from the cones of pines and spruces. Their winter wanderings depend largely on the crop of conifer seeds; in years when seeds are abundant in the northern forests the birds tend to remain there. When the crop fails they come south in large numbers and may often be seen in quiet flocks, clinging to clusters of cones like little parrots. Their travels sometimes take them far to the south of their breeding range, and the species has managed to establish itself in the pine forests of Hispaniola in the West Indies.

414, 424 **Pine Grosbeak**
(*Pinicola enucleator*)
Grosbeaks, Buntings, Finches, Sparrows (Fringillidae)

Description: 8–10″ (20–25 cm). Robin-sized. Male dull rose-pink with *two white wing bars*. Female dull gray with yellow-green tinge on head and rump and two white wing bars. Bill conical and stubby. White-winged Crossbill similar but smaller, with crossed mandibles; female shows faint streaks.

Voice: Musical warble like a softer version of the Purple Finch; clear whistled *tew-tew-tew* like that of Greater Yellowlegs.

Habitat: Coniferous forests; in winter, spreading to mixed woodlands and wherever fruiting trees are found.

Nesting: 3 or 4 pale blue eggs lightly spotted with warm brown in a shallow saucer of twigs, moss, and rootlets lined with fine grass and placed on a conifer branch up to 30 feet aboveground.

Range: Alaska, northern Quebec, and Newfoundland south to northern New England and Manitoba, and in the Rockies to New Mexico. Winters south to Pennsylvania and Kansas. Also in northern Eurasia.

Largest of the northern finches, it is less common than siskins or redpolls. When these birds do appear their preference for the seeds and fruit of trees such as mountain ash and cedar makes them more conspicuous than their smaller relatives. They are very tame and slow moving, allowing close approach. On their northern breeding grounds they avoid unbroken forests and occur mainly in brushy clearings and forest edges.

425 Gray Jay
(*Perisoreus canadensis*)
Jays, Magpies, Crows (Corvidae)

Description: 10–13" (25–33 cm). Gray above, whitish below. Forehead and throat white; nape and stripe through eye dull black.

Voice: *Whee-ah, chuck-chuck,* also scolds, screams, and whistles.

Habitat: Coniferous forests.

Nesting: 3–5 gray-green eggs spotted with dark olive-brown in a solid bowl of twigs and bark strips lined with feathers and fur and placed near the trunk of a dense conifer.

Range: Alaska and Labrador south to northern New England, northern New York, New Mexico, and northern California. May occasionally wander south in winter to Pennsylvania and the central Great Plains.

This bird is well-known to anyone who has spent time in the north woods, for like certain other birds of that region it is very tame and habitually enters camps to take food; hence one of its many names, "Camp Robber." Gray Jays will eat almost anything, but in winter they are partial to conifer seeds. They glue together masses of seeds and buds with their thick saliva and store them for use when food is scarce. Because of their confiding nature and general coloration they have often been described as giant chickadees.

446, 514 Black-throated Blue Warbler
(*Dendroica caerulescens*)
Wood Warblers (Parulidae)

Description: 5″ (13 cm). Male blue-gray above, white below, with black face, throat, and sides; female dull olive-green with conspicuous white eye-line and usually a square white wing patch.

Voice: Buzzy, rising *zwee-zwee-zwee,* sometimes rendered as *please-SQUEEZE-me* or *please-please-SQUEEZE-me.*

Habitat: Mixed deciduous and evergreen woodlands with thick undergrowth.

Nesting: 4 brown-spotted white eggs in a nest made of leaves and grass lined with cobwebs and hair, set near the ground in a shrub or a young tree.

Range: Breeds from southeastern Canada to northeastern United States and in the mountains to northern Georgia. Winters in the Gulf states as well as in the Greater Antilles.

The male is one of the easier warblers to identify since it retains its strikingly patterned plumage the year-round. These warblers are among the tamest and most trusting of this family. If the observer moves very deliberately, the bird may be approached to within a few feet without taking alarm.

447, 448 Northern Parula
"Parula Warbler"
(*Parula americana*)
Wood Warblers (Parulidae)

Description: 4½" (11 cm). A small warbler; blue above with a yellow-green "saddle" on its back; yellow throat and breast and white belly; two white wing bars. Male has an orange-brown chest band.

Voice: Single or several rising buzzy notes dropping abruptly at the end; *bzzzzz-zip* or *bz-bz-bz-zip.*

Habitat: Breeds in wet, chiefly coniferous woods, swamps, and along lakes and ponds; more widespread on migration.

Nesting: 4 or 5 brown-spotted white eggs in a woven basket-shaped nest of grass, bark, and vegetable fibers neatly hidden in Spanish moss in the South, in beard moss or *Usnea* lichen in the North.

Range: Southeastern Canada to the Gulf of Mexico. Winters from southern Florida to the West Indies and from Mexico to Nicaragua.

This species is almost entirely dependent upon either Spanish moss or beard moss for nest sites. Although breeding mostly in coniferous forests in the North, during migration these birds frequent deciduous trees and shrubs. In such situations they are seen in large numbers in spring along roadsides and in parks, yards, orchards, and gardens as well as woods. Until recently this species was called "Parula Warbler."

450 Solitary Vireo
(*Vireo solitarius*)
Vireos (Vireonidae)

Description: 5–6" (13–15 cm). Sparrow-sized. Olive-green above and white below, with dull yellow flanks. *Crown and sides of head slate or bluish gray* with bold white "spectacles."

Voice: Rather slow series of sweet, slurred phrases like that of Red-eyed Vireo but slower and more musical.

Habitat: Coniferous and mixed forests.

Nesting: 3–5 white eggs lightly spotted with brown in a pendant cup of bark strips and down placed in a forked twig of a small forest tree.

Range: British Columbia, Manitoba, and Newfoundland south to Connecticut and Michigan, and in the mountains to Georgia and Mexico. Winters from the Carolinas and the Gulf Coast south to Nicaragua.

This species was formerly called the "Blue-headed Vireo." Handsome and distinctively patterned, it is known to most people as a fairly common migrant, usually arriving somewhat earlier in the spring than other vireos. It is extraordinarily tame and seems to ignore humans near its nest; an incubating bird will frequently allow itself to be touched. Like other vireos it moves slowly and deliberately through the trees, peering with head cocked to one side in search of insects.

451 Philadelphia Vireo
(*Vireo philadelphicus*)
Vireos (Vireonidaẽ)

Description: 6″ (15 cm). Sparrow-sized. Olive above, *yellowish below;* indistinct eye-lines are white above, blackish through the eye. No wing bars.

Voice: Like the Red-eyed Vireo but higher and slower. *See-me? Here-I-am! Up-here. See-me?*

Habitat: Open second-growth woodlands, old clearings and burned-over areas, and thickets along streams and lakes.

Nesting: 4 brown-spotted white eggs in a cup of bark strips, grasses, and mosses, the nest lined with bits of lichen and thistledown.

Range: Southern Canada and northeastern and north-central United States. Winters from Guatemala to Panama.

Because this vireo was first described by John Cassin in 1842 from a specimen collected near Philadelphia, both its common and Latin names refer to Philadelphia, but it is by no means confined to that area. These are the least numerous of the family in the East. They are easily overlooked in spring since they do not sing much on migration; in addition, arriving chiefly during the last week in May, they are present when the foliage is already dense.

457 Tennessee Warbler
(*Vermivora peregrina*)
Wood Warblers (Parulidae)

Description: 5" (13 cm). In spring, greenish above, white below with a gray cap, white line over eye, black line through eye; in fall, olive above, yellowish below.

Voice: Sharp, staccato *di-dit-di-dit-di-dit-di-dit-dit-dit-dit-dit,* fastest at the end.

Habitat: Open mixed woodlands in the breeding season; in trees and bushes during migration.

Nesting: 5 or 6 brown-spotted white eggs in a nest lined with fine grasses, placed on the ground usually well hidden under a shrub or in a moss clump under a tussock.

Range: Yukon, Manitoba, and Labrador south to Maine, southern Ontario, Wisconsin, and British Columbia. Winters from southern Mexico to northern South America.

This warbler was discovered in 1811 by the noted ornithologist Alexander Wilson, who chose its common name because he first saw it in Tennessee. Its numbers fluctuate from year to year; at times it is very numerous with a dozen or more observed in a single tree while in other years very few are seen.

458 Golden-crowned Kinglet
(*Regulus satrapa*)
Old World Warblers (Sylviidae)

Description: 3½–4″ (9–10 cm). Tiny. Olive-green above, paler below, with two dull white wing bars. Eyebrow white; crown orange bordered with yellow (adult males) or solid yellow (females and young males), *crown patch separated from white eyebrow by a narrow black line.* The Ruby-crowned Kinglet lacks the conspicuous face pattern.

Voice: Thin, wiry, ascending *ti-ti-ti* followed by a tumbling chatter.

Habitat: Dense, old conifer stands; also in deciduous forests and thickets in winter.

Nesting: 8 or 9 cream-colored eggs speckled with brown in a large mass of moss, lichens, and plant down with a small feather-lined cup at the top, suspended between several twigs in a densely needled conifer, less than 60 feet aboveground.

Range: Alaska, Manitoba, and Newfoundland south to Massachusetts and Michigan, and in the mountains to North Carolina, New Mexico, and southern California. Winters south to Florida, the Gulf Coast, and Guatemala.

These kinglets are best known as winter visitors, often joining mixed flocks of chickadees, woodpeckers, and creepers. They seem to be entirely insectivorous and are adept at finding hibernating insects in twigs and bark.

459 Ruby-crowned Kinglet
(Regulus calendula)
Old World Warblers (Sylviidae)

Description: 3¾–4½" (9–11 cm). Tiny. Similar to the Golden-crowned Kinglet but greener, with no face pattern except for a narrow white eye-ring. Males have a tuft of red feathers on the crown, kept concealed unless the bird is aroused.

Voice: Song an excited, musical chattering.

Habitat: Coniferous forests in summer; also deciduous forests and thickets in winter.

Nesting: 6–9 cream-colored eggs lightly speckled with brown in a large mass of moss, lichens, and plant down with a small feather-lined cup at the top.

Range: Alaska, Manitoba, and Newfoundland south to northern New England, Ontario, New Mexico, and southern California. Winters from southern British Columbia and southern New England to Florida, the Gulf Coast, and Guatemala.

In the northern states this bird is scarce or absent in winter but is often seen during migration. It frequently sings on its way north, a song surprisingly loud for so tiny a bird. In the South it is a common winter resident and more apt to be found in deciduous woods than the Golden-crowned Kinglet. It takes a sharp eye to see the male's red crown patch, which is usually erected for a few seconds at a time when the bird is displaying aggressively. It has a characteristic habit of nervously flicking its wings.

460 Connecticut Warbler
(*Oporornis agilis*)
Wood Warblers (Parulidae)

Description: 5½" (14 cm). Olive-green above, yellow
below; head, throat, and upper breast
gray in males and dull brownish in
females. Has conspicuous, *unbroken white
eye-ring.* No wing bars. Mourning
Warbler similar but has broken
eye-ring.

Voice: A loud, ringing *beecher-beecher-beecher-
beecher* or *chippy-chipper-chippy-chipper.*

Habitat: Open larch-spruce bogs; in migration
in low wet woods and damp thickets.

Nesting: 4 or 5 whitish eggs, blotched with
brown, in a nest of grass concealed in a
clump of moss.

Range: South-central Canada to Michigan,
Wisconsin, and northern Minnesota.
Winters in northern South America.

Named for its place of discovery, this
species is only an uncommon migrant
in Connecticut. It is seldom seen except
by observers who know where to look;
it feeds close to the ground in dense
swampy woods during spring
migration, and in the fall occurs most
often in woodland edges where the
growth is rank.

470 Olive-sided Flycatcher
(*Nuttallornis borealis*)
Tyrant Flycatchers (Tyrannidae)

Description: 7½" (19 cm). Large-billed and heavy-
headed; deep olive-drab with dark sides
of breast and flanks separated by *white
down the center of breast;* white feather
tufts protrude from lower back at base
of tail.

Voice: Distinctive and emphatic *quick-three-
BEERS.* Call is a loud *pip-pip-pip.*

Habitat: Boreal spruce and fir forests, usually
near openings, burns, ponds, and bogs.

Nesting: 3 brown-spotted buff eggs in a twig

nest lined with lichens, mosses, and grasses near the end of a branch among the foliage well up in an evergreen tree.

Range: Northern portions of Alaska and Canada to the mountains of North Carolina, Arizona, and California. Winters in northwestern South America.

This flycatcher almost always perches at or very near the tops of the tallest trees in an exposed position on dead branches. Its name *Nuttallornis* honors Thomas Nuttall (1786–1859), an early American ornithologist; *borealis* is Latin for "northern."

---

463 Yellow-bellied Flycatcher
(*Empidonax flaviventris*)
Tyrant Flycatchers (Tyrannidae)

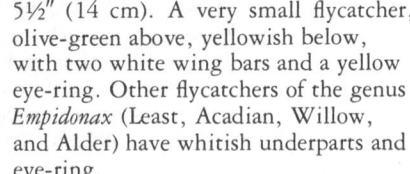

Description: 5½" (14 cm). A very small flycatcher, olive-green above, yellowish below, with two white wing bars and a yellow eye-ring. Other flycatchers of the genus *Empidonax* (Least, Acadian, Willow, and Alder) have whitish underparts and eye-ring.

Voice: On the breeding grounds, a flat *chilk* or *killic;* also a rising two-note whistle, *per-wee?*

Habitat: Thickets of alder and willow in northern coniferous forests; on migration in second-growth woodlands.

Nesting: 3 or 4 whitish eggs with brown spots, in a nest of moss and rootlets on the ground.

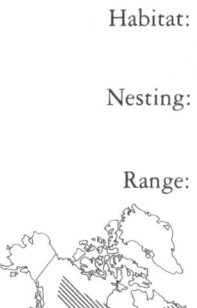

Range: British Columbia, Manitoba, and Newfoundland south to Maine, Wisconsin, and North Dakota, and in the mountains to Pennsylvania. Winters from Mexico to Panama.

This retiring little flycatcher spends most of its time on migration in dense thickets, and so is easily overlooked. With its yellowish underparts and

yellow eye-ring, it is the easiest of the
Empidonax flycatchers to identify.

487 Winter Wren
(*Troglodytes troglodytes*)
Wrens (Troglodytidae)

Description: 4–4½″ (10 cm). A tiny, dark brown
bird with a very short tail and a narrow
pale eyebrow. Similar to the House
Wren but darker, with a shorter tail.

Voice: A high-pitched, varied, and rapid series
of musical trills and chatters; call note
an explosive *kit!* or *kit-kit!*

Habitat: Dense tangles and thickets in coniferous
and mixed forests.

Nesting: 5–7 brown-speckled white eggs in a
bulky mass of twigs and moss, with an
entrance on the side, lined with softer
material and often concealed among the
upturned roots of a fallen tree.

Range: Alaska and Newfoundland south to
Connecticut, Michigan, and southern
British Columbia, and in the
mountains to California and Georgia.
Winters south to southern California
and the Gulf Coast. Also in Eurasia.

This wren moves like a mouse, creeping
through the low, dense tangle of
branches covering the forest floor. Its
nest is among the hardest to find; even
when an observer has narrowed the
search to a few square feet, he must
sometimes give up, so cleverly is the
nest concealed. Its song, when recorded
and played back at half or quarter
speed, shows a remarkable blend of
halftones and overtones all sung at the
same time.

498 Gray-cheeked Thrush
(*Catharus minimus*)
Thrushes (Turdidae)

Description: 6½–8″ (16–20 cm). Bluebird-sized. Dull olive-brown with pale, lightly spotted underparts and *no rust color in plumage; sides of face tinged with gray; no eye-ring.* Swainson's Thrush is similar but has a buff eye-ring and buff, not gray, cheeks. Other spotted thrushes show rust color on upperparts or tail.

Voice: Series of thin reedy notes inflected upward at the end.

Habitat: Nests in coniferous forests, especially in dense stands of stunted spruce and balsam; widespread in migration.

Nesting: 3–5 pale blue-green eggs, finely speckled with brown, in a solidly built cup of grass reinforced with mud and placed in a low conifer.

Range: Breeds from northeastern Siberia, northern Alaska, and Newfoundland south to Massachusetts, New York, British Columbia, and southwestern Alaska. Winters in West Indies, Central and South America.

On migration it spends most of its time feeding quietly on the ground, and while not especially shy, it is inconspicuous and easily overlooked.

501 Hermit Thrush
(*Catharus guttatus*)
Thrushes (Turdidae)

Description: 6½–7½″ (16–19 cm). Smaller than a Robin. The only one of our brown, spotted thrushes with dull brown upperparts and a rusty tail. Frequently flicks its tail.

Voice: Series of clear, musical phrases, each on a different pitch, consisting of a piping introductory note and a reedy tremolo. Call note a low *tuck*.

Habitat: Coniferous and mixed forests; deciduous

woodlands and thickets in winter.

Nesting: 4 blue-green eggs in a well-made cup of moss, leaves, and rootlets concealed on the ground or in a low bush in the forest.

Range: Alaska, Saskatchewan, and Labrador south to Long Island and Michigan, and in the mountains to Virginia, New Mexico, and southern California. Winters from Washington and southern New England south to Florida and Guatemala.

To many, the song of this thrush is the most beautiful of any North American bird. Outside the breeding range it may occasionally be heard late in spring, before the birds head north to nest. The Hermit Thrush is the only one of our spotted thrushes that winters in the northern states, subsisting on berries and buds. During the warm months, however, it feeds largely on insects taken from the ground.

502 Swainson's Thrush
(*Catharus ustulatus*)
Thrushes (Turdidae)

Description: 6½–7¾″ (16–19 cm). Uniformly dull olive-brown above, spotted below, with a *buff eye-ring and cheek.* The Gray-cheeked Thrush is similar but has grayish cheeks and lacks the conspicuous eye-ring.

Voice: Song a series of reedy spiraling notes inflected upward.

Habitat: Coniferous forests and willow thickets.

Nesting: 3 or 4 pale green-blue eggs, finely spotted with light brown, in a well-built cup of moss and lichen lined and strengthened with twigs, leaves, and grass, concealed in a small forest shrub or tree.

Range: Alaska, Manitoba, and Newfoundland south to northern New England, Michigan, and British Columbia, and

in the mountains to West Virginia, Colorado, and southern California. Winters in South America.

This bird is named after the English naturalist William Swainson (1789–1855). Like the Hermit Thrush, it is a furtive, ground-dwelling bird of the northern forests. Its song, while perhaps not as beautiful as that of the Hermit Thrush, is better known to most bird-watchers because the species sings more frequently during migration. It was formerly called the "Olive-backed Thrush."

507 Bohemian Waxwing
(*Bombycilla garrulus*)
Waxwings (Bombycillidae)

Description: 7½–8½" (19–21 cm). A sleek, gray-brown, crested bird. Similar to the Cedar Waxwing but larger, with conspicuous white wing patches and rusty (not white) undertail coverts.

Voice: High-pitched, lisping *seeee,* harsher and more grating than call of the Cedar Waxwing.

Habitat: Open coniferous forests.

Nesting: 4–6 pale blue eggs, heavily spotted and scrawled with black, placed in a loose, flat saucer of twigs, lichens, and grass in a conifer.

Range: Alaska, Yukon, Mackenzie, Saskatchewan, and Manitoba south to southern Alberta, northwestern Montana, northern Idaho, and central Washington. Wanders irregularly farther south and east during the winter. Also in Eurasia.

This handsome bird of the north woods is a rare winter visitor to the northeastern United States. When it appears, often in large flocks, it feeds on berries. A hundred or more of these birds perched in the top of a leafless tree in midwinter, calling shrilly, is an unforgettable sight. These highly social birds usually move about in tight formations, descending en masse on a clump of bushes and stripping them of fruit.

511 Boreal Chickadee
(*Parus hudsonicus*)
Chickadees (Paridae)

Description: 5–5½" (13–14 cm). Crown and back brown, cheeks white, throat black, flanks rufous, underparts white.
Voice: *Chick-a-dee-dee* more lazy, buzzy, and nasal than the Black-capped's.
Habitat: Coniferous forests.
Nesting: 5–7 white eggs, lightly speckled with red-brown, in a cup of plant down, feathers, and moss in a natural cavity, often only a few feet from the ground.
Range: Northern Alaska and Labrador south to northern New England, New York, Ontario, Manitoba, Montana, and Washington. Occasionally wanders southward in winter.

Every major forest habitat in North America has its species of chickadee, and this is the one found in the great spruce forests of Canada. Unlike the Black-capped Chickadee, this species spends most of its time in the interior of dense spruces, coming less readily to the tips of branches, and so it is much less easily observed.

544 Lincoln's Sparrow
(*Melospiza lincolnii*)
Grosbeaks, Buntings, Finches, Sparrows (Fringillidae)

Description: 5–6" (13–15 cm). Crown with two rusty stripes. *Upper breast has a buff band finely streaked with black.* Similar to the

Song Sparrow but more finely streaked and *shyer*.

Voice: Rich, gurgling wren-like song rising in the middle and dropping abruptly at the end.

Habitat: **Brushy bogs, willow, or alder thickets;** winters in woodland thickets and brushy pastures.

Nesting: 4 or 5 pale green eggs heavily spotted with brown in a cup of grass well concealed in forest undergrowth.

Range: Alaska, northern Quebec, Labrador, and Newfoundland south to northern New England and California. Winters from the Gulf Coast and California south to Guatemala.

This unobtrusive bird of northern bogs was first described by Audubon in 1834 from a specimen he collected in Quebec, and was named by him for Robert Lincoln, a companion on his trip to Labrador. Although not uncommon in migration, Lincoln's Sparrow is seldom noticed because of its shyness and its resemblance to a Song Sparrow.

---

557 Pine Siskin
(*Carduelis pinus*)
Grosbeaks, Buntings, Finches, Sparrows (Fringillidae)

Description: 4½–5″ (11–13 cm). A dark, streaked finch with a notched tail and small patches of yellow in the wings and tail. Usually seen in flocks, which have a distinctive flight pattern: the birds alternately bunch up and then disperse in undulating flight.

Voice: Distinctive rising, *bzzzzzt*. Song like a hoarse goldfinch.

Habitat: Coniferous and mixed woodlands, alder thickets, and brushy pastures.

Nesting: 3 or 4 pale green eggs lightly speckled with dark brown and black in a shallow saucer of bark, twigs, and moss lined

with plant down and feathers and
placed in a conifer.

Range: Alaska, Mackenzie, and Quebec south
to Nova Scotia and Nebraska, and in
the mountains to Pennsylvania.

The Pine Siskin is another of the
northern finches whose winter visits to
the United States occur mainly in years
when the seed crop has failed in the
boreal forests. In some years large flocks
may appear as far south as Florida.
Their principal foods are the seeds of
hemlocks, alders, birches, and cedars.
Like most northern finches, they are
also fond of salt, and can be found
along highways salted to melt snow.

---

563 Blackpoll Warbler
(*Dendroica striata*)
Wood Warblers (Parulidae)

Description: 5½″ (14 cm). Breeding male gray
streaked above with *black cap,* white
cheeks and underparts, blackish streaks
on sides. Female and nonbreeding male
greenish above with streaking. *Feet
usually flesh-colored.*

Voice: Rapid series of high lisping notes all on
one pitch, increasing and then
decreasing in volume; *seet-seet-SEET-
SEET-SEET-SEET-seet-seet.*

Habitat: Breeds in coniferous forests. During
migration is found chiefly in tall trees.

Nesting: 4 or 5 brown-spotted white eggs in a
twig-and-grass nest often lined with
feathers, usually placed in small
evergreen trees.

Range: Alaska and northern Canada to southern
Canada and northeastern United States.
Migrates through the West Indies and
winters in northern South America.

The Blackpoll is one of the most
abundant warblers in the East and has

an enormous breeding range in the northern part of the continent. During migration in late May, and again in September and early October, hundreds may be seen in a single day. Like all wood warblers they migrate at night; sometimes large numbers, attracted to bright lights on overcast or stormy nights, collide with such obstacles as lighthouses, television towers, and tall buildings.

569 Rusty Blackbird
(*Euphagus carolinus*)
Orioles, Blackbirds (Icteridae)

Description:	9″ (23 cm). In spring, adults are black, with a bluish and greenish iridescence; in fall, much more rust-brown, especially the head, breast, and back. *Conspicuous pale yellow eyes in both sexes.*
Voice:	Like the squeaks of a rusty gate.
Habitat:	Wooded swamps and damp woods with pools during migration; boreal bogs in the breeding season.
Nesting:	4 or 5 blue-green eggs with brown blotches in a bulky stick nest lined with grass, moss, and lichens set in a dense shrub or low tree near or over water.
Range:	Alaska and northern Canada to southern Canada and northeastern United States. Winters south to the Gulf Coast.

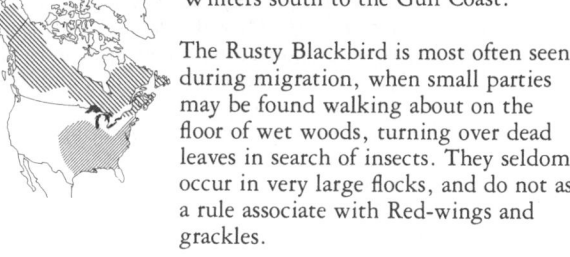

The Rusty Blackbird is most often seen during migration, when small parties may be found walking about on the floor of wet woods, turning over dead leaves in search of insects. They seldom occur in very large flocks, and do not as a rule associate with Red-wings and grackles.

581 Common Raven
(*Corvus corax*)
Jays, Magpies, Crows (Corvidae)

Description: 21–27″ (53–68 cm). Similar to the
Common Crow but larger, with a
heavier bill and a wedge-shaped tail. At
rest, the throat appears shaggy because
of long, lance-shaped feathers. Often
soars like a hawk.

Voice: Deep, varied, guttural croaking; a
wooden *wonk-wonk*.

Habitat: Coniferous forests and rocky coasts; in
the West also in deserts and arid
mountains.

Nesting: 4–7 dull green eggs spotted with
brown in a large mass of sticks
containing a cup lined with fur, moss,
and lichens placed on a cliff or in the
top of a conifer.

Range: Resident from Aleutians, northern
Alaska and northern Greenland south
to northern New England, the
Appalachians, the Dakotas, and, in the
mountains, to Nicaragua. Also in
Eurasia and North Africa.

The Common Raven is common only in
wilderness areas, for despite its large
size and intelligence it is very sensitive
to human persecution and has long
since been driven out of settled areas by
shooting and poisoning. Ravens are
primarily scavengers, and around towns
in the North they compete with gulls
for garbage. They also raid seabird
colonies, consuming many eggs and
young. They regularly ride on rising air
currents and frequently indulge in
aerial displays with mock fighting,
tumbling, and other forms of
acrobatics.

584 Black-billed Magpie
(*Pica pica*)
Jays, Magpies, Crows (Corvidae)

Description: 17½–22½" (44–57 cm). Unmistakable. A large *black-and-white* bird with a long black tail.

Voice: Ringing *wink! wink!* or *oink! oink!* Also scolds, chatters, and whistles.

Habitat: Open coniferous woodlands, range lands, and river thickets.

Nesting: 6–8 brown-blotched dull green eggs in a large domed structure of sticks, twigs, and rootlets lined with fine grass and hair, placed in a bush or a tree. Often in loose colonies.

Range: Alaska, Alberta, and Manitoba south to Utah and New Mexico. May wander east in winter. Also in Eurasia.

Magpies are frequently shot because they steal grain, but since the most important items in their diet seem to be insects and small rodents, they are more beneficial than destructive to agriculture. In captivity a magpie may be trained to imitate the human voice. These birds frequently associate with cattle and sheep, perching on their backs and picking off ticks and maggots. In the process they sometimes open sores on the animals that eventually prove fatal.

Part III
Appendices

LIST OF ACCIDENTAL SPECIES

Accidentals are species that have strayed from their normal ranges, reached our shores, and have been seen in North America only once or a few times. The following list includes only those species that have been either collected or photographed in eastern North America at least once; species that have been observed but never collected or photographed are not included.

The list is broken down into the five following categories, based on the regions they come from:

Oceanic. Coming mainly from the southern oceans and usually but not always driven to our shores by tropical storms.

European. Coming mainly from western Europe but also from the eastern portions and even as far as western Asia, and reaching our east coast.

Caribbean. Coming from the West Indies and various small islands throughout the Caribbean Sea, and found in our area mainly in southern Florida and along the Gulf Coast.

Central American. Species that wander north into extreme southern Texas.

South American. Several South American species that have wandered to eastern North America, usually along the Atlantic and Gulf coasts.

Oceanic   Yellow-nosed Albatross, *Diomedea chlororhynchos*
Little Shearwater, *Puffinus assimilis*
Black-capped Petrel, *Pterodroma hasitata*
Scaled Petrel, *Pterodroma inexpectata*
South Trinidad Petrel, *Pterodroma arminjoniana*
European Storm-Petrel, *Hydrobates pelagicus*
White-faced Storm-Petrel, *Pelagodroma marina*
Harcourt's Storm-Petrel, *Oceanodroma castro*
Lesser Frigatebird, *Fregata ariel*

European Little Egret, *Egretta garzetta*
Smew, *Mergus albellus*
White-tailed Eagle, *Haliaeetus albicilla*
Eurasian Kestrel, *Falco tinnunculus*
Corn Crake, *Crex crex*
Eurasian Coot, *Fulica atra*
Eurasian Lapwing, *Vanellus vanellus*
Greater Golden Plover, *Pluvialis apricaria*
Eurasian Woodcock, *Scolopax rusticola*
European Jacksnipe, *Lymnocryptes minimus*
Eurasian Curlew, *Numenius arquata*
Spotted Redshank, *Tringa erythropus*
Bar-tailed Godwit, *Limosa lapponica*
Black-tailed Godwit, *Limosa limosa*
White-winged Tern, *Chlidonias leucopterus*
Fieldfare, *Turdus pilaris*

Caribbean Red-billed Tropicbird, *Phaethon aethereus*
Red-footed Booby, *Sula sula*
White-cheeked Pintail, *Anas bahamensis*
Caribbean Coot, *Fulica caribaea*
Red-necked Pigeon, *Columba squamosa*
Ruddy Quail Dove, *Geotrygon montana*
Key West Quail Dove, *Geotrygon chrysia*
Antillean Palm Swift, *Tachornis phoenicobia*
Bahama Woodstar, *Calliphlox evelynae*
Antillean Crested Hummingbird, *Orthorhynchus cristatus*

Stolid Flycatcher, *Myiarchus stolidus*
Bahama Swallow, *Callichelidon cyaneoviridis*
Caribbean Martin, *Progne dominicensis*
Bahama Honeycreeper, *Coereba flaveola*
Tawny-shouldered Blackbird, *Agelaius humeralis*
Black-faced Grassquit, *Tiaris bicolor*

Central American Jabiru, *Jabiru mycteria*
Hook-billed Kite, *Chondrohierax uncinatus*
Roadside Hawk, *Buteo magnirostris*
Double-striped Thick-knee, *Burhinus bistriatus*
Ruddy Ground Dove, *Columbina talpacoti*
Gray-breasted Martin, *Progne chalybea*
Brown Jay, *Psilorhinus morio*
Clay-colored Robin, *Turdus grayi*
Orange-breasted Bunting, *Passerina leclancherii*

South American Scarlet Ibis, *Eudocimus ruber*
Band-tailed Gull, *Larus belcheri*
Fork-tailed Flycatcher, *Muscivora tyrannus*

BIRD FAMILIES IN
EASTERN NORTH AMERICA

Sixty-eight bird families are represented
in eastern North America. Many of
these occur also in western North
America and not a few are distributed
widely throughout other parts of the
world. Becoming familiar with these
families helps one to know where the
many species are placed by learning
certain characteristics that separate one
family from another. Family names are
capitalized and always end in "-idae."

Accipitridae *Hawks, Eagles, Kites, Harriers*
280 species: Worldwide. At least
twenty species breed in North America.
This widespread group of birds ranges
from the very large eagles to small
hawks not much larger than a Robin.
These birds are primarily meat eaters,
the smaller ones feeding also on insects.
In order to be able to catch and eat their
prey, they are provided with powerful
hooked bills for tearing meat apart, and
extremely sharp talons or claws for
grasping the live prey, whether it be
mammal, bird, reptile, or insect. Most
hawks breed in stick nests high up in
trees or on cliffs. A few, like the
harriers, nest on the ground. These
birds are much maligned and persecuted
in the mistaken belief that they kill
poultry and carry off lambs and calves.
Only very rarely do they kill chickens or

domestic livestock, and only when the latter are sick or injured.

Alaudidae *Larks*

75 species: This almost exclusively Old World family is represented in America by one species, the Horned Lark. Larks are birds of open country, nesting on the ground. The Horned Lark is an exceedingly early breeder, laying its eggs in late winter, even with patches of snow on the ground. These birds feed on seeds and small insects.

Alcedinidae *Kingfishers*

90 species: Chiefly tropical regions in the Old World, especially numerous in Australasia. Six species are limited to the New World, of which only two breed in North America. Many are brilliantly colored but ours are relatively plain, although conspicuously crested. These birds dig tunnels into earthen banks and lay white eggs. As their name suggests, they feed on fish, but many tropical species catch insects and lizards on land.

Alcidae *Auks, Murres, Puffins*

21 species: Exclusively northern coasts of the Northern Hemisphere. Twenty-two species breed in North America, all except four of these occurring in the north Pacific. These birds are chiefly black-and-white and live along rocky coasts where they breed chiefly on precipitous cliffs and lay their pointed eggs on bare ledges, or in crevices or burrows. They spend the winter at sea where they dive for their food, primarily small fish and squid.

Anatidae *Swans, Geese, Ducks*

150 species: Worldwide. At least forty species breed in North America. In the swans and geese, the sexes are alike, but many species of ducks have marked sexual dimorphism, with the males the brighter. All have webbed feet and

most are aquatic, although the geese are primarily terrestrial. As might be expected from such a diverse family, food habits are extremely varied, some forms being vegetarians, others eating fish, snails, insects, and so on. This successful family has been able to colonize very remote oceanic islands in all parts of the globe.

Anhingidae *Anhingas or Darters*
4 species: Tropical and subtropical portions of the world. One species breeds in North America. Large, web-footed birds with long, pointed spear-like bills with which they impale fish. They inhabit inland, freshwater lakes, streams, and marshes, and nest in trees and bushes.

Apodidae *Swifts*
70 species: Worldwide. Four species breed in North America. All of the members of this well-known family are aerial feeders, catching insects on the wing. They never perch, but cling to vertical surfaces such as the walls of caves, buildings and trees. These birds get their name from the fact that they are among the speediest of all birds. The sexes are alike and colors run from drab grays and browns to black-and-white. The eggs are pure white and clutches run from three to six eggs.

Aramidae *Limpkin*
1 species: Restricted to tropical America, and breeding as far north as southern Georgia. This is a swamp-loving, secretive, rail-like bird. It feeds exclusively on aquatic snails which it extracts without breaking the shell. It lays up to six eggs in a nest in reeds.

Ardeidae *Herons, Bitterns*
64 species: Worldwide. Twelve species breed in North America. Large- to medium-sized, long-legged birds, some of which have extremely long necks.

They are long-billed for catching fish; their toes unwebbed. Many species nest colonially in trees and bushes. Some species have elaborate plumes during the breeding season.

Bombycillidae *Waxwings*

3 species: Temperate portions of the Northern Hemisphere. Two species breed in North America. These handsome, sleek, and crested birds are named for the red, wax-like patches on the wings of the adults. They feed both on insects and berries. Waxwings are among the tamest of birds, often permitting a very close approach. They are very gregarious, often forming large flocks, except in the nesting season, which is usually in late summer.

Caprimulgidae *Nightjars*

76 species: Six species breed in North America. These mottled, cryptically colored birds spend most of their time resting on the ground, but feed on flying insects at dusk or at night. They have long wings and short bills, with a wide mouth opening for catching insects. American species, such as the Whip-poor-will, have musical calls, but many Old World species have dry, buzzy notes.

Cathartidae *New World Vultures*

7 species: Tropical and temperate America. Three species, including the nearly extinct California Condor, breed in North America. These scavengers are adapted for feeding on carrion and refuse. Unlike their nearest relatives, the hawks, they possess weak feet instead of sharp talons for holding their prey. Vultures are very large, mostly blackish birds and are broad-winged and bare-headed for getting inside carrion; this bare-headedness prevents their feathers from becoming fouled. They nest in tree cavities or on the ground.

Certhiidae *Creepers*

5 species: Eurasia and North America. Only the Brown Creeper is found in North America. These birds crawl up the trees and probe for spiders and soft-bodied insects in the crevices of the bark. Their curved bills are well suited to this. Creepers are dull-colored birds.

Charadriidae *Plovers*

60 species: Worldwide. Nine species breed in North America. Plovers are small to medium-sized shorebirds with short bills. These birds run along the sand or mud for a way, suddenly stop and probe for food in the soft ooze, and catch worms, small crustaceans, and insects. Some of the species have characteristic black or brown breast bands on white backgrounds. The largest are called lapwings; some species have a conspicuous crest, while others possess lappets and wattles. Golden and Black-bellied plovers are long-distance migrants.

Ciconiidae *Storks*

17 species: Chiefly tropical portions of the world. Only one species breeds in North America. Large, long-legged, long-necked, and long-billed birds that live chiefly in open, marshy country. They nest either singly or colonially in trees and bushes, often with herons and ibises. They feed on all sorts of animal matter and a few species eat carrion.

Columbidae *Pigeons, Doves*

290 species: Worldwide. Only eleven species breed in North America. The larger species are usually called pigeons; the smaller ones are known as doves. Nearly all members of this family lay two white eggs, but a few lay only one. Most species nest in trees but a few nest on the ground. The New World species are generally drab brown and gray, but many of the Old World tropical species are brilliantly colored.

Corvidae *Crows, Jays, Magpies*

107 species: Worldwide. Fifteen species breed in North America. Birds in this family are among the largest of the perching birds. The crows and ravens are a somber black, but the many jays and magpies are a colorful group. The sexes are either alike or very similar. The voices of these birds are mostly harsh and raucous and can hardly be called a "song." These birds are omnivorous in their feeding habits and eat meat, fruit, insects, and various vegetable substances.

Cotingidae *Cotingas*

90 species: American tropics. One species breeds in North America. These are mainly brightly colored, fruit-eating birds of tropical forests. A few, such as the Rose-throated Becard of North America, are adapted for capturing insects in flight. Among the more unusual cotingas are the bright red Cock-of-the-Rock and the all-black umbrella birds.

Cracidae *Chachalacas*

44 species. Tropical and subtropical forests of the Western Hemisphere. One species occurs as far north as the Rio Grande Valley in Texas. These large, long-legged, long-tailed, chicken-like birds spend much time in trees, where they run nimbly along the branches, searching for the buds and tender new leaves that are an important part of their diet.

Cuculidae *Cuckoos, Roadrunners, Anis*

125 species: Nearly worldwide, of which only six species breed in North America. Although some Old World species are parasitic in their nesting habits, American cuckoos lay eggs in their own nests. Besides the familiar but secretive cuckoos, this mostly tropical family includes the comical, ground-inhabiting Roadrunner of the

southwestern deserts and the two all-black anis.

Falconidae *Falcons, Caracaras*
60 species: Worldwide. Seven species breed in North America. This family includes the true falcons and also the caracaras, which are structurally akin, although convergent with vultures, being somewhat terrestrial and feeding to some extent on carrion. The typical falcons have long wings and tails, and are among the fastest flying birds in the world. They inhabit mainly open country and many of them pursue birds on the wing. Unlike other hawks, they do not build nests of their own, but utilize other bird's nests or lay eggs in hollow trees or tree holes, on cliffs, or on the ground.

Fregatidae *Frigatebirds*
5 species: Tropical oceans of the world. In North America one species breeds in extreme southern Florida on the Marquesa Keys off Key West. Large, extremely long-winged birds with forked tails, hooked bills, inflatable throat pouches (males only), and webbed feet. Nesting mainly on oceanic islands, they are piratic on other seabirds, forcing them to disgorge the fish they have caught.

Fringillidae *Grosbeaks, Buntings, Finches, Sparrows*
Over 500 species: Worldwide. Seventy-two species breed in North America. This is the largest bird family in the world and probably the most successful. It is well-represented in nearly all parts of the world. Most species are seedeaters but take insects on the side. Some, like the numerous sparrows and so-called winter finches, flock in great numbers on southward migrations.

Gaviidae *Loons*
4 species: Northern Hemisphere. All four species breed in North America.

Appropriately called "divers" in the Old World, these birds are also excellent swimmers. They are web-footed, have long, pointed bills, and feed primarily on fish. Loons breed on freshwater lakes and along rivers and winter mostly on the seacoast.

Gruidae *Cranes*

15 species: Fairly widespread, but absent in South America. Two species breed in North America. One, the nearly extinct Whooping Crane, is strictly protected; the other, the Sandhill Crane, is more numerous and has a fairly wide range. Cranes superficially resemble herons but are not related to them. They are among the tallest birds in the world and inhabit open country, where they nest on the ground and lay only two eggs. Their colors run to black, white, and gray; most of them have a bare patch on the head.

Haematopodidae *Oystercatchers*

7 species: Widespread in warm regions. Two species breed in North America. Large, boldly patterned in black or in black-and-white, with reddish bills and legs. They inhabit seacoasts and, less often, inland rivers, where they feed on shellfish, crustaceans, and sand worms. They are conspicuous birds whether feeding on mudbanks or nesting on the sand, where they lay from two to five eggs.

Hirundinidae *Swallows*

80 species: Worldwide. Eight species breed in North America. Swallows have long, pointed wings and are marvelous flyers, and, like swifts, are aerial feeders. Their bills and legs are exceedingly short. They commonly perch on wires. Many species use man-made structures, such as buildings, bridges, and culverts, as sites for their nests. In autumn, enormous flocks of

swallows may be seen on their
southward journey.

Hydrobatidae *Storm-Petrels*
21 species. Worldwide in tropical and
temperate oceans. Four species breed
in North America. These small birds
are usually seen fluttering over the
surface of the water. They feed on small
crustaceans, fish, and plankton. They
nest in burrows on offshore islands and
isolated coasts, which they visit only at
night. The Wilson's Storm-Petrel,
which visits North American coasts in
the summer, is probably the most
abundant bird in the world.

Icteridae *Blackbirds, Orioles*
94 species: This exclusively American
family contains such familiar species as
the Bobolink, the meadowlarks,
orioles, grackles, and cowbirds, as well
as the many blackbirds. Twenty species
breed in North America. Members of
this family are diverse in appearance,
nesting habits, and habitat. The orioles
are master nest builders, weaving bag-
like, hanging nests. The Bobolink and
meadowlarks are ground nesters, while
the cowbirds are nest parasites.

Jacanidae *Jaçanas*
8 species: Worldwide in the tropics.
One species is an occasional visitor to
North America. Jaçanas have very long
toes and claws, and are adapted for
walking on lily pads and other floating
marsh vegetation. They are aggressive
birds, several species being armed with
spurs with which they defend their
territories. In their exposed habitat,
they have no need for cryptic
coloration; most species are boldly
patterned, and several have brilliantly
colored frontal shields.

Laniidae *Shrikes*
74 species: Chiefly Old World, mostly
from Australia; lacking in South

America. Only two species are found in North America, one of which is also widespread throughout Eurasia. These birds commonly inhabit open country, mainly areas where there are thorn bushes on which to impale their prey—either insects or rodents and small birds. Shrikes are solitary birds and, since they have hooked bills and many species have masks, they look the part of "killers." Nevertheless, they are extremely beneficial.

Laridae *Gulls, Terns*
80 species: Worldwide. Thirty-one species breed in North America. Many gulls occur in colder latitudes, most of the terns in warmer climates, but there are exceptions in both groups. Both possess webbed feet; gulls alone have hooked bills and are generally more predatory, while terns have straight and pointed bills used chiefly for catching fish. All of these birds are primarily colonial nesters, breeding on oceanic islands and coastal beaches and on inland marshes, lakes, and rivers. Sizes range from the large Great Black-backed Gull to the diminutive Least Tern.

Meleagrididae *Turkeys*
2 species: North and Central America. One species occurs in North America. These large, brightly colored gamebirds inhabit dense forest. They are not normally shy, but become secretive when hunted. They have bare heads and necks, the skin bright red or blue.

Mimidae *Mockingbirds, Thrashers*
30 species: The New World. Ten species breed in North America. In this family are included such well-known birds as the Catbird, the Mockingbird, and several thrashers. They are good-to-excellent singers and the familiar Mockingbird is a mimic of other birds, which gives it its name. These birds

are long-tailed and short-winged, and have slender, slightly curved bills.

Motacillidae *Pipits, Wagtails*
50 species: Primarily an Old World family, of which only five species breed in North America. These two are the widespread Water Pipit and the localized Sprague's Pipit of the Great Plains. As with the similar larks, the pipits are birds of open country, inhabiting short-grass fields. These birds are plain brown and streaked. Like larks they feed and nest on the ground, walk rather than hop, and bob their tails.

Pandionidae *Ospreys*
1 species: Nearly worldwide, including North America. Ospreys have highly specialized feet for catching fish, their exclusive food; they have spike-like scales on the bottom of their feet for holding their slippery prey. They nest colonially as well as singly, and construct their stick nests on the ground (rarely), in trees, on buildings, and on utility poles. They are very long-winged and plunge vertically into the water, seizing fish with their feet.

Paridae *Titmice, Verdins*
65 species: North America, Eurasia, and Africa. Twelve species breed in North America. These familiar birds, called tits in Britain, include the tame and trusting chickadees, which not only come to feeders, but even take food from the hand. They are mostly hole or cavity nesters and will utilize bird houses. The sexes are alike and most of the species are of small size. Some have crests and nearly all travel in mixed flocks outside the breeding season.

Parulidae *Wood Warblers*
125 species: The New World. Fifty-two species breed in North America. A

group mostly of brightly colored, active insect eaters. These birds are, however, misnamed, as the vast majority of them have nothing more than buzzy, insect-like songs, hardly what could be called a warble. These birds in spring are the delight of the bird-watcher, with their distinctive patterns and bright colors. In autumn, however, many of them are in dull plumage and are known as the "confusing fall warblers" and are the despair of the beginning birder.

Pelecanidae *Pelicans*
8 species: Nearly worldwide. Two species breed in North America. Huge birds with webbed feet, very long bills, and enormous pouches. The White Pelican inhabits inland freshwater lakes and catches fish from the surface of the water, while the Brown Pelican is strictly coastal and dives from the air into salt water lagoons and estuaries, as well as the ocean.

Phaethontidae *Tropicbirds*
Three species. Tropical and subtropical oceans of the world. These birds are numerous and easy to see in the vicinity of their nesting colonies on oceanic islands, but outside the breeding season they roam widely over the ocean and are usually seen singly. They feed on squids and small fish.

Phalacrocoracidae *Cormorants*
33 species: Worldwide. Six species breed in North America. These are large birds, usually black, or black-and-white, with long, hooked bills and webbed feet. They swim and dive well, obtaining fish from beneath the surface of the water, and they nest in trees or on the ground both inland and along the coast.

Phasianidae *Pheasants, Partridges, Quails*
189 species: Worldwide. Nine species breed in North America.

Members of this diverse group are also called the gallinaceous or game birds. They are all good eating and are preyed upon by man and beast alike. They range in size from the huge peafowl to the diminutive quails.

Phoenicopteridae *Flamingos*
6 species: Widely distributed in saline desert areas of the world. Feeds on aquatic micro-organisms, filtering them with its peculiarly modified bill. All species have some pink on their plumage.

Picidae *Woodpeckers*
210 species: Widespread, but absent from Australia, New Guinea, and Madagascar. Twenty species breed in North America. Woodpeckers are noted for their sharp, pointed bills for boring and digging into trees. Most species nest in holes in trees. The stiff, spiny tail is used as prop, and the claws are sharp for clinging to the trunk and branches.

Ploceidae *Weaver Finches*
143 species. The Old World, mainly in tropical regions. Two species have been introduced into North America. Many of these small to medium-sized songbirds are clad in bright yellow, orange, or red. A large number of species weave beautifully elaborate nests, from which the group gets its name. Most weavers are quite gregarious, nesting in colonies and gathering in flocks outside the breeding season.

Podicipedidae *Grebes*
20 species: Worldwide. Six species breed in North America. Similar to loons, but smaller and with lobed feet. Grebes also dive expertly and eat fish, but also partake of a vegetarian diet. They breed on lakes, ponds, and marshes and build floating nests. They winter primarily on the coast.

Procellariidae *Shearwaters, Petrels, Fulmars*
65 species: Worldwide. Only two species breed in North America. Chiefly pelagic or oceanic in the nonbreeding season, nesting on islands and along coasts where they are chiefly nocturnal. Web-footed and with long, pointed wings, adapted for gliding over the waves. They feed on fish, crustaceans, and plankton.

Psittacidae *Parrots*
320 species: Widespread in tropical regions. Only the now-extinct Carolina Parakeet bred within the United States. The now very rare Thick-billed Parrot of Mexico formerly was a straggler to southern Arizona. Members of this well-known family are characterized by their strong hooked beaks. The species ranges in size from the very large cockatoos and macaws to the tiny pygmy parrots of New Guinea.

Pycnonotidae *Bulbuls*
123 species: Old World tropics. One species has been introduced into Florida. Bulbuls are generally rather dull-colored birds that travel in flocks and eat fruit or insects. Some are noisy and conspicuous, while others are very retiring and difficult to detect.

Rallidae *Rails, Gallinules, Coots*
130 species: Worldwide. Nine species breed in North America. These are aquatic birds, mostly living in marshes which they rarely or never leave, except for their fall migration south. This family also contains the gallinules and coots, the latter having lobed feet adapted for swimming in open water. Gallinules are brightly colored, but most other rails are cryptically colored in grays, browns, and buffs, blending in with the reeds. Their nests are well hidden among the dense rushes and other aquatic growth.

Recurvirostridae *Avocets, Stilts*

7 species: Fairly widespread in w
regions. Two species breed in No
America. Avocets and stilts are fla
shorebirds with vivid patterns of b
white, tan, and pink. They are lon
legged; the long bills are upturned
avocets, straight in stilts. The avoce
have partially webbed feet, presumal
as an aid in swimming in deeper wat
than most waders.

Rynchopidae *Skimmers*

3 species: Chiefly tropical and
subtropical areas, although the single
species in North America breeds
commonly north to Massachusetts.
These curious birds have specially
adapted bills for skimming the surface
of the water, which gives the birds
their name. Their unique bills are
compressed laterally like a knife blade,
but the most unusual feature is a lower
mandible that is much longer than the
upper.

Scolopacidae *Sandpipers*

90 species: Worldwide. Thirty-six
species breed in North America.
Sandpipers range in size from the large
Long-billed Curlew to one of the
smallest, the Least Sandpiper. They
occur on the seacoasts and on inland
lakes and rivers, and most of them nest
on the Arctic tundra. Many perform
tremendous migrations to the Southern
Hemisphere in autumn and back north
again in spring. This family includes
curlews, godwits, snipes, woodcocks,
turnstones, phalaropes, dowitchers,
yellowlegs.

Sittidae *Nuthatches*

22 species: North America and Eurasia.
Four species breed in North America.
Like the titmice, these birds are cavity
nesters. Their chief peculiarity is their
habit of crawling on trees head
downward; they can progress in any

direction, even creeping along
branches, but they rarely come to the
ground. The sexes are similar and are
chiefly identified as to species by their
various head markings.

Stercorariidae *Jaegers, Skuas*

5 species. Oceans and seacoasts in
higher latitudes of the Northern and
Southern hemispheres. Four species
occur in North America. These fast-
flying, predatory, gull-like birds feed
mainly on small rodents, the eggs or
young of other birds, and on fish they
rob from other seabirds. They nest
on the ground in open tundra, and are
vigorous in the defense of their eggs
or young.

Strigidae *True Owls*

130 species: Worldwide. Seventeen
species breed in North America.
Members of this well-known family
range from the huge horned and eagle
owls to the diminutive Elf Owl of the
arid Southwest. Nearly all of the species
are nocturnal, but the beautiful Snowy
Owl of the Far North hunts in the
daytime. Owls do not build their own
nests but use abandoned nests of other
birds, such as stick nests in trees. They
also nest in hollow trees and more
rarely on cliffs or on the ground. All
species lay white eggs. During the cold
months, many of these birds roost in
dense evergreen groves. Although like
hawks they have sharp talons and hooked
beaks for killing their prey, they are
not related to hawks.

Sturnidae *Starlings*

111 species. Tropical and temperate
regions of the Old World. Two species
have been introduced into North
America. They are medium-sized
songbirds with large feet and strong
bills, often with brilliantly glossy,
black plumage. They are mainly birds
of open country, although a few are

adapted for living in forest. Most species are gregarious, and some form huge flocks outside the breeding season.

Sulidae *Boobies, Gannets*
9 species: Nearly worldwide on islands and coasts. Only one species breeds in North American waters. Large-sized birds with long, pointed bills, webbed feet, and pointed wings, adapted for plunge-diving from great heights into the ocean for fish. They nest on steep cliffs.

Sylviidae *Kinglets, Gnatcatchers*
300 species: Worldwide. Five species breed in North America. These birds are among the smallest in the world. They live entirely on insects and spiders.

Tetraonidae *Grouse*
16 species: Temperate regions of Eurasia and North America; ten species occur in North America. Grouse are closely related to pheasants and quails, but differ from them in having densely feathered toes. Most are forest birds, but four species in North America are adapted for living in open grasslands. Most species have elaborate courtship displays, often on communal display grounds where several males gather to dance and strut before the females.

Thraupidae *Tanagers*
240 species: Chiefly tropical America, only five species breeding in North America north of Mexico. These brightly colored birds are mainly forest inhabitants and are chiefly insectivorous but also eat small fruits. They occur in our area in the warmer months and spend the winter well within the tropics.

Threskiornithidae *Ibises, Spoonbills*
33 species: Chiefly tropical regions of the world. Four species breed in North

America, including the very colorful Roseate Spoonbill. The bills of Ibises are long and curve down; those of spoonbills are straight and spatulate. They are aquatic birds and feed on fish, frogs, insects, etc. These birds nest colonially in trees and bushes, often with herons.

Trochilidae *Hummingbirds*

320 species: This strictly American family is most numerous in South America, especially in the Andean region. Only fifteen species breed in North America, and of these only the Ruby-throat occurs widely in the East. These are among the most colorful birds and have glittering, iridescent plumage. They are the only birds known to fly backwards and, like swifts, they do not perch while feeding. They hover in front of a flower and sip nectar and pick off insects while on the wing. They lay two white eggs in a soft, very compact down nest.

Troglodytidae *Wrens*

60 species: The Western Hemisphere, except for one wide-ranging species (the Winter Wren) that also occurs in Eurasia. Ten species breed in North America. These mostly small birds are clad in browns, grays, and buffs. They are mainly secretive in habits, although the familiar House Wren builds its nest in man-made bird houses. While some wrens build their nests near man's dwellings, others construct their homes in wet places, such as the marsh wrens in cattails.

Turdidae *Thrushes*

310 species: Worldwide. Thirteen species breed in North America. Many members of this family are excellent singers. The best-known species in America are the American Robin and the Eastern Bluebird. The last-named, a member of a group of three species, is

a hole nester, but most others build open, cup-shaped nests. Young of all species have spotted breasts. The family also includes the brown-backed thrushes of the genus *Catharus,* and wheatears and solitaires.

Tyrannidae *Tyrant Flycatchers*
367 species: A strictly American family with by far the greatest number of species in South America. In North America no fewer than 32 species breed. The sexes are alike, with few exceptions. These birds characteristically sit on wires and bare, exposed branches on the water waiting for flying insect prey. The flycatchers then dart out, grab the insect, and usually return to the very same spot before eating the insect. Many species in certain genera look much alike but may be identified by their songs.

Tytonidae *Barn Owls*
12 species: Worldwide. Only one species, the Barn Owl, occurs in North America. These long-legged, densely plumaged owls have well-developed, heart-shaped facial disks. They are found mostly in forests, but several species in the Old World tropics are adapted to open grasslands.

Vireonidae *Vireos*
43 species: New World, mostly tropical and subtropical. Twelve species breed in North America, all in the genus *Vireo.* These birds are small, mostly plainly colored, and inhabit woodland and forest edge. They are usually sluggish in movement and live on insects found among the foliage and small branches. Vireos are persistent and tireless singers. They lay from three to five eggs in nests usually suspended from branches.

BIRD-WATCHING

Bird-watching is a hobby that can be made as inexpensive or as costly as one wishes. One may begin without purchasing anything, relying on eyes and on memory. But sooner or later a watcher will want to buy that most basic piece of equipment, a pair of binoculars.

A major consideration is weight; a lightweight pair is better for hours of continuous use than a heavier one. Choose a pair with an adjustable right eyepiece and central focusing; this will permit you to adjust the focus quickly from a nearby sparrow to a distant soaring hawk. In general, the best magnification will depend on how steadily you can hold your field glasses. Seven- or eight-power glasses will provide adequate magnification, but after years of experience and, if you are really steady-handed, you may be able to use a pair of ten-power glasses.

For adequate light, the objective (front) lens should have a diameter in millimeters of at least five times the magnification. Thus, a seven-power binocular should have an objective diameter of not less than 35 millimeters (7 x 35), an eight-power glass should have an objective diameter of 40 millimeters (8 x 40), and so on. A pair of binoculars with an objective wider than this will let in more light. This may be useful in dimly lit forest, but on an open, strongly illuminated beach there may be too much glare to allow you to see the birds well. Then, too, glasses with wider objectives are generally heavier than those of the same power but with a smaller objective. The best advice on binoculars is to buy the best you can afford. A binocular suitable for brief use at the opera or race track may cause eyestrain and fatigue when used for hours at a time under the varying conditions of an all-day field trip.

Most experienced bird-watchers also purchase a telescope, which, if mounted on a sturdy tripod or gunstock, is an excellent way to view and identify distant shorebirds and waterbirds. Many of the considerations that apply to binoculars apply here. Choose a good telescope, one that will last for years. A suitable telescope may have adjustable eyepieces, offering various magnifications such as 15-, 20-, 40-, and 60-power. At higher magnifications—above about 30-power—one may have trouble with vibrations caused by the wind or with distortion of the image by shimmering heat waves.

Another useful piece of equipment is a pocket notebook. It is wise to jot down a description of unfamiliar birds immediately after observing them. Not only will this enable you to remember critical field marks but it will train you to notice small but important details that might otherwise be overlooked. One can also record other observations, such as numbers of birds seen, dates of their arrival and departure, peak numbers of migrants, and interesting behavioral or ecological details.

Sooner or later you may decide to preserve these notes in a more permanent form, using larger, bound notebooks or a system of file cards. Notes can be grouped according to date, locality, or species, or by whatever arrangement best suits your needs and purposes. A gradually increasing store of notes is a valuable record not only of past field trips, but of your own steadily growing knowledge of birds.

GLOSSARY

Accidental A species whose normal range is in another area, and has appeared in a given area only a very few times.

Auriculars Feathers covering the ear opening and the area immediately around it; often distinctively colored. Also called ear coverts.

Boreal forest The northern coniferous forest belt stretching from Alaska to Newfoundland; also called the taiga.

Breeding plumage A coat of feathers worn by many birds during the breeding season; often more brightly colored than the winter plumage.

Casual A species whose normal range is in another area, but has occurred in our area somewhat more frequently than accidentals.

Cere A fleshy, featherless area surrounding the nostrils of hawks, falcons, pigeons, and a few other groups of birds.

Circumpolar Of or inhabiting the Arctic (or Antarctic) regions in both the Eastern and Western hemispheres.

Clutch A set of eggs laid by one bird.

Colonial Nesting in groups of colonies rather than in isolated pairs.

Cosmopolitan Worldwide in distribution, or at least occurring in all continents except Antarctica.

Coverts Small feathers that overlie or cover the bases of the large flight feathers of the wings and tail, or that cover an area or structure (e.g., ear coverts).

Crest A tuft of elongated feathers on the crown.

Crown The top of the head.

Cryptic Form or coloring that serves to conceal.

Cup nest A nest built or woven in a cup shape.

Domed cup A cup-shaped nest completely covered or arched over.

Eclipse plumage A dull-colored coat of eathers acquired immediately after the breeding season by most ducks and worn for a few weeks; it is followed in males by a more brightly colored plumage.

Ecosystem An ecological unit consisting of interrelationships between animals, plants, and their environments.

Eyebrow stripe A conspicuous strip of color arching above, but not including, the eye.

Eye-stripe A stripe that runs horizontally from the base of the bill through the eye.

Field mark A characteristic of color, pattern, or structure useful in distinguishing a species in the field.

Flight feathers The long, well-developed feathers of the wings and tail, used during flight. The flight feathers of the wings are divided into primaries, secondaries, and tertials. See also rectrix.

Frontal shield A fleshy, featherless, and often brightly colored area on the forehead of jacanas, gallinules, and a few other groups of birds.

Gorget A patch of brilliantly colored feathers on the chin or throat of certain birds, such as male hummingbirds.

Immature A young bird not under parental care but not yet fully adult in appearance; a juvenile.

Lek A place where males of some species of birds, such as the Greater Prairie Chicken and the European Ruff, gather and perform courtship displays in a group, rather than courting females individually and in isolation from one another; females visit a lek to mate, but generally they build their nests elsewhere.

Lore The space between the eye and the base of the bill, sometimes distinctively colored.

Mandible One of the two parts of a bird's bill, termed respectively the upper mandible and the lower mandible.

Mantle The back of a bird together with the upper surface of the wings. A term is used for groups of birds (e.g., gulls) in which these areas are of one color.

Molt The process of shedding and replacing feathers; usually after breeding and before the autumn migration.

Mustache A colored streak running from the base of the bill back along the side of the throat.

Naris (*pl.* nares) The external nostril; in birds located near the base of the upper mandible.

Pelagic Of or inhabiting the open ocean.

Phase One of several distinctive plumages worn by members of certain species, such as the Screech Owl and some hawks and herons, irrespective of age, sex, or season. Also called morph.

Platform nest A large, flat-surfaced nest built of sticks and similar material.

Plume A feather larger or longer than the feathers around it; it generally serves for displays.

Primaries The outermost and longest flight feathers on a bird's wing. Primaries vary in number from nine to eleven per wing, but always occur in a fixed number in any particular species.

Race A geographical population of a species that is slightly different from other populations; a subspecies.

Range The geographical area or areas inhabited by a species.

Raptor A bird of prey.

Rectrix (*pl.* rectrices) One of the long flight feathers of the tail.

Resident Remaining in one place all year; nonmigratory.

Riparian Of or inhabiting the banks of a river or stream.

Secondaries The large flight feathers located in a series along the rear edge of the wing, immediately inward from the primaries.

Scapulars A group of feathers on the shoulder of a bird, along the side of the back.

Scrape A shallow depression made by a bird on the ground to serve as a nest.

Shoulder The point where the wing meets the body, as in the Red-shouldered Hawk.

The term is also loosely applied to the bend of the wing when this area is distinctively colored.

Spatulate Spoon-shaped or shovel-shaped; used to describe the bill of certain birds, such as spoonbills.

Speculum A distinctively colored area on the wing of a bird, especially the metallic patch on the secondaries of some ducks.

Subalpine The forest or other vegetation immediately below the treeless, barren alpine zone on high mountains.

Subspecies A geographical population of a species that is slightly different from other populations of that species; also called a race.

Taiga The belt of coniferous forest covering the northern part of North America and Eurasia from coast to coast.

Tarsus The lower, usually featherless, part of a bird's leg.

Territory An area defended by the male, by both of a pair, or by an unmated bird.

Tertials The innermost flight feathers on a bird's wing, immediately adjacent to the body. They are often regarded simply as the innermost secondaries. Also called tertiaries.

Tules Certain species of bulrushes abundant in California.

Window A translucent area in the wing of certain birds (such as the Red-shouldered Hawk) visible from below in flight.

Wing bar A conspicuous crosswise wing mark.

Wing stripe A conspicuous mark running along the opened wing.

Winter plumage A coat of feathers worn by many birds during the nonbreeding season, and often less brightly colored than the breeding plumage.

CONSERVATION STATUS OF EASTERN BIRDS

Federal laws in the United States and Canada prohibit the taking or molesting of birds, their nests, eggs or young, other than those species that damage property or agriculture, or that are covered by hunting regulations. In addition, rare or endangered species are protected by special measures and by bird management agencies. Increasingly, the states are also passing conservation measures and are studying the status of their bird populations with the aim of protecting this precious natural heritage. In our species descriptions we have noted those birds that have a special conservation status. But it should be understood that the status of birds changes and that they may be differently categorized by different authorities.

Unprotected Birds Two introduced species, the Starling and the House Sparrow, have become so numerous and widespread that they are not protected in the United States or Canada. A few other species, including the Rock Dove, the Black-billed Magpie, and members of the blackbird family, may damage crops or other birds and are therefore not fully protected in some areas.

Gamebirds These may be hunted during an open season regulated by the various states and provinces. Information on limitations, licenses and so forth can be secured from local agencies.

Rare or Endangered Species

Virtually Extinct Eskimo Curlew
Ivory-billed Woodpecker
Bachman's Warbler

Seriously Reduced in Numbers Peregrine Falcon
Whooping Crane

Threatened Brown Pelican
Wood Stork
Everglade Kite
Bald Eagle
Osprey
Greater Prairie Chicken
Lesser Prairie Chicken
Red-cockaded Woodpecker
Kirtland's Warbler

PICTURE CREDITS

The numbers in parentheses are plate
numbers. Some photographers have pictures
under agency names as well as their own.
Agency names appear in boldface.

Peter Alden (46, 319)

Ardea Photographics
Peter Alden (468)
Graeme Chapman (58)
Kenneth Fink (48, 571)
Dr. P. Germain (80)
M. E. J. Gore (434)
Edgar Jones (408, 538)
B. L. Sage (102) J. S.
Wightman (84)

Peter Arnold
Stephen Krasemann
(123, 206)

John Arvin (31, 179,
321, 324, 387, 397,
481, 495, 496)
Ron Austing (294, 295,
296, 297, 300, 304,
305, 308, 352, 359,
363, 378, 396, 403,
417, 435, 450, 554)
Bob Barrett (6, 101,
249, 274, 283, 333,
412)
Erwin Bauer (100, 270)
Greg Beaumont (527)
Tom Brakefield (107,
110, 114, 115, 132,
140, 145, 149, 150,
153, 172, 267)

Fred Bruemmer (39, 96)
Steve Cannings (338,
344)
James Carmichael (19)
Ken Carmichael (47,
360, 361, 380, 404)
Robert Carr (52, 216,
548)
Patricia Caulfield (29,
166)
Leslie Chalmers (291,
453, 521)
Herbert Clarke (91,
130, 148, 160, 165,
181, 199, 222, 244,
287, 398, 449, 471,
475, 490, 570)

Bruce Coleman, Inc.
(299) F. J. Alsop III
(375, 388, 513) Ron
Austing (293, 298,
309, 310, 311, 313,
314, 368, 372, 376,
427, 443, 447, 545,
551, 556) Jen and Des
Bartlett (89, 103, 118,
186, 187, 209, 230,
232, 239, 245, 405,
406) Bob and Clara
Calhoun (437, 550,
562) Brian Coates (484)
Thase Daniel (407, 549)

Harry Darrow (190) L. R. Ditto (213, 312) John Dunning (442, 452, 482) Francisco Erize (72) Kenneth Fink (20, 157, 211) Jeffrey Foott (303) Keith Gunnar (425) Eric Hosking (84) M. P. Kahl (195) T. D. Mangelsen (180) John Markham (565) R. E. Pelham (192) Hans Reinhard (315, 581) Laura Riley (306) Leonard Lee Rue III (94, 159, 163, 185) L. M. Stone (167) Joe Van Wormer (197, 201, 441) Gary Zahm (215) D. Zingel (92)

Cornell Lab of Ornithology
John Dunning (509)
Bill Dyer (444) Brower Hall (349, 394, 395)
Michael Hopiak (156, 252, 322, 335, 362, 382, 386, 419, 458, 462, 494, 499, 500, 530, 540, 561, 567)

Betty D. Cottrille (51, 234, 337, 341, 366, 448, 457, 460, 461, 463, 511, 512, 537)
Lois Cox (164, 483)
Allan Cruickshank (69, 71, 572)
Helen Cruickshank (15, 38, 62, 65, 68, 75, 99, 136, 175, 176, 221, 227, 233, 243, 246, 409, 426, 477, 478, 528, 552, 568, 574)
Thase Daniel (1, 4, 17, 106, 125, 154, 174, 183, 254, 347, 351, 364, 439, 492, 519, 522, 566, 575, 582)
Harry Darrow (3, 51, 53, 67, 98, 139, 152, 194, 301, 318, 413)
Ed Degginger (8, 18, 50, 76, 111, 317)
Jack Dermid (251, 278)
Ed Dutch (271, 273, 418, 430, 578)
Bill Dyer (564)
Harry Engels (259)
William Ferguson (78, 194)
Davis Finch (33, 55, 198, 200, 218, 275, 336)
Kenneth Fink (25, 109, 112, 113, 117, 120, 121, 126, 128, 135, 138, 144, 161, 162, 188, 208, 231, 261, 280, 281, 515)
Jeffrey Foott (472)
Jean-Louis Frund (241, 282, 290)
David Gill (32)
William Griffin (27, 42, 134, 238, 329, 526, 573)
Robert Hamer (13, 24)
Russell Hansen (83, 292)
Gene Hornbeck (30)
Joseph Jehl (57, 204, 223)
Isidor Jeklin (170, 256, 277, 285, 393, 422, 464, 506, 526, 555, 569)
M. P. Kahl (2, 9, 23, 43, 59, 61, 64, 390)
Peter Kaplan (577)
Michel Kleinbaum (224, 225, 414)
Stephen J. Krasemann (268, 342, 353, 384, 392, 426, 560, 579)
Stephen Kress (97, 424, 451)

193, 247, 248, 385,
421, 479, 580)
Arnold Small (21, 22,
143, 147, 189, 196,
203, 205, 284, 535,
557, 559)
Sandy Sprunt (12)

Tom Stack & Assoc.
Peter Urbanski (377)
Leonard Lee Rue III
(263)

Alvin Staffan (279, 354,
357, 369, 370, 371,
383, 420, 432, 440,
486, 488, 489, 503,
504, 525, 541, 542)
Gayle Strickland (533,
534, 546)
Arthur Swoger (416)
Ian Tait (355, 358,
433, 456, 487)

Bill Thomas (10)
Mary Tremaine (35,
141, 142, 171, 207,
236, 536, 576)
John Trott (326, 373,
446, 474, 498, 539,
558)

Verda International
M.P. Kahl (16, 70)

Larry West (14, 133,
137, 339, 514)
Ron Willocks (237,
255, 257, 325, 502)
Richard Wood (510)
Michael Wotton (169,
219)
Richard Wright (268)
Dale and Marian
Zimmerman (86, 343,
399, 410, 454, 459,
514, 529, 544)

INDEX

Numbers in boldface type refer to plate numbers. Numbers in italics refer to page numbers. Circles preceding English names of birds make it easy for you to keep a record of the birds you have seen.

NOTES

NOTES

NOTES

NOTES

STAFF

Prepared and produced by Chanticleer Press, Inc.

Publisher: Paul Steiner
Editor-in-Chief: Gudrun Buettner
Executive Editor: Susan Costello
Managing Editor: Jane Opper
Project Editor: Susan Rayfield
Associate Editors: Mary Suffudy, Kathy Ritchell
Production: Helga Lose
Art Director: Carol Nehring
Picture Library: Edward Douglas
Drawings and Silhouettes:
Paul Singer, Douglas Pratt
Range Maps: Paul Singer
Map of North America:
Herbert Borst, Francis & Shaw, Inc.

Design: Massimo Vignelli

THE AUDUBON SOCIETY FIELD GUIDE SERIES

Also available in this unique all-color, all-photographic format: